John Ruskin and the Ethics of Consumption

STUDIES IN RELIGION AND CULTURE

Frank Burch Brown, Gary L. Ebersole, and Edith Wyschogrod, Editors

John Ruskin and the Ethics of Consumption

David M. Craig

University of Virginia Press
CHARLOTTESVILLE AND LONDON

University of Virginia Press

Printed in the United States of America on acid-free paper

First published 2006

9 8 7 6 5 4 3 2 1

Library of Congress Cataloging-in-Publication Data

Craig, David Melville, 1965–
John Ruskin and the ethics of consumption / David M. Craig.
p. cm. — (Studies in religion and culture)
Includes bibliographical references and index.
ISBN-13: 978-0-8139-2558-5 (cloth : acid-free paper)
1. Ruskin, John, 1819–1900—Ethics. 2. Ruskin, John, 1819–1900—Political and social views. 3. Consumption (Economics)—Moral and ethical aspects—Great Britain—History—19th century. 4. Didactic literature, English—History and criticism. I. Title. II. Series: Studies in religion and culture (Charlottesville, Va.)
PR5267.E8C73 2006
828'.809—dc22

2006009478

To Jocelyn
my beloved consumer

Contents

Acknowledgments

In dedicating this book to Jocelyn Sisson, I would like to recognize the many forms of support she has given me throughout this project. I thrive on the creative spark of our marriage, whether that is in our differing styles as consumers, in her editorial comments about my writing, or in the exchange of ideas that has enriched this book. Jocelyn's bracing honesty and deep acceptance have both rocked and steadied me through the twists and turns of my work on a project that is older than our daughters, Claudia and Eliza Craig. I am grateful to each of them, too; for Claudia's active imagination and love of nature and for Eliza's spirited sense of play and heartfelt generosity. They lift my spirits and remind me to delight in life's abundance. Such delight is no duty at all.

The contributions of my parents, Ann and Norman Craig, to my intellectual growth and moral convictions are greater than I can recount or repay. I have learned so much from their examples of the gifted character of life. I have appreciated Kenny and Phyllis Sisson's keen interest in this project, and I am sad that Kenny did not live to see its completion, which he would have enjoyed in his inimitable way.

Turning to my academic debts, I thank Jeff Stout for asking the key questions that helped me pick my way through the early stages of the research and into the moral sources of Ruskin's criticism. More importantly, Jeff is one of those teachers who makes having one's own moral identity central to the activity of education, and I thank him for helping me learn how to say what I wanted to say in this book.

The two readers who prompted me to begin the changes that transformed this study were John Bowlin and Peter Simonson. In the years since, I have appreciated the time for research and the helpful comments that I have received from my colleagues in the Religious Studies Department at Indiana University Purdue University Indianapolis: Conrad Cherry, Matthew Condon, Tom Davis, Philip Goff, Kelly Hayes, Bill Jackson, Ted Mullen, Tony Sherrill, Peter Thuesen, and Rachel Wheeler. I mourn Tony's death; he was an engaging conversation partner and a sharp reader of my work. My good friend Kevin Cramer volunteered to read drafts of several chapters. In addition to his clarifying phrases and his historical perspective, I am grateful for his unflagging sense of solidarity and his liberal instincts. I thank Darrick Northington for the stimulating discussions that intersected with the ideas in this book. I also thank Cornel West, who provided invaluable encouragement at a key moment.

At the University of Virginia Press, I want to thank Cathie Brettschneider for her quick and wise decisions in guiding this book to its completion. I appreciate Jane Curran's careful and sensitive work on the manuscript. I also thank the editors of Virginia's Studies in Religion and Culture series and Victorian Literature and Culture series. George Landow gave me a memorable lesson in grace as a reviewer. I thank him and an anonymous reviewer for the astute observations that improved the book, especially their encouragement that I be more explicit about the role of religion in Ruskin's writings and in my own argument. Thanks to James Wetzel for the same good counsel.

The Religion Department at Princeton University supported my early work on this project. I appreciate the conversations I had with Leora Batnitzky, Beth Eddy, Bob Gibbs, Jennifer Herdt, Mark Larrimore, and Alan Ryan, each of whom made suggestions that influenced my words and thoughts. My two years at Villanova University as an Arthur J. Ennis Fellow in Core Humanities deepened my sense of the aesthetic, literary, and Augustinian aspects of Ruskin's thought, and I thank Jack Doody for this first opportunity and Maura Lafferty for our conversations about writing. While at IUPUI, I received a summer research grant from the School of Liberal Arts, which became the basis for my analysis of the "capabilities approach," enriching chapter 6 and my argument for the lasting significance of Ruskin's criticism.

Parts of chapters 3 and 6 originally appeared in my article "The Virtues and Limits of Good Consumption: John Ruskin's 'Work of Iron,'" *Soundings* 84 (2001): 337–63. I thank the current editors for granting permission to reprint these materials. Parts of chapters 5 and 7 originally appeared in my "Naves and Nukes: John Ruskin as 'Augustinian' Social Theorist?" *Journal of Religious Ethics* (Blackwell) 32.2 (2004): 325–56. I thank Blackwell and the current editors for permission to use these selections.

John Ruskin and the Ethics of Consumption

INTRODUCTION

Why Ruskin Now?

John Ruskin is one of the towering public intellectuals of the Victorian period, and yet the history of his reception testifies to the rewards and risks of achieving such acclaim. More important than the rewards of fame that the title "public intellectual" brings is the acknowledged ability certain thinkers have to make powerful connections that reveal something of the current state of their societies. Ruskin was adept at reading his moment and arranging it into dramatic scenes and expansive portraits that sought to capture the character of Victorian public life. That he was read in his day as a social thinker and critic with whom every intellectual had to come to grips only confirms his success as an interpreter of the public. The risk of this accomplishment is fleeting influence, however, and even worse the faint praise of scholars studying a dated style, the occasional references of a historical period, or the errors of a thinker transcended by another later and favored theorist.

Although Ruskin has sometimes been subjected to such treatment, he has also been seen as more than just a Victorian public intellectual. The magnitude of his influence and the lasting interest of his normative vision and critique of modern society are still recognized in pockets of the academy. He is studied by the historians and theorists of art and architecture for his contributions to those disciplines. There are literary scholars who discuss the majesty of his prose, debate his role in Victorian social movements, or borrow some element of his thought for political purposes. He still attracts both conservative and radical admirers. But the reasons that most of Ruskin's contemporaries took his vision seriously have slipped out of view. The time is ripe for a thoroughgoing reappraisal of what he might be able to teach us.

This study is a reappraisal, not a straightforward recovery. There is much in Ruskin's corpus that deserves serious scrutiny. There are parts of his social vision that should be rejected. The variety of his interests and the sweep of his writings make it possible to select out portions of his work while dismissing the integrated drive toward a holistic vision that animates so much of Ruskin's criticism. Rather than chop up his corpus piecemeal to counteract his tendency toward didacticism, I focus on the conceptual sources and ethical concerns that carry forward despite his changes of mind, shifts in vocabulary, and appeals to new audiences. Throughout, my aim is to examine his constructive contributions, seeking to disentangle the moral resources and critical lessons that still have lasting value from the elements in his criticism that should be rejected.

Among the most important and least understood sources of Ruskin's normative vision are the Christian and classical approaches to the moral life that he adopts and revises in his criticism. Reading him as a representative of a long-standing, if increasingly suspect, approach to the moral life clarifies why he is difficult to read with appreciation today and why it is important to read him with a critical eye. This book offers a critical appreciation of Ruskin to assess and argue for his lasting contributions to the history of ethics and to show where he can still help in meeting the challenges of human development, social justice, and environmental health.

Ruskin's approach to the moral life is "teleological." By this I mean that he understands the moral life as shaped by the pursuit of some telos, or some set of ends that is recognizably good. A crucial feature of the teleological approaches from which Ruskin draws is the idea that a person comes to know what is good only by developing the character needed to recognize, pursue, and achieve key aspects of "the good." On this type of approach, the central tasks of ethical reflection include trying to envision the good itself and describing the moral character and the social roles, relationships, and obligations required for people to be able to pursue the ends of a good life. Although Ruskin is continually engaged in these tasks throughout his corpus, almost no attention has been paid to his ethics.

One reason is that Ruskin hardly qualifies as an ethicist, at least as understood now. The term "moralist" fits him better, for he exemplifies both the preacherly tone that we associate with the word "moralism" and also the searching inquiry into the interrelated aesthetic, economic, political, religious, and social aspects of good lives that, in my judgment, is the defining mark of a moralist. Like Ruskin, this study aims to blur the disciplinary lines that separate these aspects of our lives, and it offers him as a model for an engaged ethics still useful for today.

The narrow abstraction of much contemporary ethics and the disciplinary preoccupations of other fields are not the main obstacles to recovering Ruskin's contributions, however. Rather, by emphasizing the teleological features of his criticism, I call attention to some of the more troubling aspects of his writings. He does not just seek to envision the good—he instructs his contemporaries about how their lives, roles, and duties should conform to his vision of the good life and the common good. Here we begin to see why Ruskin is difficult to read with sympathy today. Although teleological approaches like his have a long history in Western ethics, they can appear to run counter to movements toward political self-determination and the individual rights and freedoms central to democratic liberalism. Can a teleological approach like Ruskin's be trusted, given the many harms that have been committed in the name of hierarchical visions of the good and elitist notions of good lives?

While I challenge Ruskin's writings on these very points, I also claim that we can grasp the force of his criticism and its lasting value only if we take seriously what his normative approach still has to offer. Ruskin the critic is continually engaged by the question of character. What kinds of people are his contemporaries, and how do they form themselves for good or ill in the myriad activities and different spheres of their lives? It is this life-long concern with character that joins Ruskin's writings on art, architecture, labor, nature, religion, politics, and economics, the topics discussed in this book. As he ranges through these topics, he comes to think about character in new and innovative ways. He not only borrows from older teleological approaches, but he puts them to novel uses.

Here we arrive at another difficulty in reading Ruskin—learning to see how innovative he was as a critic of industrial capitalism. As noted, the teleological approach to the moral life that he represents has fallen considerably out of favor. In order to understand his contributions as a critic in his own day, we have to address the historical and conceptual distance that intervenes. I argue in this book that we can appreciate his innovations and their continued usefulness only by first "reconstructing" a central, though neglected, strand in his writings—what I call his moral vocabulary of the virtues. The tasks of understanding Ruskin's ethics in his period and assessing its lasting value today both depend on what we make of this moral vocabulary.

I can clarify my aims in reconstructing this vocabulary of the virtues using a distinction made by Richard Rorty. In studying the history of philosophy, or here the history of ethics, one can distinguish between the genres of "historical reconstruction" and "rational reconstruction." Both genres construe the history of thought as a plausibly imaginable conversation, though for different purposes. Historical reconstruction aims to reconstruct the conversations occurring in a particular time and place in order to locate figures from the past in a vocabulary that they would have used as they would have understood it. Rational reconstruction, by contrast, draws past figures into conversation with us today on the terms set by current vocabularies and concerns.[1]

My interpretation of Ruskin moves back and forth between these two genres. On the one hand, I argue that identifying his vocabulary of the virtues helps us read him more on his own terms. Too often Ruskin is read, if he is read at all, on the terms set by the emerging aesthetic, social, and moral theories that largely displaced his own character-based critical approach. In the book I detail the formative and constructive roles that this vocabulary plays in his writings and his remarkable uses of it as a critic of Victorian society and industrial capitalism.

On the other hand, I am ultimately interested in what Ruskin still can teach us and whether or not the terms of his moral vocabulary can be translated for today's readers. Given the renewed attention to character and community in recent academic discussion, does Ruskin's example offer ways to think more critically about current social, political, economic, and environmental challenges? At the same time, do the problems in his vision of good societies call into question attempts to revive the kind of character-based moral language that he uses? Taken together these two questions reflect my goal of disentangling the lasting resources of Ruskin's criticism from those parts of his writings that should be rejected.

This effort culminates in my thesis that Ruskin's most valuable contributions as a social critic combine in his ethics of consumption. Here I am thinking of his attempts to articulate the obligations that consumers incur to other people and to the world. Ruskin does not undertake this imaginative effort only for himself. He constructs his ethics of consumption in public lectures, essays, and letters, striving to make it "practical" in two different senses. His criticism is practical, first, in that he does not stop at a theoretical account of how the virtues relate in general to the proper ends of human flourishing. Instead he closely observes and details his contemporaries' activities and interactions, illustrating how their chosen endeavors enhance or diminish their character, their capacities for excellence, and the broader political and social commitments needed to extend this development to everyone. Ruskin's ethics of consumption is also practical in that he invites his audience to become critics in their own right. He models his virtues-centered approach to ethics so that other people might begin to evaluate their choices as consumers, seeking out the activities and the shared goods and just relationships that help make for an abundant life both for themselves and for others.

This study of Ruskin's moral vocabulary, practical criticism, and ethics of consumption intersects with several larger conversations. In the rest of this introduction, I address, in turn, the book's relevance to consumption studies, to the existing literature on Ruskin's life and work, and to ongoing efforts to reexamine our ethical options as we move beyond the Marxist-liberal debates that structured discussions of political, economic, and social issues in the twentieth century.

Production and Consumption, Past and Present

In beginning an inquiry into Ruskin's ethics of consumption and its continued relevance, we should acknowledge Ruskin's historical distinctiveness in granting priority to consumption. Colin Campbell rightly notes the "productivist bias" prevailing in mid-nineteenth-century economic, political, and social thought.[2] One thinks of Ruskin's contemporaries, John Stuart Mill (1806–73) and Karl Marx (1818–83), who both made increased material production and, more importantly, the production of new human liberties and capacities primary goals of their theories. Ruskin, by contrast, locates the "end" of economic life and the ethical issues pertaining to it squarely in the realm of consumption.

Although this focus on consumption was remarkable in Ruskin's period, it no longer is. There has been a boom in consumption studies of late. Jean-Christophe Agnew's review of this vast literature is a useful point of departure in raising the question, why have Ruskin's contributions gone largely unnoticed not only in these recent discussions of consumption but also in the continuing reception of nineteenth-century debates about industrial capitalism?

Facing the burgeoning literature on the origins of consumer culture and interpretations of its effects, Agnew begins by identifying two historical strands that shaped the mostly negative assessments of consumerism prevailing up until recently. He traces the first strand back through

George Orwell to Thomas Carlyle's (1795–1881) "caustic denunciations of advertising puffery." The second strand starts with Marx's analysis of commodity fetishism and runs through the Frankfurt School. Despite their significant divergence, Agnew writes, "both picture western history and culture—time and space—as invaded and colonized by commodities and commodity-relations." Agnew cites this dual lineage to emphasize how closely allied, in fact, were the two seemingly opposite poles that have typically bound earlier debates about consumerism.

Among the developments Agnew canvasses, the most important to note here is the clear reversal in the relative importance of consumption and production. Consumers are no longer pictured as the hapless dupes of a manipulating capitalist and advertising elite. Nor are they seen as blindly devoted to the symbolic "value" of fetishized commodities. What emerges in recent studies instead is the ability of consumers to resist the meanings affixed to the things they buy in favor of creative rereadings of these goods in fashioning their lives according to their own desires and purposes. Summing up this newfound appreciation of consumer agency, Agnew describes one resulting vision of consumption as "'cultural work,' productive of 'cultural capital,' and grist for cultural 'resistance.' From the ashes of the dead author (or producer) arises the heroic figure of the restless reader (or consumer)."[3]

This emphasis on consumers' agency as readers stands Marx's focus on production on its head. Indeed despite Marx's analysis of commodity fetishism—that the "value" of commodities is mysteriously generated by the market's relating all useful goods in money terms—he largely dismisses consumption as irrelevant to his critique of industrial capitalism.[4] Carlyle's "caustic denunciations" offer far less insight into the mechanics of exchange, not to mention an ethics of consumption. It is Ruskin who puts consumption at the center of his political economy. It is Ruskin who charges his audiences of consumers to look beyond the surface measures of market pricing and social status in order to "read" the value and meaning of the goods they buy.

Why then is Ruskin not remembered as scholars move to reconsider consumers' agency? Here I propose a deeper divide between Agnew's two strands of nineteenth-century thought to indicate why Ruskin seems so distant today and what he still has to offer.

Celebrations of consumers' agency, whether Ruskin's or the more recent ones that Agnew canvasses, emphasize the power of consumers to read the meaning and value of things in light of the desires and purposes that people bring to them. In this sense Ruskin is closer to current approaches to consumption than is Marx. Marx's productivist bias and his notion of alienated consciousness leave consumers with little room to fashion their desires and purposes, at least for the time being. Nevertheless, Ruskin is arguably much more distant than Marx from today's discussions of consumption. The reason is that Ruskin insists that questions of character always intervene between people's desires and purposes. He asks, for example, what have people made of themselves, and what have they been made by others to be? What activities, excellences, and enjoyments are people capable of or not? What desires and purposes inform people's assessments of goods and their choices as consumers? It is this "moralism"—which I define as the readiness to subject people's virtues, vices, and desires and their chosen activities and ends to ethical inquiry and critique—that so distances Ruskin's approach from today's thinking about consumption, even though he appreciates, more than Marx, consumers' imaginative powers for reading the many meanings of things.

Marx's legacy remains clearer in the suspicion that consumers' desires are constructed (a theme that also figures centrally in Ruskin's criticism). One's own "internal" desires reflect an array of cultural meanings and social relationships. Although for Marx these constructed desires lie beyond individuals' control, scholars today are sanguine in their estimates of consumers' abilities to recognize the cultural meanings constituting their desires and to appropriate or renegotiate these meanings for their own projects and goals. Thus, in place of an older politics of labor empowerment centered in workers' agency and their collective efforts, we now have a diffuse politics of consumer resistance. In this politics there is no need to articulate common goals with others or to act for shared purposes. Instead, today's politics of resistance emphasizes the multiplicity of consumers' choices and their fashioning of alternative identities. The source of consumers' creative and oppositional responses to "external" control is, paradoxically, the very plenitude of desires and purposes available to them as individuals.[5]

This emphasis on consumers' liberty finds a different nineteenth-century antecedent in J. S. Mill. In *On Liberty* Mill argues for the removal of legal controls on consumer choice. His principle of individuality—that people should be free to pursue their self-defined projects so long as they do not injure other people—is extended here into the realm of consumption.[6] The liberalizing that Mill champions in general depends on the development of new institutional mechanisms, from electoral politics to press freedoms to the market in this case. His commitment to the growth of people's creative powers and to the expression of individuality is a hallmark of newer studies of consumption, too. Indeed, these studies tend to combine Marx's cultural suspicions about desire with Mill's embrace of consumers' liberty.

These broad historical connections need further argument than I can provide here. For now I simply want to mark where I see the real divide in nineteenth-century debates about industrial capitalism and how that divide informs past and present discussions of consumption. This divide can be characterized, on the one hand, by Ruskin's moralistic sense that the formation of good character and the contents of human flourishing are both central concerns of ethics and social criticism. Thus, he intrudes himself on his contemporaries' desires, and he offers imaginative renderings of just societies and abundant lives. We see in Marx and Mill, on the other hand, a deep distrust of this moralism. Without responding to Ruskin directly, both authors criticize, often rightly, the inherited notions of good character, just societies, and human flourishing that Ruskin is all too ready to valorize at times. A similar refusal of moralism characterizes recent studies of consumption. In my judgment, though, if we reject out of hand the ethical tasks that Ruskin undertakes and the moral vocabulary that he uses to sustain them, we will have to do without valuable critical resources needed for articulating an ethics of consumption.

Although Agnew praises recent work on consumption as a "sea change," he admits that despite the wealth of new studies and of commodity consumption in general, we are not much more aware of "the remote consequences of our acts" as consumers or "our responsibilities for them."[7] Here we stand at another important divide. Looking back over the twentieth century, the theoretical visions of Marx and Mill have been deeply influential on subsequent politics as well as on current thinking about consumption. I do not see, however, how the legacy of these theoretical visions can sustain an adequate ethics of consumption. Something like Ruskin's attention to the formation of character is also needed. As he moves to develop his own ethics of consumption, his scrutiny of character motivates his keen awareness of the ways that consumers' choices shape their own and others' well-being, their shared commitments, social relationships, and the health of the environment. He articulates and combines all of these concerns using his vocabulary of the virtues, as we shall see. First, though, a brief sketch of his corpus and career as a "practical critic" is in order.

Ruskin as Practical Critic

On the matter of style, it must be said that reading Ruskin is not a passive affair. He provokes his readers with a parade of images, examples, and judgments, often commanding them to "Observe!" the lessons he teaches. It is this vivid, expansive, authorial style that invites labeling him a "Romantic prophet" or a "Victorian sage." These titles are no longer honorific, if they ever were.[8] Instead they reflect an understandable need to deflate his magisterial tone. Such labels also have the unfortunate effect, however, of presenting Ruskin as a critic who simply pronounces judgment from on high and who defends his claims with stylistic brilliance alone. This portrait is misleading if we learn to read him more on his own terms.

Although taken together the labels art critic and social critic describe much of Ruskin's work, a better label is "practical critic." By this I mean that he approaches the critical task as a practitioner whose judgments require at least some engagement with the subject at hand, whatever it may be. In his art criticism, for example, he uses his own detailed sketches of natural objects and architectural features to illustrate his points. This practice of illustrating his art criticism contributes to his practical interest in the actual working of artists. This leads, in turn, into his first area of concern as a social critic, the numbing effects of factory production and the conditions for good labor.

Art criticism and social criticism are intertwined throughout much of Ruskin's corpus. The first two decades of his career are defined by his five-volume *Modern Painters* (1843–60), begun as a defense of landscape painter J. M. W. Turner (1775–1851). A series of architectural treatises interrupt this massive undertaking from 1848 to 1854. As seen most clearly in his famous chapter on "The Nature of Gothic" (1853), these studies of medieval edifices and the labor that built them redirect Ruskin toward the social criticism of *The Political Economy of Art* (1857), "The Work of Iron, in Nature, Art, and Policy" (1858), *Unto This Last* (1860), *Munera Pulveris* (1862–63), "Work" and "Traffic" (1865), and *Time and Tide* (1867). Even as he moves beyond this period during which he hammers out his ethics of consumption, his preoccupations with art and society continue to move in tandem.

The range of Ruskin's interests would be incomplete without mentioning other subjects close to his heart but further afield from his art and social criticism. An amateur geologist and botanist, he published several works on natural history late in his career. He also wrote essays and books on educational reform. Finally, as the influence of his Evangelical Anglican upbringing receded, he turned to the study of mythology, folklore, and comparative religion.

Ruskin's chief literary endeavors of the 1870s and 1880s reflect the main trajectories of his work and his ultimate frustrations as an art critic and social critic. In 1869 he became the first Slade Professor of Art at Oxford University. His use of art works in his lectures helped to define the new field. In addition, every month, when his health allowed, he wrote a public letter to the "workmen and labourers of Great Britain" under the title *Fors Clavigera* (1871–84). Neither his Oxford audiences nor the intended readers of *Fors* met his expectations for social and economic transformation. With his hopes of finding acceptance of his critical vision having gone largely unrealized by either class, Ruskin resigned both endeavors due to failing mental health. This finally incapacitated him, and he lived out his last decade in quiet seclusion.[9]

The contrast between the productivity and influence that Ruskin enjoyed throughout most of his career and the decline of his final decades colored his initial posthumous reception. His editors' lavish care typified the first stage. There soon followed a period of unmasking Ruskin and other "eminent Victorians." We are now well past these first two stages of hagiography and psychobiography. The pendulum swings less wildly today thanks to valuable studies that locate his writings in the currents of nineteenth-century British intellectual, social, and cultural history and in the context of the parts of his biography neglected or possibly suppressed by his editors.[10] The best recent work on Ruskin challenges the view of him as irretrievably idiosyncratic or paternalistic by demonstrating his prescience about the conceptual deficiencies and moral shortcomings of the Victorian faith in markets, science, and empire. Against the backdrop of this rethinking of Ruskin's late writings, this study returns to the sweep of his corpus, showing how these new interpretations fit the teleological framework of all of his writings.[11]

Where this book departs most sharply from other studies of Ruskin is that I read him more philosophically. This deserves some comment given Ruskin's disdain for abstraction. He derides "German metaphysicians and divines" for building theoretical systems with little purchase on the things they profess to describe. In a similar vein he takes the painter Sir Joshua Reynolds to task for involving "himself in a crowd of theories, whose issue he had not foreseen" (5.425, 42). It might be objected, then, that in reconstructing Ruskin's vocabulary of the virtues I build into his use of the term "virtue" a conceptual framework that is absent from and antithetical to his practical criticism.

Although meeting this objection is a task for the whole book, let me begin by explaining more precisely why I call Ruskin a "practical critic" and how this label helps us understand his critical approach and his style of argumentation.

From the early 1850s onward, a commitment to the practical integrates Ruskin's corpus. We see this commitment in his work as an art critic and, increasingly, in the attention he devotes to a wide range of his contemporaries' activities. This focus on human activity is my interpretive key to Ruskin's inquiries into moral character and human flourishing. He argues that individuals succeed in cultivating, or fail to cultivate, their virtues as a result of the activities in which they choose to engage. This participation in specific activities also helps to define the ends and goods that people pursue, especially the ends and goods that they share with other people. One further aspect of Ruskin's critical vision enters in, too. People's activities reside within broader patterns of cultural significance and social organization. What people value and how they arrange their roles and relationships affect the types and variety of activities available in a society as well as different individuals' access to and abilities to participate in them. In sum, Ruskin's focus on practical activity joins three goals of his criticism: to foster the development of good character, to determine the legitimate ends of human flourishing, and to promote a shared commitment to the just conditions and relationships needed to extend these possibilities to everyone.

These conceptual links have not been identified as I have done here or elaborated as I do throughout the book. Ruskin never sets them forth just so, nor does his criticism conform to this framework in all respects. His evocative style, interpretive skills, and creative eclecticism all contribute to a body of criticism far more detailed and varied than this framework suggests. Yet Ruskin is also remarkable for his ability to draw powerful connections, illuminating how his contemporaries' endeavors, commitments, choices, and relationships enhance or injure their own and others' well-being. Reading him as a "practical critic" clarifies how he achieves this richly contextual moral vision.[12] It also proves central to three organizing claims of the book.

The first claim is that reconstructing Ruskin's vocabulary of the virtues brings into view the argumentative basis of his criticism. In staking this claim, I must stress that my interest is in his *evolving* use of the vocabulary. He does not always relate people's activities, virtues, goods, and ends in the ways that I just outlined. At first he sees all virtues, those of human beings and of other living creatures, as set by God's Creation. Only when Ruskin comes to appreciate culture as the arena within which people adopt and work out their goods and ends with each other does he become a practical critic in my full sense of the term. Other scholars have noted the shift in Ruskin's focus from God's Creation to human creativity. James Sherburne's comment on this transition is typical. He writes that "Social dogmatism grows on Ruskin as Evangelical fades."[13] Similarly, George Landow's study of Ruskin's aesthetic theories emphasizes the uncertainties that enter, or should enter, his art criticism as he increasingly doubts his Evangelical upbringing and abandons his early "theocentric" theory of beauty.[14] Why then does Ruskin continue to offer his aesthetic and moral judgments as if they came with the imprimatur of God's truth? If he initially "argues" from a theological conception of the good that he later rejects, what other than the mere assertion of his own personal authority can sustain his confidence beyond this point? I answer these questions differently than do other scholars.

I argue that we can understand Ruskin's continued confidence and grasp the reasons behind his critical judgments only if we reconstruct his vocabulary of the virtues and pay careful attention to how he adapts it as a means of *cultural* critique. Here the focus on practical activity is crucial. Whether Ruskin is detailing the moral characteristics of a Gothic cathedral, praising the excellence of a wrought-iron fence, or condemning the idolatrous use of money, he calls his readers to see how certain cultural activities and their attendant virtues, ends, and goods are productive of the best kinds of life, while others are not. He is not merely asserting "subjective" judgments. Instead he examines activities that are available for others to investigate, too. He analyzes how these endeavors shape their participants and help define their commitments and obligations in ways that can be judged as good or ill. A vision of the good remains in force in Ruskin's arguments, therefore, but the good is now specified through his detailed descriptions of the activities constituting human cultures at particular historical junctures. As a result, his moral vision becomes more practical, multifaceted, and contestable.

The second claim follows from this point. Ruskin's approach to culture makes for an instructive contrast with those of Marx and Mill. Ruskin comes to understand culture as a human production. At times he envisions this construction of culture as happening behind people's backs in a way similar to Marx. Unlike Marx, though, he finally places culture in the hands of its makers, charging people to examine how their chosen activities form their own and others' character and what goods and ends they uphold as a result of those choices. The contrast can be extended to Mill, too. While Mill acknowledges the effects of cultures on people, he has little to say about how cultures are or should be made. He is more interested in how the new institutions of industrializing and democratizing societies open up space for individuals to expand their civilization. This primary concern with the role of institutions in freeing up the development of stifled human potentialities marks another way that Mill and Marx stand largely on the same side of nineteenth-century debates. I develop this point in the following section.

The third claim looks ahead to Ruskin's ethics of consumption. He develops his virtues-centered approach to consumption out of his practical conception of culture, and this constructive development transforms the critical possibilities of his tradition of British social thought. This tradition includes such predecessors as William Wordsworth (1770–1850), S. T. Coleridge (1772–1834), and Thomas Carlyle whose own accounts of culture look to the shaping powers of the poet, the genius, and the hero. By contrast, Ruskin shifts the responsibility for culture and the locus of critical judgment from the poet, genius, and hero to individual consumers. It is more accurate to say that he *begins* this shift. I exaggerate to make a point about the tensions in Ruskin's ethics.

Constructing an ethics of consumption requires an exercise in moral imagination that looks past the moment of market exchange and the prices that people pay for economic goods. This effort at moral imagination becomes an increasingly complex task as British imperialism, industrial capitalism, and global commerce transform economic relations, social conditions, and political power throughout Europe and the world. Ruskin's response to these developments is both cautionary and instructive. On the one hand, he remains devoted to the quest for a common vision of the good that characterizes his tradition. Sometimes his way of presenting the "wisdom" taught by nature, community, history, and religion does make him resemble a prophet or a sage who simply calls others to heed his authority. On the other hand, the movement of his criticism toward an ethics of consumption makes the achievement of such a seamless moral vision as untenable as it would be undesirable. Consumers will continue to disagree about the good life. Nevertheless—and this is a crucial point—consumption cannot be cordoned off as a realm of life in which individuals' tastes function as the sole norm. Instead, efforts to achieve a broader view of economic life are demanded by any ethics of consumption, as Ruskin realizes.

Imagination is required to fathom the ends and the commitments reflected in consumers' choices and to reveal the effects of work and other activities on individuals' development or lack thereof. Imagination is also required to trace out the networks of interdependence in which people participate along with the justness of the relationships and opportunities available to them as individuals given their contributions to the larger community. Ruskin's social criticism aims to provoke consumers to exercise their moral imagination in all of these ways. That is why he engages so many facets of contemporary culture in his wide-ranging, richly descriptive accounts. That is also why he works out an assortment of critical tools to illuminate where common ends and shared commitments either do or should guide consumers' choices. Ruskin's "practical" approach and critical tools can still help us imagine how consumption continues to interact with character, culture, and community, making our own choices as consumers more responsible.

Liberalism, Marxism, and the Good

Ruskin, Marx, and Mill were contemporaries. After Marx's removal to Britain, all three lived and wrote in close proximity to each other, but there is no indication that any of them knew the others personally. Ruskin criticized and caricatured Mill's writings, notably his *Principles of Political Economy* (1848). Ruskin makes no mention of Marx, not surprising given Marx's relative obscurity and Ruskin's dislike of German theorists. Neither Mill nor Marx acknowledges Ruskin, which is perhaps more surprising considering the public nature of his project and his direct attack on Mill. One reason for Mill's and Marx's silence could be that both of them had engaged earlier figures in Ruskin's line of criticism, borrowing from Coleridge and Carlyle while refusing the metaphysical sanction that these other thinkers sought for their respective visions of the good.

Why then do I draw Ruskin into conversation with Mill and Marx? As noted before, I do so partly because Ruskin attends to consumption more than they do. Reading the three of them together has another salutary effect, too. It complicates the twentieth-century reception of nineteenth-century debates about industrial capitalism. For most of the twentieth century, disputes between democratic liberals and Marxist socialists predominated, with Marxism emerging as *the* critical lens on capitalism. Reading Ruskin's criticism alongside Mill's and Marx's theories helps unsettle this polarizing picture.

The nineteenth-century response to industrial capitalism did not divide into two, or even three, neat categories. Ruskin's sophisticated and remarkably thoroughgoing critique represents one among a variety of options. Recovering Ruskin does more than add to the options available in nineteenth-century debates, though. It also helps us appreciate more fully Mill's and Marx's complex analyses, a key feature of which is their shared distrust of the kind of teleological approach that Ruskin takes.

Although I want to explore the complexities of Ruskin's approach and Mill's and Marx's criticisms, let me start a bit more simply. In one important respect Ruskin stands on one side of an intellectual divide, Mill and Marx on the other. In Ruskin's teleological approach, ethics, society, economics, art, work, and so forth, can be judged only in light of some authoritative vision(s) of the good or, at the very least, shared goods. Mill and Marx, by contrast, are deeply suspicious of all such appeals. Their distrust is closely tied to the liberating thrust of their theories, a chief reason why each of them becomes so significant for progressive politics in the twentieth century.

Consider here Ruskin's scorn for Mill's emphasis on liberty. Ruskin reserves some of his harshest criticism for the "modern Liberal politico-economist of the Stuart Mill school" (27.180). If we can look beyond Ruskin's inflated rhetoric, he raises a crucial issue. He is adamant in his criticisms of Mill because he reads Mill's writings on economics, politics, and society as denying legitimacy to sources of authority that extend beyond individuals' preferences. Although unfair to Mill's corpus, this is a fair reading of his reasons for embracing utilitarianism. Marx is equally suspicious of authoritative visions of the good—and even of more modest appeals to shared goods—in his critique of ideology. In sharp contrast to both Mill and Marx, Ruskin frequently directs his audience's attention to the arrangement of goods that he thinks should guide their lives and join their efforts. He finds his evidence in a range of sources, appealing to divine revelation, the natural order, the good life, the common good, and people's everyday practical activities. These various sources of moral vision shift in priority over the course of his career, but Ruskin remains convinced that there are "prior" goods that rightly shape people's character and communal relationships.

Mill and Marx, for their part, both reject the idea that knowledge of the good is in any way prior to individual freedom. There are legitimate historical concerns motivating this line of criticism. Appeals to the good and to shared goods reflect the privileged definitions of some group, usually an elite. The alternative, however, is not entirely clear. It is one thing to suspect appeals to divine revelation, the natural order, and the good life for legitimizing the interests of some powerful group. It is another to reject all such appeals and whatever other vehicles people use to construct and sustain shared cultural agreements about their commitments. Indeed, before we reject the full-blown teleological approach to ethical reflection that Ruskin represents, we should acknowledge two problems with Mill's and Marx's responses to it.

The first concerns the "teleological" elements in each of their theories. Mill's embrace of a utilitarian form of consequentialism and Marx's utopian accounts of humanity's eventual self-realization are both conceptual attempts to arrive at some "good" independently of any prior specification of those activities, desires, and ends that are taken to be normative, at least for some group of people. These latent teleological elements in both figures' theorizing help justify Mill's emphasis on individual preference and Marx's critique of ideology.

The second problem relates to the close connection between these teleological elements and Mill's and Marx's assessments of industrial capitalist societies. Both of them applaud the ways that industrialization acts to loosen the hold of entrenched elites. But Mill's reliance on utility as the measure of value reflects a confidence in market competition that Marx's analysis of the irrationalities of capitalist production and exchange finally does not allow. Despite this crucial difference, however, both theorists view the emerging institutions of industrial capitalist societies in a similar way. They observe that these institutions are increasingly becoming the primary mediators of collective choices. Although this judgment seems largely right historically, it is not the full picture. But here the "minimalist" teleological features of Mill's and Marx's theories cause a kind of conceptual overkill. To the extent that these features are emphasized, Mill's and Marx's writings tend to be reduced by their proponents to arguments for either the market or the state as *the* institutional mechanism for producing societal goods.

Ruskin's attention to culture, community, and character begins to look more promising against this backdrop. Certainly there are ways that people fashion common commitments independently of the two institutional mechanisms of the market and the state, as the recently renewed interest in civil society testifies. We are not merely individuals who juggle our diverse and often competing desires and goals through the intermediaries of the market and the state. Nor did Mill or Marx view things so narrowly. In fact, if we embrace the narrow readings of their writings that all too often dominated twentieth-century debates, we lose much of the richness of their theoretical visions. Even if we remain at the level of institutions, Mill accepts the need for government action to support and regulate the economy, while Marx sees benefits accruing from the relentless growth of industrial capitalism. Mill is no blind loyalist to laissez-faire, just as Marx is aware of the limitations of statist control. More significantly, both figures are acutely aware of the importance of culture.

Mill's concerns with democratic culture show in his recognition of the pernicious effects of the Victorian family on women's rights and aspirations. Noting that the family serves as a "school" of character, he rejects how its Victorian configuration imposes virtues and role-based duties in sex-specific ways.[15] More generally, Mill modifies strict Benthamite utilitarianism by building in a recognition that certain pleasures of "higher" culture may be qualitatively different from ordinary satisfactions.[16] Marx, for his part, is a keen observer of the symbolic character of capitalism—notably, of how money and commodities assume cultural meanings quite different from their apparent uses. His early forays into the critique of religion also highlight the cultural construction of gender roles, the issue that Mill interrogates more fully later on.[17]

I emphasize Mill's and Marx's analyses of culture for two reasons. First, these theorists' influence has been and continues to be so extensive partly because of the integration and breadth of their critical visions. That is not to say that the richness of their writings is always recognized, however, as I have said.

Second, there is an instructive irony here. One reason why Mill's and Marx's writings on culture receive relatively little attention is that their conclusions about industrializing societies are now so widely accepted. Note that I have praised them for their insights into culture. While they are astute observers of *culture,* even if not to Ruskin's extent, they depart from him in their suspicions of the stultifying effects of *character* and *community.* Ruskin sees grave threats to culture, character, and community from market competition, the division of labor, the extension of the franchise, movements for women's and workers' rights, and so forth. By contrast, Mill and Marx largely welcome this institutionalized transformation of society. They applaud industrial capitalism for eroding hierarchical patterns of social roles, duties, and privileges and the religious, moral, and metaphysical appeals invoked to sustain these orders of dependence. For Mill and Marx, then, culture warrants scrutiny, but mostly to diagnose the pernicious effects of established patterns of *community*-sanctioned duties and *character*-based roles.

This shared conviction figures prominently in twentieth-century debates between liberals and Marxists. It appears in the narrow focus on institutional mechanisms and the relative disregard for considerations of culture.[18] It also highlights an assumption held by both sides. There is a basic premise that conceptions of culture and ethical approaches that presume the need for broad agreement to shared goods are ideologically suspect.

The example of Ruskin indicates that there is merit in this premise. His own portrait of the family as a school of character is not one to celebrate. Even as he champions a role for upper- and middle-class women in Victorian reform movements, he circumscribes women's roles and virtues in ways that justify social hierarchies in the interests of promoting good character and achieving a communal good. Nevertheless, I reject the blanket assumption that any ethics that appeals to shared goods is ideological. The premise is too broadly dismissive, and it limits the range of critical resources available today, including Ruskin's own vocabulary of the virtues, which proves so vital to his ethics of consumption. We must try, if it is possible, to separate Ruskin's valorization of social hierarchies from the appeals to shared goods at work in his assessments of his contemporaries' character, their personal and communal well-being, the vitality of their culture, and the justice of their society.

Reading Ruskin, Marx, and Mill together marks a historical crossroads of sorts. One of the roads is the full-blown teleological—and, in Ruskin's hands, largely Christian—approach to normative reflection that centers in his vocabulary of the virtues. On this approach people are defined as participants in the cooperative endeavors and shared goods that define them as interdependent members of a community. It is a well-traveled road in the history of Western ethics, especially leading up to the nineteenth century, but beyond it as well. The other road reflects more secular modes of theorizing individuals' interactions through institutional structures. This increasingly more populated path is represented by Mill, Marx, and many others.[19] The prospect offered by my own interpretation of Ruskin is that it may be possible to dwell at this intersection without having to abandon one road to pursue the critical concerns that delineate the other.

Recall my comments about the place of culture in Mill's and Marx's writings. I read in their writings something of this creative exploration of how these roads come together. Their arguments, however, are often in the service of demonstrating that only one road is viable. This line of argument is particularly apparent in Marx's scientific utopianism. The communism of the future will have its own culture, but it can emerge only through capitalism's dismantling of the ideological norms and standards inscribed in past cultural forms. A similar faith can also be seen in Mill's corpus. In his political economy, for example, he acknowledges that a "Stationary State" economy will eventually arrive when concerns about culture, education, good work, leisure, and the environment—in other words, Ruskin's concerns—can finally emerge to the fore. For now, though, industrial growth must rule if the existing conditions of scarcity and relations of dependence are to be overcome.[20]

Looking around the world today, we see that the Marxist narrative of the revolutionary transformation of the relations of production and the unleashing of humanity's potential has lost much of its following. More hopeful, it seems, is Mill's reformist conviction that the expansion of capitalist and democratic institutions is necessary to liberal commitments to individuality and equal participation for everyone. Are these the only options available for progressive politics? If so, then must we follow Mill, agreeing that expanding people's opportunities for individual well-being and fuller participation requires relying on institutions as the principal mediators of social goods and the guarantors of justice?[21]

Although there are strong historical reasons to side with Mill, he recognizes the limitations of this vision. Someday the "Stationary State" economy will arrive, and then other ethical issues will become more pressing. But when exactly does this future arrive? And how are these concerns to be articulated when the time comes? Ruskin already engages the questions that Mill and Marx postpone. He asks, what priorities should people set together, especially as consumers? What activities, ends, and goods are best for fostering people's character and well-being and are most productive of a good community, a just society, and a sustainable environment? The urgency of the questions is clear. What remains unclear is whether Ruskin's way of addressing them can still help.

Recovering Ruskin

I opened this introduction by noting the decline in Ruskin's influence. One cause is our distrust of the kind of teleological moral language he uses. Although there are good reasons for this distrust, I have tried to indicate how a critical appreciation of his vocabulary of the virtues can enhance our options as we move past the Marxist-liberal debates of the twentieth century.

This effort to recover Ruskin conflicts with two influential scholarly narratives that also help explain why he is read so little today. In different ways and in different periods, Raymond Williams and Alasdair MacIntyre have expanded the prospects for ethical and critical thought through their respective historical narratives of nineteenth-century British social criticism and Western traditions of the virtues. Both narratives, however, leave Ruskin with almost nothing to say.

Consider Williams's *Culture and Society.* This study recounts an "anti-individualist" tradition of British social thought running through such figures as Edmund Burke (1729–97), Coleridge, Carlyle, and Ruskin. When the book first appeared, it helped to diagnose and correct the neglect of culture in mid-twentieth-century Marxist-liberal debates. It remains exceptional, too, as a major study of the formative social theorists and cultural critics of the period that takes Ruskin seriously. Yet Williams discusses Ruskin mostly to demonstrate that his approach to culture is irretrievably compromised by a devotion to unity and hierarchy. In narrating the emergence of a culturally attuned Marxism in Britain, Williams positions Ruskin as *the* transitional figure who brings cultural analysis to bear on economic life. Although Williams praises this contribution, he rejects Ruskin's idea of culture as both holistic and elitist.

While Williams is right to see the seeds of Ruskin's hierarchical portrait of good societies in his early association of beauty with a "perfect life in man," Williams neither recognizes nor allows for the changes in Ruskin's vocabulary of the virtues. Certainly the perfectionist connotations of this vocabulary presume that human development in society is ordered toward "prior" goods, but the details of how those goods are fashioned, pursued, criticized, and refined matters a great deal. Rather than sorting these issues out in Ruskin's case, Williams's narrative presses on. For him a more open-ended conception of culture, stripped of religious appeals and hierarchies of "values," is the achievement of Ruskin's follower William Morris (1834–96). Morris not only secularizes culture, Williams argues. He radicalizes the relationship between art and labor by identifying the working class as the active transformer of both.[22]

Reading Ruskin as a stepping stone toward the triumph of Western democratic, secular, and humanist Marxism makes certain features of

Ruskin's criticism seem to warrant little comment or scrutiny. Nothing can be salvaged. Among these features are Ruskin's religious appeals, his evocations of nature's beauty, his portraits of craftwork, his communal sense of abundance, and his calls for the responsible use of power and the just spending of money, all of which relate to his focus on character and community and his vocabulary of the virtues. No doubt Morris's arts and crafts movement represents one of the trajectories of Ruskin's legacy. The movement itself, however, draws more from the "unsalvageable" parts of Ruskin's criticism than it does from the supposed progressivism of a secularized and revolutionary working-class culture. Nor is Morris alone in citing Ruskin's influence. Other leading figures who express their debts to Ruskin include Leo Tolstoy, George Bernard Shaw, J. A. Hobson, and Mohandas Gandhi. A 1906 survey of the first Labour Party members elected to the British Parliament found Ruskin cited as the most influential author for the group as a whole.[23]

It is surprising to discover Ruskin's remarkably political influence on the generation that followed him. Once again we must ask, why was this influence lost? MacIntyre's narrative offers a possible explanation. Ruskin is irrelevant to current debates about economics, politics, society, and the environment because his moralism is at odds with the bureaucratic and market languages of rights and utility that we rely on so heavily in negotiating these matters. While Ruskin's appeals to the good might have retained an aura of plausibility in his day, the early-twentieth-century critiques of Victorian sages by members of the Bloomsbury group "unmasked" these moralistic pretensions.

For MacIntyre what is so significant about these early-twentieth-century critiques is what they reveal about modern moral discourse not only in Britain but throughout the West. The older teleological approaches to ethics from which Ruskin draws have become unintelligible, MacIntyre argues. At one time the term "good" and evaluative judgments were generally understood to be "objective" because there remained intact traditions in which the virtues proper to a human life could be organized in light of a community's shared narrative of the "good-for-man-as-such." In such a context rational moral discourse was possible; claims about the goodness of some course of action could be defended with reasons. According to MacIntyre, the Bloomsbury critiques reflect a very different theory of language. With the twentieth-century emergence of "emotivism" as the reigning philosophy of moral language, the term "good" is seen as having no other warrant than assertions of individual preference. To say something is "good" is simply to assert that "I like this . . . and so should you," but appeals to mere preference are coercive. For MacIntyre we are all "emotivists" now. Although we may aspire for "impersonal" moral judgments and invoke "universal" principles in defense of them, we recognize that our moral views are just as subjective as our aesthetic tastes. The present state of affairs, he concludes, is the result of the historical loss of the teleological approaches to the moral life that I claim Ruskin represents.[24]

Given MacIntyre's interest in the fate of teleological ethics, it is odd that his narrative passes over Ruskin.[25] Filling in the gaps in the story, the Bloomsbury critique would seem to go as follows. Ruskin offers little more than an aesthetics of highbrow taste dressed up as "good" for workers, consumers, and society at large. Just as his art criticism might strike us today as richly imaginative *and* deeply personal, so too, his renderings of the virtues, his appeals to shared goods, and his portraits of good lives cannot be "objective" moral claims. With this judgment MacIntyre would seem to agree since he names Jane Austen and William Cobbett the last representatives of a coherent tradition of the virtues.[26] The Victorian period comes "after virtue." Ruskin's writings must therefore lack the intelligibility required for serious engagement either by MacIntyre or by other scholars interested in the critical possibilities of his ethics.

MacIntyre's narrative would be strengthened—or, in my judgment, challenged—by a careful examination of Ruskin. Here is a critic who often appeals to "the good" and who issues "objective" aesthetic and moral judgments in that light. Here is a critic who uses a vocabulary of the "virtues" and who describes the "character types" and the "social roles" that form a good society. What then are we to make of Ruskin's virtues-centered critique of industrial capitalism? Is he relying on the vestiges of a once-potent form of argumentation, the lost coherence of which is confirmed by his own fleeting influence?

A survey of recent communitarian critiques of modernity would suggest as much. With few exceptions, these critics of liberal modernity's perceived lack of cultural meaning, common purpose, and civic engagement ignore Ruskin and other members of his tradition. This silence is doubly disturbing. On the one hand, it suggests a worrisome refusal by communitarians to examine whether their chosen language of virtues, roles, character, and community is compatible with democratic individuality. On the other hand, it contributes to the narrowing down of communitarian concerns to a set of overly theoretical questions about the conditions for coherent moral discourse and the role of civil society in fashioning selves. Lost here is Ruskin's trenchant critique of economic injustice.

The Good Economy, Religion, and Moralism

John McGowan crystallizes the two issues at stake in the refusal to engage with Ruskin and his tradition. McGowan argues that communitarians, among whom he includes MacIntyre, Christopher Lasch, and others, should be more forthright about their affinities with nineteenth-century Tory radicals such as Coleridge, Carlyle, and Ruskin.[27] To take one of McGowan's examples, he notes that Lasch "leaves out all the elements characteristic of [the older Tory radicals'] positions that most consistently offend modern readers," including their "nostalgic, elitist, and antidemocratic overtones" and "appeals to the irrational." At the same time, McGowan highlights these earlier figures' importance in raising "absolutely vital questions about authority and legitimacy which both the left and the right find too tricky to tackle."[28] These issues of authority and liberty, on the one hand, and legitimacy and community, on the other hand, are both essential to, and difficult to negotiate in, any ethics of consumption. Regarding authority and liberty, we citizens of liberal democracies leave ample room for consumers to determine and express their individual preferences, provided, that is, they have the requisite purchasing power. Regarding legitimacy and community, we also recognize that there are shared goods, including the world's resources, nature's beauty, excellent craftsmanship, creative work, public spaces, and vibrant cultures, that require our mutual support and frequently demand changes in our buying patterns.

The tensions between liberty and authority are clear enough, and the critics of socialism have successfully redrawn these tensions as an inescapable trade-off, citing the ample historical evidence of authoritarian communist regimes in support of their arguments. The deeper issue, however, is the legitimate hold that shared goods should have on us as consumers and would clearly have if there were better ways to deliberate together about what these shared goods are and how we might take responsibility for them as a community.

In the coming chapters I argue that Ruskin gives us many tools for deliberating together about which commitments should guide our consumption. As such his writings include critical resources to help overcome the "nostalgic, elitist, and anti-democratic" tendencies of his tradition. One crucial lesson he teaches is that a practical criticism, attentive to the imaginative resources of religious traditions, not only can serve aspirations for a more democratic economic life, but also corrects against the zeal for abstract theorizing and institutional tinkering that sometimes narrows the vision of the secular left. Here I must clarify the cultural conception of religion that I bring to this study and that Ruskin adopts over the course his career.

Ruskin's development as a critic proves that he was an astute observer of the intellectual turn from theology to culture occurring in Victorian Britain. What puts him ahead of his time, however, is his growing sense that religions should be studied as part of the cultural mix, not viewed as a sphere of privileged knowledge grounded in a prior faith commitment. In the first half of the book (chapters 1–4), I chart his movement away from a belief-centered to a practice-centered model of religions.[29] Most obviously, the disparagement of "modern Protestantism" in his later writings reflects his moralistic critique of the idea of religion as centered in an inner-life of belief that precedes and stands apart from religious practices and social ethics. He not only locates the meaning and value that people find in their traditions in the rituals, liturgies, and other enculturated forms of worship they perform. He also comes to view the normative offerings of religions as one more set of ethical resources—one more cultural source of moral visions of the good—to bring to the forum of public discourse.

For much of its history, the study of religion has been dominated by a belief-centered view of religions, so it is remarkable to find Ruskin diagnosing and rejecting this largely Protestant idea. It is also instructive to see how he puts religious appeals to use in his later social criticism, interpreting mythic figures, scriptural vignettes, and religious artworks in novel ways, always seeking to make these interpretations fully persuasive to the "public" of his day. The important point for this book is that the more Ruskin locates religions in historical cultures, the more "reasonable" his religious appeals become. At the same time, he never wavers from his conviction that religious symbols, examples, and attitudes are vital to the moral task of imagining the full extent of the vulnerability and interdependence in human life.

It is odd, then, that Ruskin is rarely read by scholars in my own field of religious ethics. Although this omission is partly because the study of Christian ethics, in particular, has focused unduly on theologians and church officials, I would still expect to find Christian critics of capitalism mining his corpus as a resource for ethical reflection. In perhaps the greatest irony in the twentieth-century reception of nineteenth-century debates, however, Christian ethicists mainly looked to Marx, the critic of religion, for their guiding vision and vocabulary.[30] I still view aspects of Marx's analysis of industrial capitalism as illuminating. His critical vocabulary remains an important source of insight and inspiration, too. Yet as the Marxist narrative loses its intellectual hold, the danger is that ethical critiques of global capitalism will disappear along with it. We may see this happening already in the methodological preoccupations of critics like the later MacIntyre.

Another oddity worth noting is Ruskin's absence from two recent studies that praise nineteenth-century "moralists." Stefan Collini describes the Victorian heirs to Mill's liberalism as "public moralists"—those "well-connected . . . intellectuals [who] persuaded themselves they had a special duty to remind their more self-interested contemporaries of the strenuous commitments entailed by the moral values embedded in the public discourse of their society." Likewise, Terry Eagleton portrays Marx as an unwitting "classical moralist" who, despite himself, "believed that moral inquiry had to examine all of the factors which went to make up a specific action or way of life, not just personal ones." Collini's and Eagleton's shared sense that public life incorporates moral values and moral factors that must be accounted for in judging the goodness of people's lives and the justice of their society matches Ruskin's critical concerns. When Eagleton cites "the good life," "virtues," and "flourishing" as central concepts in any progressive vocabulary committed to human development, he repeats Ruskin's moral vocabulary.[31]

Collini's and Eagleton's reasons for passing over Ruskin are unconvincing. Collini notes Ruskin's eclectic borrowings from religious myths and his bad manners in the clubby environs where the other public moralists swapped their ideas. Eagleton absorbs Ruskin, along with Leo Tolstoy, into the history of "Western Marxism," without acknowledging that the religious sources and convictions informing their writings put both of these authors beyond the pale for many Marxists. It is clear that misgivings about religion contribute to the neglect of Ruskin, but the real issue is his moralism—his readiness to subject his contemporaries' character, desires, and ends to ethical scrutiny. Certainly "character" can be reduced to the "self-restraint, perseverance, strenuous effort, courage in the face of adversity" that Collini cites as the defining concept for his public moralists.[32] But Ruskin's conception of character as the full development of the range of aesthetic, intellectual, practical, and moral virtues needed to live well is better suited to the integrated moral vision of an ethics of consumption. His searching imagination and religious sensibility also sustain the powerful connections he draws for his contemporaries. To the extent that he resists predicating the authority of this ethics on the prior faith commitment of an insular set of beliefs, his arguments and his religious appeals remain open to debate by others who are free to draw their own conclusions either as participants in or as practical observers of the cultural activities that take the center stage in Ruskin's social criticism.

There is a tendency in Ruskin's moralism toward insular communities joined by a unified vision of the good. More valuable, though, are his evocative, descriptive readings of specific artworks, buildings, practices, institutions, myths, rituals, commodities, symbols, and the myriad other aspects of the cultures he interprets. It is this piecemeal, descriptive criticism, informed by his religious sensibility, focused on character, grounded in his analysis of cultural practices, and dedicated to working out common goals and shared goods, that demands our attention as a model for an engaged ethics today.

Overview of Chapters

The book's argument divides into three parts. The two chapters in part 1 introduce the theological structure of Ruskin's early readings of natural beauty and landscape painting and the cultural reorientation that occurs in his studies of Gothic architecture. Chapter 1 explores the normative aims of his early aesthetics, rejecting the epistemological conundrums that have dominated Ruskin studies. His own phrase, "The Duty of Delight," is a striking reminder that the dichotomies of obligation versus desire and virtue versus happiness in modern moral theory are foreign to the teleological ethics that frames his entire corpus. Drawing from Aristotle and Richard Hooker, this chapter sets aside the "subjectivist" premises of early nineteenth-century romantic and empiricist aesthetics and reconstructs Ruskin's initial critical vocabulary as answering to a singular idea of God's virtue as the source and aim of all life. This theological metaphysics provides a benchmark against which to measure his innovations as a critic.

Chapter 2, "The Spirit of Labor," explores Ruskin's search for a new moral vocabulary appropriate to his growing awareness that people's desires and ends are cultural, the products of the activities in which individuals participate whether by choice or by necessity. In his fictive portrait of Gothic character, he reorients his critical lens from God's seminal virtue and fixed purpose to the many human virtues and ends that people develop, pursue, extend, and revise through those "social practices" that are akin to Gothic craftwork. The chapter also contrasts Ruskin's and Marx's models of work to mark the basic tensions in their analyses of the cultural construction of economic life and human agency under industrial capitalism.

As Ruskin turns from God's Creation to human creativity, he transforms himself into a practical critic of the activities and institutions, the ideals and symbols, the individual desires and social goods, the virtues and vices, that constitute historical forms of life like Victorian culture. The chapters in part 2 explore how he adjusts to the cultural realities that are now the focus of his criticism and that mark the limits of his normative appeals. Ruskin's précis to his new endeavor in culture-reading and culture-making is his proposed "modern" curriculum of natural history, religion, and politics, and the chapters in part 2 follow this outline in answering three leading questions of his ethics of consumption: What do we make of the world's resources? What do we make of the products that other people have made? How might the making of good things and the recognition of other people's gifts be promoted in a just polity?

Chapter 3, "The Nature of Imagination," examines Ruskin's increasingly cultural understanding of "nature" and his growing appreciation of the shaping power of the imagination on individuals' perceptions of things. Still resistant to "subjectivist" accounts of individual taste, he now allows that the value of natural resources can be known only through the cultural creations of human activity. Nevertheless, he models a virtues-centered approach to examining which practical activities make the most of participants and the world itself, and he seeks to persuade his audience that they can arrive at shared judgments of the "intrinsic value" and the "natural limits" of the world's resources and alter their consumption accordingly.

The fourth chapter, "The Vision of Religion," traces out the dramatic changes resulting from Ruskin's reconception of religions as ensembles of practices dependent upon individual imagination and communal performance to make them meaningful. This chapter also explores his use of religion as a model for the symbol systems, social relations, and practical attitudes that bind people in cultures. Comparing Marx's analysis of "commodity fetishism" to Ruskin's critique of capitalist "idolatry" underscores the centrality of worship and agency to Ruskin's practical criticism (by contrast with Marx's theoretical suspicions about both) as well as the ideological liabilities of Ruskin's continued metaphysical appeals.

Chapter 5, "The Politics of Medievalism," relates Ruskin's advocacy of the virtues of natural and communal piety to a raft of other virtues—justice most importantly. His classical ideal of politics as the "science of the human good" is that portion of his writings most closely aligned with communitarian interests in a civil society of intermediate associations that foster social virtues, distributive justice, and rational deliberation, all under a coherent vision of the good. While Ruskin's concrete proposals anticipate and help legitimize some of the reforms of the twentieth-century welfare state, his hierarchical view of the good society should give us pause.

The constructive argument of part 3 claims that Ruskin's ethics of consumption is his most lasting contribution to the history of ethical and critical thought. In it we see modeled a public practice of moral imagination, to be undertaken by individual consumers and centered on visions of the human good. In his ethics of consumption, this practical effort is open to democratic contestation and committed to the cooperation and inclusion of democracy at its best.

The sixth chapter, "The Value of Virtues," demonstrates the constructive role of Ruskin's vocabulary of the virtues in his critique of Mill's classical political economy. Ruskin argues that economic value depends on the development of a range of human virtues, and this chapter reconstructs his account of value on that basis. It also demonstrates how his concept of "effectual value" corrects against his metaphysical tendencies and anticipates what is now called the "capabilities approach" to human development. A comparison with Amartya Sen shows the affinities between Sen's account of the standard of living and Ruskin's criticisms of income- and utility-measures of the quality of life. It also shows that commitments to democratic equality can be made compatible with and even enhanced by a culturally contingent teleological ethics.

Chapter 7 asks, "Is Good Consumption Possible?" and considers the charges of elitism and paternalism issued to Ruskin's ethics of consumption by Marx and Mill, respectively. In their writings they segregate the normative from the descriptive largely because they both view capitalism as a progressive force and so distrust the appeals to the good and the moral restrictions found in Ruskin's writings. In defending Ruskin's teleological approach and the practical implications of his ethics, this chapter analyzes his theory of money and his argument that money is no neutral meeting place of mere exchange. Rather, money is always a moralized power that can represent things well only if consumers practice the virtues of justice and piety in their buying decisions.

The conclusion returns to Ruskin's efforts to cultivate "Moral Vision in Religion, Culture, and Consumption." I defend his innovative and eclectic practice of a teleological ethics as offering a risky, though vital, set of critical resources, with its moral vocabulary, conceptual tools, and cultural engagement. Ruskin's hope is the creation of shared spaces of moral regard and interdependence where people might come together in the interests of their own and others' full development and a just distribution of good things. Paradoxically, creating this common space begins with individuals imagining good lives and purchasing these lives for themselves and other people. In this sense every ethics of consumption is prescriptive and therefore jarring to the distaste for moralism typical of today's secular left. It also reminds us, however, of the need to accept the discomfort that comes when religious and cultural visions of the good are offered and debated in public life. Thus, in the end, Ruskin's criticism offers not only resources for articulating an ethics of consumption but also an occasion for revitalizing progressive politics more generally.

I read Ruskin to be encouraging a great many practices of good consumption. The educational initiatives, political movements, and public debates that these spaces of common purpose and moral reflection might sustain can be made his most lasting contribution to ethical and critical thought. Taking up that challenge requires acknowledging the legitimate misgivings about his politics and then putting his vocabulary of the virtues to new uses. Political movements for social justice today need a searching and compelling moral vision. They can be helped along by consumers' creative imaginings of better lives, a provisional offering that must be open to revision and debate but that is possible only if people ask what activities, virtues, ends, and goods are worth committing to with others. Consumption will never be a realm of full agreement about the good, which is why efforts toward good consumption are both needed and will always, thankfully, be incomplete.

At its best democratic liberalism has championed inclusion, but the idea of inclusion implies that there is something worthwhile being included in, and Ruskin's teleological ethics and practical criticism offer ways of discussing and imagining what we care about, where these commitments show, and how either these or other common concerns might help in promoting economic justice, communal flourishing, environmental health, *and* democratic individuality. If we read Ruskin as standing at a crossroads of nineteenth-century moral thought, then his vocabulary of the virtues, his critical interests in social practices, his creative readings of culture, his evocative religious appeals, and his imaginative search for shared commitments can all be made useful tools serving ends that he himself did not foresee.

PART ONE

The Sources of Ruskin's Moral Vocabulary

ONE

The Duty of Delight

This opening chapter begins at a distance from Ruskin's ethics of consumption. Its focus is the theory of beauty that he elaborates early on in the second volume of *Modern Painters* (1846). The distance between this volume and Ruskin's mature ethics can be measured not only by topic and time. Dramatic changes also occur in the teleological structure of his criticism, and marking those changes requires clarifying at the outset both the sources of and the initial developments in his moral vocabulary. Those sources and developments are the organizing concerns of the two chapters in part 1.

In this chapter I approach the "sources" of that moral vocabulary more as a conceptual challenge than a historical question. There are important historical questions, of course. How is Ruskin's early aesthetics influenced by past writers and artists? How does he distinguish his theory of beauty from other leading theories of the day? How do his early writings reflect his Evangelical Anglican upbringing and his historical context more broadly? As I read his early aesthetics, however, history presents another challenge that must be addressed first, specifically, the conceptual distance that intervenes between Ruskin's character-based approach as a critic and the interlocking aesthetic, political, economic, and moral theories that increasingly become dominant in and around his period.

These emerging theories are more familiar to us today, making the task of reading Ruskin well partly a matter of setting them aside and reading him more on his own terms. In general what characterizes these theories is that they take as their starting point the premise, the promise, and the problem of "subjectivity." This trend toward seeing the individual subject as sovereign judge and creator of value is most apparent in aesthetic and economic theories. Partly because we are influenced by nineteenth-century intellectual developments, we are inclined to take people's desires and preferences as they are, especially in our discussions of aesthetic taste and economic behavior. That Ruskin is responding to these same trends helps explain why he concentrates so much of his criticism on art and economics.

Throughout his writings Ruskin remains opposed to the trend toward locating the source and measure of value in individuals' preferences and desires, where these preferences and desires are abstracted from the shaping and binding influences of character, community, and culture. In his early aesthetics, culture plays no role at all, in fact, and community is mostly a side effect of a person's aspiring love for the beauty of God's Creation—what Ruskin calls the "duty of delight." Indeed it is Ruskin's fervent conviction in *Modern Painters* 2 that God is *the* sovereign judge and creator of all things' goodness that makes this volume so useful for understanding the moral vocabulary of his early writings. It is crucial to emphasize as well, however, that Ruskin's corpus is not beholden to a static dogmatism. What is so remarkable and instructive about his criticism is how widely he ranges over the course of his writings in his arguments, illustrations, interests, language, and appeals, all the while trying to teach his audience to see—and how to see—the connections between their character, community, and culture and the commitments that he argues they do or should uphold together.

This way of framing the argument of *Modern Painters* 2 suggests that Ruskin begins with a self-conscious project of resisting the turn toward subjectivity. That is not my claim. Indeed, despite the systematic argumentation and theoretical structure of the volume, we can read in his tone the passion and exhilaration of a young man following out his heart's desires and delights in the world around him and on the canvases of those artists who move him deeply. While Ruskin wrote the first volume of *Modern Painters* to defend his contemporary J. M. W. Turner, he draws much of the inspiration for his argument in volume 2 from his encounters with the paintings of the sixteenth-century Italian Jacopo Tintoretto. As Ruskin proclaims in a letter home to his parents in September 1845, he "never was so utterly crushed to the earth before any human intellect" as on his visit to the Tintoretto gallery of the Scuola Grande di San Roco in Venice (4.xxxviii). Tintoretto's *Crucifixion,* in particular, illustrates the kind of delight that the young Ruskin finds in the ordered, symbolic vision of beauty that this painting exemplifies.

Tintoretto's *Crucifixion* overwhelms, reaching forty feet across. The scene teems with people, while a palace, hills, trees, and tools crowd its open spaces. Except for the crucified Jesus Christ who looms centrally above the action, the other figures gesture, lean, and look in seemingly countless directions and with equally varied expressions. Some grieve, some labor, some observe, some cower; no one laughs or mocks. The apparent confusion of the frenetic scene stands in sharp contrast to Tintoretto's ordered composition. Indeed on closer inspection of the painting, the grouping of people resolves itself into a radial pattern bisected by the towering crucifix and oriented by the crosses of the two thieves. These crosses lie heavy on the ground, exalting the Christ figure and accentuating the unified, symbolic vision pointing toward God by which Tintoretto held together all of this swirling energy.[1] So great is the "joy, admiration and gratitude" that Ruskin feels before such artistry that he endeavors to make these moral responses common to all of his readers (4.47).

Throughout *Modern Painters* 2 and much of Ruskin's later criticism, there is often this expectation that readers will see things just as he does. If they are not as awed by Tintoretto's representations of the range of human passion and the scenic splendor of a landscape, then it is Ruskin's task to instruct them in how to appreciate the true worth and loveliness of these things. A term of Ruskin's captures this expectation best. The goal of *Modern Painters* 2 is nothing less than the cultivation of "community" in people's tastes, a shared sense of which things are most beautiful and what their beauty means (4.25). Looking back today, this hope for a lasting and genuine consensus about the value and meaning of beautiful things is difficult to fathom. One reason is that our aesthetic and moral theories have departed from the kind of teleological thinking that motivates the premises and aims of Ruskin's early aesthetics and the theological conception of the good that he details there.

An argument for art's moral purpose propels all of volume 2 from the opening assault on the "vanity" that art serves in these "days of despatch and display" (4.27) to the exhortation that closes the discussion of beauty. Ascribing to J. C. F. Schiller the view "that the sense of beauty never farthered the performance of a single duty," Ruskin rejects such a separation of art from ethics. Instead he urges upon his readers the "duty of delight" as the surest moral course in all things spiritual and practical. "We cannot say how far it is right or agreeable with God's will, while men are perishing round about us; while grief and pain, and wrath, and impiety, and death, and all the powers of the air, are working wildly evermore, and the cry of blood going up to heaven, that any of us should take hand from the plough; but this we know, that there will come a time when the service of God shall be the beholding of Him; . . . and there shall be 'no more curse, but His servants shall serve Him, and shall see His face'" (see Rev. 22.3–4). This passage recalls the confusion of Tintoretto's *Crucifixion* and its symbolic promise of an eventual ordering of life according to God's purposes. In volume 2 Ruskin does not look to this eschatological end, however, but to the natural world around him. He counsels his readers to turn their attention and affections to "nature undestroyed" to find their chief aid in the "struggle with nature fallen." And he closes his celebration of natural beauty by charging the clergy to attend more closely to the "duty of delight" than the "duty of self-denial." Chastising parishioners about their everyday failings is less edifying of moral character than is encouraging people to revel in the goodness of God's Creation as revealed in the world's beauty (4.215–18).

This phrase the "duty of delight" is my interpretive key to the moral vocabulary at work in *Modern Painters* 2. Drawing on a central theme in Christian thought extending well back to Augustine, Ruskin locates the moral task of human life chiefly in the aspiration to delight in God's goodness. This chapter reconstructs his early critical vocabulary on that basis and begins a reading that locates him as an innovator in a tradition of ethical reflection on character, virtues, and goods. Since these aspects of his critical thought stand in tension with intellectual developments in his period, this may be why his ethics and his life-long concern with character have not been treated as aspects of an integrated vision.

Ruskin's harmonizing of duty and delight strikes a discordant note even in his day. Schiller is not alone in differentiating art from ethics, and Ruskin is arguing against the tide of aesthetic theory in claiming that the pleasures of painting have any bearing on moral obligations. Yet, arguably, this juxtaposition of duty and delight seems even more out of place from the standpoint of modern moral theory. Although Ruskin was no reader of Immanuel Kant (1724–1804) and Jeremy Bentham (1748–1832), the historical developments that elevate their moral philosophies are well underway as he begins his career. In Britain this is particularly true of utilitarianism, and Ruskin's disdainful use of the label "utilitarian"—emblematic of the "hurry of crowds and crash of innovation" (4.32)—is typical of such predecessors to Ruskin as S. T. Coleridge and Thomas Carlyle. For all three figures, the pleasures weighed by utilitarians have little to do with ethics beyond the weakening of character. Simply accepting individuals' pleasures as they are distracts people from the delights that ought to command their desires. Ruskin's polemic against utilitarianism is as pronounced in *Modern Painters* 2 as it is frequent. More implicit and more important is his appeal to an ideal of flourishing—articulated here as a theological conception of the good—that unites duty with delight and virtue with happiness. Indeed because Ruskin does not start from, or really even consider, the premise of "subjectivity" in his early art criticism, he is unconcerned by the conflicts between moral duty to others and vital happiness for oneself that define so much of modern moral theory.

On the approach to ethical reflection that Ruskin presumes in his early aesthetics, the moral task is not to set aside one's desires, or "inclinations," in favor of a Kantian categorical imperative. Nor is the moral task to regulate one's actions and measure one's pleasures by a utilitarian calculus of "the greatest happiness of the greatest number." The task is to form one's character, to train one's desires, so as to be able to seek out the proper ends of a good and full life, a life that consists in meeting obligations to others while living bountifully. In *Modern Painters* 2 Ruskin bases this correspondence between duty and delight on a Christian idea that aspiring to the good that God intends for all creatures brings not only the fullest happiness to the individual but also right relations with every other being. This chapter recovers that Christian moral framework as the source of much of Ruskin's initial critical vocabulary. Although the terms of his criticism change and develop considerably, this focus on character and on the related ideal of flourishing remains central to all of his later writings.

Good Character and Good Taste

An intriguing instance of the merging of aesthetics and ethics in *Modern Painters* 2 is Ruskin's criticism of the "appetite of tasteful cruelty." Even as the elite of his day flaunt their supposed "good taste," their display of refinement is little more than social posturing and often involves outright cruelty. With his ethics of consumption still more than a decade away, Ruskin's phrasing rings prophetically, and he writes with his usual verve: "we pamper the palate with deadly meats, until the appetite of tasteful cruelty is lost in its sickened satiety, incapable of pleasure unless, Caligula like, it concentrate the labor of a million of lives into the sensation of an hour" (4.61–62). This incisive conjunction of cruelty and taste, of the pain inflicted on others through the enjoyment of certain kinds of pleasures, might seem out of place in a study with the subtitle "Of Ideas of Beauty." As Ruskin excludes Edmund Burke's category of the "sublime," with its focus on terror and pain, from the first two volumes of *Modern Painters,* the appearance of these themes of power and suffering is surprising (3.128–30). Nevertheless, the passage is not out of keeping with the volume's thesis of the necessarily moral relation between human desire and divine delight.

We should not read too much of a political edge into this excerpt, however. Despite the injunction against wasting other people's lives in momentary luxuries for oneself, Ruskin offers no sustained analysis in *Modern Painters* 2 of how the powerful abuse their privileges. A critical interest in power awaits his later writings. The lesson he draws here is that his readers must seek the antidote to their corrupted appetites in a "deep delight from the meanest objects of creation;—a delight which shall not separate us from our fellows, nor require the sacrifice of any duty or occupation, but which shall bind us closer to men and to God, and be with us always, harmonized with every action, consistent with every claim, unchanging and eternal" (4.62). Learning to appreciate the least detail of nature's beauty can return people's sympathies to their proper objects, leaving no "direct contradiction between the unselfish duties and inherent desires of every individual" (4.61). In positing this congruence between moral duty and good taste, Ruskin goes much farther than criticizing the rapaciousness of a Caligula. He appeals to God's Creation as the original ordering of the good that human beings should seek in all things, and he reads in natural beauty the signs that guide people to this eternal harmony of the true ends of life. This vision of the good motivates his theory of beauty in ways that are insufficiently appreciated by other commentators.

Modern Painters 2 has been a puzzle and a problem for many scholars. Take what is perhaps the most widely influential reading of it. In *Culture and Society,* Raymond Williams's classic study of an "anti-individualist" tradition of British writers ranging from Burke to twentieth-century Marxists, Williams builds his largely critical interpretation of Ruskin on the theory of beauty that he constructs in the second volume. In Ruskin's definition of "vital beauty"—"the felicitous fulfilment of function in living things, more especially of the joyful and right exertion of perfect life in man" (4.64)—Williams finds the earliest expression of Ruskin's ideal of good societies.[2] Williams argues that the language of "function" and "perfection" that pervades this volume legitimizes a hierarchical ordering of society and that the same thinking compromises all of Ruskin's corpus.

While there is merit in Williams's drawing attention to the social implications of this language, his conclusions are misplaced in two ways. First, he along with most Ruskin scholars fails to explore how "function," "perfection," and other related terms operate within the teleological framework of *Modern Painters* 2. Based on Ruskin's references, he borrows that framework from the sixteenth-century Anglican theologian Richard Hooker, and Ruskin's initial vocabulary of perfections, functions, characteristics, powers, and types needs to be read in light of Hooker's theological metaphysics. Second, although Ruskin continues to use some of these terms in his later writings and his approach remains teleological, Williams misses the extent of the changes introduced into Ruskin's moral vocabulary by his turn from God's perfect Creation to human beings' imperfect creativity. That change comes as Ruskin moves from the landscape paintings of *Modern Painters* 1 and 2 to the studies of architecture that occupy him from the late 1840s through the early 1850s. Those developments are the subject of chapter 2.

There is another strand of Ruskin commentary that relates more directly to the argument of this chapter. Unlike Williams, other Ruskin scholars acknowledge significant changes in his critical approach, and the issue of "subjectivity" is prominent in those interpretations. The basic argument runs as follows: Ruskin's early art criticism is flawed because of his blindness to the diversity of people's "subjective" tastes and his insistence on "objective" standards of beauty. George Landow develops the most careful and influential version of this argument. In summing up his assessment of Ruskin's theory of beauty, Landow writes, "Ruskin's aesthetic theories are the product and the type of irreconcilable dilemmas in his thought. When he wrote the second volume of *Modern Painters,* he wished to take into account the subjective nature of beauty and yet make it a universal, objective phenomenon. Having begun with the premise that emotion is the basis of art, beauty, and morality, he wished to avoid the disordering, as well as the subjective, nature of emotion."[3] But Ruskin does not use the terms "subjective" and "objective," except to reject them. Nor, as I argue in the coming pages, does he make "emotion" the basis of art, beauty, or morality.

Certainly Ruskin's use of John Locke's empiricist terminology can be read as evidence of an interest in epistemological problems of perception. Gary Wihl goes so far as to call Ruskin "arguably, the most important epistemological critic in English." He bases this interpretation on Richard Rorty's definition of epistemology as the "labor of sorting out the 'given' from the 'subjective addition made by the mind.'" But Rorty offers this definition in *Philosophy and the Mirror of Nature,* where he seeks to dismantle the philosophical picture of a world out there, the "objective" truth of which must be known apart from the "subjective" accretions added by the perceiver's mind. Amazingly Wihl never mentions Rorty's therapeutic aim of overcoming the philosophical disputes between realists and idealists and the epistemological problems of perception that Wihl reads into Ruskin's criticism.[4] That Ruskin goes out of his way in *Modern Painters* 3 (see chapter 3) to reject the terms "subjective" and "objective" and that he defines "realism" and "idealism" in a nonphilosophical way means that we should read him in light of his own language and the structure of his teleological criticism. We can understand Ruskin's initial vocabulary and his later distancing from *Modern Painters* 2 only if we appreciate that this volume answers not to epistemological questions about the subjectivity of human perception but to ethical concerns about the human pursuit of the good.[5]

None of Ruskin's writings causes him such deep ambivalence as *Modern Painters* 2, and it is worth noting the twists and turns in its publication history. In 1871 Ruskin vowed never to publish any parts of volume 2 again "except the pieces relating to natural history." He dismissed the rest as the errors of a youthful dogmatism and affected style. A decade later, however, he changed his mind and re-issued the volume in a "carefully revised reprint" (4.3, cf., 18.31–32). In the preface to this 1883 revision, Ruskin explains the distance he now feels from this early study chiefly in terms of his religious biography. No longer is his Evangelical Anglican upbringing so formative of his criticism, and he singles out his earlier use of the beatitude "Happy are the pure in heart, for they shall see God" as a likely source of confusion for his readers. An emphasis on "the heart" suggests a focus on emotions alone. Even worse for Ruskin, it might be taken as licensing a "subjective" inwardness that seeks only its own self-justification. As he puts it looking back from 1883, the "spurious and prurient self-condemnation which is the watch-word of modern Protestantism" has nothing to do with the "general theorem" of the second volume (4.4–5).[6]

Instead, both here and throughout Ruskin's criticism, happiness is a way of being in the world that orients one beyond oneself and toward the good. It is not an internal state of self-satisfaction. Indeed one's desires and preferences cannot be analyzed except in relation to the things one admires and the ends one seeks, all judged according to their relative worth and loveliness in the scale of goodness that the early Ruskin equates with God's ordering of all life in the Creation. To be "pure in heart" is not merely to be cleansed of sin, though Ruskin the young Evangelical certainly sounds this resonance of the phrase at times.[7] More importantly, being "pure in heart" is a process of becoming more capable of exercising a loving regard for everything in the world.[8] This is why Ruskin calls the perception of beauty a "*moral* perception," a phrase that, when read against the backdrop of his use of the Lockean term "idea," causes considerable confusion (4.35; my emphasis).

On the original 1843 scheme for *Modern Painters,* Ruskin divided his intended subject into three classes of ideas, "ideas of truth," "ideas of beauty," and "ideas of relation" (3.130). In volume 1 he analyzes the workings of "ideas of truth" in landscape painting, arguing that "truth to nature" is the standard of all good art. Volume 2 picks up the remaining two classes of ideas in the original outline, and Ruskin posits the existence of a "faculty" corresponding to each one. People perceive beauty through the "theoretic faculty," and artists compose what they perceive in the world through the "imaginative faculty." And by these two faculties, Ruskin adds, "all things external to man are . . . *turned to good*" (4.242; my emphasis). This "turning to good" must be read in the context of his critical interests in the connections between a person's desires and character and the goods or ends he or she seeks. Yet Ruskin's terminology masks his focus on the virtues of good character. It implies instead an inward movement from the "external world" toward the "perceiving subject." Consider here his use of an image of the eye to organize the main topics of *Modern Painters* 2 and their corresponding faculties. He figures the theoretic faculty as a "moral retina" and the imaginative faculty as an "intellectual lens" (4.36). There is a gap, it seems, between a person's "subjective" sensations of beauty and any intellectual effort to judge things according to a common "objective" standard.

Much of the discussion of Ruskin's early aesthetics has examined the epistemological problems of perception posed by this empiricist-sounding mechanism of the eye. How is it that individuals respond to the same paintings, images, and scenes so differently? What is the source of these diverse preferences? What mental or emotional mechanisms contribute to them? These epistemological concerns fit the intellectual trends in Ruskin's period and assumptions about the subjectivity of taste. That he resisted those trends, however, makes it all the more important to acknowledge the actual terms of his project and to examine the lineage he claims for them.

Ruskin admits that people's preferences do differ, and he engages in debates with other theorists who seek to explain these differences in light of the subject's contributions of mental associations or personal emotions. Here Landow's study of Ruskin's aesthetic theories helpfully locates him in relation to the two main branches of early-nineteenth-century British aesthetics, known by the labels "associationist" and "romantic." As Landow notes, Ruskin criticizes the empiricist psychology of the associationist Archibald Alison. In his *Essays on the Nature and Principles of Taste* (1790), Alison ascribed the perceiving subject's enjoyment of beautiful things to pleasurable "associations" with past experiences recalled by the mind. A hill, for example, might become beautiful to people who associate it with the glory of a military victory or a fond personal memory. Similarly, a "romantic, emotionalist" aesthetics, to use Landow's words, also accords to the subject the activity of infusing things with a sense of beauty. In this case, though, the individual's emotions color external objects as beautiful, and the different feelings that a painting inspires in viewers will lead them to see it their own ways.

In each of these theories, the diversity of individuals' tastes is explained by some internal mechanism that brings a person's past associations or present emotions to bear on the thing being perceived. This emphasis on subjectivity is not found in Ruskin's aesthetics, and as Landow notes, Ruskin's theory of beauty counters the turn toward the subject as the creator of value. But Landow allows no other options than these associationist and romantic mechanisms for explaining differences in personal taste, even as he alludes to a "divine element in [human] nature," or what Ruskin would call, with greater conceptual precision, "character." In the end, Landow argues, Ruskin's early theory of beauty reduces to a "theory of uniform emotional reactions" that belies the evidence of this diversity. He adds that, in the coming years, Ruskin increasingly allows that the associations that people bring to their perceptions of art and nature do contribute to the beauty and meaning that they find there.[9] But if we read Ruskin through the lens of these emerging theories, we lose sight of his moral concerns and normative language.[10]

The questions of Ruskin's early theory of beauty are ethical, not epistemological. His main question is, how is the perception of beauty "moral"?[11] Put differently, what do a person's perceptions of beauty reveal about his or her character? In reconstructing this concern with character, we must heed Ruskin's references, both explicit and implicit, to Aristotle's *Nicomachean Ethics.*

One of the curious features of Ruskin's early aesthetics is the extent to which he borrows from classical discussions of pleasures and the good, even as he disparages the Greeks as pagans who are incapable of contemplating the highest pleasures of beauty. Ruskin read Aristotle as an undergraduate at Oxford, and though overt references to Aristotle are few in *Modern Painters* 2, they are basic to the argument of that volume. Ruskin names his theoretic faculty after the Greek term "theoria," or "contemplation." He introduces this faculty's operation by relating Aristotle's account of the virtue of temperance to the training and governance of desire in matters of bodily pleasure. Ruskin elevates the pleasures of sight and hearing over those of taste, touch, and smell. Only sight and hearing are marked by the finality and self-sufficiency of Aristotle's *eudaimonia* (4.42–45). Ruskin also rejects "the mere animal consciousness of the pleasantness I call aesthesis" in favor of "the exulting, reverent, and grateful perception of it I call theoria. For this, and this only, is the full comprehension and contemplation of the beautiful as a gift of God, a gift not necessary to our being, but added to, and elevating it, and twofold, first of the desire, and secondly of the thing desired" (4.47). I return to discuss this aspiring dynamic to "comprehend and contemplate" God's good through the highest pleasures of beauty in the following section. Important for now is how the language of "elevating desire" signals Ruskin's critical interests in the states of character that inform the pleasures an individual derives from "ideas of beauty" and that structure the feelings or attitudes he or she has toward them.

Given the focus on pleasure and the life of contemplation in Book 10 of the *Nicomachean Ethics,* it is not surprising that Ruskin advised in the first edition of *Modern Painters* 2 that "the concluding Book of the Ethics should be read carefully. It is all most valuable" (4.145n).[12] There are clear echoes of Ruskin's own approach to beauty in Book 10. When Ruskin introduces the category of "ideas of beauty" in *Modern Painters* 1, for example, he claims that "Why we receive pleasure from some forms and colors, and not from others, is no more to be asked or answered than why we like sugar and dislike wormwood." The pleasures of beauty are instinctive for people in a "*healthy and cultivated state* of mind." Those who "lack taste" are similar to people who find little sweetness in sugar, while those with "bad taste" actually prefer bitterness (3.109–10; my emphasis). Similarly, Aristotle argues that, although some people may enjoy "disgraceful pleasures," this is no reason to conclude that pleasure itself is bad. We would not expect, he continues, that "the things that are wholesome or sweet or bitter to sick people" are really so. Nor should we base assessments of pleasure on the enjoyments of people who have a "vicious constitution."[13]

For Ruskin, as for Aristotle, certain pleasures are "naturally" good for people. Yet in Aristotle's *Ethics* it is only through the process of cultivating one's character, and thus the attitudes, pleasures, and judgments of the virtuous, that one's "instinctive" desires become what they should be. Likewise, if we ignore the connection that Ruskin charts between good taste and a well-formed character—what he means by the "blessedness" of "the pure in heart"—then we neglect his normative concerns and the moral argument of his early aesthetics that people can and should take responsibility for their tastes. Indeed is it really the case that an individual's desires and preferences are fixed by past experience or present mood? Are people incapable of evaluating and regulating their desires and preferences because these are determined by factors outside one's control? A more critical question arises here, too. Can the "subjectivist" aesthetic theories that Landow canvasses account for the intersections between individual taste and shared moral standards? We should, I contend, be prepared to criticize an "appetite of tasteful cruelty," a love of pleasures gained through feasting on other people's suffering. Moreover, it is the taste itself that we should criticize, not simply the harmful actions undertaken to satisfy it. In this regard the aesthetic theories of empiricism and romanticism offer little critical help. They explain subjective differences through internal mental and emotional mechanisms that operate free of the shaping influences of character, community, and culture on desire.

No doubt Ruskin focuses narrowly on character in his early aesthetics. His analysis of the cultural construction of desire and its communal consequences awaits his social criticism. At this early stage of his writings, his vocabulary of the virtues lacks sophistication and is largely hidden by the Lockean terminology of *Modern Painters* 2. But before dismissing this theory of beauty as insufficiently attentive to subjectivity, we should learn to read its animating moral argument in light of Ruskin's nascent vocabulary of the virtues. He does not, in fact, appeal to emotions alone. In his contrasting lists of good and bad traits, we find more substantive moral attitudes and attributes alongside mere feelings. The people who receive beauty well combine gratitude, hope, and love with compassion, strength, and patience. Ruskin contrasts these praiseworthy characteristics of the seekers of beauty with selfishness, worldliness, vainglory, dissimulation, enervation, and apathy (4.30). These traits are not emotional reactions to, or filters of, beauty. For Ruskin they are the cultivated states of character that orient a person's whole life toward or away from happiness in all of one's pursuits, making art, nature, and beauty vital sources of the moral compass needed for devoted worship of God.

"Community" in Taste through Christian Loves

As noted, *Modern Painters* 2 builds from the 1843 outline of the three "ideas" at work in landscape painting—ideas of truth, beauty, and relation. If we take Tintoretto's *Crucifixion* as an illustrative example, we can enjoy the painting's "truthfulness" to the details of nature ("ideas of truth") and judge the canvas as an imaginatively ordered composition ("ideas of relation"). But there is something more in this artwork ("ideas of beauty") that first attracted Ruskin before he stepped back to marvel at Tintoretto's "crushing" intellect. For the rest of this chapter, I leave aside the topics of truth and imagination, returning in chapter 3 to discuss Ruskin's evolving approach to these two topics, specifically, how "truth to nature" can remain his standard of good art even as he allows more independent powers to people's imagination in his mature aesthetics. My concern in what follows is to develop and explore his argument about the moral implications of good taste.

In *Modern Painters* 1 Ruskin contrasts "taste," or the reception of beauty in general, with all forms of "judgment," a term "expressing definite action of the intellect." He insists that taste "properly so called . . . is the instinctive and instant preferring of one material object to another without any obvious reason, except that it is proper to human nature in its perfection so to do" (3.110). In this definition we see once again the important tension in Ruskin's argument—there are so-called *instinctive* pleasures that, nevertheless, require the *perfection* of human desires through the development of character.

A related tension opens *Modern Painters* 2. It is the tension between the apparent diversity in people's "mental impressions" of beauty and Ruskin's insistence that good taste is uniform. As he moves from the "obvious and visible facts" of the natural world to individuals' "instinctive and instant" responses to beauty, there is a sense in which he sees himself turning from an external world of facts to people's inner perceptions of "the value and meaning of mental impressions." Yet despite the language of this opening paragraph, Ruskin refuses the fact-value distinction. He offers instead two warnings that capture the integrating moral purposes of his theory of beauty. On the one hand, he calls for "modesty and cautiousness proportioned to the difficulty of determining the likeness, or *community*, of such [mental] impressions, as they are received by different men." On the other hand, he demands "seriousness proportioned to the importance of rightly regarding those faculties over which we have *moral power*, and therefore in relation to which we assuredly incur a *moral responsibility*" (4.25–26; my emphasis). These warnings reflect Ruskin's implicit, motivating question: is it possible—and if so how—to arrive at "community" in taste by exercising control over the theoretic faculty and its "moral perception and appreciation of ideas of beauty" (4.35, cf. 4.75)? Thus, the (finally unanswerable) question of whether or not people have the same "mental impressions" of beauty is significant for him only because it suggests how far both critic and reader must travel if they are to arrive at the normative goal of community in good taste.

Ruskin traces out the journey toward community in taste early on in *Modern Painters* 2. Although he misquotes volume 1 by omitting the task of development in arriving at a "healthy [and *cultivated*] state of mind," he now approaches the uniformity of good taste not as a foregone conclusion but as a goal to be attained (cf. 3.109, 4.51). How can this "healthy state of mind" be judged? What justifies the boldness of probing another person's taste, a domain where each individual, it seems, "has a right to his opinion," say, in "prefer[ring] the scent of violets to roses"? The force of these questions reflects the prevailing view that aesthetic matters are not subject to "voluntary choice," and yet for Ruskin it falls to each person to take pleasures from the proper "sources" and not from others. If everyone exercised his or her "moral duty" in seeking out the right sources of pleasure, he adds, then the differences in people's tastes would abate (4.52). This shift away from the perceiving subject to the sources of pleasure once again mirrors Aristotle, who claims that "some pleasures *are* desirable in themselves, differing in kind or in their sources from the others."[14] That some pleasures are intrinsically desirable and that pleasures can be ranked as good, better, and best fits Ruskin's theory of beauty exactly. For him the ability to distinguish and order pleasures is the necessary outcome of good taste.

Choosing to make his case on the worst possible grounds, Ruskin argues that even "lingual taste," what Burke called that "most ambiguous of the senses," arrives at a common ordering of pleasures.[15] The tongue's pleasures seem quite naturally varied among different people, and Ruskin acknowledges that when first tasting some new flavor, people lack the "power to prevent or command the[ir] instinctive preference." But he draws a distinction between people's "immediate preferences" and their "ultimate preferences." Over the first we have no control, but "ultimate preferences" are another matter, he argues. Empirical observation teaches that through testing and comparing flavors, people learn to discern new qualities in food and drink beyond those that dominated their palates initially. As a result, their preferences are changed. That this reordering of preferences moves "from variation of opinion to unity of opinion" is reflected, Ruskin claims, in the authority granted to the good taste of expert chefs and other judges in culinary matters. All of this shows, he concludes, that good taste is uniform and that even the tongue is designed to prefer "those qualities which are calculated finally to give it most pleasure" (4.54–55).

Compared with the leading aesthetic theories of Ruskin's day, his claim that good taste is uniform seems dogmatic, and perhaps hopelessly so. But the argument is not unprecedented. It stands in a long tradition of reflection on the relationship between character development and the good. The early Ruskin, however, understands the process of self-cultivation rather differently than Aristotle. For Aristotle the standards of pleasure's goodness show directly in the authority of the judges whom Ruskin cites. In Aristotle's words, since "virtue and the good man as such are the measure of each thing, those also will be pleasures which appear so to him, and those things pleasant which he enjoys."[16] Learning to enjoy the good man's pleasures requires taking on the activities and ends that form his virtues, thus becoming capable of pursuing the "good life" that he models for the community. By contrast, in Ruskin's early account of good taste, although the goal remains "community," the measure of goodness is not the example of the wisest, but the glories of God's Creation. It is God who ordains that some qualities of food and drink will be the most pleasurable. It is God who makes them the most "permanent" and "consistently agreeable" to the palate (4.54). And for Ruskin what holds for the tongue holds for the higher senses, too, for the sights of nature's beauty are made to be the most pleasurable of all.

Ruskin's initial teleological approach to ethics is Christian, not Aristotelian. His praise for the *Nicomachean Ethics* reflects the passing of four decades in his work as a critic. Ruskin's early definition of "theoria"—again, "the full comprehension and contemplation of the beautiful as a gift of God, a gift not necessary to our being, but added to, and elevating it, and twofold, first of the desire, and secondly of the thing desired" (4.47)—brings out the crucial connection between human desire and God's gifts that are the two poles in classical Christian accounts of the ethics of "love." The goal is to move human desire toward a reverent reception of God's loving purposes. A similar dynamic is seen here in the movement of good taste from immediate to ultimate preferences, an aspiring effort to direct one's desires toward the objects made proper to them by God's creating the world in all of its glory. The closer the beholder of beauty comes to this sanctified or "blessed" state, the truer his or her "moral perception" becomes.

I introduce the term "sanctification" to convey this ascending movement of aspiring love, the continual orientation of desire toward delight that underlies Ruskin's account of good taste. In his own use of the word "love," he includes people's "likes" and, by extension, "dislikes." This corresponds to a Christian notion of "loves" as the desires that people have for "goods," namely, all that attracts one, from art and beauty to fame and money. On Ruskin's way of thinking, one's loves are the substance of one's moral being in that "the whole culpability or propriety of actions" out in the world depends on an inward "power" of governing these likes and dislikes. As he puts it, "men are guilty or otherwise, not for what they do, but for what they desire, the command being not Thou shalt obey, but Thou shalt love, the Lord thy God; a vain command if men were not capable of governing and directing their affections" (4.54). If we read outwardly directed "affections" as inner feelings, then we omit the Christian and teleological thrust of the argument. Ruskin is not concerned with a subjective "inner life," but with character. He locates the reception of beauty "in" the heart because for him one's moral character depends on whether or not one's loves have been sanctified by placing the love of God first in all things.

This orientation of human loves toward God extends to the loves that every creature has for the divine purposes appointed to it. Here Ruskin looks beyond the strictly human happiness of Aristotle's *eudaimonia* to a Christian notion of the flourishing that all creatures seek. When Ruskin writes that he calls "any creature 'happy' that can love, or that can exult in its sense of life" (4.7), Landow responds that "loving and exultation are activities which would require consciousness in some form." For Landow, anyone who perceives love, exultation, and happiness in a plant or animal must be projecting his or her emotions onto it, indicating that Ruskin falls back on a "romantic, emotionalist theory."[17] But this move misapplies epistemological concerns to Ruskin's theory of beauty by ignoring the broader Christian teleological ethics that Ruskin reads in Richard Hooker. For Ruskin, love and exultation are not the "internal" emotions of "conscious" beings. He means these terms in the teleological sense that all creatures "love," that is, tend toward, those ends that mark their perfections and "exult," that is, attain full flourishing, in those efforts that make for vital living for them.

The Christian conception of the person as a bundle of loves to be directed and ordered properly is at the center of Ruskin's early aesthetics. It is why he rejects a romantic aesthetics of emotions as a false theory of taste.[18] Locating the perception of beauty in the subjective coloration of a person's feelings only licenses a prideful self-assertion, a taste "forever meddling, mending, accumulating, and self-exulting, its eye is always upon itself, and it tests all things around it by the way they fit it." Here self-love replaces love of God, and the taste for beauty answers not to the ordering of the Creation but to the fancy of the individual. By contrast, a true taste flows from a temper "forever growing, learning, reading, worshipping, laying its hand upon its mouth because it is astonished, casting its shoes from off its feet because it finds all ground holy, lamenting over itself and testing itself by the way it fits things" (4.60). For the young Ruskin, loving God is a moral duty at odds with a mental or emotional subjectivity. Loving God and, with it, aspiring to recognize the true significance of every aspect of nature's beauty both entail the cultivation of a character that upbuilds the right dispositions needed to comprehend and contemplate the world as God's gift.

The "duty of delight" reflects the continual effort to receive the fullest enjoyment from the world's beauty by learning to love God first. Only then can the pleasures proper to "human nature *in its perfection*" be grasped in terms of their true "value and meaning." Always in Ruskin's early aesthetics, there is this aspiring movement to love the world's beauty well and, thus, the need to be "perfected," to cultivate a pure heart, to develop one's character. But while the introductory argument of *Modern Painters* 2 suggests that the focus will be on the *human virtues* required for good taste, Ruskin's theory of beauty attends to *God's virtue,* to the "divine work and character" stamped on all of nature's beauty. So dominant is the focus on the divine sources and significance of beauty that it is hard to discern Ruskin's interests in human character at all. In the coming sections I reconstruct his initial vocabulary of the virtues by showing how his early theory of beauty is structured throughout by Hooker's theological metaphysics.

Beauty's Part in God's Character and Work

Following the classical distinction between useful pleasures and self-sufficient pleasures, Ruskin defines two kinds of pleasure taken in nature's beauty. There are pleasures "given to us as subservient to life, as instruments of our preservation"—for example, the pleasures of seeing ripened fruits and grains. Although beautiful in a way, people's enjoyment in this case lies in these things' true end of satisfying hunger and giving nourishment. There is, however, another class of pleasures, such as the delight in a flower. Why is a single flower more beautiful than a field of grain, Ruskin wonders, even though the flower serves no end beyond the sheer delight it invites? It must be that this pleasure derives not from any "means or instrument of life, but [from] an *object of life*. Now, in whatever is an object of life, in whatever may be infinitely and for itself desired, we may be sure there is something of divine; for God will not make anything an object of life to His creatures which does not point to, or partake of, Himself" (4.46; my emphasis). On the basis of this passage, Robert Hewison has argued that Ruskin had to "prove that beauty was an independent and objective reality." But clearly the word "object" carries its ethical sense as an "end" of human activity, rather than its epistemological sense as a "thing standing apart" from the perceiving subject. Ruskin does not associate beauty with "objectivity," but with such terms as "perfection," "ideality," and "attractiveness."[19] Again we see the Christian themes of aspiring love for and reverent acknowledgment of God's gifts in moving individuals toward the telos, or the good of life, and forming the character needed for the "moral perception" of beauty.

Ruskin's appeal to the "objects of life" disclosed by people's responses to nature testifies to the teleological structure of his theory of beauty. The pleasure of a flower is an end in itself. It has an "attractiveness of inherent beauty" that inclines the observer to love it wholeheartedly (4.64). This emphasis on the intrinsic "loveliness" of the natural world's greatest beauties resembles Burke's definition of beauty in *The Sublime and Beautiful* (1756), the most cited treatise on aesthetics for the young Ruskin. For Burke beauty is "that quality or those qualities *in* bodies by which they cause love, or some passion similar to it."[20] Once again the focus is on the sources of beauty and their relation to human passions. Yet Ruskin looks beyond the flower as a source of pleasure and asks why something with no apparent purpose in maintaining human life should excite so great a love. As this pleasure is so inherently attractive and so complete in itself, he concludes that such beauty must be of the highest good and so must "point to, or partake of," God "Himself."

That beauty signifies the "participation" of God's goodness in the world marks Ruskin's theory throughout. It marks the theory quite literally. As he puts it in charting the path of his argument, the "common and general sources of pleasure" that are the ultimate objects of good taste consist in "a certain seal, or impress of divine work and character, upon whatever God has wrought in all the world" (4.59). His two-part scheme of beauty—as "typical" and "vital"—builds from this conviction that the signs of "divine character" and "divine work" are stamped everywhere in the world. "Typical beauty" reveals God's own character; "vital beauty" discloses God's work in the natural world.

"Typical beauty" shows throughout the Creation from inanimate stones on up. What attracts the lover of beauty in this case are the signs of the "Divine attributes"—infinity, unity, repose, symmetry, purity, and moderation—wherever they appear in the formal patterns and lines of nature or in a landscape painting. "Vital beauty" is found in animate creatures, as already defined, in "the appearance of felicitous fulfilment of function in living things, more especially of joyful and right exertion of perfect life in man" (4.64). Ruskin devotes most of *Modern Painters* 2 to reading the evidence of these signs of God's character and work in the natural world. He gives his interpretations consistency and credence by systematically interrelating God's "types" and creatures' "functions" and "perfections." All told, it is a vision of the good that looks to Richard Hooker's incarnational view of God's participation in the world and of creatures' participation in God's goodness.

Good taste's aspiration toward the divine, as that which all objects of life "partake of," highlights Hooker's prominence in *Modern Painters* 2. Although Ruskin read extensively in Hooker's *Laws of Ecclesiastical Polity* (1593, 1595, 1648, 1661) while writing this volume, scholars have tended to limit the Anglican theologian's influence to its systematic style and preacherly tone.[21] Malcolm MacKenzie Ross stands out for crediting Hooker's theology with informing much of the volume's content, and he captures the bounded dynamism of the early aesthetics when he notes that Ruskin's "rapt naturalism" is shaped "to the image of Richard Hooker's Thomistic structure of Law."[22]

Ruskin's "rapt naturalism" shows in the loving detail he lavishes on the form, structures, and features of everything he finds in nature. Each sunset and rock, each plant and animal, has a distinctive beauty that makes it, in a word, "lovely." The powerful attraction Ruskin shows in his readings of nature's beauty exemplifies the aspiring urgency of the "duty of delight," and he sees in the movement of his own exhilarating love something of the fullness of all life. If, as he claims, people's "use and function" are "to be witness to the glory of God, and to advance that glory by . . . reasonable obedience and resultant happiness" (4.28–29), then other creatures also have their role and purpose.

Hooker provides a model for this aspiring love of beauty, matched, in turn, by every creature's pursuit of its appointed "perfections." Hooker writes, "all other things besides [God] are somewhat in possibility, which as yet they are not in act. And for this cause there is in all things an appetite or desire, whereby they incline to something which they may be: and when they are it, they shall be perfecter than now they are. All which perfections are contained under the general name of *Goodness.* And because there is not in the world anything whereby another may not some way be made the perfecter, therefore all things that are, are good." The duty of delight directs people to revel in all creatures, from the lowest to the highest. At the summit of this great "chain of being" is the source of goodness itself. In Hooker's words, "since there can be no goodness desired which proceedeth not from God himself . . . : all things in the world are said in some sort to seek the highest, and to covet more or less the participation of God himself."[23] In Hooker's teleology it is incumbent upon every creature to love God in its own way, thus bringing to fruition God's gifts in creating life. In Ruskin's use of this theological metaphysics, it is the exalted task of humanity to delight in natural beauty as the guideposts of a moral life and the signs that this original ordering of divine purposes is realized, here and there, moment to moment, in the ongoing life of the world.

Too often, though, people ignore the signs of the world's flourishing because their loves miss their mark. A person's loves, which are the measure of a person's desire for things, of his or her esteem for things' relative worth, are liable to gross misrepresentation. Note that Ruskin's phrase "moral perception" captures this coupling of goodness and truth. In loving things well or ill, evaluative judgments of goodness are a matter of true or false representation. The "truth" of art has ethical significance, just as a corrupted sense of taste has moral consequences. Lesser pleasures may become the preferred objects of desire, and even the "objects of life" designed to give the most pleasure may not be received as a gift. For Ruskin the twin failures of "bad taste," in preferring the wrong things, and "want of taste," in refusing to receive good things as gifts, occur when people are dead to natural beauty, which is why the duty of delight, the right recognition of beauty as God's "stamp" on the Creation, is so edifying of the "heart," or character.

This image of God's marking the worth of everything in the purposes it serves is the key to how beauty secures the right ordering of human loves. Ruskin's theory of beauty elaborates a system of signification whereby the true value and meaning of every beautiful thing and creature is known in the "types," "functions," "perfections," "powers," "characteristics," and "virtues" that it teaches to those who love it well. This moral vocabulary structures his whole theory of beauty. Each time one of these terms appears, he adds another detail to the wondrous designs of the Book of Nature. Thus, loving beauty as God's gift, as the sign of God's participation in life's goodness, orders a person's desires and brings delight and duty into their perfect correspondence.

Typical Beauty: God's Perfect Nature

Various scholars have noted that Ruskin's interpretations of nature's "typical beauty" resemble the "typological" readings of the Bible common among British Evangelicals and well documented in Ruskin's early life.[24] His autobiography *Praeterita* (1885–89) and his diaries and letters record his daily memorization of Bible verses with his mother and the sermon reviews he exchanged with his father. Ruskin's readings of the moral and religious significance of the smallest details of nature's beauty mirror the readings of the "types" in the Old Testament as a foreshadowing of the fulfillment of God's purposes in Jesus Christ. Clearly Ruskin's language of "types" reflects the influence of his religious upbringing on his early aesthetics and the shaping effect of this exegetical practice on his criticism. As he comes to see later on, worship is always expressed and performed through enculturated "practices," whether of one's upbringing or one's choosing. But he does not make anything of the connection between religious practices and theological convictions at this early stage of his writings.

While acknowledging that this typological exegetics is one source of Ruskin's early critical vocabulary, I focus on how his language of "types" reflects Hooker's Aristotelian approach to divine "character." I do so for two reasons. First, although typological readings are open to innovation by interpreters who are well versed in the echoing words and stories of scripture, Ruskin's theory of typical beauty is constrained by his own metaphysical sensibility and the theological framework of the good that he initially borrows from Hooker. Second, the concern with character that Ruskin derives from Hooker's stream of Christian ethical reflection has greater explanatory power across his whole corpus.

In charting the parallels between Ruskin's theory of beauty and Hooker's metaphysics of the good, let me begin with Hooker's understanding of the relationship between God's nature and the created world. Beginning with God's nature, Hooker describes the attributes of the divine legislator of eternal law as "an original draught written on the bosom of God himself."[25] God's perfect nature as author is prior to God's external work as maker. Likewise, for Ruskin, the six "types" of divine character have precedence over the many "functions," "powers," and "virtues" displayed by living creatures. Thus in the scheme of *Modern Painters* 2, typical beauty precedes vital beauty.

Taken together, the types of infinity, unity, repose, symmetry, purity, and moderation describe an ordered and largely static collection of divine traits. There is little movement in the nature of this eternal being. This view of God's nature and its participation in all creatures' goodness frames and ultimately constrains Ruskin's discussion of beauty. The idea that the beauty and, thus, the perfections of all things participate in God's own perfection helps explain why Ruskin's early writings on art display both a keen appreciation of the diversity and particularity of the world's countless instances of beauty and also the certainty that each one of them testifies to God's immutable, unchanging ordering of the Creation.[26]

This two-tiered scheme of nature and divinity, with each side participating in the other, contributes to the bounded dynamism of Ruskin's early aesthetics. Although his metaphysical sensibility is evident throughout the chapters on typical beauty, it is pronounced in his account of the divine attribute of unity. Hooker's theology structures the argument yet again, beginning with the chapter's opening quotation on Hooker's dual conception of "natural law" (4.92). For Hooker there is the law by which individual creatures follow their appointed ends, and there is another law touching "them as they are sociable parts united into one body." The first treats individuals' flourishing, which Ruskin discusses under the category of vital beauty; the second is the "law which bindeth [each part] to serve unto other's good, and all to prefer the good of the whole before whatsoever their own particular."[27] In Hooker's dual structure of natural law, all creatures are individually imperfect and so must depend on each other for their greatest perfection.

Ruskin finds a similarly high degree of perfection in the instances of "unity" that appear in the world's beauty. He cites the perfection exhibited in the unity of bodies composed of lesser parts, of waves flowing from the same current, of branches and petals growing from the same stem, and of succeeding notes in a melody. These are his examples, respectively, of essential, subjectional, original, and sequential unity. The powerful attractions of these unifying forms, he claims, can be contrasted with the blight of patched garments, mixed forests, and inordinately colored birds (4.94–96). These instances of ugliness offend the boundaries of a well-ordered beauty, just as the poor sit outside the city gates and the wilderness extends beyond civilization.

Interestingly, Ruskin's later social criticism stands almost directly opposed to these prejudices against the poor and the wilderness, and even in volume 2, he acknowledges the need for variety within the "perfect" configurations of unity.[28] For example, regarding the subjectional unity of clouds and waves to the wind, "there is a glorious unity of rolling, wrought out by the *wild and wonderful differences* of their absolute forms, which, if taken away, would leave them only multitudinous and petty repetition, instead of the *majestic oneness of shared passion.*" Translating that unity of passion to the "waves and clouds of *human* multitudes," he praises earlier Italian painters' simple formula of depicting the greatness of God's works by mixing a common gesture of uplifted hand with infinite variation of expression on the faces of all the human figures on the canvas (4.99–100; my emphasis).

Tintoretto's *Crucifixion* comes to mind here and also helps bring out how Hooker's metaphysics joins with Ruskin's Evangelical diatribe against sin in his early and deeply flawed idea of community in his chapter on "vital beauty in man." Like Hooker, Ruskin views people as the lone species whose members differ in their individual traits and social roles and who must, therefore, conform to the "relations of charity which are the privilege of humanity." But people can attain to the heights of love only so long as their differences serve to "bind" them, not to "separate" them, and the young Ruskin finds little more than "evil diversity, and terrible stamp of various degradation" among his fellows. This distance between the prospect of perfect community and the reality of individual sinfulness mirrors the tension between the frenzy of Tintoretto's canvas and his arrangement of its centrifugal energy around the centralizing figure of Jesus Christ. The disordered scene on the ground directs the viewer toward God's promised order. Unity is imposed symbolically on disunity. Similarly, Ruskin suggests that only a divinely sanctioned hierarchy of social roles and ranked offices can rectify communities rent by sin. These binding "varieties of office" appoint "some to be in authority and others in obedience, some in solitary functions and others in relative ones, some to receive and others to give" (4.176, 183–84). Although Ruskin's explication of the duty of delight exhibits an enthusiasm for the diversity found in nature, his overall theory of beauty answers to his metaphysical sensibility, which in the human realm, legitimates a rigidly hierarchical ideal of community as the necessary corrective to the failures of human love. Here Raymond Williams's cautions about the social implications of Ruskin's early aesthetics apply with force. Ruskin makes "nature undestroyed" both the source of the pleasures of "unity" and also the model of community. Modeling the social order on the natural order is always a dangerous strategy, especially when the reading of nature is as selective and bounded as Ruskin's account of typical beauty.

Vital Beauty: Creatures' Functions, Virtues, and Characteristics

In Ruskin's discussion of vital beauty, the focus on formal patterns of order is replaced by a celebration of nature's abundant diversity. The movement of love is not toward God's perfect nature but toward the myriad perfections of the world's creatures. The vivid green of new leaves in the spring and the chattering of birds at dawn inspire delight in the vitality displayed by all plants and animals, each in its own distinctive way. For Ruskin it is in the "right accepting and reading" of these signs and traits that the theoretic faculty's moral perception of beauty most fully realizes its task of orienting people toward their duties. Delight in vital beauty discloses three lessons in particular: all living things have intrinsic value; nature should be heeded as a moral guide; and the economy of nature answers to God's ends, not human desire.

It is in the lessons of vital beauty that we see most clearly the contributions of Ruskin's vocabulary of the virtues to his normative argument. In fact, at this early point in his criticism, identifying his critical vocabulary with just one term—that is, virtue—is misleading, and as I discuss in the next section, he is initially more interested in God's virtue in the singular than in human virtues in the plural. Among the other terms that structure Ruskin's readings of the world's vital beauty are "power" and "function," "characteristic" and "ideal," "happiness" and "habit." I trace out the constructive role of this language in detailing vital beauty in its "relative" and "generic" forms.

That vital beauty is filled with moral content is clear from the outset of Ruskin's analysis. As we turn from the patterns and forms of typical beauty to the vitality of living things, "There is now uttered to us a call for sympathy, now offered to us an image of moral purpose and achievement, which, however unconscious or senseless the creature may indeed be that so seems to call, cannot be heard without affection, nor contemplated without worship, by any of us whose heart is rightly tuned, or whose mind is clearly and surely sighted" (4.147). This "sympathy" for other species is the theoretic faculty's "first perfection" with regard to vital beauty.

In keeping with Ruskin's overall approach, this sympathy begins with good character, for only then can a person recognize the "felicity" or happiness of other creatures. A "kindness and unselfish fulness of heart, which receives the utmost amount of pleasure from the happiness of all things," allows the beholder of beauty to delight in living things that "exhibit most of power, and seem capable of most quick and joyous sensation" (4.147–48, 155). These indications of power and joy are what draw people's love, and they direct the beholder of beauty onto the creature's own flourishing. The soft green of new spring leaves is so lovely not just because of its unique hue but because of the returning life that its vibrancy signifies. It is this vitality for the sake of the tree's own flourishing that calls forth human sympathy, not the human needs that it might serve. Ruskin writes, "I wish particularly to impress upon the reader that all these higher sensations of beauty in the plant arise from our unselfish sympathy with its happiness, and not from any view of the qualities in it which may bring good to us, nor even from our acknowledgment in it of any moral condition beyond that of mere felicity" (4.152). Describing a tree cut down and laid over a stream as a bridge, Ruskin despairs the sacrifice of its vital beauty: "it has become useful; it lives not for itself, and its beauty is gone, or what it retains is purely typical, dependent upon its lines and colors, not on its functions." This sense of loss extends into an "abhorrence of all utility to one creature which is based on the pain or destruction of any other" (4.153). Thus, the theory of vital beauty proceeds from a non-human-centered conception of flourishing that places other creatures' happiness before any claim of human use.

This heartfelt sympathy for other creatures' well-being is the first aspect of vital beauty that causes delight. There is also an "image of moral purpose and achievement" to be read in every living being, and it is here that we see what Ruskin means by "relative" vital beauty. He shifts from creatures' "felicity" for their own sake to their "moral functions," by which he means their role in signifying a range of virtues and vices. "There is not any organic creature but, in its history and habits, will exemplify or illustrate to us some moral excellence or deficiency, or some point of God's providential government, which it is necessary for us to know," he writes. Each living being's history and habits teach moral lessons, testifying to its "position in creation," whether "as sufferer or chastiser, as lowly or having dominion, as of foul habit or lofty aspiration; and [to] the several perfections which all illustrate or possess, courage, perseverance, industry, or intelligence, or, higher yet, love, and patience, and fidelity, and rejoicing, and never wearied praise." Although every species exhibits its own measure of happiness, people do not regard all animals as equally delightful. A close reading of their moral functions clarifies these different levels of esteem. In Ruskin's words, "the beauty of the animal form is in exact proportion to the amount of moral or intellectual virtue expressed by it; and wherever beauty exists at all, there is some kind of *virtue* to which it is owing." As examples, he praises the "majesty of the lion's eye [as] owing not to its ferocity, but to its seriousness and seeming intellect." Higher still, "the gentle eye of the gazelle is fairer to look upon than the more keen glance of men, if it be unkind" (4.156–60). Ruskin charges his readers to heed these varying degrees of delight as a moral guide that corrects the errors of people's ways.[29] As he ranges through examples of the moral functions of different species, he constructs a hierarchy of virtues and vices for his readers to imitate, extending the duty of sympathy for all other living creatures into a duty of cultivating the moral character needed to relate virtuously to fellow human beings.

Finally, Ruskin turns from the "relative" beauty of nature's creatures to the "generic" beauty of each species. Here the duty of delight shifts away from judging creatures according to "that standard of moral perfection by which we test ourselves." Now, "taking it for granted that every creature of God is in some way good, and has a duty and specific operation providentially accessory to the well-being of all," there is another source of delight in the "Ideal of the species." Regardless of the relationship a species has to human beings, there is "beauty in the magnificent binding together of the jaws of the ichthyosaurus for catching and holding, and in the adaptation of the lion for springing, and of the locust for destroying, and of the lark for singing" (4.164). But in each species this "Ideal" beauty will be found in the most "characteristic or general" member of the species in terms of its display of "noble generic form" and "the full development of all the powers and properties of the creature as such" (4,166–68).

In this juxtaposition of the terms "characteristic" and "nobility," it is clear that Ruskin's vocabulary of characteristics, functions, and adaptations operates very differently from the ways that this same terminology gets used, in the coming decades, in Charles Darwin's revolutionary *Origin of the Species* (1859). Rather with a reverence for God's design typical of the early-nineteenth-century British fascination with natural theology,

Ruskin posits an ideal operation of every species' "natural functions," where that ideal is fixed by the species' role, place, and purpose in God's economy of nature. I argue in chapter 3 that Ruskin moves away from natural theology, replacing its emphasis on God's fixed designs with a new interest in natural history that is both subject to historical change and defined, in part, by what people "make" of the world (11.258). The sovereignty of God as the creator and judge of value casts aside all such considerations here. Consider how, in *Modern Painters* 2, Ruskin describes the ideal beauty of trees. Unable to ensure "the full development of all the[ir] powers and properties" as animals do through mobility, a tree's vital beauty testifies to "perfections" that unsettle any equation of beauty with balanced form. Instead the theme of active striving marks all "ideal" beauty and Ruskin's use of the term "perfections" in general. A species of wild oak, "intended and created by the Deity for covering those lonely spots where no other plant could live," achieves its "ideal" in these conditions, even if it could grow in strength and size under a gardener's protection. The wild oak is meant to fill "places comparatively unfit" with "greenness, and coolness, and ornament, and oxygen." The lovers of nature must not allow "unkind comparisons" in denying this oak its beauty. Its stunted growth in poor soil and its contorted limbs that reach for the light are evidence of its "enduring power, patience in waiting for, and ingenuity in obtaining what it wants." Nor can its "ideal" beauty be improved through "human interference," for even a cultivated park oak is less beautiful than this twisted wild oak precisely to the degree that it strays from its natural functions and loses the characteristic powers and virtues that mark the moral character of its perfections (4.169–71).

There are hints of an environmental sensibility in Ruskin's early aesthetics, but we must be clear about how his initial moral vocabulary structures and limits it. One way to get at this issue is to ask, how would he respond to a reader who objected that a park oak is more beautiful than any wild oak? Assuming, with Ruskin, that a "taste" for beauty does not involve "judgment," as I noted earlier, he could offer the objector few reasons in support of his argument. Instead he would invite the objector to go to nature with sympathy, witness the wild oak in its proper place, and revel in the purposes its beauty signifies. In Ruskin's words, "the right and true happiness of every creature is in this very discharge of its function, and in those efforts by which its strength and inherent energy are developed; . . . and that happiness which is indeed beautiful is in the bearing of those trial tests which are appointed for the proving of every creature, whether it be good, or whether it be evil; and in the fulfilment to the uttermost of every command it has received, and the out-carrying to the uttermost of every power and gift it has gotten from its God" (4.172–73). In other words the objector would be invited to a sympathetic contemplation of the oak's natural and moral functions. The language of "gift" that concludes this passage returns us to Ruskin's idea of "theoria" and his claim that "the beautiful" is above all else "a gift of God" elevating one's desire and all that one rightly desires. Here we arrive at the conviction that underlies his entire theory of beauty. For the young Ruskin, the beauty of art and nature are necessarily moral because they train human desire by drawing it toward the Christian virtue of charity.

Implicit in all of Ruskin's readings of the powers, virtues, functions, characteristics, and habits of creatures is his conviction that the "inherent attractiveness" of their most beautiful features is a sign of the Creator's charity in giving life. What makes the perception of beauty a "moral perception," therefore, is the reciprocal act of charity on the part of the lover of nature's beauty. Here charity is not simply an act of generosity; indeed taking delight in a wild oak does little for the plant other than encouraging a protective sympathy for its survival. Charity, understood in classical Christian terms, aspires to a full moral vision of God's goodness, leading in turn to a character, or a purity of the heart, that is keenly receptive to all of the sights, sounds, smells, and pleasures of beauty that signify God's greatest gifts. These gifts are the greatest because, as "objects of life," they serve no other purpose than to inspire an elevating delight, a delight that requires the perceiver to accept these gifts as gifts and nothing more. The "moral perception" of beauty is the proper response to God's many gifts, instilling an expansive charity not restricted to fellow human beings, but extended to every living creature in the world.

Simply put, charity is the moral virtue taught by vital beauty. Yet it is important to understand how this charity—this vision of God's goodness and the accompanying loving regard for other creatures—operates in Ruskin's early aesthetics. His argument proceeds from a teleological conception of nature in which every species has its God-given ends and each creature plays its moral and natural functions, to varying degrees, in participating in the flourishing of the whole. At times Ruskin's early criticism exhibits a delight in a certain wildness in the natural world, in the vitality of a creature's living for its own sake entirely. But in the end this independent worth is systematized and domesticated within a theocentric system of value predicated on Hooker's theological metaphysics and reinforced by Ruskin's own metaphysical sensibility, which at this stage in his criticism, is far stronger than any proto-environmentalism. Earlier I cited a passage from Hooker in which God's "goodness" is seen in all things' "appetite or desire" for their "perfections," a striving both on their own and in mutual dependence with other creatures. Both here in this passage and throughout Ruskin's theory of beauty, we see that the genre of his early aesthetics is drama, the drama of all life aspiring toward the perfections that mark God's "work" in giving life. Just as the static "types" of God's "character" precede the diversity of vital beauty, however, behind this drama of abundance and flourishing there is a settled "logic" of charity that specifies the "value and meaning" of every part of nature, all arranged in a bounded hierarchy of rankings and relations.

Summing up, vital beauty is delightful in three ways—in a creature's flourishing for its own sake, in its "moral functions" for human instruction, and in its dignified obedience to the "natural functions" set by God's Creation. The independent "felicity" of creatures is thus finally referable to their appointed moral functions and ideal characteristics, for these "virtues" and "powers" are granted and determined in God's gift of life. I am arguing that if we attend closely to Ruskin's early moral vocabulary and the connections he charts among the functions, powers, characteristics, virtues, and other traits that vital beauty signifies, we find that he is describing an economy of nature, which while ascribing an intrinsic value to each and every creature, ultimately answers to a circumscribed notion of flourishing.

God's charitable work as creator seeks the flourishing of all things, and yet God can accomplish this goal only by establishing a hierarchical natural order to which every creature must conform. In response, human charity is a loving regard for all other beings, regulated by a currency of delight that orders and trains human desire. A person's regard for the full value of each creature is distributed according to the "logic" of that creature's "participation" in God's grace as creator.[30] This grace—as mediated by the world of nature—fixes the relative worth of each creature, its natural functions, and its part in the hierarchy of moral traits that serves as the template of good character for human beings. Thus, God's grace dictates a logic of charity that governs people's relations to the world and with one another. That logic is there in natural beauty to be recognized by the pure-sighted, but if one is blind to it, then Ruskin's theory of beauty offers a remarkably detailed and systematic sermon on God's "work and character" as creator and the moral teachings that follow from this revelation.

God's Singular Virtue and the Created Order

Reading Ruskin's account of vital beauty in light of Hooker's theological metaphysics clarifies the initial moral vocabulary of Ruskin's criticism. Instead of emphasizing with Aristotle the different virtues of the "good man," Ruskin grounds his entire analysis of creaturely virtues and the supreme human virtue of charity in a singular conception of God's virtue as the source, goal, and limit of all life. This grounding of each and every virtue in God's virtue reflects Hooker's account of God as divine legislator and gracious creator. An important question for Hooker is, why would a perfect being create the world? His answer is that the Creation shows God's boundless grace. Another question follows: what is the relationship between the perfect "character" of God as author and the external "work" of God as creator? Hooker responds, "The general end of God's external working, is the exercise of his most glorious and most abundant virtue: Which abundance doth show itself in variety, and for that cause this variety is oftentimes in scripture expressed by the name of *riches*. . . . Not that anything is made to be beneficial unto him, but all things for him to show beneficence and grace in them."[31] In this passage Hooker names God's "virtue" the source of the world's rich diversity and also the self-derived limit that God embraces in making all things. God's virtue is both inexhaustible and yet structured by the goodness that is God's nature. This interplay between manifold variety and eternal law is foundational to Ruskin's theory of beauty.

In discussing his final type of typical beauty, "moderation, or the type of government by law," Ruskin quotes approvingly from a related passage in Hooker's *Laws* (4.135–36). The full passage reads: "The immutability of God [all creatures] strive unto, by working either always or for the most part after one and the same manner; his absolute exactness they imitate, by tending unto that which is most exquisite in every particular." The correspondence between the virtues of individual creatures and the law-like precision of God's perfect virtue is reinforced when Hooker describes how creatures take their part in the good by "affecting resemblance with God, in the constancy and excellency of those operations which belong unto their kind."[32] That God's virtue produces rich abundance all flowing from, tending toward, and circumscribed by God's singular virtue echoes throughout Ruskin's readings of the types, perfections, functions, powers, and characteristics—that is, the virtues—that are displayed throughout nature's bountiful beauty.

It might be objected that I read too much into Ruskin's early moral vocabulary, given that he rarely uses the term "virtue" in *Modern Painters* 2. He provides his clearest statement of his initial notion of "virtue" when he names moderation the supreme artistic virtue. Moderation "is that virtue which men last, and with most difficulty attain unto." Yet moderation "is essential to the conduct and almost to the being of all other virtues; since neither imagination, nor invention, nor industry, nor sensibility, nor energy, nor any other good having, is of full avail without this of self-command, whereby works truly masculine and mighty are produced" (4.140). It must be said that this is not a traditional list of the virtues, though the emphasis on God-given powers does fit Hooker's portrait of God as a virtuous creator who "gifts" creatures with the perfections vital to their place, role, and purpose in the Creation.[33] Even more clearly we see Hooker's image of God's virtue as an ever-productive yet self-regulating source of "His" manly Creation. But why does Ruskin name each of these virtues a "good having"?

Perhaps Ruskin is playing on the Aristotelian theme of a virtue as a "good habit" that disposes one toward the ends proper to human flourishing. Certainly the later Ruskin enjoys wordplay, but the frequent disparagement of "custom" and "habit" in the first two volumes of *Modern Painters* suggests otherwise.[34] Indeed, despite Ruskin's observation that moderation is often the last virtue to be attained, he gives no attention to the arts, sciences, and other activities through which people learn and develop their virtues. His practical interests in human activity await his later writings, as I discuss at the chapter's end. The mode of "good having" here is not a developed habit, or better, a cultivated excellence; it is instead a pure gift of grace. This idea of virtue as a "good having" reflects Hooker's emphasis on creaturely "participation" in God's goodness. Just as creatures "have" their appointed goodness to the extent that they fulfill their perfections, so too here these artistic virtues allow artists to "have" a role in—literally, to take part in—God's goodness by being able to intuit and mirror what nature's beauty signifies and thus reveals about the proper direction of human desire toward delight and duty. While Ruskin's "theoria" may aspire to great heights of "moral perception," what it sees, or contemplates, is God's glory as creator. Indeed so decisive is God's virtue in determining the "value and meaning" of every detail of natural beauty that

God's Creation subsumes all *human creativity* in *Modern Painters* 2, making good taste a matter of conforming one's loves to God's perfect designs and leaving no room for independent aesthetic or moral judgment, as Ruskin insists in his definition of taste.

Before pointing the way beyond Ruskin's early aesthetics, let me broaden my reading by drawing out the teleological elements in the critical visions of other figures in his tradition of British social thought. Stressing the "Puritan" and "republican" background to Thomas Carlyle's ideas of "wonder" and "heroism," Christopher Lasch helps detail the various shadings of the word "virtue" that I read in Ruskin's early art criticism.[35] Lasch notes the long-standing associations of "virtue" with "courage and manly vigor, with vitality in general, and more broadly still with life-giving creative force." He argues that Carlyle's sense of the term depends upon an even richer mix of associations, however, and he offers John Milton as the likely influence. In *Paradise Lost* Milton portrays Adam and Eve's fall from their original endowment of "superhuman" goodness as a loss of virtue. In Lasch's words, "Milton conceives of goodness as a grateful and obedient disposition of the human will but also as abundance, plenitude, and fullness of being, gifts bestowed by a beneficent creator—the loss of which, accordingly, awaits those who refuse to acknowledge them as such (and thereby to acknowledge their dependence on a higher power) and who aspire instead to godlike powers and knowledge of their own."[36] Lasch locates "virtue" at the intersection of creaturely obedience and divine grace. Virtue is manifested in an active flourishing that receives all things as gifts from God and therefore knows how to value them. The connection between good character and true vision that typifies all teleological approaches to ethical reflection shows clearly, in Carlyle's criticism, in his examples of celebrated historical heroes. These "superhuman" heroes display their prodigious virtue in modeling a new way of living by imagining how all things cohere in a whole vision of the good.

Although Ruskin read around in *Heroes and Hero-Worship* (1841) before writing *Modern Painters* 2, no evidence contradicts his claim to have come under Carlyle's influence at a later date.[37] Even so, there are striking parallels between the understandings of "virtue" found in these two works. Common to Carlyle and Ruskin is the belief that virtue is inseparable from grace—specifically, that virtue flows from the plenitude of Creation. Moreover, faced with the bounty of goodness in nature, the task of "wonder," or, in Ruskin's case, "delight" is to perceive the world rightly by being open to the particular marks of God's abundant charity on everything. Thus,

Lasch describes Carlyle's "heroic gift" as a "sincerity and depth of vision." In Carlyle's words, "to know a thing, what we can call knowing, a man must first *love* the thing, sympathise with it: that is, be *virtuously* related to it." Ruskin also sees love as necessary to the "moral perception" of beautiful things. A good character, or state of heart, is essential to the proper regard for beauty, to grasping that beauty marks the divine gifts that are creatures' perfections.

One more similarity unites Carlyle's and Ruskin's shared understanding of virtue as the mirror of God's bounteous grace in creating life. Each creature's vitality depends entirely on its dignified obedience to the place, role, and purpose assigned it in the natural order. These echoing themes of vitality and obedience, gratitude and limit, appear in Lasch's comment that "Carlyle's affirmation of freedom is balanced by an acknowledgment of our dependence on higher powers." Heroes approximate "the life-giving-powers of the creator . . . only to the extent that they recognize their source."[38] We have already seen Ruskin praise the dignified obedience of those creatures who live up to their species' particular exquisiteness by mimicking God's "absolute exactness" as maker.

In my reading of *Modern Painters* 2, God's virtue marks the "inherent attractiveness" of every instance of typical and vital beauty. This is true not only of the "Divine attributes" seen in the formal patterns of beauty. Much more so, God's *virtue* is apparent in the countless *virtues* of all living beings. Every creature's virtues flow from God's virtue as creator. The functions, perfections, powers, characteristics, and virtues signified by nature's beauty are all specific expressions of the fullness of life that begins in God's original act. In witnessing the glorious participation of every creature in God's goodness, people need the requisite virtues, too, most notably, the charity, or the "purity of heart," that makes possible the "moral perception" of beauty.

What unites Carlyle's and the young Ruskin's approaches to "virtue" is the singularity of the term. Instead of detailing and analyzing the range of virtues needed for good human lives, they appeal to an all-encompassing, unifying, productive, and masculine virtue. Despite this similarity, however, Ruskin's early understanding of virtue differs from Carlyle's in a way that distinguishes Ruskin. Although Carlyle's heroes recognize the source of virtue in the creator, he presents these historical figures as co-creators of unique, cultural conceptions of the good. There is a cultural dynamism in Carlyle's writings that is absent from *Modern Painters* 2. Here the participation of creatures' virtues in God's virtue produces a static vision of flourishing. Ruskin's detailed portrait of God's eternal nature and the bounded dynamism of vital beauty both reinforce the assumption that the Book of Nature was "sealed" by God at the beginning and is not subject to change. Each creature's functions and purposes bind it into a harmonious whole governed by God's abundant grace in the Creation, with its original, paradisiacal standard of perfection. In the metaphysics of the good that Ruskin derives from Hooker, "striving after" God's "absolute exactness" is in fact an attempted return to this one-time, perfect ordering of life. Ruskin's early idea of flourishing, even though couched in a dramatic language of desire and delight, appetite and aspiration, is best read as a proximate repetition of God's original work and perfect "virtue."

Modern Painters 2 makes nature, art, and beauty out to be a settled affair. A criticism by Henry David Thoreau (1817–62) is instructive. Considering Ruskin's acknowledgment of the intrinsic worth and moral guidance of the natural world, we might expect considerable common ground between these two contemporaries. But writing in his journal in 1857, Thoreau comments, "I have just read Ruskin's 'Modern Painters.' I am disappointed in not finding it a more out-of-door book, for I have heard that such was its character, but its title might have warned me. He does not describe Nature as nature, but as Turner painted her . . . though the work betrays that he has given a close attention to Nature." He adds that Ruskin "expresses the common infidelity of his age and race. He has not implicitly surrendered himself to her. And what does he substitute for that Nature? I do not know, unless it be the Church of England."[39] Although Thoreau probably had *Modern Painters* 1 in mind, he captures succinctly the way that Ruskin's love of natural beauty always seeks its justification in something more, just as his "duty of delight" ultimately proves itself by "its harmony . . . with the whole spirit of the Christian moral system" (4.59). If I am right in reconstructing Ruskin's initial moral vocabulary of God's virtue as the source of all virtues, then Thoreau is correct in his hunch that the Church of England, as refracted through Hooker's teleological conception of nature and society, is the source of the metaphysics that underlies Ruskin's early aesthetics and that Thoreau rightly rejects.

Divine Corporation Ethics and Ruskin's Tradition

I have reconstructed the teleological structure of Ruskin's theory of beauty to mark the distance he travels in the coming decades as he innovates in his moral vocabulary. Comparing this early aesthetics with J. B. Schneewind's model of "Divine Corporation ethics" provides a useful benchmark for measuring the changes in Ruskin's critical approach and a good reminder of how other figures in his tradition of nineteenth-century British social thought borrow from, while modifying, this full-blown teleological ethics.

Schneewind describes a consensus existing in early modern European thought around a Christian moral framework. His model of this framework, the Divine Corporation, bears a striking resemblance to Ruskin's early aesthetics. "Consider . . . the idea of a cooperative endeavor, in which agents join to produce a good that no one of them could produce alone. Each participant has a task or set of tasks. The tasks for each can be set out in rules laying down the duties of a station. It is the joint or successive performance by each of the duties of his or her station that brings about the good." Schneewind notes that in this corporation there will be some who have supervisory roles, but that no one is capable of envisioning the good of the whole, complex operation. Only God enjoys this perspective. Yet "even though no single worker has an assigned responsibility described as 'bringing about the good which the group aims at producing', each has some vague responsibility for keeping that good in view and adjusting his or her activities accordingly."[40]

The influence of Christian moral thought on this theoretical framework shows in two key assumptions. First, individuals are conceived as desiring subjects guided by their attractions for those things that are "goods" for them. As discussed earlier, people have "loves" that move them to desire many things, but a problem arises in ordering these loves and their correlative goods according to their specific purpose and their relative worth in a person's life. The second premise follows from this portrait of people as guided—and for Christian ethics, as often as not, *mis*guided—by their desires, attractions, and aspirations. Assessments of the purpose and worth of the goods that one loves must answer to their part in the good, or the telos, governing all of life.

Ruskin's early theory of beauty fits this "Divine Corporation" model exactly, provided, that is, that we expand out beyond the limits of the human community to the whole natural world. For Ruskin, nature's beauty discloses nothing less than the moral purposes of God's Creation and their arrangement as a whole. The task assigned to human beings in the "Corporate" body of all of life is to attend to and delight in the glory of the Creation as it shows in each and every part of nature. Only by pursuing this task of celebrating God's glory as *the* end of one's life is it possible to know the purpose and worth of things and the proper enjoyment and use of them.

Here the telos is the harmonious flourishing promised by God's Creation and known, for the early Ruskin, in nature's beauty. Indeed it is his remarkably detailed and synthetic vision of this telos that makes his early aesthetics such a clear instance of Divine Corporation ethics. In this regard it is interesting to compare Ruskin's early aesthetics with the work of such predecessors as William Wordsworth and Coleridge. In terms of Ruskin's development as a critic, Wordsworth is far more important. The poet's keen eye and capacity for evocative detail set the standard for Ruskin's studies of art and nature. Yet Ruskin is initially so enamored of the task of revealing God's ordained purposes that he disregards how an individual's ends and sense of meaning might lead to new understandings of nature's beauty, as seen whenever artists engage in interpreting and representing things to other people.

For Wordsworth and Coleridge, the task of the poet or genius is not limited to mirroring the glory of God's Creation and conforming to its specifications. The poet as "maker" brings new meanings out of the natural world. Nature's organicism is significant, therefore, not only in providing an integrated image of life's harmony, which for the early Ruskin is fixed by God's original creative act. More importantly, nature's organicism serves as a model for the growth of human cultures. In effect, God, as the chief executive of the Divine Corporation, provides the capital and defines the mission statement, but then hands over the future implementation of the entire enterprise to a cadre of innovative culture-makers whose "genius" works out of the spirit of the endeavor.

This turn toward the poet or genius as a culture-creator in the realm of art is matched in the social sphere, too. Indeed both Coleridge and Carlyle authorize their visions of the good by looking not to God's Creation but to the living "wholes" of human cultures, communities, and traditions. In other words, they see the articulation of the good as a historical effort by means of which people work out the content and structure of the telos. The vitality of common life depends for them on preserving *and* revising inherited cultural forms. Coleridge's idea of the "clerisy" as the institution of moral and cultural educators places the capacity for envisioning and producing a common good in human hands, if only in the hands of the few.[41] Similarly Carlyle celebrates a select few "heroes" who recast their societies by having the intuitive vision to imagine and institute a whole new way of life. Certainly hints of a providential guidance remain, but the minutely observant overseer of the Divine Corporation has been considerably displaced.

Two important points follow that orient my argument in the coming chapters. First, the example of Ruskin's early theory of beauty reminds us of the teleological elements all too often neglected in the writings of other members of his tradition. Although differently conceived as a vision of a divine or natural order, of tradition, community, or religion, this teleological vision joins Ruskin and these others into a recognizable ethical tradition. What unites them is the belief that individuals are desiring beings who depend upon and are largely constituted by their place within some "whole"—the natural or social order, the community, or a tradition—a basic orientation toward which and aspiring knowledge of which are necessary to a right reception of beauty and a true understanding of all things' meaning and worth. Ruskin himself holds to a teleological approach to art, society, and ethics, even as he moves in his art and social criticism toward seeing culture as a human production.

Second, although Ruskin's critical approach develops along these lines in allowing more independent powers to human beings as "makers," his later practical criticism remains closer to the moral framework that I have identified. Early on he does not allow for the shaping genius of the poet, artist, or hero, even as he himself stands in, largely unknowingly, I think, as the great critic whose taste is so finely attuned that he can perceive not only God's purposes in nature but also God's very being. Indeed in *Modern Painters* 2 the truly contemplative, the "pure in heart," do see God and, by extension, the grand design of the Divine Corporation. This notion that people can rise above the narrow perspective of their station reflects the broader shifts occurring throughout his tradition at this time. Each of the figures I have mentioned is seeking ways to translate a vision of the good from divine revelation into the cultural work of poetry, art, or criticism. Basic to all of their attempts is an embrace of moral intuitionism of the "whole" of life. But whereas Wordsworth, Coleridge, and Carlyle restrict this true vision of the good to the mysterious creative powers of a few geniuses, Ruskin allows, at least, that every individual can attain good taste by going to nature's beauty. Whereas these other figures often appeal to the vague language of mystery and feeling, Ruskin uses a moral vocabulary of the virtues that lends itself to precise arguments and conclusions in his early writings and to more reasoned analysis and persuasion in his mature criticism.

In *Modern Painters* 2 this careful argumentation makes Ruskin's metaphysics more transparent, exacting, and objectionable. The same is true of those places in his later criticism where this metaphysics retains its hold.

But I value a critical clarity that discloses strengths and weaknesses over intuitive appeals to mystery. As Ruskin develops as a critic, he remains more precise and becomes far more "practical" than the other figures in his tradition. By this I mean that he descends into the various practices and associations found in his contemporaries' artistic, social, political, and economic lives, analyzing them through an innovative, though recognizably continuous, teleological approach that describes and evaluates the ends, goods, and virtues that are helped or hindered by the cultural activities that his fellow Victorians participate in or support. Before moving onto the crucial reorientation of Ruskin's vocabulary of the virtues that occurs in his architectural studies, let me close by anticipating how his emerging practical criticism relates to three themes that unify his tradition. The moral intuitionism already mentioned is frequently joined with a strong defense of the established social order and a deep distrust of utilitarianism.

Good Taste as Worship and the Use and Abuse of Power

Schneewind's Divine Corporation model helps explain not only the moral intuitionism but also the anti-egalitarianism and anti-utilitarianism in Ruskin's tradition. First, the need to intuit the most salient truths of life mirrors the idea that God alone is privy to the overall design of life's flourishing. Similarly, members of Ruskin's tradition have often contrasted the narrow interests of science, prudence, and reason with the intuitions of beauty, faith, and the arts, with the latter being uniquely attuned to the richly integrated vision of the good required for living well. Second, Coleridge's institution of the clerisy, Carlyle's celebration of heroes, and Ruskin's early ideal of community all valorize established hierarchies. Here we see the vestiges of the Divine Corporation model in legitimizing some people's authority as capable of the broader wisdom unavailable, but essential, to the people in the stations below them. Finally, the general disdain for utilitarianism in Ruskin's tradition shows in the scorn for Bentham's famous declaration that the pleasures of poetry and push-pin are one and the same, human pleasures and nothing more.[42] By contrast, Ruskin insists, along with Coleridge and Carlyle, that there are higher and lower "goods" and that individuals' desires and preferences must be trained in accordance with that ordered scheme of valuation.

Although Ruskin remains a life-long opponent of utilitarianism, the terms of his mature critique depart sharply from the moral vocabulary of *Modern Painters* 2. Here he grounds his outright dismissal of utilitarianism in his distinction between self-sufficient "objects of life" and things "subservient to life." He posits a qualitative difference between the "theoretic" pleasures of contemplating beauty and the merely practical pleasures of ordinary pursuits. Do not heed, he tells his readers, those insolent "Utilitarians" who "speak in this working age . . . as if houses, and lands, and food, and raiment were alone useful." The practical work of the miner, apothecary, bricklayer, and plumber are only encouragements to human progress in the "theoretic" sciences and arts of geology, chemistry, architecture, and painting (4.29, 32–33).

Ruskin repeats this untenable rift between the theoretic and the practical in condemning his contemporaries' consumption, too. The perpetual grasping after the "the newness of a dress or of some kind of unaccustomed food" brings fleeting pleasures that only beget disgust for what was once a luxury but quickly becomes a necessity and a link in an encumbering chain of possessions. Ruskin sees the same deadening of the senses to delight in his contemporaries' pursuits of knowledge. His language is striking. He writes of people "who both wonder most at things new, and digest worst things old; in so far that everything they have lies rusty, and loses lustre for want of use." This decrial of idle fascination, harmful digestion, and faulty use would be at home in his ethics of consumption a decade or so later, except that here in *Modern Painters* 2 he embraces an otherworldly denial that people in their "state of probation" on earth can possess, use, and enjoy any material thing rightly! Instead he recommends the constant delights of beauty that are "bread of the soul for which the hunger is continual" (4.97–99).

Ruskin's disparagement of ordinary work and everyday consumption does not outlast the two-tiered scheme of valuation that he constructs in *Modern Painters* 2. His defense of this scheme, it should now be clear, rests on his conviction that the divinely appointed ends of human existence can be intuited from the delights of nature's beauty. In the coming years he no longer appeals to Hooker, and he abandons the terms "object of life" and "theoria." He shifts away from contemplating ideal beauty to evaluating practical activity. He turns from what is finally a passive model of good taste to a critical interest in the actual character development needed for aesthetic and moral judgment. As Ruskin moves away from *Modern Painters* 2, good character stops being the concomitant outgrowth of a reverent openness to God's charity. Instead of God's virtue, the full range of human virtues takes center stage. The aesthetic, intellectual, moral, and other excellences that people work out for themselves are among the most important products of the cultural practices and activities within which individuals pursue the ends and goods that govern their judgments of the "value and meaning" of everything they make, use, and enjoy, both as workers and as consumers.

Let me anticipate the direction and significance of this turn from taste to judgment, from theoretic contemplation to practical activity, by remembering Ruskin's response to Tintoretto's *Crucifixion.* Despite Ruskin's obvious delight in Tintoretto's paintings, the argument of *Modern Painters* 2 leaves no room for this artist's creativity or the praise due for it.[43] While Ruskin clearly had his ways of judging artistic excellence from the beginning of his criticism, the moral vocabulary of the second volume directs us elsewhere. Tintoretto's greatness lies in the unifying vision that points toward, and thus mirrors, God's moral purposes in ordering human life toward salvation. It is not Tintoretto's excellence and creativity, but rather God's charity and Creation, that mark this artist's work as "good," that is, as participating in God's goodness.

In *The Seven Lamps of Architecture* (1849), Ruskin admits that he previously failed to grasp the "human effort" involved in creating art until Turner convinced him of his error. One explanation can be found in the 1843 outline of *Modern Painters,* where Ruskin omits "ideas of power" as irrelevant to the scope of his critical concerns. By "ideas of power" he means the evidence of an artist's practical skill in overcoming some difficulty of execution. Borrowing from Burke the idea that "difficulty" is a mark of greatness in a work of art, Ruskin proceeds to define "the word excellent, as signifying that the thing to which it is applied required a great power for its production." But he removes considerations of "excellence" from the outline of *Modern Painters* because appreciating excellence demands practical experience in the activity in question, which in the case of painting most people lack. He concludes that although "it is possible, by the cultivation of sensibility and judgment to become capable of distinguishing what is beautiful, it is totally impossible, without practice and knowledge, to distinguish or feel what is excellent" (3.96).[44] In Ruskin's later criticism he makes the development of people's virtues, or excellences, and the attainment of such practical knowledge the basis of his analysis, arguments, and ethics.

This turn from intuited taste to practical judgment ushers in all of the key changes in his critical approach. Already in *The Seven Lamps,* he shifts his point of view from the single critic revering the great painting to the many artists making all kinds of art and ultimately to all of the individual consumers engaged in judging things' worth. He sets out on this new path inquiring into the goods and ends pursued in the "social practices" of Gothic craftwork and the standards of excellence worked out within them. This reorientation of his critical vision toward people's activities, virtues, and ends introduces a complex approach to judgments of art's goodness that takes seriously human creativity and power and its uses and abuses. No longer is God the sole creative agent, nor is God's Creation the fixed source of all goodness.

Ruskin's early writings on landscape painting offer a vision of a harmonious ordering of God's Creation apparent in beauty's inherent attractiveness. Similar visions of a harmony of goods recognized by individuals through an elevated love of the whole are common to his anti-individualist tradition, especially among thinkers who like him see the aesthetic as peculiarly insightful or revelatory. But an other-directed love, answering to a harmonious ordering of the whole that lifts up all who participate in it, lends itself rather easily to a loving deference, chiefly to God, nature, community, or tradition, but to one's human "betters," too. Given that love, or charity, structures the whole of Ruskin's early theory of beauty, Raymond Williams's criticisms of Ruskin's fixed hierarchies of social class and aesthetic value are borne out here. Ruskin's language of "function" and "perfection," while reflecting the upward dynamic of participating in God's goodness, never escapes the uncontestable hierarchies that he presumes in *Modern Painters* 2 and that are simply intuited by those whose "good taste" conforms to God's designs.

For the young Ruskin, beauty impresses moral duties on its beholder and makes one love one's place, role, and purpose in the created order of nature and society. As he puts it in volume 1, "love" is the "thirst" felt by the most truthful artists and poets who in going to nature "lose sight of themselves" (3.169). This focus on love is not surprising for someone who admired Burke's *The Sublime and Beautiful* as much as Ruskin did, yet as mentioned earlier, it is noteworthy that Ruskin's 1843 outline explicitly omits Burke's category of the "sublime." For Burke, the sublime and the beautiful call forth different attitudes. Beauty excites desire and is met by love, while sublimity excites terror and is met by awe. Beauty as the feminine is a sign of weakness that attracts the lover's affection or tenderness, whereas sublimity as the masculine causes delight if the danger it signals does not "press too close."

Burke's interests in both love *and* power reflect his own understanding of "delight," which he defines as "the sensation which accompanies the removal of pain or danger," notably when we realize that another person's suffering cannot touch us.[45] This distanced delight is the thrill that moviegoers experience when watching horror films and that highway gapers enjoy when crawling past car wrecks. Although Ruskin admits "much ingenuity in Burke's theory of the sublime, as connected with self-preservation," he rules out fear and terror as negative responses to power and danger and in no way elements of aesthetic experience. Sublimity, for the young Ruskin, is simply that portion of the beautiful involving "greatness."[46] Or, as he puts it more broadly, "sublimity is found wherever anything elevates the mind, that is, wherever it contemplates anything above itself, and perceives it to be so" (3.128–30). Ruskin's paradigm of "greatness" is God, the greatness of God's love as creator, and every sign of that love should move the beholder of beauty to "joy, admiration and gratitude" in return. So when Ruskin bows down before the meanest thing in nature's beauty, he is brought high in delighting in the goodness of the whole Creation. When he is "crushed to the earth" before Tintoretto's intellect, he defers to the heartfelt truth of God's loving purposes, never worrying about the use and abuse of power that occupies so much of his later criticism. At this stage, good taste and the loving worship it inspires are enough.

Recovering the moral vocabulary of Ruskin's early theory of beauty is an exercise in forgetting. Many of his terms—"delight," "appetite," "love," "power," "characteristic"—have different meanings today. The recent renaissance in virtue theory helps us recover Ruskin's later moral vocabulary, but the leaders of that renaissance have not always paid sufficient attention to the many sources and uses of a language of the virtues. There are good historical reasons why other, often more secular, nineteenth-century critics embraced theories at odds with Ruskin's character-based vocabulary and why even its adherents made adjustments to the teleological approach to ethics that he so clearly represents. Reading Ruskin as an innovator in his own right indicates some of the strengths of this teleological approach, while also posing the question, what historical and conceptual liabilities must be addressed in trying to recover his critical approach to art, nature, religion, politics, economics, and, above all else, consumption?

Grounding ethics in a "taste" that operates apart from any "definite action of the intellect" or "judgment" invites the kind of loving worship *and* deference to an intuited vision of the good that mars Ruskin's early theory of beauty. If his initial focus on love for God's Creation removes Burkean suspicions of power from consideration, then Ruskin makes up for that by delving into how an "appetite of tasteful cruelty" is constituted by the social and economic conditions of industrial capitalism. If his omission of "human effort" leaves him praising God's Creation instead of Tintoretto's creativity, then he begins to judge art in terms of the ends, goods, and excellences at work in people's activities. Ruskin never wavers from seeing art and ethics as inseparably joined. He also continues to insist that a delight in the world's beauty is incumbent upon every person. But Ruskin's emerging criticism is more than brilliant interpretations structured into the perfectly systematic vision of the great critic. Although he remains an astute interpreter and a master rhetorician, he abandons system building in favor of close descriptions of art and other forms of labor, finding in these activities the *reasons* why his readers should judge them as good and, thus, worthy of their interest and support. Human labor moves to the center of Ruskin's studies of Gothic architecture. In analyzing how others work well in "social practices," and in reconceiving his moral vocabulary of the virtues on that basis, Ruskin teaches us how to read his own development and criticism both appreciatively and critically.

TWO

The Spirit of Labor

Ruskin announces his critical interest in labor on the introductory page of *The Seven Lamps of Architecture* (1849). The importance of this new concern with "human effort" belies his claim in 1883 that *Modern Painters* 2 (1846) began his critique of political economy (8.19, 4.4). That claim erases the distance he travels between his early writings on landscape painting and the studies of architecture that occupy him for nearly a decade. In fact, only three years pass between *Modern Painters* 2 and *The Seven Lamps,* so drawing too sharp a line here exaggerates how quickly his attention to the making of art precipitates the changes in his thinking that inaugurate his social criticism. Those changes unfold through the three volumes of *The Stones of Venice* (1851–53) and several lectures on architecture in 1854 before he directly addresses the production and distribution of art in what was originally called *The Political Economy of Art* (1857) and bitingly renamed *"A Joy Forever" and Its Price on the Market.*

I must stress the transitional nature of this period. Only gradually does Ruskin work out the reconceived teleological approach and vocabulary of the virtues that structure his ethics of consumption. We can see how he moves in these directions by observing that the changes in his subject matter introduce a new set of concerns with history, society, and culture that were absent from his early aesthetics. A representational art like landscape painting can mislead the viewer into thinking that no human effort went into it. It is simply a reproduction, even if a particularly insightful one, of something out there in the world. Landscape paintings, in particular, readily become "mirrors" of God's Creation, which may be why Ruskin was prepared to equate Tintoretto's greatness with a vision so pure and clear that he could intuit God's moral purposes.

As Ruskin turns from the representational art of landscape painting to the concrete spaces that people construct for themselves, he considers for the first time how an artwork's meaning and value reflect the creative efforts and powers of the artist. The more he inquires into human creativity, the more he acknowledges the historical, social, and cultural influences that shape it. But he needs a new vocabulary to account for this expanded perspective. This chapter explores the initial transformations in Ruskin's critical vocabulary by tracing out his growing reliance on the terms "spirit" and "virtue." Although simplistic, we can say that in place of his singular interest in God's virtue in his early aesthetics, he looks first to the "spirit" of past cultures and then increasingly to the "virtues" cultivated in particular social practices as he hammers out new ways of judging the beauty, meaning, and goodness of architecture and the individual labors expended in making these works of art. Although he retains his teleological approach to ethics, he begins to relocate the source of the telos from God's perfect Creation to the cultures and the activities that people make for themselves.

Ruskin is not alone in adopting the ubiquitous nineteenth-century language of "spirit" to inquire into human production. For comparative purposes, the most important contemporary to cite is Karl Marx. This comparison is justified historically despite the fact that neither figure addresses the other. Although chronologically Ruskin follows Marx as a critic of industrial capitalism by roughly a decade, he was by no means a "follower." Nothing in his writings indicates that he read or knew about Marx, and the same is true of Marx's silence about Ruskin. If Ruskin encountered Marx, then he almost certainly dismissed him, preferring, as he liked to boast, the communism of the "old school," of the medieval craft guilds (27.116). Yet Ruskin and Marx both criticize the dehumanizing effects of the division of labor, and they both approach culture as a humanly made product. As a result, for both critics, only a social analysis of industrial capitalism can unmask the real workings of factory production and market exchange. In this chapter I contrast the models of work that motivate Ruskin's and Marx's early critiques of industrial labor, reserving for chapter 4 their respective analyses of capitalist exchange.

This comparison makes conceptual sense, too, despite the historical reasons for assuming that Ruskin might have little to add to Marx. Indeed the brief lag between their critiques of capitalism speaks partly to Marx's more immediate awareness of the terrible conditions under which many people worked and lived in industrializing Europe. Nearly from the first, Marx applied himself to challenging David Ricardo's political economy and labor theory of value as the ideological struts of capitalist production. Ruskin wends his way to a critique of J. S. Mill's revision of Ricardo's political economy, and he travels that course through journeys to Europe's most treasured art collections and scenic spots. But Ruskin's "high road" to understanding labor in relation to the arts leads him to pose normative questions that Marx's approach precludes. How should we judge the meaning and worth of a person's labor? And what conditions are needed for good work? Although both thinkers begin their critiques of industrial capitalism from the vantage point of labor, and although both move away from a language of spirit, Marx remains bound by his reliance on what Seyla Benhabib has called G. W. F. Hegel's "work model of activity."[1] I argue that the theoretical terms of Marx's critique leave him, oddly enough, without ethical resources for judging and praising the excellence and dignity of people's work.[2]

Already in *The Seven Lamps* we see Ruskin's groping appeals to the "spirit" of labor in his earliest efforts to trace out the connections between the defects of Victorian taste and the social and economic conditions of industrial capitalism. He finds an occasion for this argument in the revival of Etruscan jewelry and the use of nonfaceted gemstones by the Castellani family of Rome. Although some of Ruskin's artist friends patronized these jewelers, most wealthy Victorians preferred their jewels with facets, proving for Ruskin that they tolerated—indeed demanded—oppressive work.[3] Bemoaning the utter imbalance between the pleasures taken in wearing these faceted jewels and the tedious labor exacted in cutting them, he declares that the pleasure purchased by this expenditure of effort "is not at all compensatory for the loss of life and mental power" suffered by the gem cutter. Although he implicitly refers to class divisions and economic exploitation here, he does not press his claims any farther. Instead he cautions, even threatens, that there will be more on these "strange notions . . . which it is perhaps wiser not loosely to set down" (8.265).

As this example comes in the closing pages of *The Seven Lamps,* Ruskin may be trying to intrigue his readers with a promissory note. More likely, though, he treads carefully because his claims rest on an assertion, namely, that people generally sense that jewels are valued mostly as a symbol of status and power over other people. (Perhaps this is why we display gems in history museums not art museums—because we "sense" that they have more to do with power politics than with artistic excellence.) The image of a jeweler grinding down the acuity of his vision and the years of his life so that a lady can flaunt her position is compelling in its vividness. But this image by itself cannot sustain the more general claim that Ruskin is making—that there is a direct equivalence between the value of any product and the kind of labor expended in making it. His appeal to the broken spirit of the gem cutter rests on a broader, but no less vague, appeal to the sickened "spirit" of any society that demands soul-crushing work.

Ruskin's language of spirit lets him approach his architectural studies with an eye to the interplay between individuals' work and the standards, ideals, and symbols of their culture. But this dynamic is highly circumscribed at first. The all-encompassing "spirit" of a culture is both expressed by and impressed on all of the human effort undertaken within it. The culture's spirit is mirrored in everyone's actions, leaving little room for the individual creativity and historical change seen in a spirit-driven model of culture like Hegel's. Indeed what is instructive about Ruskin's initial appeals to "spirit" is that they operate with the same insularity of the theological metaphysics of his early aesthetics. The ends of a good culture are as ordered and fixed as the moral purposes of God's Creation. What unsettles the perfect fixity of a "whole" culture and what gives persuasive force to his emerging critique of industrial capitalism is his vocabulary of the virtues as he applies it anew to the activities that people make and choose for themselves.

Ruskin's critical interests in character and flourishing in his early aesthetics carry forward into his example of the high-society lady and the toiling gem cutter. At issue here are the kinds of people they are and could become if they developed their virtues fully. In *Modern Painters* 2 virtues are the creaturely "perfections" ordained by God's Creation. In Ruskin's architectural studies the term "virtue" assumes its sense of a socially recognized "excellence" that must be developed and evaluated in the context of some shared activity. He does not now base his judgments of good art on how closely aesthetic taste conforms to God's designs in bringing duty and delight into their perfect correspondence. Rather his ethical concerns turn toward the full range of human virtues—aesthetic, moral, intellectual, and practical—and the prospects for excellent work and individual development that are fostered or denied by the social and economic conditions and the cultural standards of taste upheld by a group of people.

Simply put, Ruskin's attention to human labor leads him to ask how people's desires and virtues relate not to God's purposes but to the ends that they pursue in their cultural *activities.* Although early on in his architectural studies he senses a connection between the gem cutter's virtues (or lack thereof) and the value of his products, Ruskin works out the critical terms for detailing this connection in the argument of his famous chapter on "The Nature of Gothic" (1853). I read in this keystone chapter of *The Stones of Venice* a model of good labor that I reconstruct using Alasdair MacIntyre's concept of a "social practice."[4] Although Ruskin uses the term "practice" carefully, he does not do so with the precise technical sense I have in mind. Nevertheless, his contrast between an "art" and a "manufacture" fits the idea of a social practice. He approaches arts and crafts as arenas of cooperative activity where the participants commit to pursuing the goods and standards of the activity, allowing them to develop the virtues needed to excel in these endeavors. It is this understanding of arts and crafts as social practices that makes Ruskin a "practical critic" and that ushers in the engaged cultural critique of his later writings, as discussed in parts 2 and 3 of this book.

The "Virtues of Architecture"

Comparing Ruskin's and Marx's critical approaches to the spirit of labor opens a window on nineteenth-century attempts to modify teleological conceptions of human activity to a society and culture far more diverse and dynamic than envisioned by any "Divine Corporation ethics" (see chapter 1). The changes in Ruskin's critical approach appear first in his growing esteem for the creative labors of great artists and master architects. Their energies, skills, virtues, and vision give artistic works their meaning and value. Over the course of 1850s, Ruskin extends his regard for the dignity and excellence of human work to the efforts of all of the people employed on a Gothic cathedral and, then, to many other kinds of human activity, too.

Artistic work is a good example of the sense of "spirit" that invests some types of labors. There is that something in certain architectural or musical styles that has the power to move or inspire people. Different buildings and performances exhibit this spirit to varying degrees, and Ruskin believes that his contemporaries need to appreciate the sources of the Gothic spirit. As seen in his titles in this period—*The Seven Lamps* and *The Stones of Venice*—he seeks those "lamps" that illuminate this spark of vitality in Gothic architecture; he asks what is it in the very "stones" themselves that inspires such a powerful sense of these buildings' grandeur and beauty. As his argument unfolds, he departs from the fixed aesthetic standards dictated by God's perfect Creation, but he does so only gradually.

Ruskin's stated purpose in *The Seven Lamps* is to establish the "constant, general, and irrefragable laws of right" by which the architecture of all time should be judged (8.21). His resistance to the idea that aesthetic standards are the creations of particular historical cultures carries forward into volume one of *The Stones of Venice.* He defines "three great branches of architectural virtue" or "functions" of a building: that it "act well" in defending us "from weather or violence"; that it "speak well" in expressing feelings and in recording facts and history; and that it "look well" in being "graceful and pleasing." The first and the last of these virtues, the building's "Strength" and "Beauty," manifest the architect's intellect and feelings, respectively. Ruskin states that only these virtues, only the architect's creative contributions of mind and emotion, provide a sound basis for architectural criticism because only they transcend the historical confines of distinct cultures. By contrast, a building's expression of its time and place is culturally bound. As Ruskin puts it, the "architectural rhetoric" of any style cannot be a "fair criterion of excellence in buildings, until we can fully place ourselves in the position of those to whom their expression was originally addressed, and until we . . . are capable of being touched by every association which its builders employed as letters of their language" (9.60–61, 64).

A master builder's genius can be so inspired, it seems, that its power and worth may be felt across the ages. Consider how similar this measure of architectural greatness is to Ruskin's earlier identification of nature's beauty with God's virtue. In *Modern Painters* 2 the world's beauty reveals God's "divine work and character"; now a building's strength and beauty testify to its master builder's singular creativity. Not surprisingly, then, in *Stones* 1 Ruskin hurries his readers by the carpenters and masons employed in building a bridge. By *Stones* 2, however, he lingers over the work of the many stone carvers, citing the excellences of their innovations and efforts as essential to the "expressional character" of Gothic cathedrals. By the end of the 1850s, he will have placed the execution and guidance of every good kind of labor in workers' hands: "All art worthy of the name is the energy—neither of the human body alone, nor of the human soul alone, but of both united, one guiding the other: good craftsmanship and work of the fingers joined with good emotion and work of the heart" (16.385). It is a mistake to read these vague allusions to energy, soul, and emotion apart from the teleological structure of his ethics. The quality of the "work" of the fingers and heart depends on the ends that people take on in the cultural activities and social relationships of cooperative endeavors like Gothic architecture.

This concern with the arrangement of ends is hinted at in the opening pages of *The Seven Lamps*, where Ruskin names architecture the "distinctively political art." Architecture is political because, just as the leaders of any good polity must determine "absolutely just and desirable" ends, raising a cathedral requires coordinating the talents and skills, the ideas and innovations, of many individuals, all toward the organizing goal of making a beautiful common work in praise of God (8.20). Not surprisingly, given Ruskin's focus on the leaders' political choices, he initially equates the greatness of medieval architecture with a master builder's harmonious arrangement of the whole ensemble. Yet as he begins to see the construction of these cathedrals not as the design of a single imagination but as the cooperative endeavor of many workers, he turns toward their joint efforts in meeting the variety of goods pursued in their different crafts. Building a cathedral may require an architect's design and may ultimately answer to the purpose of praising God, but these elaborately crafted cathedrals witness as well the myriad ends of distinct cultural activities as shaped by many hands.

As Ruskin shifts his critical lens from the singular creativity of the great architect as the source of the "virtues of architecture" to the individual contributions of the many builders, two important developments transpire. First, he recasts his model of aesthetic judgment from a kind of spiritual intuition to an engaged practical judgment. Second, he relocates the source of the ends, goods, and standards governing artistic work and every other kind of labor in the broader historical productions of human cultures.

Consider in this light Ruskin's initial definition of architecture. Although he appears to set aside "expressional character" in *Stones* 1, his definition of architecture in *The Seven Lamps* limited it "to that art which, taking up and admitting, as conditions of its working the necessities and common uses of the building, impresses on its form certain characters venerable or beautiful, but otherwise unnecessary." Architecture has little to do with function; it is only indirectly concerned with a building's remaining upright or useful.[5] The art itself shows in the moldings, arches, carvings, and so forth added to and organized in and around a building. Not only does Ruskin rank architecture as the "first of the arts" in housing all of the other plastic arts within an overarching design. It is these decorative elements that contribute to people's "mental health, power, and pleasure," by preserving the texture and character of the lives of the people who built it and who inhabited these expressive spaces (8.27–28, 21). He reinforces this emphasis on individual and cultural expression by celebrating the uniqueness of architecture among the arts. "We may live without [architecture], and worship without her, but we cannot remember without her. The ambition of the old Babel builders was well directed for this world: there are but two strong conquerors of the forgetfulness of men, Poetry and Architecture; and the latter in some sort includes the former, and is mightier in its reality" (8.224). The "reality" and "memory" of architecture clarify his initial use of the term "spirit" for culture.

The "reality" of architecture distinguishes this art from poetry, painting, and sculpture. Architecture is not the "mere picturing of stories and dreams" found in poetry and painting because it exerts "continual influence over the emotions of daily life" (8.251). Architecture is "a real thing," not "the representation of an idea." It differs from sculpture, therefore, because architecture may "be left colorless, and colored by the beholder's mind: but a reality ought to have reality in all its attributes" (8.176). The creations of architecture must be entirely "real," in Ruskin's sense of the term, as they are "capable of no other life . . . being not essentially composed of things pleasant in themselves," such as the melodies of music and the images of poetry. The decorations of architecture, he continues, "depend, for their dignity and pleasurableness in the utmost degree, upon the vivid expression of the intellectual life which has been concerned in their production" (8.190–91). What attracts people to architecture resides directly in the building in the expression of its builders' efforts. This art is the most "real," therefore, because it requires the most life poured into it. Its materials are inert, offering no sources of delight beyond the energies of the people who made it. Indeed architecture signifies nothing more than the human spirit embodied in it through all of the active thinking, feeling, and handling impressed in every nick of the chisel and every choice in the arrangement of its elements. It is, for Ruskin, a soul-shaped art form.

If architecture is soul shaped, then it is also soul shaping in being the memory of an age. More than just a chronicle of historical events, it records the spirit of its builders. But while this memory remains alive as long as the encircling culture is still vital, Ruskin is acutely aware of the modern world's distance from the spirit expressed in the architecture of the past. That is why he opposed the art restoration movement of his day. Restoration denies the culturally located character of all expression—the need to enter into the "letters" of the builders' "language." That "which I have insisted on as the life of the whole, that spirit which is given only by the hand and eye of the workman, can never be recalled. Another spirit may be given by another time, and it is then a new building; but the spirit of the dead workman cannot be summoned up" (8.242). The memory of architecture stands at a distance, calling forth sympathies with the expressed values, ideals, symbols, and, above all else, the vital spirit of a culture, even as it is impossible to recapture the *"life of the whole"* that infused the builders' efforts, aims, and hopes.

Ruskin's sense of the soul-shaped and soul-shaping spirit of the labor invested in great architecture is understandable. Some forms of work have a "spirit"; they serve as arenas for people's self-development and self-expression. Although Ruskin does not use language that places so much emphasis on the "self," he denounces industrial capitalism for failing to sustain the working conditions needed for good labor and the well-developed people produced therein. Calling attention to the "spirit" of certain types of work is not his only purpose, however. His condemnation of factory work and his distancing from the expressional character of the past both speak to his assumption that the spirit of a people's labor is a mirror reflection of the spirit of their culture. He posits that there is a "life of the whole" seen in the good work of vital cultures. Recapturing the spirit of Gothic architecture would require climbing back into that "whole" culture and learning to see how, by contrast, the entirely misbegotten ends of industrial capitalism rule out all forms of good work.

Ruskin's argumentation presumes a self-enclosed conception of culture—that cultures are the seamless fabric of a people's unifying ideals, symbols, standards, and ends. That is why he first equates a building's strength and beauty with the architect's contributions. Cultures are the product of the ideals, symbols, standards, and ends that people create, but there are very few culture-creators, it seems. The spirit of the culture that they produce is mirrored in the spirit of everyone else's labors. What is noteworthy in Ruskin's movement from *Stones* 1 to *Stones* 2 is that when he tries to climb back into the Gothic spirit, he does so through an imaginative rendering of its "characteristic or moral elements." Not only does expressional character move to the center of his model of good labor, but he also relates the character of Gothic cathedrals to the character of their many builders.

I return later in the chapter to this model of good labor where, I claim, Ruskin retools his vocabulary of the virtues and works out the practical basis of his emerging social criticism. The more he looks to the activities of a culture and to the various virtues, ends, goods, and standards that people make for themselves, the more he calls into question any holistic conception of culture. This movement from the encircling spirit of a culture to the specific ends of different activities is never complete, but in his later analyses of the production of Victorian culture by industrial capitalism, he works much more at the level of close detail. We can appreciate both the distinctiveness and the normative significance of this model of labor by first examining Marx's materialist conception of labor, which has exerted far greater influence on our own theoretical approaches to the human production of cultures.

Marx's Work Model of Activity

In Ruskin's language of spirit, we see his continued attention to the ends governing the development of people's character and their judgments of things' beauty and worth. We also find the suggestion that people create their cultures, but Ruskin's holistic conception of spirit divides historical periods and styles into self-enclosed wholes, and it leaves creative control of a culture's commitments and interpretations of things' goodness in few people's hands.

Marx's early social theory proceeds from his suspicions of the kind of deification of a culture's singular arrangement of ends that I read in Ruskin's early architectural studies. Indeed Marx constructs his own critical vocabulary in opposition to, and through a materialist revision of, Hegel's concept of "Spirit." Already in Hegel's *Phenomenology of Spirit* (1807), there is a dialectical movement that escapes the cloistered notion of culture seen in Ruskin's identification of the workman's labor with the "life of the whole." Marx borrows this dialectic from Hegel, but he turns his attention away from the history of ideas and institutions that Hegel portrays as the unfolding activity of Spirit to the material conditions of human life in different historical periods. For Marx, cultures are not only dynamic and developing; they are constructed through people's efforts to meet their economic needs. Marx's materialist history views human activity as neither self-conscious nor self-directed, however, despite the need for people to band together in various forms of cooperation that then become patterned as culture. Just as Hegel presents the unfolding activity of Spirit as an endeavor that transcends human consciousness, so too Marx's account of the social construction of reality is characterized by a blind automaticity.

Seyla Benhabib argues convincingly that Marx's social theory founders insofar as he retains the vestiges of what she calls Hegel's "work model of activity." In her words, "underlying Hegel's concept of the activity of Spirit is a model of labor as the cumulative generator of wealth."[6] In Hegelian terminology this wealth is the content of Spirit's consciousness recognized as the total product of Spirit's activity through history up to that point. What appears to consciousness as its object is not some independent existing thing out there in the world; rather it is the result of Spirit's earlier efforts to know the world, by means of which every object is first "externalized," and thus transformed, before being "appropriated."[7]

This work model operates at two levels, the interpersonal and the historical. At the interpersonal level, it posits that all human activity is, in Benhabib's words, "intersubjective," that is, embedded in the communicative media and expressive forms of a culture. In addition to this first level, which Benhabib sees as Hegel's great insight, however, Spirit also functions as *the* subject of all history, thus denying people control of their own cultural creations.[8]

Hegel's "work model" inheres in the first moment of externalization (Entäusserung), during which individuals undertake actions that make sense, that is, that take on meaning and reality in the context of existing cultural forms. Yet cultural change is ongoing. Individuals' actions do not conform to fixed cultural patterns, as there must always be room for new self-expression. The moment of "externalization" captures both the need for actions to be made intelligible in light of current forms of expression and the possibility that innovation will occur. We might compare this moment to a poet's effort to find the words to convey something never said before. The search for the right words takes place in a literary and social context informed by the work of other poets, both past and present, and the sensibilities of the contemporary reading public. What the poet "expresses" calls attention, therefore, to the cultural contexts in which his or her words make sense and to the ways that these contexts have been constructed and reworked over time. Not everyone will appreciate the poem's significance, not initially at least, because culture is so subject to new expressions. In addition, the poem may be interpreted and reinterpreted in various ways. It is in the dynamics of creative self-expression and the cultural innovation and negotiation that ensue that we see Benhabib's realm of "intersubjectivity."

The problems with Hegel's work model lie both in how he conceives work and in how all human activity gets reduced to this model. For Hegel, "work" is an act of working out, of *ex-pressing*, inner potential by shaping the world to embody that potential as real. Benhabib rejects this model as insufficient to the varieties of human activity. Do consumers "ex-press" some inner potential in choosing what to consume? Does the art critic do the same in interpreting the meaning of an artwork? Is today's service sector rightly described in terms of work that "ex-presses" some as-yet-unrealized potential? Moving to the heart of Benhabib's critique, there is a difference, she notes, between Hegel's views of Spirit's "work" and human "action." He accepts that human action is fraught with the uncertainties implicit in the linguistic and cultural competencies needed to be able to express oneself to others. But the unfolding telos of Spirit's self-externalization through history demands a tighter correspondence between inner intention and outer expression than is possible in human action. This is why Hegel makes human cultural development and, with it, every meaningful individual expression the work of Spirit itself. Not only does his "work model" reduce all human action to "ex-pressing" untapped potentialities, but in addition, "meaning" can only be realized and appropriated in line with the course of Spirit's unfolding activity. In Benhabib's words, human "intersubjectivity" is thereby reduced to the "transsubjective" standpoint of Spirit. Thus, in the end, Hegel's work model takes the historical level as decisive in determining what new "ex-pressions" have lasting significance and which cultural standards, forms, values, and symbols make them meaningful. Culture is open to ongoing transformation, but human history is reduced to Spirit's activity, for Spirit is both the accumulated substance of culture and the author of it.[9]

Although Marx rejects much of the drama of Spirit's self-unfolding, he acknowledges his debts to Hegel. In the *Economic and Philosophical Manuscripts of 1844* (published 1932), he celebrates Hegel for seeing "the self-creation of man as a process"—namely, of "objectification [Vergegenständlichung] as loss of the object, as alienation [Entäusserung] and as transcendence of this alienation." Hegel "grasps the essence of *labour* and comprehends objective man . . . as the outcome of man's own *labour.*"[10] Marx affirms two things here. First, the basic outline of Hegel's dialectic rightly describes the mechanics of the social construction of reality—"the self-creation of man" is a social and historical process achieved through human labor. Second, this process takes place without people recognizing what is happening because they are "alienated" from the products of their labor and dependent upon the moment of "transcendence" when the blinders are finally lifted.

Despite these parallels, Marx, as is also well known, replaces Hegel's attention to the unfolding of Spirit's consciousness with a concern for the working out of human needs. The priority of needs to consciousness is emphatic in *The German Ideology* (1845, published 1929): "life involves before everything else eating and drinking, housing, clothing and various other things." From the labor to satisfy the most basic needs, Marx derives the more complex need for cooperation in production, and only then does consciousness arise as a "social product" of these material activities and interactions.[11] Consciousness, as the governing ideas of a culture, is the product of human labor directed toward specific material needs. It is not, as with Hegel, the real engine of human history. Rather, Marx sees in Hegel's philosophy of Spirit an apology of sorts for industrial capitalism. In identifying Spirit's work with the successes of the dominant culture, Hegel offers ideological support for the social arrangements, ideals, and values of this society. Marx adopts his materialist starting point and constructs a "naturalistic" social theory to rule out precisely this sort of valorization of the inherited ideas legitimizing some group's preferred way of life.[12]

That is why Marx translates Spirit's "externalization" into labor's "alienation" under industrial capitalism. To say that human labor is "alienated" from its products is to say that the things that people make escape their control and come to exert independent power over them. Machine production conveys this sense of misbegotten powerlessness poignantly. People build machines that they must then serve as slaves. "Alienated labor" (*die entfremdte Arbeit*) is the central category of Marx's early critique of capitalism. It provides an invaluable vocabulary for confronting people's subordination to work and commodities in industrial life. Marx uses it as well to depict capitalist production because the commodities that people produce are made solely for their resale value on the market. The "ends" of commodity production reach no farther than turning a profit for the capitalist and paying the workers' wages that, when presented in this light, are exposed as the wages of self-impoverishment.

Although Marx departs sharply from Hegel, his resolution of the situation of alienated labor under industrial capitalism leads him right back to Hegel's work model. The model persists in Marx's category of "objectification." Labor conforms to the model of working out, or ex-pressing, inner potential as a largely automatic historical process. As Marx puts it, "The product of labour is labour which has been embodied in an object." He is thinking here of the production of goods. Laborers take the materials they find at hand (what has been made of the world by previous generations) and produce new goods for other people. Thus, when Marx writes that "Labour's realisation is its objectification," he would seem to have two outcomes in mind, both of which require attention to people's cultural interpretation and negotiation. First, workers "realize" their efforts in the things produced—presumably, that is, they have a sense of the value and meaning of what they make in a way parallel to a poet's finding the "right words" to express some thought in a novel though intelligible manner. In addition, workers achieve "self-realization" because their interactions with other people and the recognition they receive as a result of their labors transpire within the "intersubjective" realm of the ideals, symbols, ends, values, and standards of a shared culture.

These possibilities for individual expression and mutual recognition require that people be the agents of their own activity, however, and like Hegel before him, Marx rules this out. He posits a philosophy of history that delays the self-conscious pursuit of one's own ends, either by oneself or with others, until the arrival of communism. For Marx, capitalism is dehumanizing precisely because it prevents people from seeing the purposes of their endeavors, their "conscious life-activity."[13] As he observes, bees build hives by instinct, not by an architectural plan.[14] But under capitalism work is ruled by the sole aim of making profits, turning people into animals who lack all recognition of the ends that they pursue. Nor do people see the "social" character of their labors. They are no more aware of the interdependence of their efforts than bees making a hive. In fact, people are worse off because their blindness perverts society into the disintegrating competition of all against all that defines bourgeois civil society.

For the early Marx, these failures of vision can be corrected only if people grasp the true ends of their labors by recognizing their "species-being" (Gattungswesen). "Man is a species-being, not only because in practice and in theory he adopts the species as his object (his own as well as those of other things), but—and this is only another way of expressing it—also because he treats himself as the actual, living species; because he treats himself as a *universal* and therefore a free being." The term "species-being" reflects the interdependence of human life within a society and across generations. Present activity builds on the past production of the material wealth that serves as the basis of current efforts. And crucially, these ongoing efforts will eventually realize the species' full potential, the final goal of labor as objectification. "The object of labour is" nothing less than *"the objectification of man's species life."*[15] This progressive endeavor of labor to make the world fully human is what will ultimately lead people, or so Marx's social theory prophesies, to realize their "species-being." Understanding that this fulfillment of the species' potential is the necessary outcome of history also means that, no matter how alienating work is today, it will some day allow people to grasp the true ends of their labors.

Marx's insistence on workers' blindness to larger purpose captures well the myopia of the division of labor. Yet he delays resolving the problem of freely chosen cooperation in pursuit of self-conscious ends until the eventual realization of "species-being." That delay has the perverse effect of stripping decision-making power from individuals. It also curbs ethical reflection. Indeed, his ostensibly historical analysis is compromised by a philosophy of history differing from Hegel's drama mainly in its casting. Instead of Spirit, the species assumes the leading role. Ultimately, every person's labor contributes to the realization, not primarily of individual talents, skills, and capacities but of the essential potential of "man" as the species. The early Marx lays his hopes for labor's self-emancipation in the development of capitalism itself because he sees in it the penultimate stage of human history's working out the unrealized potential of "man" as a free, social being. The later Marx substitutes in the "universal proletarian class" as the bearer of that outcome.

The echoes of Spirit's labor in Marx's theoretical terms make his approach to the human production of culture more historical and comprehensive than Ruskin's idea of the spirit of whole cultures. But because Marx remains beholden to Hegel's work model of activity, he finally does not descend into engaged cultural analysis, and as a result, his theoretical approach postpones critical reflection, discussion, and argument about the ends that people want to guide their work and society.

Ex-pressive Labor versus Artistic Expression

Benhabib argues that if Marx took human needs more seriously, he would flesh out his understanding of the cultural creation, negotiation, and interpretation that constitutes "intersubjectivity." In this interpersonal layer of relationships, she sees the arena of cultural agreements that is itself a work in progress and that serves as the creative domain for truly self-expressive labor. Given Ruskin's attention to arts and crafts, Benhabib's extension of this argument is striking. She criticizes Marx's idea of labor as "objectification" for implying an instrumental model of work akin to machine production. For Marx, "the line between production for use and aesthetic production seems to disappear." Machine production of a useful object, Benhabib continues, is different from the production of a "work of art [or] a crafts object." These forms of work tend toward self-expression by remaining within their makers' control and, more importantly, by moving other people to make interpretive and evaluative sense of these efforts. How do other people receive works of art and craft, she asks? How do they discuss, for example, a painter's manner on a canvas? In Benhabib's words, they "characterize" it in "ethico-moral terms"—as "'impatient,' 'gentle,' 'precise,' or 'angry.'" Thus, "an object that expresses the self is one that allows the identity of the individual person to become manifest." In other words, for Benhabib, it is not the "objects" of labor that are expressive, but the subjects of labor as they participate within the "mediums of language, culture and social interaction." If work is to be made expressive and received in intelligible terms like these, then the painter and the audience must have gained this "intersubjective" knowledge, knowledge very different from that found in the "medium of object production."[16] Without shared cultural competencies and standards of judgment, no one could paint in any manner at all, nor could other people interpret their meaning and style and assess their work's relative worth.

Benhabib's criticisms are apt, but they do not go far enough. She treats Marx's work model as blinded by inattention to artistic endeavors like painting. She does not refer to his disparagement of craftwork—his scorn for "petty handicraftsmen who have been ruined by industrial freedom and are morally 'indignant.'"[17] In fact, the line between production for use and artistic production does not simply "*seem* to disappear" in Marx's writings; he suppresses it. No doubt he has his reasons. Marx's blanket dismissal of craftwork reflects a legitimate worry about power relations within medieval craft guilds and between the guilds and those dependent upon them. "Industrial freedom," in his view, liberates people from these entrenched forms of domination, and this social progress justifies the dismantling of craftwork. Yet the kind of self-expression that Benhabib celebrates depends, as she recognizes, on the forms of labor prized by Ruskin and other critics whom he inspired, such as the arts and crafts leader William Morris.

Marx's confidence in the value of "industrial freedom" speaks to the "productivist bias" of his social theory. By this I mean he bases his critical thought on an idea of production that envisions individuals' labors and the collective labor of humanity as an act of ex-pression, a working out of inner potential, as if all that it took to develop one's abilities was following a mechanical blueprint in a fairly straightforward means-to-end fashion, even as the end goal of that process remains out of sight.[18] As Benhabib points out, this work model serves to deify capitalist productivity and growth, representing, ironically, the "fulfillment" of bourgeois norms. She herself argues that the resources to correct these problems are found in Marx's focus on human needs in his social theory.[19] The question must be asked, however, does he admit the cultural forms of expression and the attendant "ethico-moral" resources needed to imagine, evaluate, and choose among the ways that people might transform their needs, their work, and their capacities?

For Ruskin, as we shall see, the goods, ends, and standards that participants take on in "social practices" enable them not only to create and judge good work but also to cultivate their excellences. Marx's ideal of emancipation as the inevitable outcome of humanity's labor eschews this layer of ethical reflection. Emancipation means freeing oneself from the prevailing cultural norms, ideals, and symbols that uphold the values of the dominant class. Consider in this light Marx's reveries about the communist future. Once freed from the division of labor, he would "hunt in the morning, fish in the afternoon, rear cattle in the evening, criticise after dinner, just as I have a mind, without ever becoming hunter, fisherman, shepherd or critic."[20] But why choose these activities? What reasons can he give for seeing these activities in that mix as a better way of life? Does anything inform his "mind" other than an innate or pure desire that he is moved to ex-press for no reason that could be defended on normative grounds? Marx's acute insights into the cultural construction of desire and the need for critical analysis seem lost on him here.

Marx is forthright about not wanting to have any entailments like a vocation influencing his choices. Nor, as we see in *The German Ideology,* does he want people's achievements to be measured by the standards of some practice. Under "a communist organisation of society," he writes, "there disappears the subordination of the artist to local and national narrowness, which arises entirely from division of labour, and also the subordination of the individual to some definite art, making him exclusively a painter, sculptor, etc.; the very name amply expresses the narrowness of his professional development and his dependence on division of labour." It is easy to think of institutional arrangements that promote an "exclusive concentration of artistic talent in particular individuals, and its suppression in the broad mass." Ruskin himself benefited from the nineteenth-century cult of genius, supported as it was by the institutions of publishing, journalism, museums, universities, and the lecture circuit. But although he would agree that this state of affairs results from the division of labor and should be criticized in that light, Ruskin would find Marx's quest for a universal and untutored art unintelligible. When Marx writes that in the future there will be "no painters but only people who engage in painting among other activities," he implies that it will be enough to engage in painting without engaging, even if only critically, the social practice that makes one a painter.[21] This blithe vision obscures how participation in such activities, along with a commitment to their governing goods and standards and an acknowledgment of any past greats, informs and enables people's expression.

For Ruskin, individual development and creativity require cultivating one's excellences, while for Marx "ex-pression" is an act of self-creation by which we make ourselves in the same way we manufacture an object. In Marx's ideal day he imagines choosing to be a critic after dinner, ex-pressing a seemingly inborn potential. But the whimsy implicit in this choice, as he portrays it, is unjust to his own excellence in crafting the revolutionary transformations that he brought to the practice of social criticism.

The early Marx sees individual labors as an act of "ex-pression" that develops the full potential of humanity. This helps explain the little he writes about art—both why he has so little to say about art and why art is for him inextricably related to emancipation. Marx has two main ways of appreciating art.[22] On the one hand, he takes art as an ideal of unalienated labor. The expressive, cooperative yet self-directed activity of making art models the kind of labor that everyone will enjoy in the future, though presumably apart from inherited practices. Until that time, however, artists must serve the revolutionary values that can hurry this day's arrival.[23] On the other hand, Marx distances himself from, almost curbs his desire for, art as a nostalgic legacy of the past. He, like many nineteenth-century German thinkers, favored Greek art, with its presumed basis in a mythological understanding of human beings' relationship to nature. While he admits that such art has an undeniable charm in conjuring up images of organic relations to the world and to other people, he insists that this charm must now be denied as unattainable and undesirable given the progress toward emancipation from the older organic bonds of a dying social order.

Marx senses the appeal of art, and he hopes that everyone may enjoy the benefits of such self-expressive work in the future. For the present, though, he restricts the measure of good art to its potential for manufacturing change. This reflects again his ex-pressivist model of work, which leaves him without recourse to the shared ends, goods, and standards that people adopt and adapt in their activities. Marx's ideal of emancipation through the ends-less production of capitalism, the transformation of past cultural products, and the inevitable realization of humanity's essential potential leaves no way of appreciating and evaluating those activities and achievements that occur within a shared context of acknowledging "excellence," even as we remain wary of the possible abuses that go with such forms of praise and such orders of merit. It is this cultural space of "social practices" that Ruskin explores in his account of Gothic craftwork where he addresses the questions that Marx's social theory cannot fathom. What kinds of work are good for people? And what does it mean to work excellently?

Ruskin's Crafted Labor

Thomas Carlyle's growing influence on Ruskin shows decidedly in his writings on architecture. It can be seen as early as the introduction to *The Seven Lamps.* From the invective against the new "necessities" rising "strange and impatient, out of every modern shadow of change," to the warmly reported counsel of an artist friend, "'Know what you have to do, and do it,'" Ruskin's emerging voice as a social critic echoes with Carlylean themes (8.21, 19). The counsel mimics Carlyle's Gospel: "Know thy work and do it." Carlyle preaches old-fashioned work as the salvation from the double ills of industrial capitalism, the aristocratic idleness to which factory-owners aspire and the numbing labor that they impose on workers. He affirms work as participatory in the divine: "Giant Labour, truest emblem there is of God the World-Worker, Demiurgus, and Eternal Maker."[24] Metaphysical overtones resound in Ruskin's vision of good labor, too, along with something of the Carlylean tradeoff between fully honoring the lowest types of work while insisting that people in these lesser stations remain satisfied with their lot in life. But these are not the fruits of Ruskin's vision. Rather, his accounts of the actual workings of arts and crafts celebrate the freedom of their makers and bring into view an idea of labor as a "social practice."

For William Morris, Ruskin evokes the conditions for and the dignity of good labor most powerfully in "The Nature of Gothic."[25] Early in that chapter, Ruskin asks, "what kinds of labor are good for men?" His way of answering is instructive because he describes the "character" he sees recorded in the stones of Gothic cathedrals. That is, he now reads the "expressional character" of this style, the virtue of architecture he set aside in his initial outline of *The Stones of Venice.* All told Ruskin details six "characteristic or moral elements of Gothic": savageness, changefulness, naturalism, grotesqueness, rigidity, and redundance (10.196, 184). The first three are most important for measuring the extent of his movement beyond the language of spirit as he works out his mature vocabulary of the virtues.

Noting the derision signified by the term "Gothic," Ruskin embraces the rough-hewn rudeness of the style. "Savageness" speaks to "the hard habits of the arm and heart" required of the inhabitants of the more strenuous northern climes where the Gothic spirit originates. Beyond these virtues of industry and fortitude, the Gothic style testifies to the animating "religious principle" of the Christian acceptance of human imperfection.[26] "Christianity having recognized, in small things as well as great, the individual value of every soul . . . not only recognizes its value; it confesses its imperfection, in only bestowing dignity upon the acknowledgment of unworthiness" (10.189–90). Simply put, people do their best work where imperfection is accepted as the condition for all human effort and excellence. For Ruskin, the Gothic style and its forms embody the Christian spirit of forgiveness, and he claims that this ideal shaped the culture that gave rise to the Gothic aesthetic. But he is making a broader claim, too. Not only in this culture, but in all cultures, labor will be accorded its full dignity only when the value of people's work is measured not on a standard of perfection but in terms of an imperfect striving to bring forth the excellence that one can attain.

This appeal to imperfection marks a notable departure from Ruskin's early aesthetics. There the worth of a landscape painting depended on how well it mirrored the beauty of God's perfect "work and character." Aesthetic value and divine perfection went hand in hand. Ruskin now invokes a merciful forgiveness as the chief offering of Christianity, and he argues that this ideal infuses the Gothic style. When compared to Greek and Renaissance architecture, the Gothic is characterized by freer working conditions for laborers and better relations between masters and workers, too.

As evidence, Ruskin contrasts the kinds of ornamentation found in each of these three periods. The "constitutional" ornament of the Gothic is preferable to the "servile" ornament of the Greek and the "revolutionary" ornament of the Renaissance. The savageness of the Gothic results from the combined freedom and guidance enjoyed by the stone carvers: their "executive inferior power is, to a certain point, emancipated and independent, having a will of its own, yet [also] confessing its inferiority and rendering obedience to higher powers." On the one hand, the style's acceptance of imperfection gives individual workers ample latitude for "invention" as it does not confine their work to the goal of perfection. On the other hand, the work is carried out under the direction of master artists and, higher still, toward praise of God, serving to further the stone carvers' burgeoning excellences and to elevate their aspirations. The latitude for creativity joins with the ennoblement of imperfect effort, allowing individual workers to express their self, that is, their character or "constitution," in their labors (10.188).

By contrast, the "servile" ornament of the Greeks reveals that inferiors were "slaves" to their masters whose exacting designs allowed nothing to their independent abilities. If the Greeks sought a perfection too low, however, then the Renaissance sought a perfection too high. Its "revolutionary" ornament abrogated the Christian forgiveness of imperfection by denying all "executive inferiority" and demanding "in all things, the utmost completion or perfection compatible with their nature. This is a noble character in the abstract, but becomes ignoble when it causes us to forget the relative dignities of that nature itself, and to prefer the perfectness of the lower nature to the imperfection of the higher" (10.189–90). Reminiscent of Marx, Ruskin contrasts perfect animals that lack all conscious aims with grandly imperfect humanity. But for Ruskin, the Renaissance erred in losing sight of the relative ordering of "natures," all arranged as a harmony of purpose. This appeal to a hierarchical ordering of all things' "natures" clearly echoes with the metaphysics of the good presumed in his early aesthetics. While it is unsurprising that he holds to such a perfectly ordered conception of nature seven years later, the continuing hold of this metaphysics underscores one historical reason why Marx so adamantly rejects craftwork in favor of the relentless growth of capitalism. Ruskin is not alone in transferring God's perfect design of the natural order onto the harmony of "master" and worker that stands at the center of his imagined medievalist social order. Nostalgia for the presumed lost coherence of a society fully joined by a common faith and completely unified in a vision of the common good is one of the standard tropes of Ruskin's tradition, and as I argue in chapter 5 on Ruskin's politics of medievalism, they warrant the kind of scrutiny that Marx brings to them.

More promising than this idealized portrait of medieval life is Ruskin's retreat from the language of perfection. Indeed perfection is anathema to him in the realm of human work, and his criticisms of standards of perfection call into question the metaphysical framework he earlier borrowed from Richard Hooker. In Hooker's model of all things' flourishing, "perfection" is an upper limit or ceiling. Toward the "absolute exactness" of God all things strive. But Ruskin now associates "perfection" with the Renaissance and its bastard child, industrial capitalism. As heir to the Renaissance, the modern world adheres to the goal of perfection in all things—perfect lines for every building and perfect precision in every stroke of the loom and crash of the press. Modernity levels all work down to those undertakings that can be executed perfectly, whether they be bland architecture or refined sugar. Left only with the goals of perfect art and repetitive production, the desiccated spirit of modernity leaves people unable to innovate or delight in any endeavor. For Ruskin these modes of work cannot accommodate the wide variety of human striving, the pursuit of which makes for the freedom of individual expression.

The "changefulness" of Gothic cathedrals allows for this variety of ends, and that is why it is the "*only rational* architecture." Its main structural elements are capable of infinite variation and innovation. Whatever the building's requirements, the architect can adapt these flexible forms, innovating with new combinations that answer to the needs of the moment while holding true to the forms of the style. So too, individual workers participate in the living "school" of the Gothic with its "vital principle" being "the love of *Change*. It is that strange *disquietude* of the Gothic spirit that is its greatness" (10.212, 214). Like the jazz musician who unnerves the listener with a rapid succession of variations never heard before, the medieval stone carver invented an abundance of designs unrestricted by the demands of perfection and repetition. The cathedral as a whole joined all the sparks of imagination and inspiration of the individual workers as they buttressed the novel notes, chords, and riffs they each struck in the rough stone.

The analogy to jazz falters, however, with the introduction of the third trait of Gothic, its "naturalism." Even in jazz, innovation works within or against some form, but jazz forms need not conform to "nature" in the way that Ruskin believes his stone carvers did. In going to the natural world for their designs, these workers displayed a naturalist tendency. He defines naturalism as "the love of natural objects for their own sake, and the effort to represent them frankly, unconstrained by artistical laws." The natural world provided a diversity of objects inviting the Gothic carver's "love of *fact*" (10.215, 232). But Ruskin clarifies his understanding of naturalism by praising those artists who are capable of perceiving both good and evil in the world. Naturalists display a "kind of *divine grasp and government of the whole*, sympathizing with all the good, and yet confessing, permitting, and bringing good out of the evil also." This sensibility contrasts with the tendency of "purists" who see only the good, an outlook that falters on a "narrowness of understanding the *ends of things*" (10.222, 231; my emphasis). Architecture may be the "political" art and, thus, the most reflective of a society's arrangement of its governing ends, working conditions, and social relations. Nevertheless, for Ruskin, the greatness of the Gothic ultimately harkens beyond human self-governance back to God's created order. The teleological structure of Ruskin's ethics has been stretched by his newfound love of human creativity, but it still remains joined to his early metaphysics of the good. The naturalism of Gothic decoration reflects an expansive view of the ends of art, but it finally answers to the vision of nature detailed in *Modern Painters* 2—that every part of the natural world and the ends they all serve are ordered into a perfect harmony where nothing is out of place and where evil only enhances good, just as ugliness heightens the attraction of beauty.

In sum, the freedom enjoyed by the builders of Gothic cathedrals answers both to the cultural forms developed within this "living school" and to the harmony of ends revealed in nature's perfect order. In this tension between the freeing up of individual creativity through the forgiving forms of the Gothic and the ordering of all human effort toward God's perfect designs, we see two religious appeals. Ruskin celebrates imperfection for its freeing up of individual efforts toward a range of expression. Yet he professes a dimly seen theology of perfection sanctioning a hierarchy of "relative dignities" perceptible by those who exhibit a "divine grasp" of the harmony of ends served by each part of God's Creation. This tension between human imperfection and divine perfection is not surprising in a religious thinker deeply influenced by Christianity, but Ruskin's thesis that medieval culture uniquely combines freedom of expression with perfect unity of purpose is not the only way of resolving it. That resolution is the product of his holistic conception of the spirit of cultures, not an inherent feature of his evolving vocabulary of the virtues.

I have synthesized Ruskin's account of Gothic character to demonstrate how his reading reflects his initial assumptions about cultures. But his steady turn toward the ends that his fellow Victorians pursue in their social practices and other cultural activities unhitches his vocabulary of the virtues both from the theological metaphysics of the good in his early aesthetics and from his idea of the "whole" spirit of cultures in his architectural studies. Indeed, Ruskin is far more eclectic than his language and his idealized portrait of the Middle Ages suggest. This portrait need not be bought whole cloth. Instead it is possible to extract from his architectural studies a model of good work that motivates his best reasons for favoring Gothic craftwork over factory production. It is also possible to separate his dual religious appeals to the imperfections of human creativity and the perfections of God's Creation.

Although both appeals continue to operate in Ruskin's later social criticism (along with other religious appeals), his praise for the Christian acknowledgment of imperfection and the varieties of human ends and endeavors that it encourages overshadows his earlier metaphysics of God's perfect Creation. As this metaphysical sensibility wanes, he calls into question the premise that only by returning to the integrated spirit of the Middle Ages, or some other "whole" culture, can the ills of industrial capitalism be mitigated. These changes in his emerging social criticism relate to his new virtues-centered approach to judging the goodness of art and labor.

Arts and Crafts as Social Practices

I have sketched Ruskin's portrait of Gothic architecture to derive from it the idea of a "social practice." My analysis proceeds from his critical interests in character and his claim that only certain "kinds of labor" allow for the development of the capacities for excellence that enable people's expression. "The Nature of Gothic" argues that individual creativity and expression can flourish only where people follow the "everlasting laws" of "effort and mercy." As life requires imperfection for change and growth, "to banish imperfection [in labor] is to destroy expression, to check exertion, to paralyze vitality." Ruskin applies this law of "Effort" to the "signs of the life and liberty of every [Gothic] workman." Moreover, this dependence of human achievement on imperfection leads him to cite the need for "Mercy" in passing judgment on other people's work (10.203–4). He cautions, "in our dealings with the souls of other men, we are to take care how we check, by severe requirement or narrow caution, efforts which might otherwise lead to a noble issue; and, still more, how we withhold our admiration from great excellencies, because they are mingled with rough faults" (10.191). A vital and thriving human imperfection replaces the perfections of "divine work and character." All of the best artists proceed, Ruskin observes, by striving toward imperfect, though majestic, excellence, rather than stopping short at a lowly perfection or being frustrated by a vain quest for an unattainable perfection. Imperfection enables freedom of expression and human excellence.

The closest correlates to the notion of a social practice in "The Nature of Gothic" are the terms "art" and "craft." Ruskin specifically distinguishes art from "manufacture."[27] He writes, "Nothing is a great work of art, for the production of which either rules or models can be given. Exactly so far as architecture works on known rules, and from given models, it is not an art, but a manufacture." Manufacture demands instrumental knowledge as reproducible as the products churned out by factories; repetitious efficiency is the aim. Comparing the glass work of medieval Venice and modern England, Ruskin praises "the old Venetian [who] cared not a whit whether his edges were sharp or not, but . . . invented a new design for every glass that he made, and never moulded a handle or a lip without a new fancy in it" (10.207, 199).

Antithetical to this crafted novelty is the modern taste for mass production. In detailing the costs of this preference for "perfect manual skill" over a person's imperfect but "whole" effort, Ruskin directs his readers to the aesthetic standards governing the design of English homes. He traces the lesser enjoyments of "accurate mouldings" and "perfect polishings" out beyond the sitting rooms of his day into the working conditions that they mandate. "Men were not intended to work with the accuracy of tools, to be precise and perfect in all their actions. If you will have that precision out of them, and make their fingers measure degrees like cog-wheels, and their arms strike curves like compasses, you must unhumanize them. All the energy of their spirits must be given to make cogs and compasses of themselves." The learned preference for works devoid of individual expression is inseparable from labor dictated by standards of "steely precision" (10.193, 192).

The relation is not accidental. Work lacking human content requires a systematic regulation of working conditions that either squeezes all of the life out of people or simply prepares them from the start for no life at all. "We have studied much and much perfected, of late, the great civilized invention of the division of labour; only we give it a false name. It is not, truly speaking, the labour that is divided; but the men:—Divided into mere segments of men—broken into small fragments and crumbs of life. . . . And the great cry that rises from all our manufacturing cities, louder than their furnace blast, is all in very deed for this,—that we manufacture everything there except men" (10.196). While Marx and Ruskin both criticize the division of labor as the cause of industrial capitalism's woes, their divergent analyses and critical responses show in their models of labor's expression. Marx's "ex-pressivist" model of labor envisions a working out of human potential regardless of the working conditions or ends of production. For Ruskin, expression depends on the existence of forms of labor like those of Gothic craftwork—the "kinds of labor" that "are good for men."

In laying responsibility for workers' lack of freedom on his contemporaries' taste, Ruskin challenges his readers to imagine "reading a building as we would read Milton or Dante." Just as repeating the same ideas over and over would not be honored in literature, so too the capacity for variation and excellence in expression should be the goal in architecture as it was in the Gothic style. Gothic forms were neither ruled by repetition nor locked into set elements, and the "Gothic spirit broke through" established laws wherever it found them "in existence." It "not only dared, but delighted in, the infringement of every servile principle; and invented a series of forms of which the merit was, not merely that they were new, but that they were *capable of perpetual novelty*" (10.206, 208).

Although Ruskin emphasizes the Gothic capacity for novelty, the accent should fall on the claim that it was the working of the style's forms that enabled the laborers' freedom. Indeed, a central argument in "The Nature of Gothic" is that crafts are so shaped—both the products are so shaped by their makers and also the crafts themselves are so shaped by their participants and the goods and ends that they jointly pursue—that craftwork generates a freedom of activity and expression eliminated under the working conditions requisite to modern taste and industry.

This view of arts and crafts as realms of achieved excellence is best understood in light of Alasdair MacIntyre's idea of a social practice. MacIntyre defines a practice as "any coherent and complex form of socially established cooperative human activity through which goods internal to that form of activity are realized in the course of trying to achieve those standards of excellence which are appropriate to, and partially definitive of, that form of activity, with the result that human powers to achieve excellence, and human conceptions of the ends and goods involved, are systematically extended."[28]

All of the main features of this idea of a practice can be found in Ruskin's discussion of Gothic architecture. Gothic craftwork represents a *cooperative activity* that shapes its participants by enabling their freedom of expression. Ruskin's insistence on encouraging the imperfect efforts of people engaged in a craft demonstrates as well his belief that practices are necessary to the *cultivation of human powers* for excellence. Likewise, in his account of Gothic changefulness, he places the *extension and revision* of the ends pursued by architects within its "great system of perpetual change"—that change being "a necessary and constant condition of the life of the school" (10.212–13).

Integral to MacIntyre's idea of a social practice is the distinction between "internal" and "external goods." For MacIntyre, external goods lie outside of practices in the domain of institutions. They are relatively easy to name because they are the ubiquitous ends of human activity, not the ends of specific practices. Wealth, fame, and power are external goods, and as MacIntyre notes, external goods tend to be distributed through institutions, such as the market, press, or political process. By contrast, the internal goods of practices are not "contingently and externally attached to . . . practices by the accidents of social circumstance." Wealth, fame, and power may be gained in all sorts of ways and used to obtain other goods in various spheres of life. Wealth, for example, often buys power and fame. But "the goods internal to the practice of chess [for example] cannot be had in any way but by playing chess or some other game of that specific kind."

This understanding of internal goods is reflected in Ruskin's claim that Gothic is a "*rational* architecture." The variability of its forms afforded ample room for innovation for the architects and the stone carvers who both worked within and changed the style, provided that they held to the authority of those cultural forms and their governing goods and standards. Similarly, in the novelty of Venetian glasswork, Ruskin sees evidence not of blundering error but of a designer fully cognizant of the room for expression afforded by his materials when worked by someone skilled in the craft. Although Ruskin does not elaborate the specific *internal goods* and *standards of excellence* of these crafts, he assumes that such a practical knowledge is necessary to the work and that the work itself allows for the ongoing revision of them.

Another instance of the distinction between internal and external goods appears in Ruskin's 1857 lecture on the "Influence of Imagination in Architecture." A more explicit focus on practices is now apparent. In concluding the lecture, he charges architects to pursue a "triple love—for the art which you practise, the creation in which you move, and the creatures to whom you minister." Clarifying the first of these loves for the "art which you practise," he declares, "I do not say you are not to desire money, nor to desire fame, nor to desire position; you cannot but desire all three; nay, you may—if you are willing that I should use the word Love in a desecrated sense—love all three; that is, passionately covet them; yet you must not covet or love them in the first place. . . . the whole question is one of first or second. Does your art lead you, or your gain lead you?" If the "art which you practise" leads the way, then its practical knowledge must have a certain authority for you. If not, and love of money, fame, or position leads the way, then you can only be "mechanics, and drudges," not artists (16.369–70). To use MacIntyre's terms, internal and external goods must be loved in the proper order, even as excellence in the pursuit of the former can on occasion secure the latter.

The practice-centered vocabulary of the virtues that Ruskin starts to work out in this period reflects his own growing recognition of the myriad goods and standards pursued in distinctive artistic practices. Responding to critics in 1856 toward the end of his architectural studies, he defends himself against the "constant allegation of 'dogmatism'" on the grounds of having "given ten years of my life to the single purpose of enabling myself to judge rightly of art, and spent them in labor as earnest and continuous as men usually undertake to gain position, or accumulate fortune" (5.4–5).

For Ruskin the same ordering of internal goods over external goods applies to anyone interested in the worth of such labor. His claim that achieving and appreciating excellence require a knowledge of practices and an embrace of their governing goods and standards is lost on a recent commentator. Poking fun at Ruskin's disdain for the Crystal Palace built for an 1851 London exposition, Thomas Richards suggests that Ruskin's commendation of the Gothic as *"capable of perpetual novelty"* sets a standard fully met by the "profusion of new sights" in the entertainments and wares displayed in the Crystal Palace.[29] Richards is proposing that the burgeoning consumer culture of Victorian Britain is just another means of self-expression not so different from the freedom that Ruskin applauds in the case of his Gothic stone carvers. This ironic jest indicates how new meanings can be given to the things we consume, including what we read. For Ruskin, what made the Gothic style so productive of novelty is its allowance for the development and expression of its builders' capacities for excellence. Only certain kinds of work, he argues, sustain these possibilities for individual creativity that move both producer and consumer to a felt spirit of vitality. Ruskin does not praise "perpetual novelty" for its own sake, but for the ways that arts, crafts, and other social practices contribute to their participants' virtues, enabling them to achieve socially recognized excellences for themselves. While consumers' choices may have been enhanced by all that the building of the Crystal Palace represented, Ruskin would argue that this choice means much less if it distracts consumers from the self-development and self-expression that some kinds of labor afford to workers.

The concept of a social practice answers Ruskin's normative questions about good work. It informs his understanding of what makes crafted labor valuable and how the worth of this work should be judged. Both points relate to important themes in his ethics of consumption. First, central to his argument in "The Nature of Gothic" is the claim that people need certain kinds of work to develop themselves. The labor reforms that

Ruskin proposes in the coming years reflect his conviction that Victorian society should be restructured to promote cooperative work in practices as much as possible. Second, these forms of work allow individual excellence not only to be achieved by their participants but also to be recognized by consumers who commit to the governing goods and standards pursued within these activities. Ruskin's critique of capitalist exchange and his alternative scheme of equating economic value with human virtue build from his critical interests in social practices. I discuss Ruskin's reforms in chapter 5. I explore his critique of capitalist exchange and this alternative scheme of valuation in chapters 4 and 6, respectively.

In Ruskin's early aesthetics the term "perfection" marks the God-given virtues that every creature might live up to. This upward, if ultimately limited, sense of striving makes perfection the measure of landscape paintings. Once he takes "human effort" seriously, perfection is no longer a mark of art's goodness: "no good work whatever can be perfect, and *the demand for perfection is always a sign of a misunderstanding of the ends of art*" (10.202). We should read this rejection of "the demand for perfection" as a caution to consumers and a chastening of Ruskin's earlier critical vocabulary and his theological conception of the good. Not the perfection of God's Creation, but the "perfecting" or "excelling" that individuals undertake as participants in social practices is now the basis for judging artistic worth. Artistic endeavor is not restricted to the singular goal of perfection, for artists pursue a range of ends, always contributing, as a result of their efforts, innovative designs and new forms of expression that transform their practice. In this contrast between the perfect ends of God's Creation and the always-imperfect ends of artistic creativity, we see Ruskin beginning to unhinge his teleological approach to ethics from the fixed metaphysics of the good that frames his early aesthetics, even as there remain the echoes of it in his appeals to the "spirit" of medieval Christianity.

The developments in Ruskin's critical approach following *Modern Painters* 2 cannot be explained in terms of his adopting a "romantic" notion of spirit. Rather, it is his concrete studies of labor that reorient his teleological approach from God's purposes to human ends, from God's virtue to human virtues. He brings his talents for evocative detail and brilliant interpretation from his early aesthetics, but his frame of reference shifts from the theological to the political. He moves, that is, from God's perfect ends in the Creation to the imperfect ends worked out by the participants in a culture's activities.

Virtue and the Virtues

Just as Marx's work model operates on two levels, the interpersonal and the historical, so too there is a practical and a spiritual level to the argument in "The Nature of Gothic." Ruskin's criticism is far more valuable if we focus on his practical interests in the cultivation of character and the construction of cultures through people's chosen activities. Even as we talk loosely of the "spirit" of a person's work, Ruskin's use of this term has grave deficiencies that I have traced to his premise that healthy cultures exhibit an organic unity of purpose. His holistic idea of spirit implies the perfect ordering of everyone's labors into a beautiful common work that lifts up all of its participants. This ideal arrangement of human purpose is still modeled on a metaphysics of the good that dictates the roles and rank of each participant. The telos stipulates the proper aims of every individual effort and measures the goodness of all labor. The beauty, worth, and meaning of human creativity and individual expression contribute in no way to working out the ends and standards, the norms and values, of a culture.

The "spiritual" character of Gothic craftwork can be construed differently. The grandeur, beauty, and expression of this style of architecture need not be justified by a metaphysics of God's Creation or the "whole" spirit of a common medieval faith. The creative expression that Ruskin finds in the record of medieval cathedrals can be described as spiritual in another sense. There is often awe, reverence, calm, or some other heartfelt response before great achievements like art and architecture. Must the "spirit" of these labors simply be felt or intuited and nothing more? Is there no way to judge their excellence in light of past cultural forms and contemporary culture, too? Certainly the vitality that people derive from making recognizably excellent work can reflect a yearning to glorify God or a delight in nature's beauty. But these are just some of the sources of inspiration that call forth people's best practical labors. If we take seriously Ruskin's denial of the possibility of good work's answering to perfect ends, then it seems that the spiritual quality exhibited by the best labors must answer in part to the ever-changing assortment of the goods, ideals, and standards that people adopt, pursue, and revise in their cultural activities. I argue in part 2 that Ruskin adapts his practice of criticism to a cultural model of this sort.

I need to address an objection to my thesis that Ruskin transforms his vocabulary of the virtues in his architectural writings. Evidence against my claim that he turns from God's virtue to human virtues comes from *Stones* 2 itself where Ruskin takes the "personification of Virtues and Vices" on the Ducal Palace in Venice as the occasion to criticize the moral bankruptcy of the medieval Church.[30] The fascination with virtues and vices in medieval art and literature reflects, he claims, the corruption of the "later Romish Church." Writing as an Evangelical at a time of heightened anti-Catholicism in Britain, he asserts that the Church had moved so far from its founding source that it sought moral guidance from the "small systems of Aristotle and Cicero" (10.369–70).[31]

Early Christians, by contrast, saw all virtues as manifestations of the "love of Christ." In Ruskin's words, this singular "virtue comprehended everything, entered into everything; it was too vast and too spiritual to be defined; but there was no need of definition. For through faith, working by love, they knew that all human excellence would be developed in due order." Here "human excellence" answers to the all-encompassing spirit of Christ's love, not to the specific character traits that people cultivate in their lives. Ruskin makes the contrast between Christ's virtue and human virtues more explicit still. Medieval Christians' readiness to "analyze character" indicates the loss of their faith's vitality, which caused them to redirect their attention from the exalted "person and offices of Christ" toward the "virtues of Christians" (10.365–68).

> The Life of the Believer became in some degree separated from the Life of Christ; and his virtue, instead of being a stream flowing forth from the throne of God, and descending upon the earth, began to be regarded by him as a pyramid upon earth, which he had to build up, step by step, that from the top of it he might reach the Heavens. It was not possible to measure the waves of the water of life, but it was perfectly possible to measure the bricks of the Tower of Babel; and gradually, as the thoughts of men were withdrawn from their Redeemer, and fixed upon themselves, the virtues began to be squared, and counted, and classified, and put into separate heaps of firsts and seconds; some things being virtuous cardinally, and other things virtuous only north-north-west. (10.368)

This analogy of Christ's virtue to a flowing stream repeats the fountainhead imagery of God's virtuous Creation of life, detailed in the previous chapter. As in *Modern Painters* 2, people are to aspire toward divine love as the source and mark of all flourishing. Instead of seeing this charity exhibited in nature's vital beauty, here it is a matter of imitating the authoritative "Life of Christ." Ruskin's general appeals to the perfect ordering of life present God's immeasurable love as the only legitimate moral guide and disdain the building up and ranking of the human virtues that take center stage in an ethics of "character analysis."

The appeal to Christ's singular virtue recalls the metaphysics of Ruskin's early aesthetics and conflicts with key themes in his architectural studies. Consider the scornful reference to the Tower of Babel in the passage above. How different this condemnation of human pride is from his earlier praise for great architects, those "old Babel builders" who expressed themselves in their architecture and left their legacy as the memory of a culture. Or remember Ruskin's charge to architects that they set the love of their practice before the love of money, fame, and position. Going so far as to "desecrate" the word *love,* he allows that these goods may be *"coveted"* so long as they are not loved first. If artists grant the goods of their practice priority and authority, their aesthetic and moral judgments will be protected against the tainting influences of money, fame, and position, or so it would seem. Why then does Ruskin now deny final authority to the practical judgments that people make as participants in their culture's activities? Must the virtues that people celebrate be justified by a unifying vision of the telos governing all activity? Is holding to a singular conception of the good the only way to engage in reasonable debates about the meanings of things, the ordering of goods, and the rankings of virtues?

These questions apply to Ruskin's emerging social criticism as well as to the tradition of British social thought in which he stands. Must there be "unity" about the good, whether that is secured through divine revelation, the natural order, community, custom, tradition, poetic genius, heroic vision, the "unity of a life" (to use MacIntyre's phrasing), or whatever other source of a singular vision is needed to assure *consensus* about good character and the common good?[32] At various times Ruskin makes most of these appeals in his later social criticism, and yet it is my contention that over the course of his architectural studies he relocates ethical reflection in people's practical decisions about how to order the ends and goods that they pursue by choosing to commit to some activities over others. It is these practical choices, which are made in the culturally productive and open-ended spaces of social practices, that lead to the development of the virtues that shape the character and judgments that people make.

Ruskin's evolving vocabulary of the virtues bears out this interpretation. Even as he now rejects the kind of "character analysis" that I read in his later work, he shows a keen interest in the topic. Following his attack on the medieval Church, there ensues a lengthy account of various systems of virtues and vices in medieval art and literature. He includes the writings of St. Ambrose, an unnamed thirteenth-century author, Spenser, and Dante, the last of whom is the source of several of Ruskin's own fabulous portraits of the vices of capitalism in his later writings (see chapter 4). In addition, he discusses the renderings of the virtues and vices in the carvings on the walls of St. Mark's and the Ducal Palace and in the paintings of Giotto and Orcagna. Three decades later, Ruskin opens *Fors Clavigera* (1871–84), his monthly series of public letters, with a handful of Giotto's portraits, suggesting that he may have initially intended these letters as a lesson in the virtues, in the character required for the revolutionary transformation of industrial capitalism that he sought.

Here in *Stones* 2 Ruskin recommends a French list of seven virtues—charity, chastity, patience, abstinence, humility, liberality, and industry—to which he appends "Honesty (or Truth)" (10.385–86). As honesty becomes the foundation of justice for him, he holds to this list of virtues (though he rarely discusses chastity, patience, or abstinence in his later writings), with the additions of magnanimity in *The Political Economy of Art* (1857), gentleness in *Unto this Last* (1862), fidelity in *Time and Tide* (1867), and hope and piety in *Fors Clavigera.* Clearly Ruskin is aware of the history of ethical reflection on the virtues within Christian art and thought. He is also cognizant of the tension between his early reliance on a Christian standard of God's perfect virtue and the distinctive human virtues that occupy him more and more.

Instructive parallels can be drawn between Ruskin and MacIntyre. Ruskin relies on an idea of arts and crafts as "social practices," as I have demonstrated. The more he attends to different social practices, the more he inquires into specific virtues, too. He sketches out model "character types," and he maps the terrain of the pleasures, attitudes, and judgments appropriate to each virtue. He offers these portraits to convince his audience of the moral implications of the virtues to which they appeal, if only in name. Ruskin does not argue for the "incommensurability" of rival conceptions of the good, as MacIntyre does, though they share the conviction, explicit in MacIntyre's case and implicit in Ruskin's, that social practices are needed for human excellence, shared goods, and just distributions of them. Finally, as we have seen, Ruskin tells a narrative of decline in *The Stones of Venice* that shares the premise of MacIntyre's own narrative of the loss of coherent traditions of the virtues, namely, that only a "medievalist" social order, fully unified in its common purpose and structured by role-based duties, can secure a virtuous community.

In light of these parallels, it is all the more surprising that MacIntyre places the Victorian period "after virtue." In MacIntyre's narrative of decline, although a critic like Ruskin may still invoke the language of the virtues, he is no longer operating in the context of a community living out the story of its telos. As a result, his arguments on behalf of the virtues offer "fragmentary" appeals that have no persuasive force for his contemporaries. Maybe MacIntyre's narrative is correct, and Ruskin's life should be read as an example of one Victorian's fall away from the coherent vision of the good secured by a tradition of the virtues. In his early aesthetics the young Ruskin is supremely confident that "community" in taste can be attained because his sheltered Evangelical Anglican upbringing afforded him an elaborate narrative of a sacred history, replete with signs of God's promise and analogies to God's nature in the world, that lent itself to the remarkably detailed accounting of the telos found in his theory of beauty. By the time of his architectural studies, however, he acknowledges that there are, in fact, distinctive communities of taste, opening up his criticism to the more complex makings of aesthetic and moral judgment in the goods, ends, standards, and virtues of particular cultures. But, curiously enough, it is when Ruskin starts to abandon the metaphysics of the good detailed in his early aesthetics that he adopts the kind of the virtues-centered ethics that MacIntyre claims was lost at the start of the nineteenth century.

Ruskin's career actually runs counter to MacIntyre's history of Western moral thought. It may be that Ruskin's attempt to articulate a virtues-centered ethics of consumption is a foolhardy enterprise undertaken at a time when consensus about the good and, thus, coherent talk about the virtues was becoming impossible in Victorian society. But why assume that the development of Ruskin's criticism and nineteenth-century critical thought more generally reflects a historical fall from a lost moral coherence? As I read Ruskin, he becomes more effective as a practical critic and more sophisticated as an analyst of the virtues the more he delves into the complexities of Victorian culture and society. As I detail in the coming chapters, he does not abandon himself to that complexity, wringing his hands over a lost coherence that prevents him from marshalling his vocabulary of the virtues in an effort to persuade his contemporaries that they do and should, in fact, hold more in common than they allow. At times he relies on a "medievalist" rhetoric of a lost social unity that must be renewed, but it is his more ad hoc religious and moral appeals, his evocative portraits of Victorian virtues and vices, and his descriptive analyses of the activities and associations of his contemporaries that prove far more compelling and valuable as a model of an engaged ethics of consumption.

One way to read MacIntyre is not as the theorist who discloses the incoherence of modern moral discourse caused by the loss of traditions of the virtues, but as a member of a tradition for whom the language of the virtues is one vital resource for promoting commitments to and conversations about good lives, the common good, and the societies and practices most productive of them. Why does MacIntyre not own up to his affinities with a critic like Ruskin? Is it because Ruskin is writing "after virtue," or is it because his recommendations of gendered roles and duties and paternal institutions and governance are not as egalitarian and inclusive in spirit as we need in modern liberal democracies (see chapter 5)? Avoiding the difficult work of disentangling Ruskin's vocabulary of the virtues from these other problems in his social vision only begs the question, however: is the Victorian period really after virtue? Or is this period too close to our own political, economic, and social debates to allow for a comfortable rendering of a tradition of the virtues—fully coherent in its vision of the telos yet sufficiently vague in the actual operations of its social structure, roles, and duties—to make a nostalgic embrace of the lost spirit of a past community seem better than the presumed chaos of contemporary life?

At issue here, in part, is the Aristotelian thesis that any set of virtues must exhibit a "unity" directed toward a telos. But perhaps we can imagine thicker and thinner notions of unity. In the case of Ruskin's early aesthetics and his architectural studies, every creaturely virtue and every human virtue is predicated on the singular virtue of God as creator or Christ as redeemer. In his later uses of his vocabulary of the virtues, he departs from this singular vision, never fully, but still remarkably, given the profound influence of his metaphysical sensibility on his early art criticism. I am not claiming that Ruskin stops making religious appeals. Nor am I rejecting his religious appeals as generally implicated in this metaphysics. I am arguing instead that his rhetoric of "spirit" gains more specific content as he investigates the practices and virtues upheld (or not) in Victorian culture. That specificity opens up his normative claims to critical scrutiny and ultimately makes his criticism more contestable and persuasive, too. Although he still has little positive to say at this juncture about the downfall of Christian virtue into human virtues, his later writings show him embracing the task of character analysis and the importance of virtues other than charity in making for good characters, cultures, and communities.

Excellence and Domination

Even as Ruskin moves away from his unitary vision of God's virtue, he holds onto his hope for a perfect ordering of the good, from social practices on up to the society as a whole. This is why Gothic cathedrals are such a potent symbol for him. He seeks a society as beautiful as these buildings, a harmonious structure of architect, master, and apprentice, all freely joined in a mutually affirming social hierarchy. This "medievalist" ideal is shared by other critics in Ruskin's tradition. It warrants the suspicions that Marx's heirs such as Raymond Williams bring to Ruskin's writings. Williams credits Ruskin as the first critic to demonstrate how a society's art records the values implicit in its social relations and economic conditions. Yet he criticizes Ruskin for formulating the relationship between good art and good societies in a manner that retains a hierarchy in the social order and in aesthetic values.[33]

Williams's criticisms have merit, but neither he nor any other scholar has noted how Ruskin's model of good labor practices changes his moral vocabulary. Instead of justifying the goodness of art and society on the basis of a fixed hierarchical conception of God's perfect designs as creator, Ruskin now judges human excellence in terms of the imperfect strivings of individuals within social practices. The very aspect of Ruskin's criticism that Williams wants to applaud—the connections he draws between art and society—depends on this reconceptualization of artistic worth in terms of socially recognized excellences. Looking back to Ruskin's cursory remarks about the toiling gem cutter of *The Seven Lamps*, we can now clarify the evaluative framework for judging human labor that he works out over the course of his architectural studies. For Ruskin the value of all labor reflects not the spirit of the work but the virtues of the workers. Working conditions must allow for the development of a worker's virtues and, thus, the possibilities for self-expression. Without social practices in which to cultivate virtues, the resulting labor, artistic or otherwise, will be deficient and oppressive.

Marx's view of labor, which presumes the industrialization of all forms of work, may be more realistic given nineteenth-century conditions. It might also seem to lend itself better to Williams's interest in working-class cultures. But recall the theoretical deficiencies of Marx's "ex-pressivist" conception of labor. Just because work is industrialized does not mean that workers cannot imagine and develop their own practices, define their own excellences, and so shape a culture to their own ends. Yet these efforts at practical criticism and culture-making are described by Ruskin's model of work, not Marx's. It is Ruskin's approach to good labor that allows for a more self-conscious and collaborative construction of a culture through the creation of new activities, associations, ideals, symbols, standards, norms, and values. We have to improvise with his understanding of practices, not restricting them to craftwork per se. Still his focus on how people join together in shaping and expressing their character through the pursuit of common ends can be applied to a range of activities, including the formation of working-class cultures and a counter-culture more broadly. Ruskin's linking of virtues and ends in people's chosen activities offers a powerful rubric for critically examining cultures and remaking them as needed.

There remains the issue of authority, which I address at greater length in the chapter on Ruskin's politics. The idea of a social practice entails the premise that participants enjoy opportunities for development and expression of their "selves" in part because they accept shared goods and standards as having authority for them. That is why Ruskin so often praises "great" art and "master" artists. He would argue that it is only on the basis of the established goods and standards of practices that excellence can be achieved and recognized. These authority relations are fraught with power, however. The ways that excellence gets recognized in societies often depend upon the ways that traditions and ideologies privilege certain forms of endeavor and certain classes of people. That is why the kind of unitary vision of the good that figures both in Ruskin's criticism and his tradition of social thought is so worrisome.

Marx would question Ruskin's readiness to embrace the cultivation of excellence as the answer to the ills of industrial capitalism. He would see in the cultural ideals and standards that Ruskin celebrates an ideological justification for a privileged kind of life. Only an art critic, Marx might say, could put so much stock in the value of crafted goods that most people cannot afford. Perhaps it is not the desire to praise but to command good labor that lies behind Ruskin's nostalgia for Gothic cathedrals. Simply put, Marx worries that appeals to "great" culture legitimize some people's domination over others more than he cares about whether some cultural forms promote human excellence.

"Excellence" becomes an apology for "domination" in "The Nature of Gothic" insofar as Ruskin takes the architect's integration of the craftwork of Gothic cathedrals as *the* template for ordering social practices and shared goods across a whole society. These practices are as varied as the ornamentation decorating Gothic cathedrals, but he imagines them as cohering into a unified ensemble. At the same time, however, Ruskin's model of good labor highlights what is wrong with Marx's refusal to assess the actual ends of people's cultural activities. Indeed the problem is not Ruskin's explicit normative attention to character and excellence, but his perfectly unified vision of a proper ordering of ends and goods.

If Ruskin is primarily concerned with the ideal of excellence and Marx with the reality of domination, then it must be said that Ruskin also shows how commitments to excellence can subvert established relations of domination. As a critic of industrial capitalism, he demonstrates the value of attending carefully to the ends that people pursue in their work and their other activities. He pays close attention to the ways that certain types of labor provide opportunities for people to develop themselves, and he stresses the susceptibility of the internal goods of practices to the external goods of money and power. Protecting these forms of work against market encroachment is vital to having social spaces within which people can enjoy the spirit of vitality that comes from having the capacities to choose, determine, and innovate in the "kinds of labor" that are "good for men" and women, too.

There are two critical visions that Ruskin aims to teach in "The Nature of Gothic." There is his idealized vision of a social order exemplified in the building of Gothic cathedrals. I argue in subsequent chapters that this unitary vision continues to valorize a divine ordering of natures and to underwrite a feudalistic ordering of social roles in parts of his criticism. But there is another critical vision that Ruskin aims to teach in making his readers engaged critics in their own right. In pursuing his "endeavour in description,"[34] and in inviting his readers to their own imaginative assessments of the broader reaches of economic life, he focuses increasingly on the practices, goods, and excellences threatened by the distortions of the money economy and the stultifying effects of factory work. As he puts this second critical vision into practice, he chisels away at the fixity of the first one. Ruskin's endeavors in description, his descriptive ethical criticism of the character, culture, and community that his contemporaries have made for themselves, should remain standing as the best of his legacy.

PART TWO

"Modern Education"
A Pedagogy of Character and Vision

THREE

The Nature of Imagination

Ruskin's architectural studies transform all of his criticism. The more he comes to appreciate the "human effort" expended in making great buildings and beautiful art, the more he begins to read other cultural forms and every kind of labor through the model of "social practices" developed in the previous chapter. This shift toward human striving in cultural activities introduces an important tension into his criticism. As we have seen in "The Nature of Gothic" (1853), Ruskin devotes his attention to the builders' "moral characteristics" as expressed in their work and as developed through their crafts. The excellences they cultivated and the goods they shared emerge within the practices themselves at a remove from God's "divine work and character." God figures only distantly in the builders' efforts as the object toward which they directed their energies of praise. Yet as Ruskin envisions these imperfect strivings to celebrate God's glory, they are ultimately justified by continued appeals to a theology of divine perfection. On the one hand, that theology forgives the imperfection of human efforts, freeing up individual creativity. On the other hand, that theology still derives every earthly good from a metaphysical ordering of the good originally dictated by God in creating life.

This tension between the perfection of God's Creation and the imperfections of human creativity motivates the three chapters in part 2. In introducing this section, I need to clarify this tension and the issues it raises. Up until this point in Ruskin's criticism, a central question has been, how should the critic judge the significance of an artwork? In the movement from his writings on landscape painting to his architectural studies, there is a decided shift in his answer to that question.

Initially, for Ruskin, all standards of judgment are determined by God's ordaining the nature, worth, and purpose of everything. The whole Creation is made good by God in its original perfection, and the artist's task is to reveal the moral lessons stamped on every detail of nature's beauty. By "The Nature of Gothic" Ruskin's attention has shifted to the human making of things in all of its variety and change. Gothic architecture is made good, not according to the standards of God's Creation, but through the human spirit invested in crafting it. How, then, should the critic judge the significance of this art? Is it still a matter of conforming to God's good, a task of judging things according to a divinely sanctioned ordering of life? If so, is there any room left for individual creativity, for the human making of things, however imperfectly?

In Ruskin's account of the Gothic spirit, this tension between God's Creation and human creativity is still muted. In praising the Gothic carvers' faithfulness to God and to natural forms, he circumscribes their creativity within an encircling framework of divine perfection. The variegated, but unified, beauty of the cathedral also serves as a model of a necessarily "whole" vision of the good—that ideal ordering of ends that organizes people's commitments, duties, and relationships, uplifts their desires, and structures their proper use and enjoyment of everything.

From this point forward, however, Ruskin becomes more aware of the tension between his growing appreciation of the individual excellences of human creativity and his ongoing quest for an integrated vision of the good. He addresses this tension directly in the third volume of *Modern Painters* (1856), the book that introduces what I call his "aesthetics of making." Having admitted the shaping "powers" of individuals' imagination into his writings on architecture, he now puzzles over whether the dictum of his early studies of landscape painting still holds. Can he continue to insist that "truth to nature" is the measure of great landscape art? If people make out the meaning of things through their own imaginative powers, then everyone's judgments of the beauty, value, and significance of the natural world would seem to be subjective, casting doubt on the claim that there can be any "truths" about "nature."

I return to the problem of nature and imagination in the body of this chapter. I allude to it here to help bring into view the main conceptual issue of part 2. Simply put, the more Ruskin takes seriously people's active role as "makers," the less tenable are his earlier attempts to define good character and to envision the good in terms of either a metaphysics of divine perfection or a unified, medievalist social order.

Let me develop this point briefly. If people have an active, determining role in "making" things, then they also make themselves and their cultures. In making themselves, people can be seen as the active fashioners of their desires, purposes, activities, relationships, beliefs, and so on. Of course, such things are never fully under anyone's control, but this image of the human "maker" introduces considerable diversity. The making of cultures adds further complications. Now the standards and norms used in judging these various facets of individuals' lives are themselves the product of a great many people engaged in a wide range of cultural pursuits. Again I exaggerate the role that individuals play in fashioning cultures, but I do so to present the tension in Ruskin's emerging critical thought as starkly as possible. In allowing for human "making" and, thus, for the individual and cultural meanings that people fashion, can Ruskin still articulate a persuasive account of the character and vision his contemporaries need to direct their lives toward common ends and shared commitments that are good for them, good for others, and good for their society?

That Ruskin retains a teleological approach to ethics demonstrates his conviction that it is both possible and vital to work toward such a common vision. At the same time, he adjusts his critical approach and concerns in ways that indicate a recognition on his part of the limitations of his earlier writings. The most significant change is his turn toward culture.

It might sound odd to claim that a student of landscape painting and medieval cathedrals *turns* toward culture over the course of the 1850s, 1860s, and 1870s. I do not mean "culture" in the narrow sense of the refined pursuits of art, literature, and music. We come closer to Ruskin's idea of culture in his account of medieval architecture. The builders' expressional character reflects their participation in a tapestry of social practices, relationships, ideals, and standards that together functions to unify their lives. Despite the richness of Ruskin's readings of Gothic craftwork, this initial idea of culture is too abstract and composed. It is as if his audience stands far across a gallery, gazing at an idealized portrait of human excellence good for all time. While this portrait of the Gothic "spirit" may help shock readers into imagining a "whole" new vision of life, it offers them little practical guidance about how best to organize their own lives and society.

Ruskin seeks to redress this deficiency through his growing attention to Victorian culture. His distant rendering of the unified "spirit" of the Gothic is different from the detailed analysis of his own culture to which Ruskin increasingly turns. This shift toward contemporary culture requires him to adapt to the demands of engaged cultural critique in two important ways. First, he grapples more with the formative effects of cultures on people's character and vision. This dynamic proves central to his ethics of consumption. Second, he realizes that his own efforts to articulate a common vision proceed from and therefore must appeal to the culture he shares with his readers. No doubt Ruskin continues at times to proclaim a vision of the good either from on high by appealing to God's Creation or from afar by invoking the spirit of medievalism. These tendencies lessen, though, as he descends into the complexities of Victorian culture.

The three chapters in this section analyze and evaluate the new strategies, arguments, and appeals that he works out in this more promising mode of descriptive cultural analysis and ethical critique. The best way to introduce these chapters is by using a remarkable, though neglected, appendix to the third volume of *The Stones of Venice* in which Ruskin outlines his plan for a "Modern Education" (1853).[1] In many ways this little tract sets the course for his emerging social criticism.

"Modern Education": A Pedagogy of Character and Vision

Ruskin proposes three disciplines—natural history, religion, and politics—for his "modern" curriculum. Together they answer the questions facing a "man" in becoming educated for life: "Where he is" (natural history), "Where he is going" (religion), and "What he had best do, under those circumstances" (politics). The teleological structure of these questions reflects Ruskin's searching interest in the telos of a human life and its role in shaping good character and accurate judgment.

"Modern Education" is Ruskin's statement of the character needed for the present age. It is progressive in the sense that it is designed to be a public education for all "men." It is also meant to replace the pedagogy of classical languages and literary genres then dominating elite education in Britain. In Ruskin's view, learning the forms of Greek and Latin literatures is "not in itself an important end of human existence," and a classical education produces "men" who know nothing of the "ends" of a "human" life.[2] Just as aping the technique of great artists cannot teach the full range of knowledge required for artistry, a pedagogy concerned only with imparting the formalistic techniques of past writers cannot acquaint students with the manner of living characteristic of their society. Instead of training in an empty technique, such as "the general discipline which a course of classical reading gives to the intellectual powers," there needs to be education in the conduct of life. The term "conduct" conveys the interweaving of knowledge with activity. The purposes that practical reason serves and the problems that it resolves arise within the ongoing cultural activities of some group of people (11.258).[3]

Ruskin is not shy about the deficiencies of his fellow Victorians' character in his earlier criticism. Examples of those failings abound in "Modern Education," too. More noteworthy is Ruskin's attempt to sketch out a program of character development, which is the clear aim of the questions listed above. The concern with character is everywhere. One of the first topics of "politics" is "the operations of the virtues and vices of men upon themselves and society." The purpose of "religion" is not "theology," or "*Talk* about God." It is "the 'binding' or training to God's service." Finally, Ruskin cites the lack of courses in "natural history" as the "chief" cause of the "vices of the upper classes of Europe." All told, his program of "Modern Education" is a training "in moral habits, bodily strength and beauty" and in "faculties of mind" (11.260, 259, 263).

Why is an art critic suddenly concerned with educational reform? What more is needed than the visions afforded by great landscape paintings and Gothic craftwork? Perhaps Ruskin's curricular innovations reflect the commitments that led him to teach at the Working Men's College in the early 1850s and to take art education directly to the public through lectures, essays, and museums. Certainly these developments are all of a piece, but Ruskin's expanding engagement with various spheres of Victorian life reflects his broader turn toward culture.

"Modern Education" is a pedagogy of character *and* vision. Adding the term "vision" is to some extent redundant. All virtues-centered ethics entail a close, almost circular, relationship between character and vision. In order to develop one's character well, one must see how certain activities and excellences have their point in the good. In order to envision the good, one must cultivate the character needed to pursue key aspects of it.[4] Thus in *Modern Painters* 2, the more one conforms to God-given virtues and orders one's loves in light of God's harmonious design, the more one recognizes the goodness revealed in nature's beauty. This relatively straightforward relationship between character and vision—that character and vision are both good insofar as they conform to God's good—becomes more complex and dynamic as Ruskin inquires into the "human making" of cultures.

Cultures are neither uniform nor inherently good as Ruskin presumes the arrangement of God's Creation to be. Cultures are human products. They consist of the activities, goods, ends, and standards that people create and pursue and around which they form their character and structure their relationships. As Ruskin moves toward cultural critique, therefore, he cannot simply direct his readers to the eternal truths of nature's beauty. He must hunt out those parts of contemporary culture best suited to making good character and communities, and he must justify his choices by appealing to the norms embedded in these cultural practices.

This change is most apparent in Ruskin's discussion of religion in "Modern Education." Again he distinguishes the theology taught in European universities from "the 'binding' or training to God's service." The impact of the Oxford Movement on Ruskin's generation and the conversion of several of his friends to Roman Catholicism are his principal objects of scorn here.[5] Likewise, Ruskin's lament that theological training on the Continent seems to produce only "rebels and infidels" echoes with worry over the 1848 Revolutions. But even as he stresses the obedience that religions teach, he is agnostic as to which "religious facts" properly "bind" people to God's service (11.259, 260). Why this sudden modesty about the dictates of God's moral purposes?

We see here an incipient, though growing, reluctance on Ruskin's part to appeal beyond cultures. In "Modern Education" he leaves it an open question whether one "had better consult the Bible, Koran, or Council of Trent" as to where one is going. Moreover, it is the "duty of a rational nation" to answer the question and to make the religious institutions and practices it supports—whether to maintain or get rid of an "Establishment" and "Liturgy"—fit their decision (11.258, 259–60). In short, Ruskin now suggests that religion is a communal affair. This shift is consonant with his emerging view of religions as repositories for and communal practices of the shared values and meanings manifested in particular historical cultures.

Consider the implications for Ruskin's teleological approach. Although he has "not yet abandoned all expectation of a better world than this," he believes that "this [world] in which we live is not so good as it might be" (11.261). But where should the critic seek for the vision needed to direct readers toward improving themselves and their society? The answer is in the culture they share. Indeed "Modern Education" surveys the formative aspects of Victorian culture and instructs readers in the best of it. Thus it is in education that we find new sources of the common vision that Ruskin seeks. Elaborating this common vision is cultural work, a matter of examining the best and worst activities and ends in a culture, sorting out the harmful and beneficial ways of patterning social interactions, and conducting this inquiry in light of the standards and ideals that people adopt and revise in their chosen pursuits.

All told in "Modern Education" Ruskin makes character and vision a function of culture. And he sees that he must operate within this framework, too, analyzing his culture's resources for improving people's character and joining individuals around common goods. As a cultural critic his task is not just to illuminate Victorian culture but to remake it in the interests of good character and community, seeking to promote personal well-being and social justice. While Ruskin has not yet assumed the roles of culture-analyst and culture-maker, his writings after "Modern Education" tend in this direction.

The three chapters in part 2 follow out Ruskin's curriculum, examining his shifting views on nature, religion, and politics as he adjusts his teleological approach to the demands of cultural critique. All three topics are closely related to his ethics of consumption. Consider, for example, a central issue that emerges in this chapter. Every ethics of consumption requires judgments about the value and use of natural resources. In his early aesthetics Ruskin accords independent worth to living creatures and the rest of the Creation by locating their goodness in the structure of God's moral purposes. But the science of natural history differs from natural theology. Natural history need not answer to God's purposes; indeed, Ruskin conceives natural history and the other physical sciences as answering to human ends. Interestingly enough, though, he continues to argue that nature has "intrinsic value," even as he admits that individuals' judgments are shaped by the cultural activities, aims, and desires that they bring to presumably "natural" things.

Something similar can be said about Ruskin's evolving views on religion. I have noted that he adopts a more "cultural" view of religions. The religious practices that people observe serve to enliven certain "binding" attitudes, symbols, and commitments that can be performed only through these practices. We see this new practice-centered view of religions initially in his acceptance of religious art as an essential tool of worship, not a cause of idolatry. Over time Ruskin argues that all worship is mediated through cultural forms like these. There is another way that he comes to see the human making of things as intimately connected with the formation of religious attitudes. I am thinking here of Ruskin's account of the "idolatry" of money. He analyzes the cultural system of valuation produced by capitalist exchange as a kind of false religious worship. The parallels to Marx's analysis of commodity fetishism clarify these critics' similarities and differences. Much of chapter 4 focuses on the lessons of that comparison, contrasting Marx's reliance on theory as a covert form of moral argument and Ruskin's explicitly ethical criticism.

Chapters 3 and 4 discuss Ruskin's way of approaching judgments of the world's value and the system of signification generated by industrial capitalism. The final chapter in part 2 takes up his vision of the ideal polity needed to produce a good society and good people. Most relevant to his ethics of consumption are the political reforms he advocates beginning with the closing lines of "Modern Education." He declares that "the first duty of a state is to see that every child born therein shall be well housed, clothed, fed, and educated, till it attain years of discretion." But he cautions that achieving this goal requires a government with "an authority over the people of which we now do not so much as dream" (11.263). This reform platform stands in sharp contrast to the laissez-faire policies that Ruskin disdains. It also reflects the rich understanding of social justice that he elaborates in his account of the virtue of justice. Chapter 5 assesses this politics of social justice and public virtue. I argue in the end that the deficiencies of Ruskin's medievalist politics, with its natural gender roles and its institutions of moralistic governance, are significant obstacles to recovering his ethics of consumption.

Imagination and Metaphysics

So far in this chapter I have introduced the tension in Ruskin's criticism between God's perfect Creation and the imperfections of human creativity. I have also indicated his movement toward a view of "culture" as a human production. This tension and that movement show first in Ruskin's new aesthetics of the imagination in *Modern Painters* 3. Analyzing his evolving idea of the imagination serves two purposes in this book. First, it distinguishes Ruskin's mature aesthetics from Romantic theories of the imagination in which "feeling" and "subjectivity" are the dominant themes. Ruskin, by contrast, maintains his conviction that there can be "community" in taste (see chapter 1). Nevertheless he opens up his theocentric model of "moral perception" from *Modern Painters* 2 to a practical effort at "moral imagination" in *Modern Painters* 3. Clarifying this idea of the moral imagination and its work within a culture's activities is the second purpose of this chapter.

Ruskin recognizes that his writings on architecture reorient his criticism. Returning to the third volume of *Modern Painters* after a ten-year hiatus, he presents himself as a traveler embarking on "an interrupted journey in a guideless country." He must climb a hill to locate the path he has taken and to decide on a new course (5.17). Scholars have cited this need for a new orientation, along with the volume's subtitle, "Of Many Things," as evidence of a haphazardness in Ruskin's critical thought during a period of transition and discontinuity.[6]

Although I agree that Ruskin radically reorients his art criticism in the ten years between *Modern Painters* 2 and 3, I read the subtitle "Of Many Things" differently. It does not signify confusion so much as it does a conscious awareness on Ruskin's part that he must reconstruct his teleological approach. This better explanation is suggested by Richard Hooker's influence on Ruskin's early theory of beauty. After cautioning that our words about God should be "wary and few," Hooker adds, "Our God is one, or rather very Oneness, and mere unity, having nothing but itself in itself, and not consisting (as all things do besides God) *of many things*."[7] Ruskin also professes God's unity and incomprehensibility as early as *Modern Painters* 2, but his modesty is belied by the massive exposition of God's attributes given there. In opening volume 3, he disowns this earlier approach as "laboriously systematic." None of the details of nature's beauty could stand on its own in *Modern Painters* 2, but now Ruskin vows to care little about "marking connections, or insisting upon sequences," among the topics he discusses. He will take up them like cherries "in their own wild way of clustering about their crabbed stalk" (5.18).

This image of receiving each offering from the natural world in its "wildness" contrasts with the initial plan for *Modern Painters* 3. The third volume was to examine in synthetic detail the characteristic beauties "in every division of creation, in stones, mountains, waves, clouds, and all organic bodies, beginning with vegetables, and then taking instances in the range of animals, from the mollusc to man" (4.142–43). This promised systematic inquiry into these "many things" can also be explained in the terms of Hooker's theology. For Hooker, God alone is self-subsistent or "one." By contrast, the "many things" that God creates cannot subsist in themselves. The manifold and imperfect "nature" of every creature requires it to reach out to others in mutual dependence. While fully comprehending God's "Oneness" transcends the limits of human understanding, working out the "connections" and "sequences" among nature's "many things" is a way of coming closer to a knowledge of divine perfection. The seeker after nature's beauty climbs the ladder of contemplation from the individual perfections appointed to each and every species toward the higher perfections of the binding and ranked relations among these "many things" as dictated by their "participation" in God's "divine work and character." That Ruskin initially assigns "ideas of relation" to the province of the imagination only underscores how fully Hooker's theology structures his early account of this faculty (3.130).

I remind readers of Ruskin's notion of Christian "theoria" to set his account of the imagination from *Modern Painters* 2 in its proper context. There he distinguishes three forms of the imagination in its "penetrative," "associative" and "contemplative" functions (listed in the order that the mind works according to Ruskin). Let me note at the outset that even here in the second volume he observes that "any very great work of art" does not come "in a form of pure transcript." The renderings of natural beauty in a landscape painting "invariably receive the reflection of the mind under whose shadow they have passed" (4.228, 223). As we proceed onto the actual workings of the imagination, though, it turns out that the only "mind" that finally counts is God's mind, not the artist's mind. There is little autonomy or creativity here. Imaginative works must be "truthful" to nature, Ruskin argues, because the imagination is an "intuitive" and "prophetic" faculty, the mysterious greatness of which lies in its recognizing and reflecting the perfections of God's Creation.

Consider the penetrative imagination. Its life "is in the discovering of truth." The "virtue of the imagination is its reaching, by *intuition* and intensity of gaze, (not by *reasoning*, but by its authoritative opening and revealing power), a more essential truth than is seen at the surface of things" (4.287, 284; my emphasis). Ruskin describes this "penetrating, possession-taking faculty" in sexualized, masculine imagery. The "piercing, Pholas-like mind's tongue . . . works and tastes into the very rock heart, no matter what be the subject submitted to it." It cracks the "invisible door in the rock," opening "a huge, obscure, endless cave, with inexhaustible treasure of pure gold scattered in it" (4.251). This portrait of the artist's commanding vision mirrors Hooker's account of God's manly "exercise of his most glorious and most abundant virtue" (see chapter 1).[8] What marks the penetrative imagination above all else is its delving into things "to trace to their farthest limit [their] true laws and likelihoods." There is "no virtue," after all, in "being unlike nature" (4.286–87).

The debts to Hooker become more overt in the movement from the penetrative to the associative imagination. Here Ruskin discusses the painter's combining various ideas on a canvas, and he draws a contrast between fanciful composition and genuine imagination. Associating ideas that tickle the fancy with novelty is relatively easy, but only those artists with a prophetic gift for "harmony" are truly imaginative. The model is once again God's Creation, the perfect harmony of arrangement that can be traced throughout the myriad of subtle and beneficent "connections" and "sequences" among the "many things" that God has wrought. In similar fashion, great artists intuit a perfect combination of imperfect ideas. Each idea in an imaginative work is lacking on its own, requiring supplement from the artist's other ideas, just as a snake's gliding movement requires "coils that go in opposing ways." Ruskin quickly cautions, though, that only God can create the perfect combinations of animal form, marking a "limit" on human imagination. The wealth of ideas available to any artist is so plentiful, moreover, that the perfect harmonies of imaginative art cannot be worked out through trial-and-error combinations. They must instead be grasped all together in a moment of prophetic insight (4.233–34, 236). Thus, while the imaginative artist may combine images of nature in ways never seen before, the standard remains nature's truth. As Ruskin puts it, "The laws of nature [the imaginative artist] knows, these are to him no restraint. They are his own nature" (4.239). By extension, this interweaving of imperfect ideas conforms to the perfect arrangement among nature's "many things" as ordered by and revelatory of divine law and, so ultimately, of God's Oneness.

For the early Ruskin the imagination's work is a spiritual exercise, a step-wise ascent toward a fuller knowledge of God that culminates in the "contemplative" imagination. Here, too, nature's truth leads to a metaphysics of divine perfection, the flourishing that is attainable so long as the "many things" of God's Creation exercise their virtues and fulfill their roles within the appointed limits. This natural order is defined by complete interdependence and hierarchical rankings. There is little "wildness" in this vision of the natural world since all of its goodness resides in a domesticated ensemble of purposes. Human beings have their role, too, as witnesses to the beauty of God's design. The function of the imagination, as Ruskin initially conceives it, is to arrange the countless details of the natural world according to that perfect plan.

In sum, Ruskin's early aesthetics conforms to a linear model of sorts. At the apex of that model, God marks divine purposes in natural beauty, and artists along with everyone else are charged with aspiring to discern these truths. Not surprisingly, then, Ruskin sees the artist's task as a matter of mirroring the glories of God's Creation to other people. The great artists' imaginative, though perfectly faithful, renderings of natural beauty can expand and uplift other people's moral vision, but finally add nothing of their own individual powers of creativity.

An Aesthetics of "Making"

Although Ruskin acknowledges the imaginative work of the "artist" and the "beholder" in *Modern Painters* 2, the beholder is clearly subordinate to the artist and the artist to God (4.260). As Ruskin accords greater independence to artist and audience alike, he explores new questions about the imagination's role in artistic representation and interpretation. These questions lead him to reconceive the *intuitive faculty* of the imagination as an *active power.*

As other scholars have observed, Ruskin adopts a more "Romantic" aesthetics in the 1850s.[9] In M. H. Abrams's classic terms, he can be seen as turning from the metaphor of the mind as a "mirror" reflecting external things toward the metaphor of the mind as a "lamp" illuminating these objects by its own light. This transition remains partial in Ruskin's case and should not be exaggerated.[10] Again the *tension* between divine perfection and human creativity persists throughout his corpus, even as his attempted mediations of it ramify considerably as he attends more closely to the human making of things through individuals' use of their imaginative powers within the practices of a culture.

We can chart out the new concerns of Ruskin's criticism by borrowing what is actually a more useful point of reference than Abrams's contrasting images of the "mirror" and the "lamp." In a scheme of the "four elements in the total situation of a work of art," Abrams positions the "work" of art within a triangle of "artist," "audience," and "universe." I substitute in the term "nature" for "universe," as this term is more appropriate to Ruskin:

NATURE

WORK

ARTIST AUDIENCE

On the basis of this scheme, Abrams outlines how each of the four main aesthetic theories in the history of art criticism derives its categories from one of these four elements. His aim, though, is to distinguish a nature-centered aesthetics from an artist-centered aesthetics, that is, the long-standing "mimetic" theories of art from the relatively recent "expressive" theories that he dates to the Romantic period.[11]

This scheme serves my purposes by showing how Ruskin's new interest in human labor and, following from it, his new idea of the imagination complicate the linear model of his early art criticism. Ruskin himself observes the change taking place. He acknowledges in *Modern Painters* 3 that others might read the new prominence he accords to the shaping powers of the imagination as incongruous with his argument that art must first aim for "truth." Responding to this challenge, he replies that truth remains the principal measure of good art. "But Truth so presented, that it will need the help of the imagination to make it real. Between the painter and the beholder, each doing his proper part, the reality should be sustained. . . . But not without that help" (5.185). In the workings of the imagination, he continues, "we recognize a supernatural operation, and perceive, not merely the landscape or incident as in a mirror, but, besides, the presence of what, after all, may perhaps be the most wonderful piece of divine work in the whole matter—the great human spirit through which it is manifested to us" (5.187). Ruskin's language of "divine work" and "human spirit" is continuous with his architectural studies. The terms "artist" and "beholder" can be traced back even farther. Nevertheless, the shift away from the artistic task of "mirroring" is clear.[12] In claiming that good art must aim for truth and *yet* that its "reality" depends on the imaginative powers of artist and audience alike, Ruskin abandons the linear model of his early aesthetics.

What complicates the picture is that the central term of Abrams's model, the work of art itself, comes to stand problematically between artist and nature and between artist and audience. Previously the artwork and the artist entered into the linear relation between nature and audience only to provide other means for revealing God's purposes in the Creation. The artist aimed for a transparency that removed both the artist and the artwork from consideration on their own. Increasingly Ruskin sees both artist and audience as independent "makers." What they make matters, as the ethical questions of his remaining art and social criticism testify. The most important of these questions are, What do people make of things from nature? What do people make of the things that others have made? What do these acts of making things and making judgments reveal about people's character, culture, and community? Although these questions are intertwined in Ruskin's emerging criticism, I take them up in order in this chapter and the next two chapters to show how his new "aesthetics of making" leads into his ethics of consumption.

The inklings of Ruskin's new aesthetics are apparent as early as *The Seven Lamps of Architecture* (1849). Two of the "lamps" concern the sources of the majesty and beauty that Ruskin finds in great architecture, and for the first time, he looks past nature's beauty to the power of human creativity. The difference between the lamps of "beauty" and "power" resembles Edmund Burke's distinction between the beautiful and the sublime. The difference between beauty and power is "the difference between what is derivative and original in man's work; for whatever is in architecture fair or beautiful, is imitated from natural forms; and what is not so derived, but depends for its dignity upon arrangement and government received from human mind, becomes the expression of the power of that mind, and receives a sublimity high in proportion to the power expressed" (8.101–2). Ruskin draws a distinction here between nature's beauty and human efforts to represent it anew. For the first time he allows that the shaping "power" of an artist's mind is significant in itself and that this human endeavor may be more valuable than the delights of the world's beauty. Asking why people are drawn to the rough stones of ruins instead of the delicately wrought weeds lying around them, he declares that a ruin's "true delightfulness depends on our discovering in it the record of [the builder's] thoughts, and intents, and trials, and heart-breakings—of recoveries and joyfulnesses of success: all this *can* be traced by a practised eye; but granting it even obscure, it is presumed or understood; and in that is the worth of the thing, just as much as the worth of anything else we call precious" (8.82).

This celebration of "the work of poor, clumsy, toilsome man" marks a radical departure from the idea of imagination in *Modern Painters* 2. There Ruskin insists that the imagination displays a prophetic intuition able to grasp all in an instant a vision of imperfect things joined as a perfect whole, an intuition of an ideal harmony that can only be recognized open-mouthed, not hammered out through human effort and judgment. There the imaginative artist disdains the hard labor of trial and error because such methods cannot rise to the level of insight needed to fathom God's purposes. Here the stone carver's work—what he himself makes of things from nature—presses forward in Ruskin's criticism.

How can we account for this changed assessment of people's powers of making things? Throughout Ruskin's writings the term "power" connotes a capacity for action, understood in the ethical sense of the ends toward which an action aims. One way to describe the opening up of his critical vision from the 1840s to the 1850s is to say that he allows a wider range of ends as God the author of all those he originally professes recedes from view. Indeed what makes the stone carver's efforts worthy are both the purposes he sets for himself and the powers he displays in overcoming the obstacles to his excellent achievement. Instead of idolizing those few great and "truly" imaginative artists whose prophetic insight transcends all reasoning, Ruskin looks here to the excellences that ordinary people achieve and the practical reason that they display in their chosen activities. Over time this standard of making things well in light of individuals' desires and purposes and the cultural practices that shape their character and ends becomes, for Ruskin, the measure of imagination in artistic, religious, social, economic—that is, in all moral matters.

Imagination's Truth and the Pathetic Fallacy

These changes in Ruskin's idea of the imagination unfold gradually. In *Modern Painters* 3 he still upholds a select few "great" poets and artists as exemplars of imaginative power. He also defines the final guide of a "true criticism of art" as an "unchanging love of all things that God has created to be beautiful, and pronounced to be good" (5.43). In addition, however, we find Ruskin asking a new set of questions about the powers and limits of the imagination. These questions reflect his growing regard for the independence and dignity of individual creativity in people's making things from the natural world.

Consider this new question about the worth of a landscape painting: "What is this in the picture," Ruskin asks, "which is precious to us, and yet is not natural?" There is something "*not natural*" in a landscape painting, and this "shortcoming" is one of the genre's "virtues." These two statements would be inconceivable in Ruskin's early aesthetics of the mirror. What he now views as so *unnatural* and yet so valuable is the artifice of the imagination, the human making that goes into any artistic representation of things' meaning, including everything in the "natural world." Well, Ruskin anticipates his readers complaining, what about all those "long dogmatic chapters of yours about giving nothing but the truth, and as much truth as possible" in art (5.176, 185)?

In answering this challenge Ruskin strikes a balance between truth and imagination, and although he modifies his views about how best to strike this balance, it remains the pivot point of his conception of the moral imagination. Here in *Modern Painters* 3 the artistic imagination works by bringing "images" and their attendant "feelings" to things. These images and feelings proceed from the artist's "attitudes," a term that Ruskin does not use but that rightly conveys the directive and relational work of the imagination as he now understands it. When working well, a person's imagination orients him or her toward other people and toward the world's many goods in an attitude of receptivity and curiosity. It does not seek to comprehend the whole scene of a landscape in any systematic way. The aim is better described using Ruskin's phrase the "science of *Aspects*," a phrase that he applies to J. M. W. Turner's watercolors (5.387).

Imaginative artists sympathize with things' aspects; that is, they relate feelingly to things through devoted study of their "external facts" by reverently seeking out their "true" significance. This connection between things' facts and their broader significance is explained by the teleological structure of Ruskin's ethics. As in Hooker's theology, the "many things" of the natural world never stand alone but are related to other things through the intertwining of God's purposes. Ruskin's new idea of the imagination is similarly teleological, only his focus starts to shift from God's purposive making of the "many things" of nature to people's making of things' meaning and their own character and cultures. In Ruskin's aesthetics of making, the "external facts" of a thing always signify more; they point to the meanings that can be seen only when individuals' desires, aspirations, feelings, and attitudes evoke the natural object's "true" purposes.

Ruskin offers an example of the imagination's necessary work. He recounts how when gazing at the Swiss Alps one day he delighted in the sun's glinting off the glass roof of a nearby building, believing it to be the grandest view of these mountains he had ever seen. Just as a once-admired piece of art loses all value the instant it is exposed as a forgery, he wonders how he could have been conned. The culprit is the imagination, for as soon as he sees this "Alp" for what it is, the conjured images and feelings set in motion by his imagination are proven false.

The emotions were good, however, Ruskin argues. Had he been gazing at an actual Alp, the same process of generating images and feelings through the imagination would have been required for a full and accurate perception of the mountain's significance. Among these feelings he cites the "wonder" before a mountain's divine majesty, the reverent "understandings of the gifts and glories of the Alps," and the "strange sympathies" with the "unknown" history of its human inhabitants, their endeavors, and their travails. In short, the observer's recognition of nature's meaning and value requires this "helpful" work of the imagination in bringing images, feelings, and attitudes that are truthful to the "facts of the thing" (5.176–78).[13]

What should we make of these odd juxtapositions of truth and imagination, of things' facts and individuals' feelings, images, and attitudes? In other words, having admitted the "not natural" in landscape paintings—and, more generally, the artifice of the imagination in the human making of anything—how can Ruskin still assert that people can share a common vision of things' meaning and value and that recognizing and extending these agreements in aesthetic (and later economic) matters is a critical task for artist, critic, and audience alike?

Ruskin is arguing that as purposive beings we do not see anything without first taking an interest in it. In other words, we are interested in things only in the flow of our lives, guided and limited as our lives are by our range of experience, breadth of knowledge, binding attachments, practical commitments, consideration for people, both near and far, and everything else that is woven into the "artificial"—that is, the humanly made—substrate of one's character. How one judges the natural world testifies to the kind of person one has made oneself and has been made by others to be.

The "helpful" feelings that Ruskin finds in his regard for the Alps are good or "true," as he would put it, in large part because they direct him beyond himself, making him interested in the manifold significance of the natural world. It is this movement beyond a narrow interest in things that makes the work of the imagination so vital, and it is this dynamic striving to envision other purposes than one's own immediate concerns that he calls to his readers' attention. There are, he claims, guiding ends and right relations in the vast economy of nature, and in imagining the full significance of things, artists and others have to proceed with curiosity, receptivity, and gratitude in tracing out those encircling purposes and connections. His allusion to the Alps' gifts and glories is meant as a reminder that the world is something upon which we depend with every breath, and yet something that has its own independent life, too. His sympathies for the life, happiness, and death of the Alps' inhabitants stretches moral regard to the ends pursued by unknown people often at tremendous cost to them. In landscape art the painter's attention is fixed on the natural world alone, a limitation that Ruskin feels acutely as his interests turn toward social criticism. Nevertheless, when a landscape painter sustains nature's "reality" by imagining it passionately and searchingly and representing it fully and well, the audience can learn "helpful" attitudes, too, guiding them toward a fuller vision of nature's beauty and worth. In the help of the imagination on both sides of the painting, character and vision relate in a dynamic, edifying interplay.

Structurally this picture of the imagination is not so different from Ruskin's early account of the imagination as a prophetic faculty able to grasp all in instant the whole of God's purposes in the Creation's design. Yet now he acknowledges forthrightly that the imagination's vision of the arrangement of things is artificial and human, not prophetic and divine. When a landscape painter chooses natural objects for devoted study and, more importantly, for passionate display on a canvas, the artist models the workings of human perception in its most acute, sensitive, and thoroughgoing mode of regarding things' meanings. Two points must be emphasized. First, the imagination has the power to move people out beyond themselves. Second, the success of the imagination's efforts must finally be assessed in the space of the interaction between artist and beholder, critic and audience.

We have before us Ruskin's new understanding of the imagination as a moral power. When people make sense of nature, art, or anything else imaginatively, their judgment of everything's meaning and value will be shaped by their own ordering of their desires, attitudes, and ends. Thus character and imagination meet, and for Ruskin, recognizing the teleological contours of the imagination's activity is a crucial step toward a broader, more relational undertaking of moral responsibility. Responsiveness to others becomes a more interesting affair, too, because now one must strive to take in one's own and others' interests, which is the "helpful" work of the moral imagination.

If we adopt this view of the imagination, then it becomes harder to hold onto two common assumptions. On the one hand, we have to abandon the idea that the imagination is an inherently "subjective" power, reflecting nothing more than the coloration given to an object by an individual's mind, images, or feelings, abstracted from all that informs his or her character. On the other hand, we need to set aside the notion that accurate perception demands that one's strictly "subjective" interests give way to the disinterested "objectivity" of truth. For Ruskin the moral life cannot be described as either merely subjective or precisely objective. It is better described by what we recognize in common with the other people who participate with us in the activities that help constitute our character and commitments as they presently stand. Thus he offers a glimpse of how his own character and commitments lead him to see the Alps, professing his reverence for their gifts and glories and for those people who made the most of them.[14]

In describing the imagination as "artificial" and "human" and its practical work as shaped by character and culture, I anticipate the directions taken in Ruskin's later criticism. For the most part in *Modern Painters* 3, he still measures the accurate making of things' meaning against the backdrop of God's making the "many things" of this world. The language of "making" is clear in the following passage: "the power of assembling, by *the help of the imagination,* such images as will excite [noble] feelings, is the power of the poet or literally of the 'Maker'" (5.29). But this poetic power poses risks, Ruskin cautions—most importantly, the threat of projecting one's feelings onto natural objects in a way that distorts their facts. He calls this error the "pathetic fallacy," and as an example, he faults Charles Kingsley's image of ocean foam as "cruel and crawling." The image attributes a life to the ocean it does not have. So too, he criticizes S. T. Coleridge's verse: "The one red leaf, the last of its clan / That dances as often as dance it can." As Ruskin observes, the dying leaf has little of its own life left to it and none of the "choice" and "merriment" that Coleridge ascribes to it. Coleridge falsifies the fact of the leaf's dying in ignoring that its redness really signifies the close of the year's bounty. Still there is something right in Coleridge's joy before nature and something admirable in Kingsley's projection of grief onto the wave. Indeed what makes the pathetic fallacy a matter of pathos, or feeling, and not an outright falsehood, is that it brings a "noble" emotion to bear on the wrong object in a way that distorts the facts of the thing—viewed, let me stress, in light of the encircling purposes that give this thing its significance (5.205–7).

The great poet, by contrast, admits the same emotions, but masters them in a way that ensures that nature is represented truthfully. Thus Ruskin praises a scene from the *Iliad* where Homer relates Helen's sadness over her brother's death. Commenting on the lack of anger in Homer's image of "the life-giving earth," Ruskin writes, "though [Helen's brother] be dead, yet the earth is our mother still, fruitful, life-giving. These are the facts of the thing" (5.212–13). Instead of being bound by the feelings and interests of the moment, Helen's character can still acknowledge the many beneficent ties that human beings have to the natural world.

Yet does Ruskin's contrast between the pathetic fallacies of Coleridge and Kingsley and the truthful imagination of Homer really settle anything? Why is the image of the earth as a life-giving mother accorded the honorary name of a "fact"? Homer's image clearly projects feelings onto a thing, granting a life to the earth and representing its "facts" in a particular way. Even if Homer's attitudes are more balanced than Kingsley's grief or Coleridge's joy, how does Ruskin determine which feelings are true and what balance is correct? Indeed having adopted his new aesthetics of making, how can he still appeal to common standards in matters of beauty and artistic representation?

Answering these questions reinforces important differences between a Romantic account of the imagination as the subjective coloring of things through individual feeling and Ruskin's teleological conception of the imagination as a moral power that seeks out the ends of things. I stressed before that Ruskin's concern with "facts" always entails the deeper issue of whether people's attitudes lead them to envision things' purposes. Here an instructive contrast can be drawn between the terms "pathos" and "ethos," that is, between emotions and ends. "Pathos" is a matter of temporary feeling, whereas "ethos" reflects the steadiness of excellent character that results from "mastering" one's passions through determined pursuit of the good. Again, Ruskin calls it the "*pathetic* fallacy," not an "*ethical* fallacy." Given the centrality of proper ends and shared goods to his teleological criticism, an ethical fallacy would be the willful distortion of things by defining them in light of one's own vision of the "bad," a harmful ensemble of ends serving no one but oneself.[15] Ruskin judges this type of fallacy more harshly, as I discuss in chapter 4 when I examine his critique of modern idolatry. Important for now is that both fallacies are corrected by attitudes of curiosity, gratitude, and, above all else, reverence. Countering the pathetic fallacy, in particular, demands a reverence for nature that motivates a searching out of its "intrinsic" ends and that prevents individuals from projecting their heightened feelings of the moment (or, in the case of an ethical fallacy, their willful misrepresentations) onto natural objects with no regard for the "facts," for these things' broader purposes in the world and, indeed, their independent worth. Such reverence entails a kind of "mastery," or practiced excellence, in a poet or anyone else, that keeps him or her mindful of the rich variety of purposes, benevolent and otherwise, served by the natural world.[16]

I have explored Ruskin's understanding of the artifice of the imagination—our bringing images and feelings to things and representing them by our own lights—against the backdrop of his changing teleological approach. This explanation clarifies how he argues that art is still a matter of truth. It also illustrates the centrality of character to his criticism, a concern that fills his overuse of the Romantic language of "feeling" with the ethical scrutiny of ends that is finally the issue for him. This explanation, however, only shifts the question of Ruskin's standards of judgment to a different level. Even if he no longer figures imaginative artists as prophetic seers of God's Creation, he presents artistic excellence as a mastery of passions, an alignment of one's interests with the good, that ensemble of ends that makes for human and natural flourishing. As Ruskin's goal remains "truth to nature," in what does this ideal ordering of ends consist?

In *Modern Painters* 3 Ruskin stands at a threshold, shifting from one set of sources of good character and moral vision to another. In this volume he appeals less often to God's perfect design in the Creation, and he rarely invokes the language of "function" from *Modern Painters* 2. But he still lodges nature's truth in a metaphysical ordering of the good. The divine perfection that shows in the natural ordering of things still regulates his teleological approach. By the third volume's end, however, Ruskin is moving toward a more cultural vision of "the natural." The conceptions of the good apparent in Greek, medieval, and modern visions of the natural world are just as *"not natural"* as landscape painting. By this I mean that the practice of landscape painting and the other cultural activities that shape people's desires, attitudes, ideals, and standards move more to the center of Ruskin's practical criticism. We see this especially in his assessments of his fellow Victorians' use and enjoyment of the world in making things from "nature." Tracing out this gradual shift from a divine metaphysics of nature toward the human practices of cultures will help introduce two issues at the heart of his ethics of consumption.

God as Maker of Nature, People as Makers of Cultures

Ruskin opens his account of the pathetic fallacy with a critique of German idealism and British empiricism. This critique takes him outside the realm of art to the broader work of the moral imagination in political, economic, and social matters. It also underscores the line he draws between his early aesthetics of the "mirror" and a full-blown Romantic aesthetics of the "lamp." Although Ruskin never crosses this line in admitting subjectivity into aesthetic or moral judgments in his later criticism, his high-wire act of claiming an independent worth for natural objects requires increasing rhetorical and analytical dexterity over time.

For reasons of "German dulness and English affectation," Ruskin writes, the terms "subjective" and "objective" have lost their meanings (5.201).

Philosophers claim that certain qualities of objects, such as taste, smell, and color, depend entirely on the subject's perception of them so that "it does not much matter what things are in themselves, but only what they are to us." Describing this "mystification" as a form of "egotism," Ruskin locates the true significance of the Lockean "secondary quality" of color, not in the "sensation" we receive, but in the object's "power." "'Blue' does *not* mean the *sensation* caused by a gentian on the human eye; but it means the *power* of producing that sensation; and this power is always there, in the thing, whether we are there to experience it or not, and would remain there though there were not left a man on the face of the earth" (5.202–3).

Playing on people's capacity to light the world by the lamp of the imagination, he continues, "Precisely in the same way gunpowder has a power of exploding. It will not explode if you put no match to it. But it has always the power of so exploding . . . whatever philosophy may say to the contrary. . . . If you find that you cannot explode the gunpowder, you will not declare that all gunpowder is subjective, and all explosion imaginary, but you will simply suspect and declare yourself to be an ill-made match." This "ill-made match" represents a faulty use of the imagination. So dependent are people on the attitudes, desires, and goals they bring to things that their perceptions may be badly distorted by the imagination's work. Though difficult to believe, a person might fail to grasp the inherent power of gunpowder—what it is good for. Similarly a person incapable of recognizing a gentian as blue would miss its intrinsic power, "its particles being everlastingly so arranged by its Maker" (5.203).

Ruskin stakes a broad claim here, one with implications for his ethics of consumption. Natural objects and manufactured substances have their inherent powers or "intrinsic value" no matter what we might make of them. A flower's color and a compound's chemistry are proof that God's created order governs human creativity, setting limits on the imagination. In the coming years as Ruskin extends the reach of the imagination beyond the realm of artistic representation into every act of valuing things, he presents all judgments of things' value as colored by the artifice of the imagination and the desires and purposes that individuals bring to what they use, enjoy, and consume.

How can Ruskin hold to his claim that the powers of natural resources are fixed by God as Maker while allowing that individuals' assessment of things' meaning, value, and purpose will reflect the feelings, images, and attitudes their imaginative powers conjure? The simple answer is that he cannot. And as he moves beyond *Modern Painters* 3, he appeals less and less often to such a direct and culturally unmediated knowledge of the inherent purposes of things. Put differently, God's making of nature is increasingly displaced in Ruskin's criticism by the human making of practices and cultures. For now, though, Ruskin secures the imagination's truth in an economy of ends, arranged by God and apparent in things' inherent powers. Indeed, the "many things" in volume 3 may appear wild, jumbled, and various, but they are shadowed by Ruskin's image of God's "Oneness." This image of nature as a uniform whole, the goodness of which stands entirely apart from people's desires and purposes, is itself a pathetic fallacy, an intense longing for the perfect harmony of all things that colors his own critical judgments.

Given how Ruskin's lingering metaphysical sensibility shapes his readings of the natural world, it is intriguing to stumble upon the brief history of nature that concludes *Modern Painters* 3. He surveys the history of Greek, medieval, and modern views of the "natural world" as represented in the literary record of these cultures. Detailing this analysis, limited as it is to Homer, Dante, and Sir Walter Scott, is tangential to my concerns, but two observations are in order.

First, Ruskin approaches this history by examining the "different forms in which art has developed itself within the periods historically known to us." He suggests that someone familiar with this history of artistic forms would be shocked by the modern genre of landscape painting with its devotions to mountains, lakes, and ruined buildings, and he allows that this newcomer might well posit that an "extraordinary change in *human nature*" had transpired (5.193, 196; my emphasis). This allowance that cultural forms may reflect transformations in "human nature" is new in his criticism.

Second, Ruskin relates the cultural forms of expression used in these three periods to different historical attitudes toward the world. The Greek's polytheistic reverence for the spirits of nature differs from the monotheistic abstraction of divine spirit from the material world. In Homer's ideal landscape of fountain, meadow, and grove, nature's value is clearly identified with the human use and working of the natural world in creating such pleasant places (5.231, 234). By contrast, medievals introduce mountains into their idealized portraits of nature, even as they retain a fear of them. Dante narrates the "soul's purification" as an arduous journey through the rocky and alien terrain of the heights, punctuated only occasionally by the pleasures of mountain glens. Mostly, though, Ruskin observes, medieval poets and artists prefer the brilliant colors of flowers to this frightful gloom

(5.294–95, 299). It is only in modern landscape painting that mountains come into the foreground. The modern landscape artists' fondness for mountains and the blackness of their canvases are witness to modernity's "free and fearless" confidence combined with a "profanity of temper in regarding" the natural world (5.319–20).

Even these few details demonstrate that Ruskin's quarry is a set of ideal types, not any actual history. What he seeks is the "mind" of these cultures, and he derives their visions of "the natural" from his readings of a select few authors without giving any attention to historical context or cultural complexity. Even so, his approach to nature has changed. No single type of landscape functions as the ideal against which all others are judged as deficient. In this sense we are some distance from Ruskin's use of the Gothic "spirit" as the benchmark for all good labor. Furthermore, he also insists that people's perceptions of the "natural" world are the product of the cultural forms that these people inherit and rework for themselves. Certainly the cultures he constructs are monolithic, the creative products of a few "great" minds. When he advances normative claims by appealing to these cultures, his appeals hardly differ from his earlier appeals to the perfect "wholes" of religion, nature, and spirit. Culture, it seems, reflects the same perfect arrangement of things' ends that is consonant with a seamless vision of the good.

Ruskin does not offer a cultural history of "nature" in today's sense. Most importantly, he gives limited attention to how conceptions of "the natural" uphold power relations in cultures and societies, though he does observe that the scenes of nature depicted in medieval art idealize the leisured pursuits of nobles (5.251–52). While Ruskin's metaphysical sensibility still shines forth, his acknowledgment that the "natural" world has a history and that people's ideas of "the natural" are shaped by the cultural practices and standards that they construct is suggestive of the transformed teleological vision motivating his ethical appeals and arguments as he moves more decisively to examine the human making of all things in his ethics of consumption.

Two issues related to that ethics of consumption are now before us. I have described Ruskin's metaphysical sensibility as a pathetic fallacy. His intense longing for a unifying vision of the good shows in his early appeals to religion, nature, spirit, and now history and culture, too. While I challenge this passionate desire for perfect harmony, I applaud a different attitude in Ruskin's criticism, the attitude of reverence that is so prominent in his writings. A reverence before the natural world is, I claim, vital to any ethics of consumption. A searching attitude of curiosity, receptivity, and gratitude before the world's "wildness" is needed if people are to recognize the extent of their dependence on the world and to accord the respect due for its many gifts. This reverence before the world can spur the moral imagination onto broader, if always partial, judgments of the value of natural resources and living creatures and the best ways to use, enjoy, and otherwise relate to them.

The second issue follows directly, namely, Ruskin's claim that natural resources have an "intrinsic value." Much of his concern in discussing the pathetic fallacy is that people not abuse the world by defining its worth in terms of their own "egotistical" ends. But why should natural objects, or even living creatures, be granted independent worth? Moreover, what is the basis for such judgments, especially once one grants a shaping power to individuals' imaginations and a culture's practices? Arguably there are no grounds to deny people's autonomy in valuing natural things nor, indeed, to assert that there is any "nature" out there apart from the idealized views of "the natural" that people make for their own purposes. Using the terms "nature" and "intrinsic value" as Ruskin does is, perhaps, the form of mystification we should avoid most assiduously. Indeed while insisting that consumers respect "natural limits" in using the world's resources, he also upholds "natural limits" on women's roles, rights, and autonomy, as I discuss in chapter 5.

For now I take up these two issues—the need for reverence before the world and the concept of nature's intrinsic value—in the remainder of this chapter. I explore these issues by reintroducing Ruskin's vocabulary of the virtues to his discussions of nature and imagination. His 1858 lecture titled "The Work of Iron, in Nature, Art, and Policy" is the crucial piece for seeing how his growing attention to the virtues revises his thinking about the imagination and the value of the natural world. In this lecture we find him pursuing the call for "nature-worship" sounded near the end of *Modern Painters* 3. Thinking of the biblical Job, Ruskin describes this "man whose piety was in other respects perfect" as having to learn a love of nature through God's Whirlwind speech (5.377–78; see Job 38–41). Ruskin seeks to cultivate the same natural piety in his audience through his imaginative readings of "The Work of Iron." In doing so he shows how his concept of nature's "intrinsic value" can be made consonant with his emerging cultural critique. If nature's value is discernible only by those who have crafted a virtuous character, then valuing natural objects rightly requires first choosing and engaging in the activities of a culture that make for the best uses and enjoyments of these things, given the standards, norms, and ideals of good lives and the good society found therein. Such judgments are not easy, but they are recognizably cultural and therefore disputable on those terms.

The Virtues and Limits of Iron

Nick Shrimpton argues that "The Work of Iron, in Nature, Art, and Policy" reorients Ruskin's criticism, culminating his search in the 1850s for a new genre of "political literature." According to Shrimpton, Ruskin follows Thomas Carlyle in abandoning the medievalist approach of *The Stones of Venice* for the hard-facts satire of Dickens's realism. He also adopts a "less reliable, but far more exciting, form of literary invention."[17] Ruskin does appeal less often to the holism of an idealized social order, and for this reason, his arguments both in this lecture and in most of his later writings are more complex and suggestive because his images, examples, and appeals operate internally to a context shared by his contemporaries. They reflect neither the past as in his architectural studies nor God's Creation as in his early aesthetics. Instead he directs his audience to imagine the things making up their lives, charging them to take responsibility for discerning the limited bounty of their surroundings.

"The Work of Iron" is an excellent example of Ruskin's emerging social criticism. It puts the teleological approach of his criticism to the purposes of cultural critique and engaged ethics. He focuses specifically on "the work of iron" in his fellow Victorians' lives. At issue for him are the ends and goods that they seek through their myriad activities. He is not reconstructing the "moral characteristics" of long-ago Gothic craftsmen and the harmonious society that sustained them. Instead he uses his vocabulary of the virtues in a self-conscious attempt to teach his audience its value as a tool of cultural analysis. In other words, he addresses his audience as a thinking public, as if their imaginative "help" really was needed to sustain the "reality" of his own readings of iron's value.

As a lecture, "The Work of Iron" details how iron functions in nature and gets used in art and policy. Using iron as a representative natural resource, Ruskin asks his listeners to imagine the "full significance" of its goodness, looking to its myriad roles in nature, art, and policy, not simply to its commercial value in industry. I concentrate here on his account of iron's roles in nature to show how the growing importance of Ruskin's vocabulary of the virtues transforms his teleological approach, in general, and his teleological conception of nature, in particular.

My thesis is that the term "virtue" ties together the lecture's seemingly disparate concerns with nature's beauty, artistic excellence, and economic justice. No other scholar has noticed the importance of this term in the lecture, even though Ruskin's aim is to inspire his listeners to undertake all of the work that they must do to cultivate their character if they are to seek out the "true" worth of iron in their lives. This interaction between the work of iron and the work of character development relates to the two ways he uses the word "virtue."

First, in talking about physical objects, Ruskin ascribes virtues to things, meaning the properties that enable these things to serve specific purposes. One virtue of iron, for example, is its strength as steel, allowing even the thinnest knife blade to withstand great force. In addition, in talking about people, he uses the term "virtue" to mean the various kinds of "excellence" that individuals can acquire in their activities. So, for example, only workers skilled in the virtues, or excellences, of the craft of forging metals can make such a strong blade.

On the one hand, things can be used well only according to their virtues, and it is our task as producers and consumers to seek out the most efficacious uses of all of the natural resources at our disposal. On the other hand, people can use things well only if they possess the relevant virtues, meaning the particular set of excellences, ranging from the skills of craftsmanship to the capacities for moral or aesthetic discernment, that are appropriate to a given activity. "The Work of Iron" follows this logic, starting from the need to recognize *things' virtues* and moving to the need to develop *human virtues.*

Ruskin delivers the lecture in the town of Tunbridge Wells. He had vacationed at this spa town as a youth, and he remembered how the town's fountains were colored by the concentration of iron in the water. In addition to these mineral springs, the charms of the town have something to do with its distance from the heavy industrial regions to the north. Yet Ruskin is aware that the wealth produced by Britain's industrial machine is more likely to be on his audience's mind than the other kind of wealth signified by the town's spas.

Based on a reporter's testimony, some of the people made rich by industry were probably in attendance, for he was received by a "fashionable and crowded audience" and with "continued and protracted cheering"

(16.lx). The warm reception stands in contrast to Ruskin's professed misgivings about his audience. What topic might draw these people out from their "comfortable houses on a winter's night"? What could he possibly say to a general audience about his own "special business of art" without the benefit of the kind of illustrations he later pioneered as the first Slade Professor of Art at Oxford? It was for these reasons, he tells the assembly, that he chose iron as his topic in hopes that a mineral so valuable to them would prove sufficiently interesting to overcome these difficulties (16.375). Indeed his listeners are plenty interested in iron already—our interests are always at play whenever we imagine things. Ruskin's challenge is to demonstrate how narrow his audience's interests really are, to scrutinize how their attitudes, desires, and purposes misrepresent iron's goodness, and to model how only a full imagination of iron's worth can offset the false construction of its value in the workings of industrial capitalism.

There is a further and more general problem of audience that Ruskin does not address. "The Work of Iron" reads like a magisterial exposition of the proper uses and enjoyments of iron in nature, art, and policy. Arguably Ruskin does little more than offer his own vision of iron's role in a personal conception of the good life, suggesting that he has not moved much beyond his metaphysical sensibility with its necessarily seamless conception of the good. But he also seeks to engage and enlist his audience's powers of imagination in new ways. As he puts it, the lecture will amount to nothing if his listeners do not "follow out the subject . . . at home"; "what I have endeavoured to lay before you to-night will only be useful to you if you do" (16.406). By appealing to his audience's powers of imagination, he calls them to examine how helpful their own idea of iron's value is. There is an important issue of character development here, of what is revealed of one's virtues and vices in the uses and enjoyments one makes of iron. There is a problem of moral vision, too, because Ruskin must somehow provoke people to look beyond the vaunted industrial machine and convince them that iron's true value lies elsewhere.

Ruskin engages the problem of moral vision directly. Referring to the "saffron stain" on the fountains of Tunbridge Wells, he asks his audience what makes this "steely element" one of the "most precious gifts of the earth." He means to shock these beneficiaries of the industrial machine, for it is not the hardened form of pure iron that makes it most valuable, but its broken-down state as rust. "It is not a fault in the iron, but a *virtue,* to be so fond of getting rusted, for in that condition it fulfils its most important functions in the universe, and most kindly duties to mankind" (16.376; my emphasis). He continues, "You all probably know that in the mixed air we breathe, the part of it essentially needful to us is called oxygen; and that this substance is to all animals, in the most accurate sense of the word, 'breath of life.' . . . we, and other animals, part with [this breath of life] again; but the metal absolutely keeps what it has once received of this aerial gift; and the ochreous dust which we so despise is, in fact, just so much nobler than pure iron, in so far as it is *iron and the air*" (16.377).

The religious significance of the phrase the "breath of life" should not be missed. Ruskin drives home his sense of the divine in iron's breathing in and holding onto oxygen. He writes, "it is impossible for you to take up the most insignificant pebble at your feet, without being able to read [a] curious lesson in it. You look upon it . . . as if it were earth only. Nay, it answers, 'I am not earth—I am earth and air in one; part of that blue heaven which you love, and long for, is already in me . . . ; [and] because there is, according to my need and place in creation, a kind of soul in me, I have become capable of good, and helpful in the circles of vitality'" (16.378). In this passage the many "circles of vitality" in which iron plays its part begin in God's life-giving spirit as creator. Building on this point, Ruskin charts the myriad ways that the broken-down forms of iron contribute to the full range of its goodness. Iron serves his purposes well because it is everywhere, from inorganic things to living systems. Its decomposition into rust illustrates the importance of decomposition to the soil, of which iron itself is a crucial part. From iron's place in the soil, he tours the landscape, celebrating the iron oxides that color the world in the reds of clay, the purples of slate, and the crimson of oxygenated blood. Here, in particular, he fashions his symbol of iron to turn his audience's admiration from the productivity of their iron machines to the gift of iron in the blood on which their continued existence depends.

To use the language of Ruskin's ethics of consumption, iron's "intrinsic value" is partly a function of the many roles it plays in the world's flourishing. His claim that iron has an intrinsic value appears to proceed here, in particular, from the idea that God orders all things toward their appointed purposes. So, if Hooker's idea of God's "Oneness" continues to shadow the "many things" of the third volume, then Ruskin's allusions to iron's "breath of life" and his insistence on the inherent limits fixed by God's Creation likely carry forward, too. The language of iron's "virtues" reinforces this apparent connection because, in *Modern Painters* 2, God's immutable "virtue" establishes the virtues, or "perfections," that every created being and thing is to measure up to in performing its part in the flourishing of the whole (see chapter 1).

Ruskin's appeal to nature's association with divinity, as seen in iron's affinity for the breath of life, does repeat the idea that things' "virtues" define the fullness *and* scope of life's flourishing. The fullness of the earth's flourishing does require observing certain limits. But to stop with the claim that nature's divinity all by itself fixes the inherent restrictions on people's use of the planet would be to ignore the other ways that Ruskin now approaches the question of how to observe the world's limits.

Consider that "The Work of Iron" does not stop at the boundaries of nature but continues into art and policy. The essay notes that iron's virtues of ductility and tenacity make it useful for producing tools and decorative work, as I discuss in chapter 6. The acknowledgment that the full significance of iron's goodness depends upon people's active participation in making the most of it parallels another shift in Ruskin's thinking, too. Iron's chief virtue—its tendency to rust—is what frees it up to play its many roles in "nature." As such, nature's goodness is defined not so much by what is original as by what is replenishing. Without iron's natural affinity for oxygen, nineteenth-century industrial capitalism might soon turn the earth into an ironclad "globe of black, lifeless, excoriated metal." Ruskin, the amateur geologist, adds that the earth may well have once been that, but a return to such an original state is as impossible as it would be undesirable (16.378).

There are two novel features in this argument. First, Ruskin approaches natural limits using an ecological model of sorts. Certainly he describes iron's chief virtue using an image of the divine in citing iron's affinity for the "breath of life." In his larger argument, though, iron's limits are set by its myriad roles in the world's "circles of vitality." And he leads his audience through a wide-ranging portrait of the work of "impure" iron in the natural world, all the while evoking the interdependence of ecological systems and the limits imposed by these relationships. Diverting iron too much from its part in any one "circle of vitality" will eventually jeopardize its many roles in sustaining life. Iron's virtues still mark life-giving limits for people to observe, but its limits reflect the internal balances of living systems, not a static ranking of all things' "nature" imposed from above.

The second change is more subtle. To grasp it, we must take seriously Ruskin's new aesthetics of making and his evolving vocabulary of the virtues. In sharp contrast to his early art criticism where any use of the natural world detracts from its beauty, he now acknowledges that people always use the natural world, working it to their own purposes. Simply put, iron's work cannot be judged apart from our work. This is true even of what might appear to be the "hands-off" appreciation of the beauties of iron in nature to which Ruskin calls his audience in this part of the lecture.

Ruskin acknowledges that his own account of iron's work in nature is partial. For him the most interesting role that iron plays in nature is "its operations as a coloring element," that part of iron's work most closely related to his own "special business of art" (16.384, 375). At one point he tells his listeners that they must "take the word of a sketcher" that the charm of English country towns is due more to a "warm purple" than to a "warm scarlet." Although the tiled roofs of their houses might appear reddish, they owe their "colour to a mingling with the vermilion of the deep grayish or purple hue of our fine Welsh slates . . . , made more blue still by the colour of intervening atmosphere" (16.381). Here is another example of the "natural" abundance made possible by iron's affinity with air. In this instance, though, appreciating the full significance of iron's goodness requires the knowledge of a sketcher. Seeing the purple hues brought out by the blue of the sky and the gray of the slate, all balanced just so, takes practice in mixing colors and understanding the interplay among them. It is a feeling for things fostered in a cultural activity that others can partake of if they commit to the ends and goods of its practice. In trying to persuade his listeners to see the world's limits and wealth in a fuller light, Ruskin calls on the practical judgment he has gained by cultivating his own excellences as a participant in the activity of sketching. He appeals to a common delight available to everyone in his audience, not restricted to prophetic seers and not without reason. It is, rather, a delight his audience can share if they take the time to observe and, more importantly, to develop the practical skills required for observing well.

This is the main point that Ruskin wants his listeners to take home: discerning the virtues of iron requires cultivating their own. Paradoxically, then, learning to imagine iron's "intrinsic value" involves searching out and either directly engaging or materially supporting those cultural activities that make the most of iron and that make the most of their participants and the society, too. I do not read "The Work of Iron" as an imperious declaration of a prophetic vision of the good, recourse to which is restricted to the great artist or wise critic. It is instead an invitation to undertake the task of moral imagination for oneself. No doubt Ruskin speaks with authority and aims to instruct his listeners to see things rightly. But he does not simply invoke a divine metaphysics as in his earlier writings. Nor does he assume the mantle of prophetic seer. Rather, his metaphorical appeals to nature's divinity are backed by argument. In these arguments he blends science and art, while displaying his excellences as a sketcher. More importantly, he calls his audience to examine the character and commitments that they have forged and may refashion through their chosen activities. For now they must take the word of a sketcher, but they might decide to take on the ends and cultivate the excellences of the practice. This directive reflects Ruskin's broader turn toward culture, and it makes his portrait of iron's intrinsic value and its natural limits a matter of a practiced discernment that is itself critical and open to other people's criticism, too.

From Natural Theology to Natural Piety

In "The Work of Iron" Ruskin emphasizes his excellences as a sketcher, but his broader concern is a virtue that his listeners can develop in a wide array of pursuits. That virtue is a piety before the natural world, the only kind of piety lacking in Job, and a virtue that Ruskin comes to see as necessary to any good life.[18] Although he does not name this virtue in "The Work of Iron," if we consider the full run of Ruskin's writings on nature, from the early volumes of *Modern Painters* through his late works on natural history, *Love's Meinie* (1873–81), *Deucalion* (1875–83), and *Proserpina* (1875–86), then instilling the virtue of natural piety emerges as a primary goal of his criticism. As he declares in *Fors Clavigera* (1771–84) near the end of his career, his "duty to the future [is] to teach the Love of the fair Universe around us as the beginning of Piety, and the end of Learning." This piety toward the natural world entails "kindness to living things, and orderly use of the lifeless" (29.465, 495).

Ruskin employs the term "piety" infrequently in his corpus and usually in its negative sense of a self-centered and showy religiosity. He scolds the pious for displaying either a fretful enthusiasm for purification or a proud conviction of chosenness (see chapter 4). But in the 1883 preface to his revision of *Modern Painters* 2, he circles back to commend the "heathen" virtues of "Righteousness," "Honour," and "Piety" alongside the "biblical" virtue of "Faith." He cites these virtues as constitutive of a "character, intelligently obedient to a moral law common to the Jew and Arab,—to the Greek and Christian." This character, he adds, is all that he ever meant to illustrate by his early theory of beauty (4.6).

Even a cursory reading of *Modern Painters* 2 refutes this claim. In fact, Ruskin scorns pagan virtue, describing its "essence" as an "abuse and corruption of the sense of beauty" (4.49). Somewhat abashedly, he now explains why this ecumenical celebration of the virtues is hard to discern behind the praise for God's sovereign authorship of nature and the critique of human pride found in second volume. "All these virtues imply radically the conception,—they lead ultimately to the revelation,—of personal and governing Deity: but they begin, practically, and themselves consist to the end, in truthful knowledge of *human power* and *human worth*" (4.6). This emphasis on "human power and human worth" accurately charts the path toward Ruskin's later criticism, but he discusses human power and worth in *Modern Painters* 2 only in terms of the "perfections" that flow to each and every creature from God's font of "virtue." Once again we are reminded of the tension between divine Creation and human creativity, and just as Ruskin turns from God's "making" to human "making" everywhere else in his criticism, he redirects his writings on nature. He stops preaching natural theology and God's perfect design and instead urges his readers to cultivate a natural piety by participating in those cultural activities that are good for them and for the world.

How does Ruskin move from natural theology to natural history? As Robert Hewison rightly notes, "Natural theology sanctifies vital beauty" in Ruskin's early aesthetics.[19] Here the dominant concern is God's design, to which human use is subordinate. As Ruskin puts it, "everything created [is] pre-eminently useful" insofar as it "rightly and fully [performs] the functions appointed to it by its Creator" (4.28). The emphasis on function in *Modern Painters* 2 testifies to Ruskin's amateur studies of science as a youth. His interests in the Rev. William Buckland's (1784–1856) geological account of Creation and his use of Charles Bell's (1774–1832) anatomical sketches display the conviction Ruskin shared with many early-nineteenth-century British naturalists, namely, that scientific inquiry would only reinforce the proof of God's illustrious plan.[20]

When Ruskin separates the study of religion from the discipline of natural history in "Modern Education," he retains his reverence for the natural world, but he turns from a theological language of "functions" and "perfections" to a naturalistic language of "instinct." Only those men whose "natural instincts urge [them] to the pursuit of the physical sciences too strongly to be resisted" learn anything of these subjects. The usual lack of instruction in the sciences "leaves the greater number of men without the natural food which God intended for their intellects"—the "perpetual, simple and religious delight in watching the processes, or admiring the creatures, of the natural universe" (11.259). This finding delight and admiration in nature recalls Ruskin's debts to William Wordsworth.[21] But in his early aesthetics Ruskin fit his Wordsworthian fascination for nature's detail into his conviction that beauty functions to reveal God's purposes. The joy and reverence before the natural world that he commends in "Modern Education" look instead to the emotional nourishment that people take directly from the "natural universe" when rightly open to it.

Ruskin identifies the concerns of the science of natural history as including "what kind of creatures live in [the world], and how; what it is made of, and *what may be made of it*" (11.258; my emphasis). Ruskin's allowance for people's making things from the natural world reflects both his growing interests in labor and his use-centered understanding of the physical sciences. He continues to insist, however, that scientific work should be conducted with grateful reverence for the inspired significance of nature's countless gifts. When Ruskin returns in the 1870s and 1880s to his abandoned studies of birds and botany, he denounces classificatory schemes based on invasive exploratory techniques. In *Love's Meinie* he observes that every book on ornithology reveals the "masters of science" in league with the "lords of land." The aristocrat is interested only in shooting the birds, while the scientist writes the "classifying epitaphs" of a procession of species rapidly becoming extinct. Ruskin cautions, the "lancet and the microscope in the hands of fools" cannot "be complete substitutes for imagination in the souls of wise men" (25.25–27). The errors of these scientists are the product of the field of natural history as then practiced. In place of its current practices, Ruskin advocates classifying plants, animals, and minerals according to what strikes the observer's unaided eye, vivifying things through the imagination rather than vivisecting them into their component parts.

It should be noted that Ruskin's critique of the science of natural history has less to do with its conclusions than with its means of taxonomic collection and the proliferation of names for individual species proposed by every new scientist seeking to make a reputation for himself. The rhetorical gibe that he scores in reference to Charles Darwin's (1809–82) *Descent of Man* (1871) is a case in point. Ridiculing disputes over the exact number of "species" into which the human race should be divided, Ruskin proposes an answer of two. A swinish species "capable only of avarice, hatred, and shame" contrasts with an avian species "capable of loyalty and of love" and of soaring into the skies (25.56–57). Clearly Ruskin's concern here is to describe the character of his contemporaries, not to dispute theories of evolution.[22] He draws the analogies to pigs and birds to categorize people into different *moral* species.[23] He neither engages nor disagrees with the genealogies that Darwin traces in his studies of evolution.

Although Ruskin is not among those moralists who directly attacked Darwin's theory, there is a deep and fascinating intellectual difference between the two figures. When Ruskin uses such terms as "characteristic" and "function," he is thinking of "moral species." The character and function of a bird or a plant can be known only in reference to the moral universe of ends that gives a species its full significance. Classification schemes should honor those purposes, Ruskin asserts, or we will be badly led astray in what we "make of things" from the natural world, the ostensible task of natural historians. Darwin, by contrast, employs the terms "characteristic" and "function" in a scientific sense, analyzing the differentiation and transformation of a species' characteristics through the chance-like mechanisms of natural selection. There is no moral universe of ends here, no perfect harmony of "natures" fixed for all time, or even to be worked out over time, in light of which the characteristics, functions, meanings, and significance of everything could be known, related, and organized, or in a word, classified.[24] Today we stand mostly in Darwin's camp in our usage of these terms—yet another reason why Ruskin's moral vocabulary is so difficult to fathom, let alone to recover. I strongly suspect, however, that Darwin himself had to struggle mightily to blunt the moralistic insistence we find in figures like Ruskin that a searching inquiry into the "natures" of things must of necessity proceed onto the moral universe of ends that marks everything's true flourishing.[25]

I have raised large issues that go beyond this book, but they reinforce a central lesson of Ruskin's late studies of natural history. He approaches the science of natural history as a moral enterprise. He commends study of the colloquial names of plants and animals found in folk languages for their "historical points of interest." He directs his readers to "mythology," in particular, as "the most important part of [a species'] natural history" (25.22, 40). What accounts for this seemingly bizarre merging of the science of natural history with studies of philology and mythology? The answer is that Ruskin's growing attention to the human making of things in cultural practices leads him to reconceive how people come to know the meaning and value of the natural world.

For Ruskin, natural history is a cultural practice, which should be judged in light of its practitioners' ends. The scientists' praiseworthy goal of knowledge is vitiated by their complicity in the bloodlust of a sporting aristocracy. It is not their tools but their attitudes that mislead them. Ruskin argues that these scientists should heed the repository of cultural wisdom about the natural world that persists in folklore and fable and that serves as a school of natural piety, especially when sung to children by "mothers and nurses" (25.25). Ruskin's lectures on ornithology are meant for his Oxford students. His work on botany is more for children. In both cases, though, his attention to moral education and his bifocal interests in careful scientific study of "natural forms" and in literary representations of species through "cultural forms" make sense only if we recall his changing views on nature and imagination.

People perceive the natural world and imagine different species' significance in light of the attitudes and interests they bring to their "making" of things from nature.[26] These attitudes and interests are culturally shaped, informed by the art, mythology, literature, and religion of the cultures that people inherit, uphold, and reform in their everyday activities. Ruskin looks to this complex assortment of cultural wisdom for sources of a full and accurate knowledge of the world's "intrinsic value." Thus nature's worth is both independent of human use and yet recognizable only through the cultural practices to which people commit. Natural piety requires using the world well and acknowledging one's continual dependence upon it. Natural piety also consists in an appreciation of the myriad ways that people are shaped and nurtured by their interactions with this larger world. Fostering natural piety requires, therefore, examining and articulating the moral universe of ends that makes for "orderly use of the lifeless" and "kindness to living things." As Ruskin now approaches these tasks, this moral universe is not the product of divine revelation, nor can it be justified by appealing beyond human cultures, even as it remains open to creative revisions of past cultures and their legacy of folklore, fable, and myth.

The distance that Ruskin travels from natural theology to natural piety can be summed up by closing with his 1867 letter in *Time and Tide* on the four theories of biblical authority. The theories range from believing that the Bible "is in every syllable of it [God's] 'Word'" to its being a collection of human wisdom having "no more authoritative claim on our faith than the religious speculations and histories of the Egyptians, Greeks, Persians, and Indians" (17.348–49). Ruskin's religious biography shows a steady decrease in his belief that God has any authorship, however remote, in writing the Bible. During the 1860s, he turns to the "philological school" of

Friedrich Max Müller and the burgeoning field of comparative mythology and folklore for new materials for his imaginative readings of the proper ends guiding his contemporaries' lives.[27] Ruskin explains these borrowings from other traditions of "human wisdom" and his own continued use of the Bible as conforming to the fourth theory of biblical interpretation. The Bible is just one more book on the virtues, though the most important one for his contemporaries because the most formative of a shared Victorian culture.

Although Ruskin abandons his early belief in the Bible's inspired authority, he lays down one prerequisite without which his readers must find his own writings unintelligible. While it is fine to allow no more authority to the Bible than to any other book, there is "one farther condition of incredulity"—"the incredulity, namely, of inspiration in any sense, or of help given by any Divine power to the thoughts of men. But this form of incredulity merely indicates a natural incapacity for receiving certain emotions" (17.348–49, 350). This emphasis on inspiration and reverence, on the emotions of joy, wonder, receptivity, and gratitude before the world's beauty, intricacy, and abundance, reiterate the centrality of natural piety to Ruskin's late writings.

The Nature of Ruskin's Appeals

An issue I have been pursuing in the background of this chapter is whether the prophetic, intuitive cast of Ruskin's appeals to religion, nature, spirit, and emotion can be stripped away. So often it seems that he operates as the "great" critic, able to grasp all in an instant a perfect vision of the "whole" of life to which his readers are expected to assent even if the reasons escape them. Such a style fits his early theory of the imagination far better than the one he works out from the 1850s onward. Artistic and critical representations demand, after all, imaginative "help" on both sides of the canvas or corpus, from artist and audience, from writer and reader alike. In attempting to recover Ruskin's criticism, part of our task becomes assessing what informs the "images" and "feelings" that he brings to his own imaginative "making" of things—specifically, the individual ends and the cultural practices that he upholds for his readers' consideration and participation.

In reconstructing his teleological approach to ethics, I have argued that there is always this movement in Ruskin's criticism toward a scrutiny of people's desires and purposes as these are ordered in their characters and fashioned through their cultural pursuits. This movement explains the role of his appeals to religion, nature, spirit, and emotion—namely, to justify some arrangement of the ends necessary to human flourishing. But whether Ruskin is offering his vision of the natural order, the common good, good lives, or shared goods, his justifications must reach beyond his own feelings, or he denies the teleological reach of the moral imagination, as he conceives it in *Modern Painters* 3 and applies it throughout his subsequent writings. I read his idea and practice of the moral imagination as one of his most important and lasting contributions to ethics and social criticism. He does not always exploit its full power, however. It is not enough to desire that everything hang together in a perfect harmony, coloring all that one sees in light of some passionate longing. To the extent that Ruskin does this himself, he commits a pathetic fallacy. If no better reasons can be given than his fond desire that it be so, unjustified by appeals to cultural practices and moral judgments in which others can share, then we are better off refusing to make his ways of articulating a "common vision" our own.

In introducing the idea of natural piety, I have relied on the word "emotion" to reflect Ruskin's usual way of describing the reverence due to the world. No matter how much my smile at a passing hummingbird comes all in an instant, I resist this Romantic language of feeling. It suggests that Ruskin's criticism is intuitive. It makes his arguments appear prophetic. I propose that his vocabulary of the virtues is a better resource because it reflects his broader concerns with character and his fuller argumentation about desires, attitudes, and ends. This moral language provokes consideration of how well people are developed and what purposes they seek and are able to attain. As Ruskin uses this vocabulary, it also requires examining where people are positioned in a society and culture and whether individuals are free to develop their excellences and pursue the full range of flourishing afforded to others. The language of emotion is the tool of the intuitive critic, while a vocabulary of the virtues is more practical.

Looking back to "The Work of Iron," these concerns with human development and social justice are sustained by Ruskin's interest in the virtues that people do or do not cultivate as participants in the best activities of their culture. But even as he works as a practical critic, we also see the tendencies of the intuitive critic. For example, after advising that iron is "eminently made for" crafting "involved form," he declares that this message from the "lips of the earth-mother" is as plain as the different uses appropriate to the properties of iron and marble. Only a fool or a show-off would choose brittle stone for carving twisted branches and tender leaves.

But "[y]our slender leaves shall not break off in my tenacious iron, though they may be rusted a little with an iron autumn" (16.387).

What should we make of the phrase "iron autumn"? That iron's tendency to rust marks a "natural limit" seems true. That iron is better suited than marble for crafting fragile foliage needs little argument. But then Ruskin adds that iron's characteristic "autumn" stain signifies its natural fit with this particular kind of artwork. Read the Book of Nature; observe the colors of fall; this is one of the things that iron is really good for. It is partly on the basis of such intuitive appeals to nature's guidance that his lecture as a whole assembles the best uses and enjoyments associated with iron and orders them into a fuller vision of the good life. Is "The Work of Iron," then, simply the performance of a virtuoso critic who can create the effect of a seamless moral vision, disclosing truths about iron's uses and abuses as if they were taught by "nature" herself?

There are good reasons to resist this moral intuitionism. Placing our faith in Ruskin's evocations of the mysterious interconnectedness of the natural world would mean embracing, without argument, his cultural vision of "the natural." Although his view of "nature" evolves, as I have indicated, it remains allied with his sanctification of a social order of "natural" roles for men and women. Ruskin's portrait of the work of iron in policy divides along gender lines. To men goes the work of the plow and the production of food, to women the work of the needle and the sewing of clothing. An important issue, therefore, is whether his call for reverence before the natural world and his concept of intrinsic value can be disentangled from his cultural vision of the natural. The more that the intuitive and prophetic aspects of his criticism are emphasized, the less likely this conceptual surgery can be performed successfully.

I examine Ruskin's gendering of roles in discussing his politics in chapter 5. The next chapter explores his evolving views of religion and his analysis of the idolatry of modern life. I have alluded in the present chapter to his early appeals to God's perfect Creation as the crux of his metaphysics. As he moves from his early studies of art and nature toward his interests in society and economics, his inquiries into human "making" expand from one question, what do people make of things from nature, to a second question, what do people make of the things that others have made. While the current chapter has focused on the artist's and critic's use of the imagination in representation, the next chapter shifts toward the role of the audience as imaginative interpreters in their own right.

With this turn we move closer to Ruskin's ethics of consumption. His analysis of modern idolatry centers on the system of valuation generated by industrial capitalism. As he investigates this historically produced system of exchange, the complexities of Victorian culture become more central to his criticism. His views on religion and his religious appeals become more overtly cultural, too. Exploring how these more provisional and cultural appeals open the way toward a more democratic articulation of a common vision helps us understand which aspects of Ruskin’s criticism retain lasting value today.

FOUR

The Vision of Religion

The previous chapter explores Ruskin's developing views on nature and imagination as both are transformed by his growing interests in the human making of cultures. As his critical lens turns from God's perfect Creation toward imperfect human creativity, his views on religion change, too, not surprisingly. We have the biographical evidence of Ruskin's self-declared "un-conversion" from Evangelical Anglicanism in 1858 (34.89). There are subtler hints of this distancing as early as "Modern Education" (1853). Simply by naming religion one part of a full curriculum and by locating the "binding" practices of different religions in the societies they shape (11.259), he adopts a different posture than the wholehearted worship that shines through every page of *Modern Painters* 2 (1846).

Ruskin's approach to religion shifts dramatically from the early 1850s onward. The more he doubts his Evangelical upbringing, the more he finds efficacy in the practices and teachings of various Christian traditions and other religions, too. Yet he retains two convictions of his early aesthetics. He never fully abandons his sense of the need for a metaphysical ordering of the good to guide individuals' judgments and to secure their moral duties. He also continues to believe that worship is necessary to human life because it enables people to recognize all of the gifts they receive. I have criticized Ruskin's metaphysical sensibility before, and I show its limitations in this chapter, too. I argue as well, however, that his calls to worship—his calls to acknowledge the "giftedness" of life in the things we enjoy from the world and buy from other people—are invaluable aids to an ethics of consumption.

I am using the term "worship" in a specific way—Ruskin's way. By worship he means the recognition of a thing's "true" goodness, where the act of recognition is predicated upon an acknowledgment of a debt to, or dependence upon, the thing's maker. Ruskin's initial paradigm is the debt to, or dependence upon, God as the creator of life. But over time he argues that worship is due both for the gifts we receive from the world's bounty, as discussed in the previous chapter, and also for the gifts we receive from other people's effort and creativity, as I begin to explore here. This idea of worship introduces the central issue of the chapter.

That issue is the problem of moral vision, the problem of how to attain the shared vision of things' goodness implicit in Ruskin's concept of worship. The three previous chapters have already addressed problems of vision related to the more complex one here. Chapter 1 analyzed his early aesthetics and the problem of how to recognize the glory of God's Creation. Chapter 2 examined his studies of Gothic architecture and the problem of how to recognize the excellence of great work from the past. Chapter 3 developed Ruskin's new aesthetics of making and the problem of how to recognize the beauty and worth of the natural world. The problem of vision in this chapter is how to see across the distances of the money economy of industrial capitalism to recognize the "true" value of all of the things that people exchange on the market.

As Ruskin turns from art and nature to society and economics, his understanding of the challenges involved in attaining a common vision of things' goodness becomes more nuanced and sophisticated. When he discusses Gothic architecture, he can appeal to the shared goods and standards of social practices as measures of craftwork and artistic excellence. When he discusses the natural world, he can identify activities like sketching and natural history that train people to appreciate the world's integral beauty and worth. In both cases the cultures that people have made for themselves serve to mediate their recognition of goodness, marking the distance from Ruskin's early aesthetics where goodness is recognized simply by conforming one's loves to God's purposes as revealed in the Creation. But the more Ruskin allows for the role of human creativity in making cultures and the more he takes in the vast range of activities in any economy, what can possibly serve to join people in their judgments of value? Put differently, the more he takes seriously the ways that an individual's imagination shapes things' meaning through the desires, ends, and attitudes that he or she brings to production, consumption, and exchange, is it still plausible to insist on the need for a shared vision of things' goodness in economic life?

These questions reach beyond this chapter. In the chapters on Ruskin's politics and his ethics of consumption, I discuss how he develops various critical tools for imagining a common good and good lives for all. My current focus is his argument that a worship for life's gifts is necessary for attaining any shared moral vision in economic life. We cannot understand this argument without tracing out his biographical movement from being raised a devoted Evangelical Anglican to adopting the "cultural" approach to religions found in his later social criticism. By this I mean that Ruskin increasingly views religions as the "binding" practices of a people, as first defined in "Modern Education." For Ruskin, religious practices form three aspects of a people's common life: they foster shared attitudes, they structure social relations, and they sustain symbol systems. All three elements are present in Ruskin's analysis of the "idolatry" of money, that part of his critique of industrial capitalism that draws together the thematic concerns of this chapter—his evolving views on religion, his ongoing calls to worship, and his critical attention to the attitudes, relations, and symbols at work in economic exchange.

I mention Ruskin's account of the idolatry of money to introduce a key comparison with Karl Marx's analysis of commodity fetishism. The parallels are striking. Both critics make a theoretical use of religion as a tool of analysis, arguing in particular that industrial capitalist exchange is characterized by a systematic distortion of the value of commodities. These distortions are generated through the symbolic operation of money in the marketplace, which allows for the projection of new meanings onto things. Both critics also agree that the workings of industrial capitalism mask a power structure that serves some people at others' expense, all the while constructing the desires that keep everyone beholden to the religious fixation, whether in the form of "idolatry" or "fetishism," that occludes these distorted meanings, power relations, and constructed desires.

Ruskin's and Marx's visions of religion are quite different, however. Marx's interest in religion is strictly as a theorist. He devotes little attention to specific forms of worship and the attitudes they foster. He names the need for consolation the sole drive toward religion and false consciousness its only product. He never enlists the practices, literatures, and teachings of Christianity or any other tradition except to illustrate his theoretical dictum that all worship is mystifying. Ruskin, by contrast, often makes religious appeals, and at times he offers insight into the virtues cultivated within religious practices. His use of the concept of idolatry, however, ultimately constricts his vision. An idolatrous worship of Mammon is opposed to the one true worship of God. This dualism between God and

Mammon is typically backed by Ruskin's familiar appeals to a metaphysical ordering of the good. In this case the choice between God and Mammon reinforces a polarizing choice between two types of society—the competitive, market-driven society of industrial capitalism and an "ideally" cooperative society, unified in its communal feeling but divided into hierarchical roles.

As Ruskin never shakes his metaphysical sensibility or his hierarchical social vision, I argue that Marx's anti-metaphysical suspicions indicate where serious scrutiny is warranted of Ruskin's portrait of the necessity of worship in human life. On my reading of *Capital* (1867), Marx's analysis of commodity fetishism functions as the culmination of his critique of religion as the primary bearer of false metaphysics. Marx would be rightly suspicious of how Ruskin's talk of worship readily translates into a hierarchical ordering of difference and deference. Is it possible, then, to salvage Ruskin's calls for worship for the gifts we receive?

There are resources internal to Ruskin's criticism that undercut his metaphysical appeals. I am thinking here of the fully cultural understanding of religion that he adopts toward the end of his career. Ruskin suggests that all religious knowledge is culturally mediated, dependent upon the forms of expression that people use and enliven in their inherited practices of worship. In other words, religion involves "human making" as does everything else in people's lives. Thus, in *Aratra Pentelici* (1871), he names the efforts of sincere religious people of his day as an imaginative "calling, in the sense of creating, things that are not, as though they were" (20.258). In presenting worship as dependent upon cultural practices and individual imagination, Ruskin allows us to read his own religiously informed arguments and metaphysical appeals as imaginative creations that make use of the cultural resources available to him. They are the imaginative attempts of a practical critic seeking to persuade his audience to read and embrace parts of their culture as the ideals, norms, and virtues that should guide their common lives. If Ruskin takes his own idea of the imagination seriously—that ethical judgments require the "help" of the artist and the audience, the writer and the reader—then these cultural guideposts require more than his own imagination to make them "real." They require the imaginative and critical response of his readers, too.

This engagement with readers is vital. It invites readers to assess and criticize Ruskin's imaginative offerings, while recovering his moral vocabulary and critical tools selectively. At the same time, readers are called to use their own moral imagination in seeking out the gifts on which their lives depend and, thus, avoiding complicity in the failure to recognize and respond to other people's efforts and suffering. As A. N. Wilson observes, Ruskin retained his respect for and attachment to Christianity, despite of all his doubts, because "he had a dread of shutting his eyes to life's imaginative possibilities." He exhorted his readers to share this dread of thinking "that one's own way of viewing the world (whether as an individual, or as a member of a class, or as a representative of any particular age or generation) was the only way."[1] This invitation to readers to become critics themselves, to imagine the broader interactions and obligations of economic life, is at odds with Marx's reliance on theoretical critique in place of moral argument.

Romanist and Protestant Idolatry

Ruskin writes by piling up the significance of his words. I mean this literally in how he layers on the meanings of his key terms. Once he introduces a concept, he adds to its relevant associations and plays out its deeper resonance. Two reasons prompt him to this writing style, both of which reflect his efforts to find common sources of authority other than God's Creation.

The first reason stems from his belief in the "vital law" of "Organic Form" as the ground of art criticism and the principle that bad art abrogates. Illustrating the truth he finds in organic form, he observes at the outset of *The Two Paths* (1859) that most people resist its unifying force not only in great art, but in their ethical reflection, too. He writes, "a sapling truth, with earth at its root and blossom on its branches; or a trenchant truth, that can cut its way through bars and sods; most men, it seems to me, dislike the sight or entertainment of. . . . And, indeed, this is no wonder; for one such truth, thoroughly accepted, connects itself strangely with others, and there is no saying what it may lead us to" (16.251).

With a similar attachment to root insights, Ruskin's style also reflects his increasing reliance on etymology as his social criticism develops. Although many of his word histories are dubious, what leads him back into classical authors for lost legacies of meaning is the hope of shocking readers into seeing a different pattern of moral reasoning than their own. He begins *Munera Pulveris* (1862–63), his essays on the conceptual elements of political economy, with a section of "Definitions." He writes, "The reader must not . . . be surprised at the care and insistence with which I have retained the literal and earliest sense of all important terms used in these papers; for a word is usually well made at the time it is first wanted, its youngest meaning has in it the full strength of its youth" (17.148). So entrenched are the habits of modern thinking, he contends, that the alternatives can be shown only by reconstructing the now peculiar significance of words. Thus, despite the variety of his interests and the range of his corpus, Ruskin's careful definition and frequent repetition of his key terms weave his seemingly disparate discussions into the fabric of his criticism.

One of these words is "idolatry," a term that expands and ramifies every time Ruskin uses it. For chronological and conceptual reasons, I begin with his discussions of idolatry in religious art. Ruskin introduces the term in arguing that the "Romanist" Church makes a mockery of the heritage of Christian art. The argument reflects the anti-Catholicism that he abandons as he moves beyond his early Evangelical devotions. More importantly, the argument reflects his new attention to the imagination's role in making and reading religious art, and it clarifies his idea of worship as a recognition of gifts.

If people are imaginative "makers" in their judgments, then how can religious art be protected from misrepresentation and misinterpretation? Ruskin answers that religious art serves magnificently so long as people create and appreciate it with the right attitude of worship, which at this stage in his writings is restricted to a reverence for God's gifts in creating life. Idolatry arises only when people fail to recognize these gifts. Thus, idolatry is a misreading of the goodness of humanly made art (and later, other things, too) caused by failing to receive gifts with the proper worship.

As a Protestant admirer of Gothic cathedrals, Ruskin stands in an uncomfortable position. He confronts the historical antipathy toward church art shown by many of the Reformers.[2] The 1850 reinvestiture of a Catholic bishop in Britain and the conversion to Catholicism by leading members of the Oxford Movement present more immediate challenges for an Evangelical caught up in the prevailing tide of British anti-Catholicism.[3] In defending his love of the Gothic, Ruskin casts the great art of the Middle Ages as Protestant in spirit. The lengths he takes the argument, and perhaps his own discomfort with it even at this time, show in the intensity of his scorn for A. W. N. Pugin (1812–52), the Catholic architect and leader of the Gothic revival in Britain.

In an 1851 polemic against "Romanist Modern Art," Ruskin warns that Pugin's architecture proves neither the superiority of Catholic theology nor the inherently tainted nature of religious art. Both claims fall prey to the basest "fatuity" of the Romanist Church, "the being lured into [it] by the glitter of it, like larks into a trap by broken glass" (9.437). As Ruskin put it several years before, the "abuse and fallacy of Romanism by which the true spirit of Christian offering is directly contradicted [is that the] treatment of the Papists' temple is eminently exhibitory; it is surface work throughout; and the danger and evil of their church decoration altogether, lie, not in its reality . . . but in its tinsel and glitter . . . ; all this being frequently thrust forward to the concealment of what is really good or great in their buildings" (8.41n). So embarrassing is this passage that Ruskin excised it from the 1880 revision of *The Seven Lamps of Architecture.* Nevertheless we see here his initial idea of idolatry. Idolatry is a misreading of things' goodness, and it manifests as a passive fascination. The idolater fixates on the superficial attractions of religious art and fails to seek out its deeper significance.

In arguing for the true significance of religious art, Ruskin cites the Israelites' history as the scriptural authority for his view of the proper function of art in worship. He notes that the prohibition against idolatry cannot mean that people may use no earthly objects in their worship, or the Hebrews would have broken the second commandment against making graven images when they built the temple and richly decorated it (Exod. 20.4). Yet God demanded "for Himself such honours, and accept[ed] for Himself such local dwelling, as had been paid and dedicated to idol gods by heathen worshippers." Despite the threat of being like the "idolatrous Egyptian," the Israelites' action testifies that things can be made in a way that promotes good worship. The proper significance of these things will be known to the people who create and receive them in the right spirit, a spirit of sacrifice. Just as there was an "external sign" of God's covenant with the Israelites in male circumcision, Ruskin writes, "so the acceptance of that covenant might be marked and signified by men, in some external sign of their love and obedience, and surrender of themselves and theirs to His will" (8.35–36).

Moving from this biblical example to the historical case of medieval art, what *marks* and *signifies* the true meaning of this work, Ruskin argues, is the same spirit of sacrifice. Religious art has always made lavish use of precious materials and human effort, he observes. The reason is not to impress worshippers with a show of opulence. The significance lies instead in the "costliness" of the expenditure of "skill," "treasure," "strength," "mind," "time," and "toil." All of these sacrifices are owed "so long as men shall receive earthly gifts from God" (8.33, 36).

Here we see how worship functions for Ruskin in the making of religious art and in the recognition of its meaning. Artists offer sacrifices in response to human beings' countless debts to God. The grateful reverence that motivates the production of religious art must be matched by the worshippers' own devotions. The artist discerns and displays the signs of God's manifold gifts in the world, and the audience grasps the giftedness of life in their own recognition of the artist's sacrifices. There can be no idolatry in religious art, Ruskin claims, when its production and reception, its making and recognition, are infused by worship.

As already stated and as developed here, worship means the recognition of a thing's goodness, where that is predicated upon an acknowledgment of a debt to, or dependence upon, the thing's maker. Ruskin's initial discussion of idolatry still operates within the framework of his early aesthetics. Although he invokes the Hebrews' covenant and thus implies the need to seek out the norms internal to and governing people's covenanted relationships, the model of God's Creation is still regulative. The goodness of all things is secured by God's purposes in making the many gifts on which life depends. Even as human making gains stature insofar as artists inspire their audience to worship by calling the gifts of God's Creation to mind, there is no suggestion that artists or anyone else "make" the standards by which people "recognize" the meaning of things.

Two years later Ruskin moves to clarify the "Proper Sense of the Word Idolatry" (1853). This piece retracts much of the vitriol he poured on Catholicism. In place of the concern with passive bedazzlement is a new concern with the idolater's active role in misrepresenting things' meaning. Ruskin now claims that idolatry is "not the mere bowing down before sculptures, but the serving or becoming the slave of any images or imaginations which stand between us and God." He shifts his ire from "the poor and untaught Christians who are this day lying prostrate before crucifixes, Bambinos, and Volto Santos" to the "many Protestants who idolize nothing but their own opinions or their own interests" (10.451–52).

This reconception of idolatry from a kind of passive bedazzlement to an active effort at misrepresentation reflects Ruskin's growing estimate of people's powers of imagination. It also augurs the more cultural and sociological directions his analysis of idolatry takes. In the earlier discussion, all that prevents the worshipper from reading the true meaning of religious art is his or her failure to adopt the requisite attitudes of gratitude and sacrifice so as to recognize the ever-present signs of God's gifts in the world. Ruskin's initial conviction that the "divine work and character" of God's Creation are clearly stamped for everyone to see still governs his critique of Romanist idolatry. In the "Proper Sense of the Word Idolatry," it seems that discerning God's purposes has become more difficult. No harm is done, Ruskin now allows, when out of "simple reverence" worshippers use images "to render conception more vivid, and feeling more intense." Idolatry threatens only when people attribute "Power to the image itself." So, while Catholics may be guilty of breaking the second commandment by bowing down before art, Protestants commit a more subtle but far worse form of idolatry. They break the first commandment by making their own "opinions" and "interests" the gods they serve before God in every aspect of their lives (10.451).

Although this new account of idolatry echoes with economic overtones, Ruskin works out these broader implications only gradually.[4] For now the most significant development is his retreat from anti-Catholicism. His initial understanding of idolatry and its corrective remains largely intact. "Protestant idolatry" involves the disordering of one's loves by failing to put the love of God first. The attitudes of gratitude and sacrifice that correct "Romanist idolatry" help to arrange one's loves, too, by calling attention to the ordering of God's gifts. While Ruskin retains this Christian moral concern with the task of arranging one's loves for the many goods of life, he addresses with increasing sophistication the obstacles to knowing how best to arrange one's loves. Specifically, in redefining idolatry as a willful distortion of things' meaning, he allows that people can make their own "opinions" and "interests" the symbolic medium of their evaluative judgments. This insight leads to his concerns with the abuses of power and the construction of desire that he associates with the idolatry of modern art.

Modern Idolatry and Imaginative Religion

In *Modern Painters* 3 (1856) Ruskin returns to discuss idolatry and art. He gives a historical account of the abuse of power and the construction of desire that mark the idolatry of Renaissance art and modern life more generally. The history of religious art since the Middle Ages is a tale of unmet promise. Medieval paintings, he claims, were highly imaginative partly because their creators lacked the technical innovations of the Renaissance. As a result, the imaginative work of medieval painters left room for their audience's imagination. In Ruskin's words, "The reader glanced at [the painting] as a glittering symbol, and went on to form truer images for himself." The symbols in medieval painting invite an active response leading the audience to ponder the highly symbolic cosmological vision of medieval iconographic art. Here the "glitter" of medieval art actually contributes to a proper worship of God when secured by this richly evocative and full vision of the good. But for Ruskin, the untutored faith of the Middle Ages is progressively displaced by the studied disbelief of modernity.

According to Ruskin, the technical advances of the Renaissance held forth the promise that artists might better "realize," or "vision forth," the two great subjects of religious art—the "history of the Redeemer" and present-day spiritual truths about the world to come. "But as soon as art obtained the power of realization, it obtained also that of *assertion*" (5.72–74). As artists produced unprecedented realism in their paintings, they undermined belief in the religious facts they ostensibly portrayed. They replaced the crude symbols of medieval paintings with "the graceful emptiness" of images stripped of the "power and presence of God." Into this void artists inserted two things. They made their own technical skills the chief attractions of their art and the admiration of their audience the sole aim of their efforts (5.83–84). They also depicted "customs [they] had never practised, and gods in whom [they] had never believed. Such art could, of course, have no help from the virtues, nor claim the energies of men." In the end, the "ideal art of modern Europe [became] the shadow of a shadow," a doubly insincere form of idolatry (5.92–93).

This brief overview of Ruskin's narrative of the decline of modern art underscores his sense that worship is inescapable in human life. The turn from Christianity that he reads in the record of Renaissance painting is not a refusal of worship. It simply replaces a true worship of the Christian God with a false worship of other gods and, more disturbingly, of people entirely undeserving of such acclaim. Not only did these Renaissance artists lord their power over their admirers, but they also instructed their audience to desire the very things they proffered—a vapid technical expertise and empty images of the good. The abuse of power that typifies Ruskin's account of the idolatry of money requires a similar but more wide-reaching training in desire, as I discuss later. Already, though, we have before us the two sins that define the double idolatry that he comes to identify with industrial capitalism—the active misrepresentation of things' goodness by capitalists and the passive fascination of consumers beholden to these false visions of the good.

In *Modern Painters* 3 Ruskin makes fleeting mention of the virtues. When he discusses idolatry and art again fifteen years later in *Aratra Pentelici,* he examines more closely the virtues that people cultivate in their production and reception of art. The dramatic shift, however, is his praise for the virtues that the Greeks developed in sculpting and worshipping their many gods and goddesses. What has happened to Ruskin's Christian conception of idolatry?

These lectures come at the end of a decade in which Ruskin borrows from Friedrich Max Müller's philological approach to comparative religion and of Greek mythology in particular. Ruskin's growing respect for Greek art, philosophy, and especially religion is evidence of this influence. I have noted the authority that Ruskin grants to the etymology of Greek and Latin terms. This appeal to the origins of language is consonant with Müller's *Science of Language* (1861) and his Oxford lecture series on the topic (1861–64). In Müller's theory "the formation of *roots*, the 'ultimate facts' of language," is pregnant with an original power. In the names of the Hindu deities in the Vedas, for example, he reads both the terms for physical phenomena, the sun, the storm, and so on, and also the infinite power that attends the accurate perception of all things. Translated into the concerns of the current chapter, the "making" of words involves the "recognition" of the higher spiritual reality that Müller believes is present in all things. When joined with a sense of the moral constraints imposed by this recognition of a higher good, religions arise. As quoted by Eric Sharpe, religion for Müller "is 'the perception of the infinite under such manifestations as are able to influence the moral character of man.'" This highly generalized theory of language and the origins of religions fits Ruskin's long-standing concern with the connection between the making of moral character and the recognition of goodness that a true vision of the telos brings.

Ruskin's references in *Aratra Pentelici* to the "unseen" spiritual forces that shadow human perceptions of material objects may reflect his dabbling in Müller's writings. In the details of the argument, however, we see Ruskin putting this theory to his own purposes. Müller posits the progenitors of a language as something akin to pure visionaries who are able to discern the infinite in its full meaning and power. There follows a decline into the childish stage of mythology.[5] Ruskin's lectures on *The Queen of the Air* (1869) acknowledge his general debts to "recent philologists," but they show a greater respect for Greek mythology than Müller exhibits.[6] In *Aratra Pentelici* Ruskin finds further reason to praise the "childishness of the Greek mind" in its earliest stages of artistic endeavor (20.247). The "mimetic instinct," the desire to imitate living creatures in the world, is the first impulse toward sculpture. Nowhere is this instinct more apparent than in children's play, Ruskin claims; and "in national as in actual childhood, it is not merely the *making*, but the *making-believe* . . . that is delightful." In sculpting and, even more so, in the performing of drama, one sees the "life-shaping" powers that animate cultures and that are at work in all imaginative activity, religious and otherwise (20.221).

Ruskin's interest in the "making" and "making-believe" of the sculptural and dramatic arts is a prelude to another grand historical narrative of artistic greatness followed by decline. Full cultural development, he argues, requires two other instincts than the mimetic, the instincts of "Idolatry, and Discipline." In progressing from mimicry to idolatry, most cultures stop imitating the creatures around them and begin to represent their creators. Thus, the "realistic or idolizing instinct" emerges as "the desire to see as substantial the powers that are unseen." What is striking here, when compared with *Modern Painters* 3, is that Ruskin now accepts idolatry, at least provisionally. Idolatry is simply an "imaginative longing," the "desire of companionship with images" (20.223, 228, 229).

The mere observation of people bowing down before church art or sculpting gods and goddesses is not evidence of idolatry. Such actions testify instead to the vital role of imagination in the "making" and "making-believe" of human life and cultures. When Ruskin first discusses the imagination in *Modern Painters* 2, there could be no doubt about which painters were truly imaginative and which were not. The work of the intuitive, prophetic faculty of the imagination directly mirrored the perfections of God's Creation. Here in *Aratra Pentelici,* however, idolatry and imagination are separated by a fine line. They are, in fact, two sides of the same coin, the capacity for forming images to make abstract things more vivid and meaningful. In Ruskin's words, imagination is nothing more than the "noble and truth-seeking phase" of idolatry—"that is to say, [imagination is] the invention of material symbols which may lead us to contemplate the character and nature of gods, spirits, or abstract virtues and powers, without in the least implying the actual presence of such Beings among us, or even their possession, in reality, of the forms we attribute to them" (20.242). This imaginative invention of gods, spirits, virtues, and powers, which may or may not exist and which may or may not have the forms attributed to them, is the vital contribution, the great gift, that Greek sculpture and drama made "to the happy and holy imagination of a sincerely religious people" (20.232).

Greek idolatry, "the invention and service of Idols," was not vicious in itself. For Ruskin, the "idolizing" instinct that led the Greeks to sculptural and dramatic representations of their deities produced religious practices that trained people in "the pure habits and perfect delights of an honest life." Greek art and religion served, therefore, as a training ground for people's virtues and pleasures. Here we see the primary role of religions for Ruskin. By directing people toward the most worthy and beneficial ideals, vividly depicted through imaginative renderings of the divine, religions serve to guide, to enliven, in a word, to train, people's desires. This emphasis on practical training is clear in the movement toward the third instinct of "discipline" (20.218, 233).

What directs the imaginative "making" and "making-believe" of artistic and religious practices either toward sincere worship or toward base idolatry is whether or not a people also has an "ethos" (Ruskin uses the Greek term) that, as he puts it, "chooses the right thing to idolize" (20.227). Note how radically different this conception of idolatry is now that Ruskin accords full power to individuals' imagination. Even as he retains the concept, judgments of "idolatry" depend not on direct appeals to God's commandments but on careful examination of the interaction between a people's religious practices and the broader culture. What ideals animate people's efforts? What do they desire above all else? What gives these cultural symbols of stature, worth, achievement, and vitality their power in individuals' imagination?

Note as well the circularity in Ruskin's argument. The Greek character was molded by artistic and religious practices that imagined gods, spirits, virtues, and powers that may or may not have been real. In the "making-believe" of art and religion, the Greeks forged the telos that guided their lives and structured their moral judgments. In other words, the act of *recognizing* things' goodness, including the goodness of their own artistic and religious productions, is itself dependent upon the imaginative *making* of the ideals and standards of these practices. A culture and its vision of the good—that is, its "Ethic law" (20.228)—are the contingent products of people's imaginative creations as they embrace and rework the cultural forms that they have inherited. Here the "making" and "recognition" of goodness and the worship that sustains these efforts all operate, for Ruskin, only within the practices of a specific historical culture.

Ruskin's foray into Greek sculpture and mythology might seem irrelevant to his views about Christianity and other "mature" traditions. In *Aratra Pentelici,* though, he presents the religious practices of his fellow Victorians as another case of "making" and "making-believe." Even Christian worship attains no higher than verisimilitude—that is, the "'[making] something trustworthy by passionate desire that it should be so'—which exactly describes the temper of religious persons at the present day, who are kindly and sincere" (20.258). The connection to the discussion of

Greek religion is clear. "Sincerely" religious people engage the practices of their traditions in imaginative ways that commit them to worthy cultural ideals. By contrast, the similarities between this portrait of a culturally mediated and imaginatively performed worship and the all-encompassing spirit of the entirely lived worship that pervades Ruskin's early aesthetics seems much more tenuous, at least until we remember the teleological shape of his ethics. Indeed his focal interest remains the proper guidance of "passionate desire" through the making of good character. But now the telos that properly structures people's desires and virtues is a culturally situated, not a divinely revealed, vision of the good.

Perhaps we should read this fully cultural conception of religion as the sour grapes of a Victorian whose early faith flagged. Scholars continue to debate how far Ruskin drifted away from his Evangelical upbringing. But as John Barbour notes, Ruskin's self-portrait of his "un-conversion" has little to do with intellectual doubts or specific beliefs. Instead Ruskin rejects the stunted imagination he finds, for example, in a monk's blindness to the beauty of the surrounding mountains or in a preacher's condemnation of all of the inhabitants of nearby Turin, except for those gathered at this one Waldensian chapel for services. According to Barbour, in passing such judgments Ruskin repeats two common themes in other Victorian deconversion narratives—an "aesthetic critique" of a Christianity deadened to the beauty of art and nature and a "moral revulsion" against the social callousness of Evangelical doctrine. Again this is not a story of lost belief. Rather, as Barbour's integrated portrait shows, the aesthetic, ethical, and social factors at work in Ruskin's recollection of his deconversion fit his newly cultural conception of religion.[7] Early on in his writings, there is no acknowledgment of the "practical" nature of his religiosity—that his desires were forged, in part, by his upbringing in the practices of his birth tradition. As he moves away from Evangelicalism, he sees how these practices helped form specific character traits, social attitudes, and aesthetic judgments, and he finds his birth tradition lacking.

Ruskin's cultural account of religion reflects his broader turn toward the human practices of cultures that I have been tracing out in part 2. One important consequence of this turn is the apparent unmooring of "right" desire from a divinely sanctioned ordering of the good. Desire remains central to Ruskin's criticism. So too, the development of good character is still a core concern of his. But it would seem that the task of imagining and articulating the vision of the good needed to direct and upbuild people's wide-ranging desires and purposes has been radically reconceived.

I read Ruskin as placing himself among the sincere religious people of his day. When he criticizes Victorian culture in *Aratra Pentelici,* he stands opposed to the "we" he condemns. By contrast with the childishness of earlier "Heathen and Christian art," he writes, "We . . . are now, in all that we do, absolutely without sincerity;—absolutely, therefore, without imagination, and without virtue" (20.254). His task as a critic, then, is partly to rekindle in his audience an "imaginative longing," a "desire for companionship with images," to enable them to seek out ideals, norms, and virtues made available by all of their cultural practices, including the religious ones, and then to remake these offerings to help foster in themselves and others an acknowledgment of the gifted character of life.[8] How faithful Ruskin is to the strictures and possibilities of this more contingent cultural analysis and engaged ethics we will see when I return to discuss the idolatry of money and the religious appeals that he invokes to justify it.

The Use and Abuse of Religion: Marx's Critique

This sketch of Ruskin's evolving views on religions and idolatry shows how he extends the reach of the shaping powers of people's imagination once again. Not only do artists bring their desires and ends to bear on the subjects and things they represent, but religious worshippers are also active makers of meaning in inventing and performing deeply symbolic practices that evoke their sense of the divine. Yet Ruskin always balances the human *making* of things with the evaluative task of *recognizing* things' goodness. Thus, he writes in *Aratra Pentelici* that the value of the best Greek sculptures lies in their "being on the side of the gods against what is base and ungodly" so that "the kind of worth which is in them is . . . indeed worshipful, as having its source with the gods" (20.226). How can the value of the things that people make have their "source" with deities, the knowledge of which depends upon people's imaginative constructions and communal practices of worship?

This question serves as a useful transition to Marx's theory of the making of religion. The oddly circular relationship between the vast energies that people devote to worship and the unquestionable authority that people "find" in their evaluative standards is precisely the kind of cultural myopia and religious mystification that Marx aims to diagnose and expose. The challenge posed by Marx for Ruskin's teleological criticism is profound. Indeed I suggest that Marx above all other nineteenth-century critics demonstrates the limitations and downright dangers of the kind of talk about ends that we read in Ruskin. We share those suspicions, and rightly so, but is it wise to labor under them uncritically? Ruskin also diagnoses social abuses of power and the cultural construction of desire, even as he affirms the possibility and, indeed, the necessity of an engaged ethics that imagines and fashions desires, virtues, and ends that are good for oneself and others. Marx's challenge to Ruskin's appeals to religion, morality, and metaphysics is whether they amount to anything more than mystification on behalf on Ruskin's idealized vision of the good. Ruskin's challenge to Marx, though, is whether we can simply refuse to imagine how religion and morality (not metaphysics) and the other resources of cultures can be made into "binding" commitments that people embrace and perform as aspects of a common vision of good lives and a good society. Here we stand at a critical divide in nineteenth-century social thought, one with lasting implications for today, even as some of the other aspects of Marx's theorizing lose their hold on political, economic, and ethical debates, for better and for worse.

The "criticism of religion is the premise of all criticism"; so begins Marx's "Contribution to the Critique of Hegel's *Philosophy of Right*" (1843). For Marx, religions are a primary source of the historical construction of ideologies, and they give insight into processes by which groups of people organize and justify their authority, power, and privilege over others. While Marx criticizes religion from the start, his analysis of commodity fetishism in *Capital* represents, I argue, the full working out of his anti-metaphysical suspicions. His analysis of the commodity sits within his broader account of industrial capitalism's relentless leveling of all existing qualitative distinctions. This historical argument is the means by which he aims to free his later "scientific" analysis from his earlier dependence on Hegel. An unfortunate though fully intended effect, I claim, is that the analysis of commodity fetishism further removes ethical resources from Marx's late social theory, making his moral arguments, such as they are, even more a matter of abstract theory. Although I applaud him for challenging the sorts of metaphysical appeals that Ruskin makes, Ruskin also offers critical tools precluded by Marx's theorizing.

Marx's account of commodity fetishism is continuous with his "projection theory" of religion. He does not, in fact, develop a full-blown theory, but one can be pieced together from his scattered remarks about religion in his early writings. The term "projection" actually comes from George Eliot (1819–80), née Marian Evans. Her 1854 translation of Ludwig Feuerbach's (1804–72) *Essence of Christianity* (1840) uses "projection" instead of "objectification" for the German word Vergegenständlichung.[9] As Van Harvey describes Feuerbach's critique of Hegel, the chief problem lies in Hegel's "inveterate tendency to treat abstract predicates as entities."[10] Rather than acknowledging that "thinking," for example, is the activity of people in the world, Hegel takes "thoughts" themselves as entities belonging to the unfolding history of Spirit. For Feuerbach and Marx, the truth in Hegel's philosophy is that people engage in a similar process of projection. People take human attributes or qualities and project them onto God, the gods, or whatever they revere. These human attributes or qualities thus become inverted in people's self-understanding, just as a slide-projector inverts the image it shines on a screen. Consider how this process might work in Christianity. Such human attributes as loving, knowing, and suffering get projected onto God as the perfect attributes of an *all*-loving, *all*-knowing, and *all*-suffering Being. But this sacrifice of human qualities to God robs people of the awareness of humanity, joined in the species, as the actual bearer of these perfections.

For Feuerbach, this inverted consciousness is the prerequisite to people's realizing their own perfection in the species. Marx, however, adds to this portrait of people's sacrifice to God, finding in it the sense of oppression that motivates the profound need that religion really serves. That is the need for consolation. For Marx, the suffering so prominently depicted in many religious traditions always expresses human suffering. Here we arrive at his main disagreement with Feuerbach. What Feuerbach sees as a "natural" process in the development of "human consciousness" is actually historical and social. By demonstrating that people "make religion" and produce its "inverted world consciousness," Feuerbach brings the critique of religion near to completion.[11] But he fails to grasp that religions serve more basic and pressing needs than those of intellectual development. As Marx puts it in his famous, though half-remembered, passage, religion is not simply an "opiate"; it is "the sigh of the oppressed creature, the heart of a heartless world, just as it is the spirit of spiritless conditions." Only after understanding the concrete needs that religions serve in historical societies will it be possible to overcome the deadening effects of false consciousness.[12]

Marx presses the argument for historical and social analysis in his *Theses on Feuerbach* (1845, published 1888). He praises Feuerbach for demonstrating that there are two worlds, "a religious, imaginary world and a real one." Yet Feuerbach "overlooks the fact that . . . the chief thing still remains to be done. For the fact that the secular basis detaches itself from itself and establishes itself in the clouds as an independent realm can only be explained by the cleavage and self-contradictions within this secular basis." In the following few *Theses* Marx identifies the "ensemble of [existing] social relations," not any human essence, as what gets falsely projected onto the heavens.[13] In this dual emphasis on social relations and symbolic projection, we see the twin problems that accompany Marx's understanding of the mystifying use of religion to express human suffering.

The primary problem that religion helps meet is the existence of social conflict and oppression. Power relationships mark every type of society, and in *The German Ideology* (1845, published 1929), Marx traces economic exploitation all the way back to the patriarchal family. The "contradictions" in the modern "division of labour" are based, he claims, "on the natural division of labour in the family . . . where wife and children are the slaves of the husband." Just as wage labor is the contingent product of industrial capitalism, the "natural" fact of male dominance is the historical product of the earliest peoples' cooperative efforts to fulfill their basic needs. With the cooperation first seen in the family, certain social relations emerge and become ordered into patterned roles, complete with enforceable sanctions against crossing the now settled divisions among different classes of people.[14] By a similar process, Marx argues, every historical type of society has been produced. Material needs lead the way, and economic cooperation follows. Only then come the ideologies that justify the ownership and labor patterns and the role-based attributes, duties, and privileges that constitute the "ensemble of social relations" in a given community.

I use the word "community" here to introduce the second problem that religions help to meet for Marx. Even as societies are riven by divisions, unity is required. Religions mask the "cleavages" between different classes, genders, and other social groups, and they engage people in upholding these unequal relations. Marx agrees, for example, with Feuerbach's discovery that the "earthly family" is the "secret of the holy family."[15] In Christian doctrine the mantle of God's divine authority passes only to the son. Yet tremendous pains are taken in the Gospel stories to ennoble Mary's virgin birth. A kind of symbolic, if practically unattainable, elevation of women's "purity" as mothers is achieved. The stories function to maintain women in their roles and to offer much needed consolation. I have filled in the details of Marx's account, adding to his argument that the gendering of social roles is the first historical form of ideology. Indeed other than claiming that in the "language of politics, laws, morality, religion, metaphysics, etc., of a people" we find symbol systems that reflect and legitimize a people's "ensemble of social relations," he offers relatively little concrete analysis. Instead he urges that the "earthly family" and similarly unjust social structures "be criticised in theory and revolutionised in practice."[16]

Marx's suspicions of the legitimizing effects of metaphysical systems apply to Ruskin's use of religious appeals to reinforce the orders of nature and society. Marx's narrative of the formation of different types of society is also more persuasive than the narratives of Greek and Renaissance art that Ruskin tells. Ruskin's trickle-down theory of high culture, which posits the willful misrepresentations of Renaissance artists as the historical cause of modernity's power abuses and constructed desires, is less plausible than Marx's own grand theorizing. There is an important difference, however, between Ruskin's approach as a critic and Marx's approach as a theorist. Ruskin continually moves back and forth between the "theoretical" level of social analysis and the "practical" level of human action. In other words, cultures cannot operate for Ruskin apart from people's choosing and, thus, evaluating their activities and commitments. Marx's analysis, by contrast, never accounts for individual agency despite his claims to ground theory in practice. That Marx remains at the level of theory and relies on a philosophy of history, not the moral imagination of engaged individuals, to correct the failings of industrial capitalism becomes clearer in his account of "The Fetishism of the Commodity and Its Secret."

Industrial Capitalism as Symbolic Machine

In chapter 2 I contrasted Marx's use of Hegel's "work model" of activity and Ruskin's model of a "social practice." I argued there that the terms of Marx's early theory leave him unable to account for the cultivation of excellences and the adoption and revision of practical ends and standards that help make for some of the best kinds of work. In opening *Capital* Marx narrates the historical construction of the division of labor and the wage system under industrial capitalism. What is so striking about the argument is that he does not merely claim that the arts and crafts celebrated by Ruskin become historically untenable. The purpose of Marx's argument is more sweeping.

For Marx the great benefit of the industrial machine is that it generates an entirely novel scheme of evaluation that supplants normative judgments.[17] Let me clarify this crucial claim by placing it within Marx's philosophy of history. The argument of the first chapter of *Capital* is that by generating a new kind of economic good (namely, the "commodity") and a new form of "value" (namely, "exchange-value"), industrial capitalism unmasks all past and present qualitative measures and their ethical justifications. Simply put, these qualitative standards and ethical appeals are necessarily ideological. In the case of bourgeois societies, the existing liberal ideals, norms, and standards are of limited use, except for conducting an "immanent critique" of how the social and economic conditions of these societies contradict their professed principles. In fact, the principles are used ideologically to prop up the dominant group's interests, as Marx argues very effectively. The "language of politics, laws, morality, religion, metaphysics, etc." always performs this function in his view. Thus, liberation from contemporary culture, not the creative use of its resources, is the route to the historical achievement of a rationally cooperative "association of free men."[18]

But if all normative standards are untrustworthy, then how does the critic imagine a "better" society? And how does the critic enlist others in the effort of societal change? In my reading of Marx, his theoretical analysis of commodity fetishism answers these questions. The critic does not imagine new principles; the critic does not detail the contents of good lives or the shape of good societies. The critic does not have to enlist others in embracing such a vision of the good, good lives, the common good, or even shared goods. Nor could this be done without committing the sin of ideology. The religious language is appropriate. Indeed the "secret" of commodity fetishism is that this peculiar form of worship is what enlists people in redeeming their society without their realizing it. I develop this argument by clarifying Marx's account of commodity fetishism and then setting this analysis and its secret in the context of his overall theory.

The fetishism of the commodity refers to the mystical power that commodities appear to take on in capitalist exchange. Only by understanding the dual character of a commodity, Marx argues, can we analyze how this power is generated and what its worship entails. "A commodity appears at first sight an extremely obvious, trivial thing. But its analysis brings out that it is a very strange thing, abounding in metaphysical subtleties and theological niceties. So far as it is a use-value, there is nothing mysterious about it. . . . The form of wood, for instance, is altered if a table is made out of it. Nevertheless the table continues to be wood, an ordinary, sensuous thing." The first feature of a commodity is that it must serve some needs, or else people would not buy it. A table meets needs through its "natural" properties, or the "use-values" produced when people take lumber and work it into a useful thing.

In addition to being useful, however, a commodity must also, and more importantly, be exchangeable. Marx continues, "as soon as [the table] emerges as a commodity, it changes into a thing which transcends sensuousness. It not only stands with its feet on the ground, but, in relation to all other commodities, it stands on its head, and evolves out of its wooden brain grotesque ideas, far more wonderful than if it were to begin dancing of its own free will." What gives a commodity its seemingly mystical power is its "exchange-value," or what Marx means by "value" pure and simple. He notes that as the system of capitalist exchange develops over time, commodities are brought into pricing relationships with one another. Each one becomes measured relative to every other commodity traded on the market. This purely relative measure of market pricing becomes so fascinating and attractive that the "use-values" that presumably motivate people's economic choices serve only as the "bearer" of the power of "value."[19]

So great is this power that further explanation is needed to understand the full process by which "value" is generated. We can understand this process best by relating Marx's analysis of commodity fetishism back to his projection theory of religion. As in his early critique of the social functions of religious symbols, the symbolic power of the commodity must reflect the social conditions of its production. The basic historical factor is the division of labor. Not only do the producers of commodities become ever more minutely divided as operatives, but they are also increasingly distanced from the consumers of their products. Nevertheless, tremendous growth in economic interdependence occurs simultaneously. Social relations multiply in number even as they become more impersonal. The burgeoning of these progressively more interdependent yet impersonal relations, all distantly mediated through market exchange, radically disrupts the existing patterns, roles, and relationships that constituted social life. It is this new "cash-nexus" that generates the mystical power of value.

This power is symbolic and productive at the same time. Most importantly, the worship of value achieves a kind of cooperation. In Marx's words, the value of "the commodity reflects the social characteristics of men's own labour as objective characteristics of the products of labour themselves." Recall that the term "objectification" echoes with the word "projection." Value is "objective" in the sense that this "socio-natural" property, which capitalist exchange projects onto everything, emerges as the decisive property of any commodity. Value dominates, defines, and even distorts commodities' meanings. This is because the whole point of commodity production is to make money, whether to pay workers' wages or to increase owners' capital. But here is where the magic of commodity fetishism transpires. Because no society could operate if making money were not only the *dominant,* but also the *exclusive,* end of people's activities, the underlying "use-values" and social relations of economic life must still figure in somewhere in capitalist exchange. For Marx both are at work, though only symbolically. That is, the value of any commodity is a reflection of the social relations between people's labors in producing what they need and use, only now projected onto the money relations between things.

In Marx's theory, industrial capitalism has a double operation as a symbolic machine. We see this in the strange situation of "material [*dinglich*] relations between persons and social relations between things."[20] In the first half of this passage, the machine-like workings of the capitalist economy are emphasized. The machined precision shows not just in the relentless drive to make money. It appears in people's relations, too, because even human labor is commodified, leaving people to interact with each other only through exchange relations. In the second half of the passage, the symbolic dimension comes to the fore. Curiously, the "value" of everything traded on the market reflects, in a mediated form, the underlying cooperation between people who work to produce goods to meet one another's needs, even though they do not grasp the true ends of their activity. The moral regard implicit in the terms "cooperation," "goods," "needs," and "ends" is kept out of view by the machine-like rounds of capitalist production and exchange. Amazingly, while these moral concerns are hidden from participants, they are still cared for by the symbolic operation of "value," which is itself the perfect product of industrial capitalism insofar as it generates ever-greater social wealth and interdependence while mirroring people's ever-more extensive social relations, though in a mystifying form. Let me stress that I have brought out the ethical element implicit in Marx's analysis. There is no hint in *Capital* that he is engaged in anything more than a theoretical description.

Theory without Ethics?

I read the broader argument of the opening chapter of *Capital* as an effort to highlight the "injustice" of industrial capitalism without relying on normative claims or engaging in an ethical debate about the good. This fits with Marx's distrust of religion, metaphysics, and morality. The mystification of all existing ideologies must be cleared away. I question, though, his strategy of relying on theory to do the work of ethics. I want to begin this argument by drawing a contrast between Marx's and Ruskin's understandings of "power." While both of them associate power with "life" and "energy," the best synonym is "capacity." Marx equates Arbeitskraft, "labour-power," with Arbeitsvermögen, "the capacity for labour."[21] This idea of the "capacity for labour" conveys a generic sense of capacity. It lacks the moralism accompanying Ruskin's use of power to mean a human capacity directed toward a good end. The difference is not accidental.

Marx's historical account of the construction of the commodity form aims to undermine the kind of moralism we find in Ruskin. As industrial capitalism progresses, Marx argues, its impersonal and value-driven production of commodities reduces every kind of labor down to "human labour pure and simple." Qualitative use-value—"the 'how' and 'what' of labour"—is replaced by quantitative exchange-value—"the 'how much', [that is] the temporal duration of labour."[22] Marx observes that in earlier economic systems what defined the properties and worth of goods were the distinctive use-values that workers produced and that consumers sought. Those use-values depended on the practical knowledge and crafts associated with the making of any good. But as clothing, for example, becomes manufactured by workers paid on the wage system, the worth of the labor that produces it gets homogenized into mere units of time. Older qualitative measures governing weaving, tailoring, and the other crafts vanish. The useful or beautiful qualities of a piece of clothing have no real significance beyond the "value" that the commodity commands on the market. More significantly, no distinctions of human excellence, as measured by the standards of social practices, continue to characterize people's work.

The relevant measure of human labor shifts from the *qualities* of discrete *kinds* of labor to *quantities* of purely *abstract* labor. In Marx's language exchange-values are "merely congealed quantities of homogeneous human labour, i.e. of human labour-power expended without regard to the form of its expenditure."[23] Due to the historical transformation wrought by industrial capitalism, all forms of labor, along with the human powers expended through them, become fully exchangeable in terms of value and are thus *e-qualized.* I hyphenate this term to convey both the movement toward "equality" in Marx's argument and his conviction that equality depends on the elimination of all qualitative distinctions. In his analysis of the commodity, all work becomes the same. And the leveling impetus of commodity production eliminates the possibility that people might realize their capacities, or excellences, by directing their efforts toward the attainment of the goods and ends shared with others in social practices. This *e-qualization* of qualities into mere quantities progressively expels the normative standards previously used to evaluate human endeavor and character. All forms of moral and social regard are replaced by the hegemonic standards of the market.

For Marx, commodity production and, with it, the emergence of "value" as the generic measure of expended human powers not only drive the modern world toward a belief in human equality, one of the professed principles of bourgeois society.[24] This leveling process, this de-ethicization of people's activities, also teaches that commodity fetishism is the form of religious *mystification* that, strangely enough, achieves the *demystification* of all metaphysical pretensions. That conclusion is the real "secret" of Marx's analysis of commodity fetishism.

Indeed, "value" is not so much an obscuring sign as it is a progressive force. Although value "does not have its description branded on its forehead," it powerfully "transforms every product of labour into a social hieroglyphic."[25] I read this passage as a reference to the biblical story of the protective mark that Yahweh put on Cain's forehead after he killed his brother Abel and before he set out to build the first city (Gen. 4.15–17). These images of an active, present God who protects and of human beings who engage in ethical reflection as they seek to build better lives both run counter to the thrust of Marx's theorizing. Like him I am suspicious of the ways that appeals to divine presence get used by the powerful to authorize their economic and moral standing. No doubt Marx's theoretical analysis of commodity fetishism is also a towering achievement that illuminates the seemingly out-of-control automaticity of the industrial capitalist economy. Yet he remains so theoretical that he removes ethical discernment and moral action from people's control, placing all agency in the hands of another god, the capitalist god of "value."

Marx himself has a fetish, his "scientific" conviction that history's progress is inevitable. His chapter on the commodity concludes with a summary contrast between the social forms found in the past and anticipated in the future. Here his normative purposes finally press through the theoretical account. The comparison among bourgeois civil society, medieval feudalism, the patriarchal rural peasant family, and "freely associated men" condenses Marx's warnings against idealizing past social forms—especially the order, faith, and community of the Middle Ages—as palliatives to industrial capitalism's ills. Feudalism is a larger version of the patriarchal family. Social relations in both are personal and mutually dependent because everyone belongs together, finding his or her place in social roles fixed by such "natural" characteristics as birth, sex, age, or talent. In theory, at least, the impersonal, isolating, equalizing, and even exploitative relations of bourgeois society are the necessary route to a better society.

Here value's activity is decisive. It clears away existing ideological norms and the social divisions they reinforce. It achieves "universality" and "rationality" in social relations. This movement remains obscured so long as commodity fetishism persists, and yet this fetishism is also the form of worship that eliminates all others, until it too stands unmasked, its historical task fulfilled. In Marx's words, "The religious reflections of the real world can . . . vanish only when the practical relations of everyday life between man and man, and man and nature, generally present themselves to him in a transparent and rational form. The veil is not removed from the countenance of the social life-process . . . until it becomes production by freely associated men, and stands under their conscious and planned control." Marx's historical narrative of the emergence and function of the commodity rejects the hope that Ruskin locates in the development of good character and the forging of shared goods through the social practices that people find and create in their cultures. It also rejects worship categorically, from the "ancient worship of nature" and "tribal religions" to modern European religions and commodity fetishism.[26] Yet Marx's own hopes for the unveiling of industrial capitalist society echo with religious allusions. Whereas, in the Creation story in Genesis, the "countenance" of the "deep" is a forbidding abyss requiring God's original ordering of things, Marx envisions a radical, new creation with humanity stepping in for God, clearing away the clutter of religion, metaphysics, and morality and attaining a now-transparent vision of "the countenance of the social life-process."

Marx's rejection of worship stands in sharp contrast to Ruskin's insistence that worship is necessary in human life. In chapter 3 I detailed Ruskin's attempts to foster a natural piety in his audience. In the rest of this chapter, I examine his portrait of the idolatry of money to show that his antidote to this form of idolatry can be read either as a "true" worship of God's perfect Creation or, better, as a communal piety, a reverence for the gifts one receives as a member of a community.

The Idolatry of Money in Practice

Ruskin's critique of the idolatry of money is impressionistic and exhortative. He devotes more of his efforts, in fact, to analyzing the proper functioning of a money economy, and I return to his debt analysis of money in chapter 7. I approach his discussion of the idolatry of money here by reading it against the backdrop of his earlier reliance on a Christian moral framework of well-ordered loves, which I have already located in his writings on art and idolatry from the 1850s.

When Ruskin shifts his attention to the "idolatry" of money in *Munera Pulveris,* we see two marked developments in his use of the concept. First, he describes idolatry as a pervasive phenomenon reaching beyond religious art into all aspects of a culture. Second, he identifies the worship of money as the crux of Victorian idolatry. In *Modern Painters* 3 Ruskin focused on Renaissance paintings as the site of artists' abuses of power, their fabrications of the good, and their corruption of their audiences' desires. Now he presents these distortions of people's imagination of things' meaning as systematized through the operation of money in the marketplace of industrial capitalism.

I use the language of "system" to capture the theoretical overtones of Ruskin's critique. He seeks to provide his contemporaries with a vision of their culture and economy and invites them to see their lives in an entirely new light. Unlike Marx, though, he does not construct a complete "theory," a fully integrated explanation abstracted from people's everyday activities and designed to reveal what they otherwise could not recognize at all. This theme of recognition and the quest for a vision of people's common life are crucial to understanding the differences between Ruskin and Marx, as critic and as theorist, respectively.

Two related questions motivate Ruskin's discussion of the idolatry of money. In what various ways do the peculiar attractions of money show in his contemporaries' desires, choices, and interactions? Why is money such a powerful force in Victorian society? Ruskin's answers to the first question fit his concerns as a practical critic more closely as he invites his audience to ponder the apparent irrationalities in their own behavior. He does not rest content with these practical concerns, however, as we shall see.

I begin, then, with Ruskin's scattered observations about the appearances of idolatry in Victorian culture. Consider, first, "one of the most curious, though commonest forms of the Eidolon, or Phantasm of Wealth," he writes. The asceticism of the rich—the arduous making of money, not to spend and enjoy all that it buys, but to accumulate and hoard it—"hardly seem[s] a covetable" kind of life. But people admire these hoarders of wealth and devote themselves to joining their ranks of austerity. How could money become so attractive when it is only a *means* to the goods people seek in life, he puzzles (17.169, 168).

Ruskin explains this phenomenon in two ways, each of which highlights an aspect of the "religious" dynamics of the idolatry of money. First, he describes the economic practices of his fellow Victorians as producing a false religiosity. Contrasting his contemporaries' avowed and actual religious practices, he muses, "Now, we have, indeed, a nominal religion, to which we pay tithes of property and sevenths of time; but we have also a practical and earnest religion, to which we devote nine-tenths of our property, and six-sevenths of our time. And we dispute a great deal about the nominal religion; but we are all unanimous about this practical one; of which I think you will admit that the ruling goddess may be best generally described as the 'Goddess of Getting-on,' or 'Britannia of the Market'" (18.447–48).

Earlier in *The Political Economy of Art* (1857), Ruskin describes the false religion of his day, using an ethnographic vignette of the merchant class. He is shocked by the disciplines his fellow urbanites inflict on themselves. "Our large trading cities bear to me very nearly the aspect of monastic establishments in which the roar of the mill-wheel and the crane takes the place of other devotional music; and in which the worship of Mammon or Moloch is conducted with a tender reverence and an exact propriety; the merchant rising to his Mammon matins with the self-denial of an anchorite, and expatiating the frivolities into which he may be beguiled in the course of the day by late attendance at Mammon vespers" (16.138).[27] The vaunted industry and rectitude of the commercial classes are, indeed, painfully wrought, lending weight to their claims to just profits. But these excellences and this standard of justice are not recognized simply by the force of their inherent authority. A set of practices legitimizes these virtues and norms in the eyes of their participants and others, too. Again, for Ruskin as practical critic, character is one of the chief products of a culture, and the activities of a culture are the primary source of a people's evaluative measures.

In Ruskin's second explanation of money's fantastic transformation from a means to an end, the practical structures of Mammon worship are complemented by the desire to worship and be worshipped by other people. As he observes in *Munera Pulveris,* there must be something in people's perceptions of money that gives great pleasure. Money itself cannot be enjoyable simply as a means; rather it is what money promises. As Ruskin argues in his account of money's proper functioning, one of the main functions of money is commanding other people's labor (17.189). But in the case of the miser, this function is held in check along with all of the goods it could obtain. The miser's pleasure is "taken *in the imagination of power to part with that with which we have no intention of parting*" (17.169). It is this perpetual anticipation of exerting power that the miser finds exhilarating. This same anticipation makes other people worship at the feet of the wealthy, further distorting and extending the reach of money's power of command.

This juxtaposition of "imagination" and "power" has broader implications in Ruskin's critique than the curious respect enjoyed by the rich simply for holding onto their money. We can begin to draw out these other lessons by remembering his earlier analysis of Renaissance art. One part of the idolatry of the Renaissance, for Ruskin, was the acclaim achieved by merely technical artists. Lacking all understanding of the ends of art, these artists made their technical means an "empty" sign of greatness. Here we turn toward the other side of this double idolatry. Not only were Renaissance paintings ill-made, but they were designed to be objects of worship. Artists took the "gifts"—the innovations—of the first generation of Renaissance masters, but instead of using them to further their audience's imaginative powers to recognize facts and ideals of true worth, they substituted in technical prowess as the standard of artistry and the sole object of their audience's desire. At the same time, they removed other evaluative measures by misrepresenting the good in the guise of unknown gods and customs. Having corrupted people's desires and falsified their standards of judgment, later Renaissance artists ensured a misreading of their own paintings as "good," all the while misleading their audience from the task of envisioning the proper ends and ordering of good lives.

Money is also a humanly made product designed for purposes of representation. And like paintings, what money represents depends, for Ruskin, on people's imaginative powers. In his debt analysis of money, as I discuss in chapter 7, he locates the actual worth of a currency in the ratio of a society's holdings of goods to the amount of the currency in circulation. In other words, money itself has a value that is subject to change due in part to the purposes and wants that people bring to its use. Money is not a neutral medium of exchange, a universal equivalent for commodities, as theorized in classical political economy. Instead, money's value depends on other factors, including the estimates that people make of the "conceived or appreciated value of what [money] represents" (17.189).

Ruskin's critique of the view of money as a neutral medium of exchange has two implications. The currency may be *"true or false"* as well as *"strong or weak."* In each case we see how money is subject to the imagination, which, in Ruskin's teleological approach, always brings a person's desires, attitudes, and ends to judging things' significance. For the currency to be "true," there must be substantial holdings of "wealth" in a society for people to claim with their money (17.189–90). Ruskin clarifies that "the term wealth is never to be attached to the *accidental object of a morbid* desire, but only to the *constant object of a legitimate one*" (17.165). The issue of the strength or weakness of a currency is similarly a matter of desire, he observes. He cites the example of a "youth" whose "love of money" compels him to steal in order to buy "pantomime tickets and cigars; the 'strength' of the currency being irresistible to him, in consequence of his [intense] desire for those luxuries" (17.190n). Thus, paradoxically, a "strong" currency is almost always a sign of disordered or excessive desires. Where people's imaginations are vital, money's "true" worth is great. Where they are unhealthy, money's falsifying power emerges with destructive force.

The Idolatry of Money in Theory

On the practical level, Ruskin's examples of the idolatry of money are meant to provoke his audience's critical reflection about the culture of industrial capitalism, the deferential worship accorded to the rich, the misdirection of desire in economic life, and, of course, their possible complicity in the culture, worship, and desires of consumerism. Shadowing these observations is another question: why is money so powerful a force? Ruskin's arguments in response to this question are more speculative. His analysis shifts from the practical to the theoretical. He turns away from the use of money to command goods and labor and from its capacity to gain undue respect for its holders. He inquires instead into its role as a sign.

Money operates something like a sign in the case of the miser, whose riches are read as a sign of power. In Ruskin's words, "The power of arithmetical comparison is . . . a great thing to unimaginative people. . . . Only few can understand,—none measure—and few will willingly adore, superiorities in other things; but everybody can understand money, everyone can count it, and most will worship it" (17.207). This general deference to the moneyed classes indicates a lazy imagination and an obvious lack of discernment, for the miser's money is only an "image" of power, not an actual power, as it is never put to use. A distinction must be drawn, Ruskin stresses, between "Iconoclasm," or "*image*-breaking," which "is easy," and "an Idol [which] cannot be broken—it must be forsaken; and this is not so easy, either to do, or persuade to doing. For men may readily be convinced of the weakness of an image; but not of the emptiness of an imagination" (17.287).

This passage sets before us the crucial phrase the "emptiness of an imagination." It also shows Ruskin acknowledging the difficulty of persuading his audience to see how the falsifying power of money emerges from their collective failures to pursue the task of moral imagination in economic life.

Recall the discussion of the imagination's seeking out the "full significance" of iron in chapter 3. Only by inquiring into the activities that make for the best uses of iron, as judged by the goods and virtues that people pursue and attain therein, can consumers assess iron's actual value. People's desires and uses for things are similarly at play in determining money's worth. Thus, like iron, the current value of money is a function of people's imaginations, as are judgments of the value of every good. But money is different from iron. It is not only a good; it is also a sign that takes on meaning in a whole economy, whether that is the good economy that Ruskin envisions or the economy of industrial capitalism that he abhors. The misuse of money, then, has a multiplying effect. Here it is not just the value of a resource that has been misjudged; the falsification of money abets the misrepresentation of everything it touches. A graver abuse of money than treating it as an end, therefore, is taking it to be *the* standard of all economic value.

I invoke the idea of a "whole" economy because Ruskin's discussion of idolatry pushes past individuals' assessments as lonely economic actors into the countless interactions mediated through money. By the "emptiness of an imagination," he is pointing out how money's value is more prone to false readings than the value of an actual thing with specific properties like iron. He is also offering an image of the way that money works in classical political economy where consumers base their choices on nothing more than current preferences and going prices. Nothing matters beyond the desires that people project onto everything they buy. It is relatively easy, of course, to make the case that people should reconsider what goals and aspirations motivate their purchases and how the value of every commodity involves more than market pricing. Again for Ruskin images are easy to break, and the image of market choice as "perfect" or even "good" choice is no exception.

Although this image is easy to break, what can individuals do all by themselves when confronted by the vast distances of the division of labor and the machinations of market exchange? There are limits, it seems, to people's abilities and responsibilities to intervene in and alter the workings of an economy. Maybe capitalism really is a symbolic machine, as Marx suggests, and the only option is to let it run its course. Put differently, although money is clearly not the exclusive end of human activities, perhaps accepting the dictates of the market is both a necessary compromise and a means to a better future and freer society. Ruskin emphatically rejects such views, and his fuller analysis of the "Eidolon" of money is central to his counter-argument.

As he puts it, the term "Mammon" is read too "narrowly" as the "power of money only," for it "is in truth the great evil Spirit of false and fond desire, or 'Covetousness, which is Idolatry'" (17.287). The "emptiness" of individuals' imaginations somehow becomes a much larger force, the attraction to which can only be explained as a kind of worship. Like Marx, then, Ruskin depicts the "value" generated by capitalist exchange as a god that remakes all things in money terms. He does not presume, though, that "value" mirrors the social relations underlying people's hidden cooperation in producing goods to meet one another's needs. For Ruskin the issue of whether capitalism serves people's cooperation, goods, and needs is very much in doubt. That is why he insists that capitalism requires an ethical critique and response, even if theory has its uses, up to a point, in indicating the broader ramifications of individuals' seemingly isolated choices.

I began this chapter with the connection between worship and gifts in Ruskin's criticism. The ethical importance he assigns to acknowledging gifts in economic life is bound up with his more theoretical view of the workings of money as a whole. As noted above, he cites the failures of Renaissance artists to recognize both the "gifts" of past masters and the proper ends of art. Similarly, money is made to serve certain purposes. Once a currency gains a people's trust, it can facilitate an extension of economic interdependence and social cooperation. If that trust is lost, interdependence and cooperation will suffer, too. Yet there are other ways that these aims may be frustrated, the most important for Ruskin is that people may place their trust in the security of a mutual "covetousness" rather than in commitments to the interdependence and cooperation required for anyone's well-being.

This mutual covetousness produces the falsifying vision of economic life that Ruskin associates with the money economy of industrial capitalism. If the Renaissance's chief product was a falsification of the good, then the idolatry of money achieves the same effect, though more subtly. Renaissance artists corrupted people's moral vision through representations of foreign gods and customs. Money can also be made to falsify a society's good through representations of things' value. In the case of art, however, the artist as "maker" is the agent who distorts the beauty of things and falsifies the recognition of their worth. Agency and responsibility are more difficult to assign with money. Money does not just allow for the misrepresentation of things on a canvas as painting does. Rather, Ruskin charges, money can generate a falsifying vision of its own, and it is this overarching vision of the market pricing of all commodities that is so hard to forsake.

This vision translates the value of everything into money terms. Indeed as theorized in classical political economy, the market gives individuals a seemingly impossible perspective from which to know the "value," that is, the market price, of every good in light of the current workings of an economy. Each change in capital investment and monetary demand is quantified in money terms, sending signals rippling through the market and readjusting the price of every commodity with "perfect" accuracy as supply and demand return to equilibrium. This theoretical portrait of money's operation is truly remarkable, for money's power is not merely the power of attraction, as in the case of the miser, or legitimation, as in the case of the merchant's penitence. Money's power is a *power of vision,* a superhuman capacity to re-present the perpetual balancing of the preferences and interests that people collectively bring to their economic interactions. For Ruskin, the only problem with the seamless operation of the capitalist economy is that the vision that money offers requires a perversely "shared" attitude of covetousness. Money's signaling of things' "value" depends on people's making the good of all the product of market competition. This embrace of market pricing as the standard of value in economic life eliminates every other way of measuring and recognizing things' goodness, entirely removing from exchange relations, he charges, ethical regard for other people and commitments to common goods.

In this portrait of money's overall operation in a whole economy, the practical elements of Ruskin's critique assume a more theoretical guise.

The practices of Victorian capitalism do not merely appear to be "religious." For Ruskin, the standards, ideals, and ends produced by these practices are the "making-believe" of a people devoted to a false god. To put it paradoxically, these cultural guideposts reflect *the "shared" vision of people who refuse to hold anything in common among themselves.* Their attitudes are impious because they worship misers and soulless commerce. Their society is unjust because their imaginations answer to ill-considered wants and aspirations. What propels their relentless desires and legitimates their exploitative economy is the symbolic operation of money in the marketplace, left unguided by any shared *moral* vision at all.

Wealthy Victorians are free to project their desires onto everything they buy, the sole constraint being the current prices of available commodities. Yet these prices are set, in turn, by people's collective desires, sorted and aggregated through the market's pricing mechanisms. So long as participants accept money as their god and have it to spend, they are free to remake the meaning of things in the manner of "Protestant" idolatry. Individuals' "opinions" and "interests" become the measure of value, displacing efforts to envision the best activities and a proper arrangement of goods in their lives. Yet, ironically, individuals' desires are themselves produced by a "great evil Spirit," a vast economy of "false and fond desire," that no one seems able to control. Ruskin's analysis of the Victorian misuse and abuse of money is, in the end, a perfect "whole," a constellation of impious attitudes, unjust relationships, and empty symbols that must finally be read as wholly idolatrous irreligion—or so he endeavors to persuade his audience.

Metaphysics and Metaphor: Christian Ethics as Mystification?

The most striking feature of Ruskin's account of the idolatry of money is how much must be shared in a society if money is to exert its visionary power over an economy. There are the mercantile practices of industry and commerce and the virtues and standards that they make normative in Victorian society. There is the widespread love of money that accords the mere holding of riches tremendous power. There are the desires generated by commodity production and reinforced through overt advertising and subtler cultural signs. Finally, Ruskin argues, classical political economy plays a vital ideological role. If the Eidolon is the god of his fellow Victorians, then the theory of political economy supplies the main tenets of their creed.

Above all else, though, what his contemporaries hold in common is their covetousness. It is this covetousness that Ruskin wants his audience to forsake because of its destructive effects on them. When consumers buy solely on the basis of going prices and current preferences, money may appear as if it were a neutral medium of exchange facilitating the diverse tastes and projects of individuals. Ruskin counters, though, that money is not a neutral sign; in capitalist exchange, it is an empty sign. Its worth depends on the imaginations that people bring to its use. Where people are joined in covetousness and engage in unchecked self-assertion in their spending, money allows them to empty out and infuse whatever they buy with false imaginations of their own making—or, rather, with the status symbols, the brand names, the marks of refined taste, all of the wants and desires that industrial capitalism generates with its welter of fashions and styles.

Persuading people to forsake this "Idol" is exceedingly difficult, however. People have good reasons to hold onto their mutual covetousness. Not only does it promote economic growth and allow for diversity in tastes, but it also affords a vision of the whole of economic life that seems impossible apart from market pricing. Given the vast distances that separate people in a money economy, how can anyone gain a clear enough vantage point on economic life apart from the vision that money affords? For Ruskin, money, properly understood and used, is vital to a moral vision of good consumption, but not as it is employed in Victorian capitalism.

Although I reserve Ruskin's critique of political economy to later chapters, a passage from *Munera Pulveris* serves as a useful transition to his correctives to the idolatry of money. He contrasts the lack of substance and vision in classical political economy with the "operations of faithful Economy . . . she the calm arbiter of national destiny, regards only *essential power for good* in all that she accumulates and alike disdains the wanderings of imagination." In a footnote written at the time of *Aratra Pentelici,* Ruskin explains that he does not mean to include here "the Right goings . . . of Imagination" (17.166, 166n; my emphasis). As seen earlier in this chapter, he comes to accept idolatry and imagination—the "wanderings" and the "Right goings" of people's visionary powers—as two sides of the same coin, the human capacity for bringing desires, attitudes, and ends to the making and recognition of things, especially such things as painting, sculpture, and money, which represent the gods, spirits, virtues, and powers that are the making-believe of a culture and that guide people's striving.

It is jarring, therefore, to find Ruskin in 1871 discussing the idolatry of money in terms that echo with the divine metaphysics of his early aesthetics. Describing the Eidolon, he names it a "phantasm, or imagination of Good," which stands in "for that which is real and enduring; from the Highest Living Good, which gives life, to the lowest material good which ministers to it. The Creator, and the things created, which He is said to have 'seen good' in creating, are in this their eternal goodness appointed always to be 'worshipped,'—i.e., to have goodness and worth ascribed to them from the heart; and the sweep and range of idolatry extend to the rejection of any or all of these." Several points warrant emphasis in this passage. Ruskin holds to his notion of worship as a recognition of the "goodness and worth" of things. Here the Maker of all goods is God, and worship is directed first to the "Highest Living Good, which gives life," under which all other "material" goods take their place in the "fixed Law of life." Either "we" remain loyal to this hierarchy of goods that sets the true worth of everything, or, he continues, "with resolute opposite loyalty [we] serve our own imagination of good, which is the law, not of the House, but of the Grave, (otherwise called the law of 'mark missing,' which we translate as 'law of Sin')." The ordering of things' "essential power for good" in a "fixed Law of life" and the language of "mark missing" recall Ruskin's early aesthetics and his discussion of Romanist idolatry (17.287). As before, the corrective to the idolatry of money and the misreading of economic goods is to refer each thing's value to the charitable whole of God's life-giving purposes in the Creation.

How can this appeal to divine metaphysics, to a perfect ordering of things not at all subject to individuals' imagination and historical practices, be squared with the cultural conception of religion that Ruskin adopts in *Aratra Pentelici*? If he argues there that the ideals, norms, and virtues that animate a common recognition of things' goodness are themselves the products of human making-believe, then how can he appeal so baldly to a timeless metaphysics that, while present in his early discussions of idolatry, would seem to have been exorcised by now?

Consider, in this light, Ruskin's own imaginative "making-believe" in his portrait of the two sins associated with the idolatry of money.[28] There is, first, the active making of money's power to misrepresent the value of goods. There is also the passive beguilement by this power that leads people away from recognizing things' actual value. Following Dante, Ruskin figures the first sin as a masculine enterprise, the other as a feminine deception.

Ruskin notes that Dante describes two types of the "avaricious and prodigal," those who can and those who cannot be redeemed. The redeemable act without "deliberate or calculated operation." They are represented by Dante's "feminine" spirit of the sirens who symbolizes the "'*Deceitfulness* of riches.'... She is lovely to look upon, and enchants by her sweet singing, but her womb is loathsome," Ruskin writes. Everyone who falls under this spirit's enchantment is guilty only of thrilling in money's falsifying power and the desires it promises to fulfill. This passive fascination, which lacks all agency, repeats Ruskin's portrait of "Romanist" idolatry. A surface reading of the attractions of consumer goods typifies most people's acquiescence in the market system—literally taking things at market value without imagining the economic exploitation and societal conditions kept out of view by the fixation on money's power. Sometimes the sirens' victims even receive their due in life, shipwrecked by their foolhardy pursuit of alluring desire.

By contrast, the irredeemably guilty in Dante's hell are consigned to battle against each other like the "*waves of Charybdis.*" That is because, Ruskin claims, the gravest abuse of money is the "*contention* for riches." The "feminine" illusion that meeting one's desires necessarily bears fruit in the form of greater economic prosperity for the whole society masks an underlying violent contest that profits the few at the expense of the many. This contest is not among the capitalists, who benefit most richly from the "mutuality" of covetousness. The contest is instead between these powerful people and the rest of the community. The capitalists are not beguiled by desire; their unjust dealings are not so easily hidden by the distances of the money economy. Rather, they willfully refuse to acknowledge their debts to those who work for them and their extensive dependence on the many others who contribute to the society from which they profit. In paying unfair wages, making little communal provision, and reaping undue rewards, they actively misrepresent all that money gains for them. This willful distortion of money's potential for fostering interdependence and cooperation is symbolized, Ruskin claims, by the impossibility of recognizing these denizens of hell as ever having been part of any human community. Thus, Dante's Plutus has "unintelligible" speech, "and no single soul of all those ruined by him *has recognizable features*" (17.209–12). The impossibility of recognizing these spirits is a fitting punishment for their own refusal to recognize other people's gifts in making the myriad goods that kept them alive and that might have sustained individual and communal flourishing, more broadly, had they not made money into an empty and, thus, meaningless sign.

This metaphorical portrait of capitalists as the Plutus's devotees and of consumers as the sirens' victims is more in keeping with Ruskin's development toward cultural critique. He takes a classic work from a cultural heritage shared by an elite, at least, and he offers his audience an evocative reading of character types to spark their moral imagination.[29] This invitation to critical engagement is more promising than his return to metaphysics, but I want to be clear about the deficiencies in Ruskin's way of presenting his contemporaries' economic options. All too often, he offers a Manichean choice between life and death, cooperation and competition, a true worship of God and a false worship of Mammon. While some Victorians are redeemable, they must first accept that industrial capitalism is wholly corrupt. It is an idol that must be forsaken; it cannot be meaningfully criticized in a more selective and partial way, Ruskin suggests, even as he does just that in his more practical criticism.

Ruskin's polar opposition between the entirely false vision of the capitalist marketplace and the perfect moral vision of God's Creation may be rhetorically powerful, but it should be rejected as a critical strategy. Stated more broadly, the attempt to recover Christian moral languages of character and community and the ethical task of ordering one's loves in light of some telos, while potentially very useful to an ethics of consumption, must remain vigilant of religious appeals and rhetorical strategies that locate the good beyond the reach of criticism and contestation. In Ruskin's case the gendering of the two sins of idolatry, as active and masculine, on the one hand, and passive and feminine, on the other, reminds us of the parallels between his claims that every created thing has its own "essential power for good" and that each type of person has his or her "natural" virtues and roles.

A remark in J. S. Mill's *On the Subjection of Women* (1861) is instructive. Mill describes a prevailing form of mystification that fits parts of Ruskin's criticism all too well. The prejudice of the nineteenth-century critique of the Enlightenment is to "accord to the unreasoning elements in human nature the infallibility which the eighteenth century is supposed to have ascribed to the reasoning elements. . . . This [current] idolatry, infinitely more degrading than the other, and the most pernicious of the false worships of the present day . . . [obscures] the real root of much that is bowed down to as the intention of Nature and the ordinance of God."[30] Ruskin's call to recognize, or worship, the goodness of all things in light of his own reading of God's Creation and the Book of Nature is the kind of rhetorical strategy that Mill warns against. If Ruskin's sole corrective to the "emptiness" of his contemporaries' imagination and the misdirection of their desires is that they embrace his own perfect conception of the good, then we have not a call to an active moral imagination, but rather something much more like the mystification of power relations that Marx finds in all metaphysics, religion, and morality.

Perhaps Ruskin's account of the idolatry of money, like Marx's analysis of commodity fetishism, finally leaves individuals powerless as moral actors. The key difference is that Marx refuses to detail a moral vision for other people, a necessarily ideological undertaking, while Ruskin's reliance on a Christian moral framework of well-ordered loves makes his audience's salvation a matter of recognizing the force of his own vision and bowing down to it.

Making and Recognition, Gifts and Piety

Throughout this chapter I have been tracing the evolving dynamic between "making" and "recognition" in Ruskin's criticism, from his early discussions of the threat of idolatry in the production and reception of medieval and Renaissance art to his later analyses of the idolatry of money in industrial capitalism and the cultural makings of all religions. The more he appreciates the range of ways that people make themselves and their culture, religion, and economy, the more tenuous any common recognition of things' goodness would have to become, it seems. This tension between individuals' making of judgments and a shared recognition of goodness is arguably most pronounced across the distances of a money economy. The nineteenth-century model of the market, with its emphasis on production and its faith in laissez-faire, is ideally suited to a model of the person as "maker" with the task of creating one's own life, pursuing one's desires, fashioning one's identity, even as other individuals are allowed the same liberties. Here the only guiding vision is the autonomous vision of the good that each person makes for him- or herself; no other organizing visions of things' worth and purpose need be recognized.

Even as Ruskin celebrates people's imaginative powers as makers, however, he still approaches the making of things and the making of judgments from the vantage point of a reader. People are not just makers, they are also readers; they are not only producers, but also consumers. Put differently, people make their lives out of an inheritance that is historical, cultural, religious, economic, and so on, and they may actively read this inheritance, imagining what best to make of it, or they may adopt it passively, forming their lives out of it unreflectively. For Ruskin, making the most of this inheritance requires a careful reading of its sources for structured ways of arranging good lives and a good society. Without these guides, a common moral vision is too difficult to create.

If we look back to "Modern Education," my organizing framework for part 2, we can put this challenge of constructing a common moral vision in the larger context of Ruskin's corpus. In "Modern Education" he first describes religion as answering the question of "where [a person] is going," meaning "what chances or reports there are of any other world besides this." Already here in the early 1850s, though, he confesses his doubts that such knowledge may be reasonably taught. If it cannot, then the nation would do better "to get rid of the expense of an Establishment, and the hypocrisy of a Liturgy; to exhibit its cathedrals as curious memorials of a by-gone superstition, and, abandoning all thoughts of the next world, to set itself to make the best it can of this [one]" (11.258, 260). In the decades that follow, Ruskin devotes his social criticism to making *this* world better, and yet he often does so by calling his audiences back to the "binding" practices of their religions and the rest of the wisdom that he sees inhering in their shared cultural legacy.

Victorian capitalism is anathema for Ruskin, in part, because it unbinds people from this inheritance as well as from each other. It unbinds individuals by falsely promising that they may make their own way in life however they choose. Contemporary Christian practices and pieties do the same, he argues. Two examples suffice to indicate the contours of his practical critique of Victorian Christianity.[31] Consider, first, Ruskin's rejoinder to the theological controversy that swept Britain in 1864 over whether or not Christians should abandon the traditional belief in hell.[32] Casting a plague on both houses in the debate, he asserts, "I do not merely *believe* there is such a place as hell. I *know* there is such a place." Then characteristically twisting the knife, he adds, "and I know also that when men have got to the point of believing virtue impossible but through dread of [hell], they have got *into* it" (17.360–61). This hell on earth results both from the partisanship among Christian churches and from the false pieties of individuals unduly concerned with the state of their souls. Such fixations on abstract matters of doctrine hinder the cultivation of a virtue of piety, rightly understood.

Thus, in "The Mystery of Life and Its Arts" (1868), Ruskin rejects sectarian bickering, urging instead a joint effort to live by the highest teaching of Christianity, the "direct contention with material evil." Averting suffering is the chief purpose served when people's imagination gives "full presence and power to the possible and true," which is the proper goal of a religion "daily founded on rational, effective, humble, and helpful action. Helpful action, observe! for there is just one law, which obeyed, keeps all religions pure—forgotten, makes them all false. Whenever in any religious faith, dark or bright, we allow our minds to dwell upon the points in which we differ from other people, we are wrong, and in the devil's power" (18.184–85). Ruskin's language of the "possible and true" harkens back to his aesthetics of making in *Modern Painters* 3. Just as he condemns the factionalism produced by idle speculation on the finer points of Christian theology, he rejects both the fretfully remorseful and self-righteously confident pieties of individuals fixated on their own personal salvation. Whether one imagines a soul corrupt beyond doubt or chosen with certainty, this concentration on the "impossible and untrue" repeats the errors of the pursuit of "the ideal" in art, the "pursuit, by the imagination, of beautiful and strange thoughts or subjects, to the exclusion of painful or common ones." Simply put, religious zeal narrows the imagination so that people "let themselves, and the existing state of things, alone (at least in the way of correction)" (5.71, 70).

Ruskin's criticisms of the false pieties of Christian practice point to the two obstacles he sees hindering the active moral imagination needed for an ethics of consumption. There is the failure to attain a broader vision of what is held in common with other people. There is also the failure to be vigilant as to how one's self-deception masks complicity in other people's suffering. Both themes appear in Ruskin's reading of Dante on the subject of idolatry, as they typically do in the ad hoc appeals in his mature social criticism to scriptural passages, biblical imagery, moral teachings, and an assortment of myths and deities from non-Christian traditions. I canvass some of these appeals in other chapters, but one example helps show how, as he pursues his interests in the cultural makings of religions, the arts, and the imagination in his social criticism, he extends the aims of worship and the virtue of piety. No longer is worship due only to God as the Maker of all good things; nor is it enough for the virtuous to cultivate a reverence for nature's gifts—the natural piety discussed in chapter 3. Increasingly, for Ruskin, what religions teach, when people enliven their inherited practices through an active exercise of their imaginations, is a communal piety, that is, a reverence for the gifts one receives from the many human makers, both past and present, whose efforts and creativity produce the gifts that maintain one's existence and that sustain a life of flourishing.

In *Fiction Fair and Foul* (1880–81) Ruskin criticizes his long-standing inspiration William Wordsworth for his narrow practice of piety. Wordsworth's poetry is falsely colored by a zealous desire to imagine beauty throughout the natural world so much so that he sentimentalizes decrepit buildings, not as signs of poverty, but as one more lovely feature of the landscape. Because he paints the world with his own longings, he remains inattentive to the human suffering around him. As Ruskin puts it, in appealing to Christ's crucifixion, Wordsworth is "incurious to see in the hands the print of the Nails" (34.320).[33] Even so capable a reader of nature's gifts and so imaginative a maker of their meanings as Wordsworth is deficient in his moral vision if he excludes from view the full range of gifts needed for human life, including decent shelter. Whenever people fill their imaginations with the "impossible and untrue," they make the world over in the image of their own narrow desires, failing to consider the cultural and social contexts in which the effects of those desires should be assessed. This deadening of the imagination prevents a broader view of the good lives and good society that might be made "possible and true." Thus, the piety of receiving life's many gifts with gratitude and reverence contrasts with the impiety of believing oneself to be the sole maker of one's life.

I want to conclude with *Aratra Pentelici* and two examples of the impiety that Ruskin finds everywhere in Victorian life. Citing the childish, if sincerely religious, art of the Greeks and medieval Christians, he denounces modern design for lacking "imagination" and "virtue," and he offers as an example the gas lamps decorating the new embankment alongside the Thames in London. In how the lamp designers "admire and imitate" the art of the past, there is no imaginative discernment and, thus, none of the vivid realization that good design requires. There is no recognition of the originality of earlier artists' creative efforts that might serve as a guide and motivation to new artistic achievements—"we are not only impotent to restore, but strong to defile, the work of past ages." So too, Ruskin charges, the choice of decoration for this riverside scene ignores the sanctity with which the Thames was held by the "imagination of our ancestors" and the usefulness of the river's "bounty of nature." By contrast, the emptiness of the lamp designers' imagination shows in their choice, simply because the lamps line the river, to have the gas "come out of fishes' tails." But these makers cannot even "cast so much as a smelt or a sprat" from the Thames, and instead they "borrow the shape of a Neapolitan marble"—"cast *that* badly, and give lustre to the ill-cast fish with lacquer in imitation of bronze" (20.255). The whole ensemble is emblematic of modern design and should prompt "a regretful piety" before "the blank stones which at once restrain and disgrace your native river," this "the final worship rendered it by modern philosophy" (20.259–60).

In this example Ruskin argues yet again for the inescapability of worship in human life. Although worship is inevitable, its cultural practice varies greatly and, with it, the desires, ends, and attitudes and the kind of imagination that people bring to the many things they make, use, and borrow in their lives. For Ruskin the vitality of religions, the arts, and the imagination requires a searching recognition of what made other people's creativity and visions of the world good. The implication is that any people unwilling to revere the gifts they receive from others will be left to their own meager resources, casting about for whatever strikes their present fancy, producing ill-made goods and swallowing the ready-made tastes of the day. For Ruskin, individuals cannot make a flourishing life whole-cloth all by themselves, even if the image of an entirely liberated "self-making" is the prevailing cultural ideal of the market as nothing more than the neutral mediator among individuals' authentic and diverse tastes.

Here we return to the importance of a people's making-believe. In deifying "self-making" as the cultural ideal and idol of the capitalist market, Victorians commit themselves to a pantheon of gods, spirits, powers, and virtues of their own manufacture—most importantly, the god of money with its power of vision and the spirit of competition with its virtues of industry and thrift. Reinforcing these wellsprings of Victorian cultural energies is another ideal/idol, namely, the "Self-made man," who "has been taught, or helped, by no one." In *Aratra Pentelici* Ruskin sets a magazine caricature of this icon side by side with an image of the Apollo of Syracuse stamped on a Greek coin (20.293). Indeed, so tenuous is the difference between the false imagination of idolatry and the true imagination of piety, they are merely the two sides of the same coin, the human capacity for imagining things' meanings. In Ruskin's interpretation the caricature of the "Self-made man" accurately conveys the lack of "grace," that is, the absence of "Beauty and Mercy" in this figure, a lack of grace that prevents the grateful recognition of the worth of everything received from other people and that inhibits the fullest making of good lives for ourselves and others (20.257). This self-made man is one of the followers of Dante's Plutus, and his misrepresentation of all that money gains for him is marked in the wizened face, the rich man's top hat, and the tired eyes of the bespectacled financier.

Grace well received requires an acknowledgment of debts to and dependence upon, not just God and nature, but the many human makers of life's gifts, too. It demands a piety that seeks out the gifts we receive from others, whether those gifts keep us alive day to day or are the inherited sources of flourishing lives preserved through vibrant cultures, religions, traditions, and communities. Such gifts cannot be adequately compensated for by money (see chapter 7). Indeed such gifts, because they are the basic maintenance and the formative sources of people's lives, require an attitude of piety akin to the ardent worship that he initially directs toward God as the creator of all life. Ruskin's vision of worship has changed dramatically and, with it, his sense of the giftedness of life, which now ranges beyond God's charity and nature's bounty to the offerings of past cultures and the efforts and creativity of the members of one's society, however widely those relationships extend across the distances of economic exchange. This conviction that life is gifted throughout is basic to Ruskin's ethics of consumption.

In taking final stock of the limits and possibilities of Ruskin's vision of religion, let me return once more to Marx. The issue of piety cuts to the core of the differences between Ruskin and Marx. Indeed Marx's dismissal of the "ancient worship of nature" and "tribal religions" seems directed at contemporary purveyors, like Ruskin, of the worship owed either to nature or to one's community as sources of the gifts that form one's existence and that finally cannot be repaid. Marx is deeply suspicious of calls to strike postures of worship for one's indebtedness because they contribute to the tendency of some people to strike deferential postures toward others in the natural and social ordering of things. As he puts it in the *1844 Manuscripts,* "A man who lives by the grace of another regards himself as a dependent being." "But," he continues, "I live completely by the grace of another if I owe him not only the maintenance of my life, but if he has, moreover, *created* my *life*—if he is the *source* of my life. When it is not of my own creation, my life has necessarily a source of this kind outside of it. The *Creation* is therefore an idea very difficult to dislodge from popular consciousness. The fact that nature and man exist on their own account is *incomprehensible* to it, because it contradicts everything *tangible* in practical life."[34] Marx's astute observation about this discrepancy between the notion that both nature and society are humanly made, and the idea that one's life has been created by a power other than oneself, highlights a fundamental difference between Marx and Ruskin and, arguably, between secular and religious strands of nineteenth-century critical thought, more broadly.

No doubt this difference is a complex amalgam of experiences, attitudes, fears, and hopes, but it can be framed simply in terms of "making" and "recognition." For Marx, the human making of cultures implies that no evaluative standards, not freely and self-consciously made by individuals, whether on their own or with others, can be trusted. It is not only historically necessary, but also morally preferable, to set aside inherited standards and to rely instead on the symbolic apparatus of the capitalist marketplace as the sole means of evaluative judgments. Marx's profound skepticism about the ideological effects of religious appeals, both to God's grace and Creation and to human debts and sacrifice, is clear in his early writings. His full-blown theory of capitalism as a "symbolic machine" answers to his subsequent need to explain how people can judge the value of economic goods in a way that effects at least a semblance of the interdependence and cooperation that any society requires, but without individuals' having to recognize any cultural ideals, norms, and ends not made directly by themselves. But how, then, is it possible to judge what is owed to other people simply for the "maintenance" of one's life? That is a question that Marx's strictly theoretical critique is ill-equipped to answer.

Ruskin envisions something very different than Marx when he asks what judgments are possible in the meeting place of people's exchange relationships. He insists on worship, on the recognition of debts and dependences, and, equally important, on the visions of the good, the common good, good lives, or shared goods that make it possible to discern why another person's effort or creative contribution is worthy of regard. This idea of worship serves two purposes in his criticism. It requires people to read the full worth of things by tracing their value back to the efforts and creativity that others have expended in producing them. It also requires a further imaginative leap to fathom the desires and purposes that motivated and guided the others' work. Recognizing the worth of people's gifts requires, therefore, appreciating how those people saw fit to arrange their lives as individuals and as a society. This act of moral imagination implies the need to judge others' efforts and creativity in light of broader evaluative standards, standards that transcend what each of the parties—producer and consumer—brings to the exchange. These broader standards can be valorized by appeals to God's Creation and the order of Nature, or they can be viewed as cultural agreements that are subject to continual revision and debate. The cultural conception of religions that Ruskin articulates in his late criticism hints at the latter possibility, though he often strays from this path himself.

Ruskin continues to appeal to God's perfect Creation despite his turn toward imperfect human creativity. In looking ahead to his medievalist politics and his ethics of consumption, I argue in the coming chapters that his critical efforts to craft a common vision for his contemporaries are most successful when he remains faithful to his sense of the contingency of the cultural makings of religions and the imaginative practices of worship. But he is sometimes guilty of the kind of idolatry that Mill describes, the idolatry of dressing up his cultural offerings in the mantle of a prophet who reads the pronouncements of God's Creation and the Book of Nature without *making* any imaginative contributions of his own.

I side with Ruskin on the importance of imagining other people's circumstances, needs, and contributions and the goods that we already do or might agree to share with others in the larger community. I also claim that a practiced piety for the sources of one's existence is a necessary reminder of these obligations. Finally I applaud his critical efforts to make explicit for his contemporaries the reasons why certain cultural agreements should be recognized as good.

An overblown sense of worship toward the makers of life's gifts is just as dangerous, however, as an impious disregard for them. In Ruskin's case, undue deference to his social vision as the final word on the moral imagination that he aims to foster will stifle the reform efforts that his criticism, at its best, encourages. That danger is clearest in *Aratra Pentelici* when he condemns the "Free man" along with the "Self-made man" (20.293). Ruskin's antipathy toward liberty is one of the problems in his overtly antidemocratic politics. To analyzing the weaknesses in that politics along with the strengths of his reform proposals and his account of political justice, the book now turns.

FIVE

The Politics of Medievalism

The two previous chapters narrate the transformation of Ruskin's views on nature and religion as he turns his critical lens toward culture. The changes are dramatic. Gone is his early conviction that great art mirrors the moral lessons of God's perfect Creation to the "pure in heart." Individuals' imaginative readings of nature's beauty and worth are shaped by the cultural activities they choose for themselves or adopt out of necessity. Ruskin still views religions as formative influences on a people's character and vision, but his analysis of the idolatry of money suggests that the religious practices needed to correct the distortions of industrial capitalism are as culturally contingent as the false worship of Mammonism.

This final chapter of part 2 extends these themes of character and vision into Ruskin's politics. Once again his tract on "Modern Education" (1853) anticipates the directions he takes in his emerging social criticism, helping to introduce three issues in this chapter. First, there is the profound ambivalence toward the modern that runs throughout Ruskin's corpus, at least after the 1840s. Indeed, given his usual care with titles, it is noteworthy that he did not propose the title of *Modern Painters*, the massive five-volume undertaking that established his reputation. His publisher suggested it, and he agreed (3.xxxi). Being known as a defender of "modern" painters suited Ruskin's early self-conception quite well. By the 1850s, however, this view of him is difficult to square with the shift in his devotions toward medieval architecture. In his writings of this period, we find polemics against "Modern Pulpits," "Modern Glass Painting," and "Modern Romanist Art," making his piece on "Modern Education" a remarkable reminder of his initial defense of the cultural achievements of his day.

Second, in "Modern Education" Ruskin defines politics for the first and only time. In his words, politics is "the science of the relations and duties of men to each other" (11.260). As he conceives the political, its boundaries are vast, encompassing all of the associations that people enter into with each other both near and far. For Ruskin politics extends beyond the halls and institutions of governments. It is chiefly a matter of governing one's conduct and complicity in the ever-widening networks of interdependence at work in modern societies. His emphasis on self-governance is clear in the first topic of the study of politics—the "knowledge of the operations of the virtues and vices of men upon themselves and society." He also includes the duties of the various "ranks and offices" in society and every "station of life" and a "practical knowledge of the present state and wants of mankind" (11.260). Ruskin's scrutiny of people's virtues and vices and his image of the good society as an organic hierarchy of roles and duties are defining features of the "medievalism" of his politics.

Third, although politics is more than government for Ruskin, he turns to the state in the final paragraph of "Modern Education." In the voice of the reformer, he declares, "I hold it for indisputable, that the first duty of a state is to see that every child born therein shall be well housed, clothed, fed, and educated, till it attain years of discretion." Then with an intriguing abruptness, he concludes, "But in order to the effecting [of these reforms], the government must have an authority over the people of which we now do not so much as dream; and I cannot in this place pursue the subject farther" (11.263). This is the first time that Ruskin advocates government activism to implement welfare policies mitigating the ills of industrial capitalism. Thus, the irony of his politics is that his "modern" reforms on behalf of egalitarian measures are justified by a "medievalist" social theory. With marvelously ambivalent phrasing, Jose Harris captures these tensions, dubbing Ruskin "the moral godfather of the modern welfare state."[1]

This chapter ranges through Ruskin's writings of the 1850s to the 1870s, reconstructing what I call the "cathedral model" of his politics. I use this term to highlight the main structural building block of that politics, his interest in "social practices" as arenas for cultivating human excellence and promoting commitments to common goods that dates to his architectural studies. The themes of excellence and common goods, human development and social responsibility, are central to Ruskin's politics, and in this chapter I show how completely his growing attention to human virtues shapes his conception of political justice and his many reform proposals.

Once again, virtues are excellences for Ruskin. Virtue connotes the vitality, achievement, and recognition that mark the best kinds of human lives. In what follows I detail his powerful arguments on behalf of individual excellence, social justice, and rights to public support, the main elements of his politics. In addition, Ruskin commends a number of moral virtues to his fellow Victorians, including providence, magnanimity, honesty, charity, and humility, but the chief moral virtue in his politics is justice. Echoing the classical idea of justice as giving other people their due, he defines this virtue as "granting to every human being due aid in the development of such faculties as it possesses for action and enjoyment" (27.147). To this end Ruskin champions public education, job training, pensions for the elderly, and a raft of other reforms as legitimate areas of government action and oversight. In evaluating his politics, we must remember how far ahead of his time his proposals were and how much argumentative effort was required to make these reforms legitimate in his day.

Along with Ruskin's vocabulary of the virtues, the issue of legitimacy is at the heart of his politics and his distrust of institutions in favor of associations. By this I mean he challenged the justice of such institutional mechanisms of modern liberalism as market exchange, individual rights, and electoral representation. These institutional arrangements can appear to operate without explicit and extensive agreements among participants. Individuals enter the market to trade money for goods and services, needing only a willingness to abide by current prices. Elected legislators gain and use their offices by currying favors with the electorate and trading votes in Parliament, bloating the state's budget without clarifying national priorities. So run the critiques of modern liberal institutions that resemble Ruskin's arguments.

The concern with legitimacy clarifies the associational structure of Ruskin's cathedral model. Starting at the level of individuals, his question is, how might individuals best exercise their authority both in directing their society and in fulfilling the obligations they incur through their standing in jobs, families, and communities? Moving onto the state, how can its policies be made to serve people's needs and foster a good society in ways that have legitimacy in the public's eyes? Characteristic of Ruskin and his tradition is the conviction that individuals and the state can wield their authority properly only if their actions answer to common interests that are recognized and upheld by some association of people. These "intermediate associations" join participants through shared commitments to and mutual benefits from their cooperative efforts. By means of these associations, members forge "political" agreements that express their common goals, meet their various needs, and structure their relations, duties, and rights. Such agreements are legitimate, Ruskin argues, because participants not only consent to them but do so after having learned to appreciate why certain associations cultivate individuals' virtues and promote public welfare. Thus, justice is possible, he claims, only where good character and communal agreements are secured, and the state must act to advance these aims by supporting the success of intermediate associations.

Given the retreat of the welfare state in recent decades, the continued legitimacy of government initiatives on behalf of the public welfare is a topic deserving renewed interest. At the same time, however, Ruskin's image of the good society as a beautiful cathedral, structured throughout by social practices and fully organized under "master craftsmen" and a "master builder," casts doubt on his rejection of the goods of liberty and the spaces for individual rights and public disagreements about the good that are protected by liberal institutions and a democratic politics.

Too often communitarian critics of modernity fail to engage the full history of their tradition. We hear praise for the language of the virtues, the character of engaged citizens, the intermediate associations of civil society, as the necessary prerequisites of a just society. We also hear the claim that liberal institutions are not only incapable of sustaining these elements of the common good, but are antithetical to it. We should assess these arguments historically, and Ruskin is an excellent case study. Although his "medieval" concerns with cultivated excellence and societal interdependence can be made compatible with "modern" commitments to basic fairness and democratic individuality, this balance is hardest to strike in his politics. That is partly because he remains so theoretical in his political reflections. Most notably, he posits an immutable dichotomy between cooperative associations and liberal institutions: "Government and co-operation are in all things and eternally the laws of life. Anarchy and competition, eternally, and in all things, the laws of death" (7.207). Either a society is organized throughout for "help," or it is entirely riven by "separation." The more that he appeals to this dichotomy between two seamless visions of social life—two antithetical ways of arranging people's "relations and duties," with one a perfect harmony of associations and the other the unrelenting clash of liberal institutions—the less helpful his politics and his account of justice become.

A close reading of Ruskin calls into question the complaints about moral incoherence, incommensurable goods, and irreconcilable conflicts sounded by today's communitarians. In his own idealized portrait of a medievalist social order of honorable characters who freely play the roles proper to their virtues, talents, and stations, there are no disagreements among masters and servants, dukes and bishops, kings and queens. In his defense of the "natural" virtues of men and women and in his denial of individual rights in these hierarchical relationships, we see why his cathedral model of the good society desperately needs the more fractured and mixed economy of practices and institutions that can be gleaned from his ethics of consumption. In fact, Ruskin's criticism is more eclectic than his political theorizing suggests, and I conclude the chapter noting that the gems of his criticism and his politics are his fragmentary observations about moral hypocrisy and social injustice in Victorian life. He is at his best as a practical critic who calls his audiences to heed the moral virtues, religious norms, and political priorities that they profess by shocking them into a recognition of the supposedly "shared agreements" of their culture and the implications of abiding by them as a community. These more fragmentary appeals to what his contemporaries do or should uphold in common provide strong reasons, interestingly enough, to support liberal economic, political, and social arrangements that carve out spaces for conflicts and disagreements about the good, which, for the most part, Ruskin himself assiduously avoids.

The Sources of Ruskin's Medievalism

Before dismissing Ruskin's politics as "medievalist," we need to consider its historical antecedents and competitors, my tasks in the first two sections. Florence Boos's assessment of Victorian medievalism is instructive. Looking back today, she writes, "one must pause to (re)conceive a society in which reflective people sometimes expressed their deepest hopes and demands for *change* in evocations of an idealized '*past*.'"[2] Charles Dellheim also notes how pervasive this tendency was at the time. He defines medievalism as "the appeal to, and the appeal of, the styles, symbols, and survivals of the Middle Ages." His typology of Victorian medievalism shows how common this symbolic language was in the period, even if different groups drew opposing lessons from its use. The most surprising of these "types" are the Whig industrialists, who in funding much of the neo-Gothic construction in the period, sought to claim the new industrial capitalist economy as heir to older English institutions of self-government and civil rights.[3]

Ruskin's medievalism is equally strategic, and his portraits of the Middle

Ages cannot be written off so easily as misplaced nostalgia. He admits as much in *The Two Paths* (1859). "We don't want either the life or the decorations of the thirteenth century back again. . . . All that gorgeousness of the Middle Ages, beautiful as it sounds in description, noble as in many respects it was in reality, had, nevertheless, for foundation and for end, nothing but the pride of life—the pride of the so-called superior classes" (16.341). Ruskin's strategic use of medievalism is meant to justify the "moralism" of his politics—his locating squarely within the realm of the political the responsibilities that people incur to others through networks of interdependence less obvious than in the past. If the "superior" classes of the Middle Ages sinned in failing to care for the many dependents attached to their kingdoms, guilds, and orders, Ruskin views the low wages paid by industrialists as an equivalent denial of the new forms of interdependence in Victorian society. Stated more broadly, he rejects any conception of politics that starts from discrete individuals abstracted from their relations and duties to others as actors in the complex political, economic, and social spheres of modern life.

Ruskin has a classical conception of politics as that art concerned with the arrangement of a society's activities and ends and the training of people's character and talents toward the common good. Recall from chapter 2 that Ruskin names architecture the "distinctively political art" (8.20). It is "political" because, in Aristotelian fashion, it is the art that encompasses every other art. The construction of a cathedral organizes these other arts' ends, products, and pleasures and directs many individuals' efforts and contributions, all toward the goal of creating a beautiful edifice that embodies the good ultimately sought through these activities and labors.[4]

Extending the analogy between Ruskin's cathedral model of politics and Aristotle's idea of politics as the science of the human good, we can outline the shape and aims of Ruskin's ideal social order. He focuses on the types of associations in a given society and the kinds of cooperation they foster or inhibit. This interest in the dynamics of social participation is well served by his cathedral model. No one can build a Gothic cathedral alone. Individuals participate only as members of specific crafts and guilds. Not only is participation in the larger "polity" of the cathedral mediated through these associations, but most "political" questions of relative authority, contribution, and reward are settled at this level, too. For example, the more skilled the members of a particular guild become, the higher their authority and the greater their contributions and rewards should be. Most importantly, they are responsible for the instruction and development of new members, and their authority is legitimate to the extent that they serve the craft and its novices well.

Beyond this basic level of Ruskin's politics, the various "intermediate associations" engaged in building the cathedral must be organized, too. The different arts have to be combined and coordinated, their contributions need to be arranged and prioritized, if the cathedral is itself to be a beautiful whole. It is easy to imagine conflicts arising at this level, as associations differ over the value and priority of their members' efforts, achievements, and rewards, but Ruskin's cathedral model functions to minimize such disputes. On the one hand, he stresses the forgiving style of the Gothic and the freedom enjoyed by the individual members of a great many associations, even as they mutually benefit themselves and their society. On the other hand, there is also the office of master builder, and Ruskin tends to frame the good society as a great hierarchy of cooperative endeavor.

This contrast between workers' fragmentary pursuits of distinctive excellences and the master's perfectly unified vision of their essential interdependence is noteworthy. Once again we see the themes of character and vision at the core of Ruskin's teleological ethics. For people to develop their virtues, there must be some shared recognition of the ends and goods necessary to a life of flourishing and, thus, some recognition of which associations can sustain individuals' development, contributions, rewards, and authority in other people's eyes. But how explicit and extensive must these agreements be, and how are they to be worked out and maintained?

Here it is useful to recall the four themes of "virtue," "authority," "organicism" and "tradition" that John McGowan cites as joining Ruskin's Tory radical tradition with contemporary communitarians.[5] The more Ruskin envisions participants choosing to join intermediate associations to develop their virtues, cooperate with others, achieve social recognition, and meet broader obligations, the more promise this politics has. To the extent that the organic hierarchies of his cathedral model predominate, the democratic potential of his politics recedes.

No one contributes more to the organicism in Ruskin's medievalism than "his friend and guide" Thomas Carlyle (17.145). Ruskin echoes his mentor's signature bombast, declaring to the readers of *Fors Clavigera* in 1871 that Carlyle remains "the only living writer who has spoken the absolute and perpetual truth about yourselves and your business; and exactly in proportion to the inherent weakness of brain in your lying guides, will be their animosity against Carlyle." Repeating the Carlylean themes of the mechanism, atomism, and amorality of the age, he names the chief of those "lying guides" the "modern Liberal politico-economist of the Stuart Mill school" (27.179–80). It should be noted that J. S. Mill agreed with Carlyle on some points, and the two discussed ideas from the 1830s into the early 1840s.[6] For Carlyle, however, classical political economy with its protagonist, *homo economicus*, the lonely utility-maximizer, epitomized the emerging liberal political order. And Carlyle never relented in castigating the utilitarians' "swine" philosophy that heeds the growl of the stomach over the edicts of the soul.

Three aspects of Carlyle's medievalism are significant for understanding Ruskin and for evaluating the renewed medievalist appeals in recent critiques of modern liberalism. First, Carlyle tells a narrative of decline in *Past and Present* (1840), related through contrasting scenes of the harmonious patronage of a medieval abbey and the chaotic competition of industrial society. Second, he uses representative character types as a tool of social analysis and critique. Finally, he calls for a common faith to counter the modern gospel of competition, offering the twelfth-century Abbot Samson as an exemplar of the salutary effects of a unifying "Hero-worship" on people's virtue and vision. Carlyle's historical narrative of the displacement of vibrant communities by liberal institutions is repeated in Ruskin's claim that the social practices required for people's character development and their vision of a common good are no longer viable in Victorian society. Similar arguments about the incompatibility of social practices with modern liberal institutions are echoed today by Alasdair MacIntyre and John Milbank.[7]

Carlyle explains his use of character types as an essential tool for diagnosing the causes of injustice in a society where terrible ills are suffered without anyone in particular to blame. An observation by Ralph Waldo Emerson (1803–82) is apt here. Gazing across the Atlantic, he reads in Carlyle's dizzying commentaries "the first domestication of the modern system, with its infinity of details, into style."[8] The great ills that people suffer, two million in workhouses, according to Carlyle, the brutal toil of factory work, are no one's fault. The evils lie in "the system," and their causes and consequences can be revealed only by describing how people's characters get warped when "all human dues and reciprocities [are reduced to the] one great due of *cash payment*." Carlyle stages his drama of modern life with an assortment of character types: the desperate poor, disgruntled laborers, idle aristocrats ("double-barrelled Dilettantes"), and industrious capitalists ("Midas-earred Mammonists"). In his retelling of the Midas fable, people devote every effort to increasing the "enchanted wealth" of capital, a glittering store of riches that like Midas's gold no one may actually enjoy. Following the industrialists' lead, the other characters scurry about "muttering . . . some vague janglement of Laissez-faire, Supply-and-demand, Cash-payment, the one nexus of man to man: Free-trade, and Devil take the hindmost, our latest Gospel yet preached." Carlyle adds, "We call it a Society; and go about professing openly the totalest separation, isolation. Our life is not a mutual helpfulness; but rather, cloaked under due laws-of-war, named 'fair competition' and so forth, it is a mutual hostility."[9]

Injustice is so endemic to the emerging system of industrial capitalism, Carlyle argues, that no solutions are possible through parliamentary laws or elections or any other institutional response. Instead, "Reform, like Charity . . . , must begin at home"—in close-quarters relationships where binding duties and good character are easier to recognize. At the level of society, the reform of character begins with the perfect authority of "Hero-worship," "the soul of all social business among men."[10] The impulse to model oneself on some exemplary figure is irresistible, Carlyle contends, because people achieve a sense of purpose, formative direction, and full commitments in their lives by having the solid substance of model characters to imitate, not by adhering to abstract principles and institutional rules that cannot themselves promote unity, build relationships, or provide inspiration. The only question is, who is worth revering?

Carlyle's portrait of Abbot Samson, the hero of *Past and Present,* indicates how little there is worth preserving in this medievalist ideal of an organic social unity and common faith. Carlyle rejects popular elections as incapable of appointing governors with Samson's traits: austerity and discipline in regulating the monastery's expenditures, justice and mercy in fending off mutinous challenges, courage and wisdom in venturing forth on crusades and standing up to the king himself. Carlyle's litany of Samson's "Herculean Labours," which are typical of "every governing man, from *Paterfamilias* to *Dominus Rex,*" buttresses his claim that "there is in every Nation and Community a *fittest,* a wisest, bravest, best: whom could we find and make King over us, all were in very truth well."[11]

I sketch Carlyle's autocratic model of authority to reinforce the reasons why Ruskin's own appeals to the "organic" warrant critical scrutiny. Yet Carlyle and Ruskin differ, especially on the subject of virtue. Ruskin employs character types as Carlyle does, and he ranks some above others, appealing to masters and titled aristocrats as models of the virtues being eroded by liberal modernity. But Ruskin does not identify human excellence with any historical figure, the one great "soul" who embodies the life of a people and is uniquely capable of envisioning the good for them all. According to Carlyle, when someone worships a true hero, "the Life-fountain [of virtue] within you [is] set flowing, what innumerable 'things,' whole sets and classes and continents of 'things,'... will then be doable and done!"[12] Certainly Ruskin, in his early aesthetics, portrays God's virtue as the fountain from which life flows, all ranked and arranged as an ordered hierarchy of the good (see chapter 1). But he abandons this unitary conception of perfect "virtue" for an analytical framework of the "virtues," those distinctive excellences that people cultivate in cooperative associations like Gothic craftwork. Carlyle's insistence on organic unity through paternal authority and a singular conception of the good indicates the need to look instead to the particular virtues, duties, and agreements that people take on and work out in their chosen associations.

Although Ruskin becomes interested in social practices through his architectural studies, as the decades pass, his politics shows clear affinities with the politics of another predecessor, Edmund Burke. When Ruskin ranks customs first among the constitutive elements of politics in *Munera Pulveris* (1862–63), the Burkean influences are evident. Ruskin's full list is "customs, laws, and councils, and their enforcements," and he clarifies his understanding of custom by detailing its three stages of "completeness." Custom is first "the manner or moral of acts." It then "become[s] a habit in the character: i.e., a constant 'having' or 'behaving.'" Finally, as custom gains "ethical power in performance and endurance," it is "the skill following on habit, and the ease reached by frequency of right doing." For Ruskin, even law proceeds from custom, for laws are either "the definitions and bonds of custom, or what the nation desires should become custom" (17.231, 236).

Burke also argued that a people's long-standing customs, mores, and associations exhibit a kind of "wisdom" that shapes a people's character and brings into view a workable vision of the common good. In Burke's view, society is threatened in two ways, but the threat is the same—the "arbitrary" exercise of power either by the state or by individuals. This concern with arbitrary power is a fixture of Burke's political writings, from his support for the American colonists to his defense of French aristocrats. In 1775 he cites the "*temper* and *character*" of these colonists, specifically, the love of freedom expressed in their history of leaving native countries, often as dissenting Protestants, in traditions of local self-governance and in various manners, not always admirable, including the "haughtiness of domination" that results from owning slaves. The tax policies of King George III run so contrary to the history, tradition, and manners of American liberty, he warns his fellow legislators, that these policies can only be viewed as illegitimate in this people's eyes.[13]

Writing on the same subject in 1770, Burke defines arbitrary state power in an important passage: "It is the nature of despotism to abhor power held by any means but its own *momentary pleasure;* and to annihilate all *intermediate situations* between boundless strength on its own part, and total debility on the part of the people."[14] Although Burke is concerned with the state's despotic powers here, individuals act arbitrarily, too, when they deny the moral claims made incumbent on them by the forms of association recognized as binding in a society. Again, for Burke, legitimacy is vested in a people's customs and associations. Political institutions, in particular, have legitimacy because they reflect past struggles by reasonable people to find practical means for promoting, as far as possible, the common aims and just relationships of a good society. Future generations should be wary, therefore, of discarding these, albeit imperfect, means of cooperation and the vision of the common good that they help to preserve. Burke's apologetic defense of the French aristocracy in his *Reflections on the Revolution in France* (1790) reflects both his sense of the vital importance of acknowledging the larger vision of justice and community at work in a people's traditional associations and also his distrust of proclamations of natural rights that rend the existing social fabric, however much in need of reform it may be.

Ruskin also upholds the established social order and opposes new individual rights for women and workers as tools of reform. We see him, moreover, appealing to an aristocratic noblesse oblige in charging well-off Victorians to meet their responsibilities to the industrialized poor. Joining the Carlylean distrust of institutional mechanisms with Burkean worries about arbitrary power, Ruskin innovates, too. Specifically, he translates Burke's analysis of arbitrary political power into a thoroughgoing critique of arbitrary economic power.

Ruskin argues that industrial capitalism licenses the unchecked power of the rich and erodes more legitimate means of forging public agreement about the ends, relations, and duties that should structure Victorian society. For him a liberal political economy of disconnected individuals secures "momentary pleasure" for some while destroying all of the "intermediate" associations where people might band together in cooperation *and* resistance, leaving money-power the new despotism. Instead of entrusting a society's direction to market mechanisms, and thus de facto to the wealthy, he proposes that people (the men at least) (re)claim decision-making power through self-governing associations. Public interests will be best served, he argues, by a network of guild-like associations where members decide and commit themselves to what the "commonwealth" asks of them. Add in the state's role in guaranteeing the conditions for creating, maintaining, and gaining access to these social practices, and the complex structure of his associational politics hints at its democratic potential, despite Ruskin's tendency to equate legitimate authority with organic consensus (Carlyle) or with customary wisdom (Burke).

Victorian Moralisms and Laissez-Faire Individualism

Burke, Carlyle, and Ruskin are members of a tradition of British *social* thought. Their contributions and their shortfalls are both worth pondering today when the very concept of the "social" seems politically unsustainable. Despite the problems in their portraits of medieval life, heroic character, and traditional authority, these figures and, to my mind, Ruskin, in particular, paved the way for early twentieth-century reformers, like Jane Addams, who argued that democracy needed to expand from a narrow focus on political representation to social participation.[15] This emphasis on the "social" shows as well in Ruskin's criticisms of Christian doctrines that blind people, he argues, to all that is or should be shared in political life. Here we must distinguish between the moralism of his politics and the more individualistic Christian moralism prevalent in the period.

Given today's disciplinary divisions, it is striking to learn that classical political economy joined politics and economics with morality, too. The Rev. Thomas Malthus's (1766–1834) *Essay on the Principle of Population, or, A View of Its Past and Present Effects on Human Happiness* is a case in point. Malthus's dire predictions about population growth and natural scarcity and his warnings against raising workers' wages directly reflect his late-eighteenth-century Evangelical worldview. He championed laissez-faire policies not because morality could be overlooked in the economic realm, but because the divinely sanctioned laws of political economy describe a world in which individuals must strive after salvation on their own. Interfering with the divine arrangement of things would only exacerbate the depravity of the poor by removing the spurs to righteousness that economic laws and natural scarcities reinforce.

In opposing this stern taskmaster view of divine providence, Ruskin identifies providence with earthly abundance in the good use and enjoyment of all of life's gifts. His antipathy for the Malthusian doctrine of providence is clear in his condemnation of preaching to the poor "the duty of remaining content in the position in which Providence has placed you." To "call the confused wreck of social order and life brought about by malicious collision and competition an arrangement of Providence," he charges, "is quite one of the most insolent and wicked ways in which it is possible to take the name of God in vain" (17.320).

Ruskin was not alone in relating notions of providence to economic attitudes. As Boyd Hilton has discussed, early nineteenth-century British Evangelicals divided over theology and politics, and Hilton's comparison of "moderate" and "extremist" Evangelicals sets Ruskin's moralism in the context of broader Victorian debates. Although Ruskin was raised a moderate Evangelical Anglican, his opposition to classical political economy and laissez-faire policies and his support for government activism all parallel the extremists' outlook.[16]

Theologically the two Evangelical camps differed over the soteriological significance of Jesus Christ's death. The moderates were post-millennialists, the extremists pre-millennialists. Hilton writes, "Where moderates 'preached Christ and Him crucified', extremists celebrated 'not Christ crucified merely, but Christ risen . . . , and Christ to be again present in person' very soon." These divergent perspectives on the world's spiritual state translate into opposing visions of the course of God's providence. As with all Christians awaiting the Second Coming in their own time, extremist Evangelicals viewed natural, social, and economic crises as proof of an imminent apocalypse. God was directly punishing and purging sinful humanity in preparation for the coming judgment day, and individuals' efforts to change the world amounted to little in comparison to God's "*ad hoc* and *ad hominem* interventions in terrestrial affairs." Whereas the extremists believed in the "special" operations of providence, the moderates saw it working "'generally' and predictably through natural and immutable laws of cause and effect." With the coming of the new age at Christ's resurrection, moderates believed that the responsibility for attaining the Kingdom of God on earth had shifted to humanity. God established the possibility of and the framework within which individuals can strive after personal salvation, and individuals succeed or fail due to their own efforts.

As Hilton shows, correlating these doctrinal views of providence with political attitudes about economic and social reform yields a curious result in the case of nineteenth-century British Evangelicals. The pre-millennialists advocated government intervention in social and economic affairs. Although no government action or social reform could prevent God's imminent wrath, an impossible feat, they might ameliorate the underlying problems. By contrast, moderate Evangelicals tended to oppose government regulation of the industrializing economy, believing that the health of society depended wholly on personal morality, not social responsibility. Thus, the expected correlations between pre-millennialism and fatalism and post-millennialism and activism seem reversed. But Hilton rejects that apparent paradox, explaining that "'improvement' then was generally envisaged in moral rather than material terms, and that the post-millenarian moderates, however callous their economic attitudes may appear to modern eyes, were actually the more paternalist in this other sense of wishing to control the morals of the nation. Indeed, they supported *laissez-faire* economic and social policies precisely because these would best nurture individual morality."[17]

For the moderates, individuals succeeded or failed morally within a divinely established framework of natural laws, among the most important of which were the laws described by the new science of political economy. Not the truly unregenerate, who were so far beyond the pale that nothing could be done to save them, but the fairly righteous, who committed the occasional peccadillo, warranted assistance in the form of intrusive moralistic uplift. The moderates' moral earnestness and their relative detachment from social and economic problems repeat the moral paternalism and laissez-faire inactivism found in Malthus. As many commentators have noted, the predominance of this moderate outlook among nineteenth-century Evangelicals and Methodists made many Christians, and most of the more optimistic and "progressive" ones, sympathetic to the individualism of utilitarian philosophy and classical political economy.[18]

Ruskin targets this laissez-faire individualism and merely moral reform in describing the true meaning and practice of Christianity. Declaring material aid and societal transformation the highest Christian duties, he writes,

> Wherever you see want, or misery, or degradation, in this world about you, there, be sure, either industry has been wanting, or industry has been in error. It is *not accident,* it is *not Heaven-commanded calamity,* it is *not the original and inevitable evil of man's nature,* which fill your streets with lamentation, and your graves with prey. It is only that, when

> there should have been providence, there has been waste; when there should have been labour, there has been lasciviousness; and wilfulness, when there should have been subordination. (16.19; my emphasis)

Condensed in this one passage, Ruskin repudiates both the extremists' and the moderates' views of providence. Human misery is not the extremists' "Heaven-commanded calamity" auguring an imminent apocalypse. Nor is it the result of "the original and inevitable evil of men's nature," an inward evil that requires constant scrutiny of one's moral rectitude and that, if left unchecked, causes the depravity of the poor who fail to improve themselves even though spurred on by the individualist framework of God's laws. Ruskin's prophetic rhetoric is directed not simply against his fellow Christians, however, for he also rejects secularized versions of Malthusian providence, in which poverty is simply a societal "accident" and is only worsened by efforts to correct against it. While J. S. Mill was no blind opponent of government regulation, his embrace of Malthus's "iron law of wages" (see chapter 7) is one example of why Ruskin lumps Christian advocates of laissez-faire individualism and liberal political economists like Mill as equally ideologically suspect.[19]

There are two broader issues here. First, when Ruskin appeals to divine providence, his goal is the full development of human excellence that his contemporaries might attain if they recognized the ills of industrial capitalism and actively opposed them. When his "moderate" opponents trumpet a moral virtue like "temperance," they imagine a different telos than Ruskin's earthly vision of an abundance of well-made people and well-made things. Indeed, Ruskin distanced himself from the Temperance Movement, praising the sacramental significance of wine and its use "as a stimulus to the powers of life" (17.370–71). Nor is this merely an instance of filial piety toward his wine-merchant father. Rather it is indicative of how his vocabulary of the virtues aims to expand human development across all social classes and imposes moral strictures mainly on the rich by charging them to observe the Christian virtues of charity and humility that they so freely commend to others.

Second, Ruskin's contrast between "providence" and "waste" in the preceding passage helps us see the limitations of the "prophetic" mode of argumentation he sometimes adopts. These prophetic appeals lend themselves to dualism, reinforcing the basic dichotomy between wise "paternal" governance and "anarchic" liberal institutions in his politics. Society either is heading for redemption or is entirely corrupt, having deviated from God's righteousness. No straying from this path may be tolerated, for with darkness all around only those seers who can discern God's vision for human life and history can make progress toward good character and societal abundance. Rhetorically such bursts of prophetic light have their shock value in exposing ideological blinders. Ruskin is right to challenge his contemporaries' complacent praise of their virtues and ready condemnation of others' vices. A better account of the virtues, he implies, not only would reveal these ideological blinders but, more importantly, would clarify, teach, and extend the moral virtues, cultural norms, practical excellences, and political ends by which his contemporaries should judge themselves and govern their society.

Here we see the constructive aims of Ruskin's criticism; his goal is always to move the conversation from social division to societal engagement. There are shared standards by which we evaluate ourselves, he insists. There are exemplary ideals we recognize in common, and we acknowledge that we incur obligations when other people contribute to our lives through direct association or distant exchange. As he paints his canvas of Victorian social life, Ruskin seeks to convince his audience of what they do and should uphold in common.

The trick is to balance these arguments for solidarity with democratic commitments to individuality. In Ruskin's case, the nostalgia of his medievalism and the dualism of his prophetic appeals reinforce the antidemocratic impulse, seen throughout his tradition, to affirm some "organic" social order of the past as *the* answer to the individualism of modern societies. When Ruskin opposes the "confused wreck of social order" and its "malicious collision and competition" to a harmony of associations, characterized by complete "agreement" to paternal governance by the wise and faithful submission by everyone else, he presents his own singular vision of the good society as nothing less than God's providential ordering of life.

In distinguishing his politics from the individualistic virtues of moderate Evangelicals and the haphazard social reforms of the extremists, Ruskin professes his hope that a politics productive of self-development and social virtue can be achieved through human governance. Although he mostly appeals to *divine* providence in his politics, it is worth noting that in 1871 he claims more modestly that providence "in its truest sense and scholarly use . . . is a human virtue" (20.306). This shift underscores the goals of his political reforms, the full development of people's capacities for excellence and the production of a more abundant commonwealth for all. As I turn from this historical backdrop to Ruskin's account of the political structures needed to achieve these aims, I examine his arguments for the right to public support, the primacy of politics over economics, and the idea of justice as "desert."

The Nation as Family and the Right to Public Support

Ruskin opens his lectures on *The Political Economy of Art* (1857) by noting the "*just* and *wholesome* contempt" that moderns have for poverty, at least when compared to classical writers. Whereas Victorians equate wealth with honor and poverty with shame, the Greeks, Romans, and medieval Christians celebrated itinerant philosophers and mendicant saints for disdaining the allure of riches in favor of the "Spirit of Poverty" (16.15–17). Ruskin applauds his contemporaries' sense of justice and flourishing in hating poverty, provided, that is, they hate the poverty and not the impoverished themselves.

Despite this apparent rejection of the ancients on the subject of political economy, Ruskin takes his general principles of "political science" from classical ideas.[20] He begins with the Greek meaning of "economy." Economy is not merely a matter of scrimping and saving. It involves saving, spending, and much more, as it means the "administration [*nomos*] of a house [*oikos*]; its stewardship." Ruskin follows this definition with an image of the happy home, "whether of the queenly housewife or queenly nation," which captures his dual conviction that, through the wise management of resources and people and through the ready cooperation of every member, a good society can be achieved for all (16.19, 20). This political vision of wisdom from above and solidarity throughout is central to Ruskin's arguments for "paternal government" and the "right to public support."

As Ruskin moves from the economy of the home to the nation as a family, he replaces the maternal authority of housewives with the paternal authority of national leaders. There are two issues here. First, there is the problem of the relative standing of women and men as leaders with different spheres of rule. Second, there is the question of whether any association, from a family up to the nation at large, can or should aspire to the unity implicit in Ruskin's imagery. Susan Moller Okin raises both concerns in *Justice, Gender, and the Family.* Citing Ruskin's 1864 lecture "Of Queens' Gardens," she focuses on his portrait of the home as the "Place of peace" and his praise for women's capacity for "self-renunciation." She rightly argues that theories of justice must apply in a world of social conflict and division and cannot presuppose that unity in affections and purposes is an attainable, or even a desirable, social ideal. Moreover, she rejects the gendering of separate spheres and duties for men and women that Ruskin claims is "natural."

Later in the chapter, I argue that any effort to recover Ruskin must confront these two challenges. But Okin raises a deeper conceptual question, too. Are teleological approaches that focus on excellence and interdependence compatible with modern democratic commitments to equality and autonomy? As she puts it, even if people exhibit nobler virtues in their interactions, "justice takes primacy because it is the most *essential,* not because it is the highest, of virtues."[21] By "justice" Okin means "fairness," and she locates this value in a framework of political, economic, and social institutions designed to ensure open access and basic "primary goods" for everyone, while allowing individuals to use these means as they see fit so long as they comply with whatever institutional arrangements they contract with one another.

Although anachronistic, comparing Ruskin's understanding of justice to Okin's notion of justice as fairness is instructive. Instead of institutional procedures, he focuses on associative commitments. Instead of founding justice on abstract principles that secure sufficient means for everyone's self-determination, he insists that justice requires concrete reflection about the ends of the activities and associations that are necessary to people's development. Two countervailing questions are raised by Ruskin's classical notion of a politics of ends. Given the problems with the organicism of his politics, can aiming at political agreement about ends actually serve democratic societies? Given the weakening of the welfare state in recent decades, can a politics of means maintain adequate public support for a social safety net?

Although Ruskin errs, in Okin's words, in placing the family "'beyond' justice," he agrees with her that justice is the primary political virtue. Compare how he ranks charity and justice in his 1865 lecture on "Work." "The one Divine work—the one ordered sacrifice—is to do justice; and it is the last we are ever inclined to do." "Yes," charity "is greater," he adds; "it is the summit of justice—it is the temple of which justice is the foundation. But you can't have the top without the bottom; you cannot build upon charity. You must build upon justice, for this main reason, that you have not, at first, charity to build with. . . . It is all very fine to think you can build upon charity to begin with; but you will find all you have got to begin with, begins at home, and is essentially love of yourself" (18.420). In rejecting the cliché that charity begins at home (and Carlyle's defense of it, too), Ruskin might have written "love of yourself *and yours,*" for he carries the argument in that direction. He illustrates the deficiencies of charity using a family all dressed up for church with nothing to spare for the ragged, young street sweeper they pass on the way. Self-love, which he implies includes undue love of family, is the main obstacle to the extensive moral regard for other people's welfare that is fundamental to a good society. It turns out, then, that Ruskin does not place the family entirely "beyond" justice. Decisions about the distribution of goods within families must acknowledge obligations to outsiders, at least.

Perhaps the deepest difference between Okin and Ruskin on the question of justice is whether her conception of "justice as fairness" can be described as a virtue at all. "Fairness" lodges more in institutional procedures than in moral traits, though certainly procedures of blind review and anti-discrimination laws can have edifying effects on people's character in fostering tolerance, for example. Ruskin's challenge to the liberal tendency to make justice a matter of constructing better institutional mechanisms is that moral education involves much more. On the one hand, justice comes in many forms—money, honor, love, pleasure, respect, aid, and so on—and knowing what all is due to others requires learning what is appropriate in the myriad spheres of cultural activity and social interaction. On the other hand, justice is also due to people whom one may never know and will have little regard for even if they pass by on the street. Simply put, giving justice, in all of its forms, to distant others whom we do not know, begins with the task of cultivating a more extensive moral regard.

Extending moral regard beyond oneself and one's near and dear is basic to any approach to justice that takes fairness as a basic criterion. John Rawls's imagined "veil of ignorance" is a clear recognition of this difficulty. What Okin calls Rawls's "central, brilliant idea" is that people will institute fair rules of justice only if they do not yet know their place in society.[22] The veil of ignorance worn by people in the "original position" of contracting the rules of their society also reveals the practical limitations of this approach, however. The need to foster moral regard for unknown others is not a one-time affair. Take the legitimacy of rights to public support. These rights are always subject to reconsideration. Maintaining their legitimacy requires more than the hope that every election day the veil of ignorance will once again drop over a people's eyes.

Contemporary moral debates about welfare programs offer a useful way into Ruskin's defense of rights to public support. On the political right, in the United States at least, the moral arguments against welfare provision range from the libertarian claim that justly gained earnings should not be redistributed through government interference to the claim that welfare programs undermine personal initiative and a host of virtues. On the political left, the moral arguments include appeals to individual rights to the "primary goods" needed to participate in society as well as the claim that a capitalist economy has structural dynamics that disadvantage some of the people whose basic welfare needs must therefore be met out of the collective pie.

Unsurprisingly, given the hybrid nature of Ruskin's politics, each of these positions is found in his arguments. Although no liberal, let alone a libertarian, he affirms the right to private property, though he proposes strict legal limits on personal incomes and holdings of wealth (17.322). He also worries about the deleterious effects that public provision has on character, especially the false sense of superiority that comes from enjoying a horse and carriage at the public expense, one of the many forms of "alms" for the elite that typically go unacknowledged, he notes (16.113–14). Finally, he echoes the arguments of the political left in detailing the systemic injustices of Victorian capitalism and in affirming rights to public support.

Ruskin's formulation of these rights reveals much about his politics. Rights, for him, do not inhere in people themselves; rights emerge from the structure of their "relations and duties" and the collective benefits and burdens thus produced. Rights also have corresponding duties, he claims, and the duties come first. He cites an argument to this effect from another predecessor in his tradition. In William Wordsworth's words, "as all rights in one party impose a correlative duty upon another, it follows that the right of the State to require services of its members, even to the jeoparding of their lives in the common defence, establishes a right in the people (not to be gainsaid by utilitarians and economists) to public support when, from any cause, they may be unable to support themselves." Ruskin's own defense of the right to public support reflects this duty-based notion of rights. It also makes much of Wordsworth's naming Britain a "Christian government, standing *in loco parentis* towards all its subjects" (16.27n).

As Ruskin sees it, "the masses" have a "right to claim education from their government; but only so far as they acknowledge the duty of yielding obedience to their government"; they have a "right to employment from their governors; but only so far as they yield to the governor the direction and discipline of their labour"; they have, in short, a "right to ask that none of their distresses should be unrelieved, none of their weaknesses unwatched; and that no grief, nor nakedness, nor peril should exist for them against which the father's hand was not outstretched, or the father's shield uplifted" (16.26–27).

The paternalism of this politics is clear. Although the destitute may be protected against the worst deprivations caused by their lack of access to education and work, they are subject to discipline and, even more intrusively, to definition of their "weakness" and "distress" by their "governors." Although examples of hierarchical governance were more common in this socially stratified era of masters and servants, and although Ruskin's appeal to God's "fatherly" solicitude is meant to urge the nation to its Christian duties to all of its "children," his language amply demonstrates his valorization of paternal and male authority. Must we, then, separate talk of individual rights from attention to social duties? Must we reject Ruskin's sense that we are all in this together and had better work out political agreements not just about the basic *means* for societal participation, but more importantly about the *ends* of good lives and the commitments to human development, social cooperation, and the public support that they require?

In calling rights to public support "entitlements," we express our deep reluctance to press the demands of political justice any farther than access to basic means. Citizens are *entitled* to these means by right, in theory at least. Of course that theory remains valid only so long as the public supports the requisite provision of aid as a legitimate task of the state, one that imposes binding financial and civic obligations on the community. The challenge of Ruskin's politics is this: is the idea of "justice as fairness," with its faith in contractual principles and institutional structures, adequate to its aim? Without some political agreements about the makings of good lives and a good society and without sufficient solidarity in embracing those requirements as social responsibilities, can basic justice be served?

The Gift of Art and Its Political Economy

Ruskin devotes the rest of *The Political Economy of Art* to demonstrating how a politics joined around shared ends helps promote human development, wise leadership, mutual aid, and public goods. It must be acknowledged that his argument is made easier by his focus on art. We accept that the cultivation of artistic excellence requires learning from wise teachers who grasp the point of a common practice. Likewise, great artworks appear to be a public good so long as they are not hidden away in private hands never to circulate again. Finally, Ruskin's belief that people have natural talents and that these are ordered to the society's benefit is less offensive in a realm where artistic genius is often viewed as an innate "gift" that nevertheless enriches other people's lives by expanding their imaginative horizons.

At the heart of Ruskin's analysis of *The Political Economy of Art* is his insistence that politics takes primacy over economics. The primacy of politics—in determining the ends of good lives and making citizens capable of realizing them—is clear in Ruskin's outline: how to discover and apply the talents and to accumulate and distribute the products of the "special genius" for art "to the best national advantage" (16.29). This "special gift" of "artistical gold" is scattered throughout every population, he declares, for "aught I know there may be two or three Leonardo da Vincis employed at this moment in your harbours and railroads." But the discovery and encouragement of this talent require two kinds of public leadership. The state, for its part, must support "trial schools" and employ young artists (whom Ruskin assumes to be men) in public projects to decorate schools and guildhalls. Master artists must assume responsibility for training these novices in the arts best suited to them (16.30–31, 88–89, 93). This combined initiative, by the state and by guild-like associations, fits the cathedral model of Ruskin's politics exactly.

This example also illustrates the two types of justice at work in these political reflections and the types of justice that Ruskin largely ignores. Again justice in general means giving other people their due, but how that due is determined varies with the kind of justice. Ruskin skips two parts of Aristotle's account of justice. He downplays "justice in exchange," the giving of equivalent amounts of different goods as agreed to by the parties to exchange. And he sets aside the judgments of punishment and compensation in criminal and civil law, claiming that, with "the advance in our social knowledge," the present need for "judicial" justice will be lessened through better governance (16.25–26). The heart of Ruskin's politics is "distributive justice," which begins with the social goods that are the shared possessions of some group of people and portions out these goods according to people's relative standing in an arena of distribution. So, for example, in the sphere of politics, the social goods of power and office are not granted to everyone, but in appropriate amounts to the appointed leaders, however they are chosen.

In addition to distributive justice, what we call "social justice" figures prominently in Ruskin's politics, despite its absence from classical discussions.[23] Appeals to social justice call attention to the gap between current and "better" distributions of goods in a society, where that gap is blamed on the economic, political, and social barriers built into the operations of existing institutions, barriers that prevent or restrict the due recognition of individuals' dignity, the due support for their development, or the due enjoyment of rewards commensurate with their contributions. This definition begs the question, of course, of what justifies the "better distributions" sought by the seekers of social justice. Here there will be considerable debate, but the common concern in these appeals is how institutions structure the access, opportunity, assistance, and respect that individuals do or do not receive as members of the public.[24]

The close connection between distributive and social justice is clear in Ruskin's proposal for trial schools and a job corps for young artists paid at the public's expense. The first question of distributive justice is, what are the social goods to be distributed in a society? As indicated by the revised title of *The Political Economy of Art,* Ruskin borrows John Keats's phrase in naming the arts *"A Joy Forever."* He not only declares the arts to be a lasting public good, however, but he points to the nation's decision to fund a National Art Gallery as proof that the public already agrees that art is one of the "Treasures" of their Commonwealth (16.17). In order to promote this public end and distribute this shared possession, art of the highest quality must be produced in the greatest quantity and made available throughout the polity. But there are barriers to overcome. The barrier of social class is redressed by the state's funding of trial schools and arts projects to allow all potential artists the chance to realize their gifts. Another barrier is the Victorian taste for manufactured goods over craftwork. This preference commits the public to factory production and capitalist exchange, making government support for a guild-like structure of arts and crafts an urgent matter of social justice.

Ruskin adds another barrier to the abundance of excellent arts that underscores the centrality of character to his politics. Too often budding artists face public criticism and apathy when what they need and deserve is the "justice of praise." By this phrase he means that the public should be quicker to praise what is worthy in juvenile endeavors than to criticize what is unworthy. Praise for these fumbling attempts is the budding artists' due. It encourages their initial growth and eventual achievement. Although it may seem odd to name this encouragement an act of justice, Ruskin's phrasing highlights both the breadth of his idea of the right to public support and the complexity of his understanding of justice.

Again for Ruskin, rights to public support sit within a framework of duties. Artists are duty-bound to use their gifts well, and the public is charged with supporting their labors because the public is the ultimate beneficiary. In knowing what is due to young artists, other people must be able to recognize the many different forms in which justice is owed. The goods due to young artists include, at the very least, practical education and access to it, public aid in launching artistic careers, and communal honors for excellence. Indeed, justice always encompasses a range of goods, but where the production and distribution of art are "governed" solely by market exchange, the "external goods" of money and fame crowd out these other goods (see chapter 2). That is why Ruskin insists on the primacy of politics over economics; market competition by itself is no governance at all. Relying on the market to determine societal priorities and to distribute social goods is, simply put, the abrogation of politics.

When riches control the art economy, Ruskin argues, the gift of art will be squandered, doing an injustice to the lost talents and to the public at large. Much of *The Political Economy of Art* describes the irrationalities of managing the arts through market mechanisms instead of wise governance. He notes, for example, the folly of using cheaply made materials in creating art, and he proposes government paper and paint factories to establish quality standards. He also laments the reluctance by Members of Parliament to commit public funds to buy the priceless works of great artists while the nation spends far larger sums in support of wars destroying some of Europe's greatest treasures (16.44–45, 53).

Turning to the art market itself, Ruskin identifies two harmful tendencies caused by inflated prices. The high prices of contemporary art are fueled, he claims, by the desire for fame. Vanity spurs most private collectors as the rich aspire to display their good taste by following the fashions of the day. This crowd-following behavior rewards the luckier artists unduly while it depresses both the market for and the makers of less trendy art works. The other cause of inflation is the typical jump in the prices that people pay for dead artists' work. Although this phenomenon can be explained by the sudden scarcity of an artist's work, Ruskin counsels, "pay your prices into the hands of living men, [do] not pour them into coffins." Above all else, he condemns collectors who hoard living artists' works in hopes of profiteering on their deaths. He sets forth a rule against buying the work of any artist whom one did not support while he was living; it does "no good to him" and "some shame to yourself" (16.82–88).

Ruskin's hopes for reform in the art market and reform of the public's taste go hand-in-hand, and the state has a role in achieving both ends. The nation should purchase the works of past masters for public museums. By displaying art's greatest gifts, "the people" will share in a collective inheritance, edifying their taste and enhancing their understanding of the past. Private buying should be encouraged, too, but limited to the works of living artists. People can explore their distinctive tastes by enjoying the works of contemporary artists in their own homes. With art prices lower on average and with more people buying art, the number of living artists will increase, and the interactions between artists and their audiences will reach more widely across all social classes, breathing new life and a more democratic spirit into the culture (16.82).

Ruskin describes a "gift economy" in the arts. His vision makes the creation of a "commonwealth" in the arts contingent on wise governance by the state, master artists, younger artists, and the people. If politics is the concerted effort to identify and uphold public ends for the good of all, then for Ruskin that means abandoning unregulated market choice and the status quo of rich and poor as the two primary determinants of economic choice. Public interest in artistic work cannot be left to the caprice of the art market. People should become artists because they have the talent, not because they have the leisure and security purchased by high social class. And as Ruskin extends the conclusions of his "political economy of art" across other arenas of economic activity, he makes a universal gift economy the corollary of a just politics. Not only art, but "all things needful" to human existence and flourishing are providentially arranged as life's "gifts," including "healthful rest," "serviceable leisure," "comfortable habitation," "good education," and "many pleasant objects of luxury" (16.18–19).

As noted at the outset of this section, the core tenets of Ruskin's politics are most easily defended in the sphere of art. In making the arts the model of a politics of individual excellence, abundant commonwealth, and just distributions, he is overly sanguine in his arguments that there are already recognized social goods and political ends that impose common commitments on the public. As well described in Lewis Hyde's work on gift economies, the arts are a special arena of masterly instruction and willing deference, of self-sacrifice on behalf of one's gifts, and of sharing the fruits of those labors. For Hyde as for Ruskin, the gift of artistry dies if an artist fails to receive it in the spirit of sharing or if the audience treats the gift of art as a dead thing to be possessed in private and removed from broader circulation.[25] The survival and increase of the arts demand mutual exchange, not just of money for commodities, but of honor, aid, imagination, knowledge, and a host of other goods, a full cultural exchange cycling through the body politic. Hiding the works of past masters in one's house, seeking to possess an artist's fame, denying young artists due praise and public aid, failing to support guild associations and instruction, all of these actions create barriers of injustice in the operation of existing institutions.

These contrasting images of cycling gifts in the body politic and unjust barriers in liberal institutions clarify both the force of Ruskin's account of the "social life" of Victorian Britain and also the limitations of his politics. That the goods of art are most abundant where they are embraced as a shared end that imposes social responsibilities on the public is a compelling argument. That it follows that this example of a "gift economy" proves the necessity of a full-fledged politics of ends is questionable, all the more so when we read in *The Political Economy of Art* Ruskin's antidemocratic idyll of the "magnanimous" government of sovereign kings.

Magnanimity or Justice

The influence of Ruskin's art criticism on his politics shows in his readings of the virtues that he commends to his contemporaries. In *The Political Economy of Art*, he interprets a fresco by Ambrozio Lorenzetti (?–1348) depicting the virtues required for "Good Civic Government." This fresco and Ruskin's subsequent use of Giotto's (1266?–1336?) prints of the virtues and vices serve as bookends around this section. In framing Ruskin's political reflections this way, we see how far he comes in assigning primacy to justice and why, for him, the virtue of justice is a matter of "desert."

Although *The Political Economy of Art* focuses on distributive justice, Ruskin gives pride of place to the virtue of magnanimity in his reading of Lorenzetti's fresco. In the fresco various virtues, all portrayed as women, attend the figure of the king. Ruskin acknowledges the central place of the virtues of faith, hope, and charity hovering around the king's head. These theological virtues serve human government, not as "heavenward" distractions from earthly rule but as persistence through adversity, reform of existing institutions, and mutual love between a sovereign king and his people. Ruskin devotes his praise, though, to magnanimity, the virtue of administering public revenues. This virtue, which "we hear too little of in modern times," is the "capacity of heart—the great *measuring* virtue" that weighs all gifts, gains, goods, and sacrifices (16.54–55, 56).

Ruskin's appeal to magnanimity is an appeal for increased spending for public welfare. But magnanimity has damning drawbacks at the political level. Simply put, while magnanimity may be a noble virtue at times, it is not a virtue of democracy. As a kingly virtue, magnanimity implies an official hold on power and largesse sufficient to institute one's own designs for other people's welfare. As a "capacity of heart," Ruskin also suggests that magnanimity is intuitive, knowing other people's needs instinctively without having to explain one's reasons even to the people being served. Magnanimity, in general, has something of this quality of a fait accompli. A remarkable gift or sacrifice is made on other people's behalf—remarkable because it is so great or so unexpected that it unsettles established norms of justice, leaving recipients to accept the offering almost speechlessly or to refuse it most ungraciously. Think of the handmade gifts of art we receive from children and loved ones. Or consider how Ruskin's ideal of a magnanimous king clarifies why it is said that monarchs transcend the law. Their solicitude for their subjects need not conform to written codes or procedural standards, and there is no quarrelling with the king's magisterial vision of the public good and his true discernment of his subjects' characters, needs, abilities, roles—in short, the kind of "nobles" they are or are not.

I am not denying magnanimity's importance in human relationships. A magnanimous gesture may be praiseworthy when the action does not reify a hierarchical relationship or power structure upon which the gift or sacrifice depends. An early retirement for the purpose of opening room in a tight job market is magnanimous partly because it undermines the vested privilege of professional status. It transcends, by challenging, the accepted procedures for gaining professional employment, which though they may be as fair as possible are not just enough. By contrast, the magnanimity that Ruskin envisions is guided and checked solely by the king's other virtues. Any other strictures on his wealth and power would defeat the potency and reach of his magnanimity. The king's sovereign command of the nation's purse, law, and policy is necessary to implement his wise designs. Indeed, there cannot be a "politics of magnanimity" apart from an aristocratic social order where the sacrifices of an elite—if they make any sacrifices at all—are guaranteed a reverent reception by the presumed beneficiaries, the people.

Ruskin's regret over a lost politics of magnanimity reflects his medievalist narrative of decline and the supposed disappearance of the organic unity, paternal authority, wise mastership, dutiful roles, mutual affections, and beneficent inequalities of his ideal communities of the past. To what extent are these medievalist holdovers unsettled as he grants a higher priority to justice?

Already in his lecture on the "Influence of Imagination in Architecture," Ruskin elevates justice. He tells the assembled architects, "your work must be associative. You cannot carve a whole cathedral by yourself—you can carve but few and simple parts of it. Either your own work must be disgraced in the mass of the collateral inferiority, or you must raise your fellow-designers to correspondence of power" (16.372–73). This argument resembles his earlier call for the "justice of praise," but now the concern is not so much the *praise* justly given as the *aid* justly demanded. This double movement of justice is central to Ruskin's politics. There is both an "upward" and a "downward" thrust to his arguments. Looking upward, the attention is directed toward the goods shared in social practices and throughout the community, toward the excellences that people acknowledge together, and toward the virtues, norms, and standards that they profess to uphold in common. Looking downward, the focus shifts toward distributive and social justice, specifically, toward the societal conditions and economic exploitation that cause direct injury to individuals.

Both of these movements are apparent in this lecture when Ruskin tells his architects that they must develop their workers to attain equivalent power in their art. He charges that "if you are morally strong enough to make . . . kindness and justice the first motive, it will be better;—best of all, if you do not consider it as kindness at all, but bare and stern justice; for, truly, such help as we can give each other in this world is a *debt* to each other; and the man who perceives a superiority or a capacity in a subordinate, and neither confesses, nor assists it, is not merely the withholder of kindness, but the committer of injury" (16.374). Notice the language of "injury" here. When an architect or the "masters" of any craft fail to aid workers' development, even to the point where the workers surpass them in capacity, excellence, and authority, a direct injury is done. The effect of this argument is to unsettle social hierarchies that maintain some people's power at other people's expense. The architect's goal should be to lessen and even displace the differences in power that currently give him authority over those in his charge. Elsewhere Ruskin bemoans the dashing of people's hopes for flourishing lives and social recognition because other people refuse to acknowledge the debts they incur through their associative activities, whether near or far.

We can now approach Ruskin's full understanding of the virtue of justice in light of the etymological links he draws between "honesty" and "honor." In *Time and Tide* (1867) he describes "justice" as "the most comprehensive word for all kind of honest dealing" (17.368). "Honesty," understood as a virtue, is not merely a principled refusal to tell lies or omit the truth. It is an active capacity for recognizing human worthiness. For Ruskin it is at bottom the capacity to stake a claim of the "honor" due someone, a claim that can be substantiated with reasons in an appropriate context of judgment and comparison. Take painting, for example, where judging appropriate honors begins with recognizing a painter's relative merits in view of the goods and standards of the practice and the past and present achievements of its participants. Seen from this perspective, it is just to give young artists praise before criticism. If they had to compete at the highest levels from the start, their growth would be stymied. In discerning both the praise *and* the aid due to young artists, the judge must look with one eye to these artists' relative standing today and look with the other eye to their future promise. For Ruskin, justice cannot be doled out on the basis of current social rankings, especially if those rankings were determined by goods of money and fame that have no intrinsic connection to the practice of painting. The goal of human development and the achievement of commonwealth both demand something more progressive, and yet, for Ruskin, it falls to the masters to know exactly what is due to—and what is good for—all of the different talents in their charge.

Ruskin emphasizes both the particularity and the paternalism of justice when he finally defines this virtue four years later in the *Fors Clavigera* letter "Honour to Whom Honour." In his words, "true justice (not to spend time, which I am apt to be too fond of doing, in verbal definition) consists mainly in the granting to every human being due aid in the development of such faculties as it possesses for action and enjoyment. . . . '*Due*' aid, you see, I have written. Not '*equal*' aid" (27.147–48; my emphasis). Ruskin proceeds to insist that this inequality of the aid due to individuals applies to education most of all; more and less talented students deserve different kinds of instruction and concern. The apparent injustice shocks procedural standards of fairness. But there is merit in the argument if justice is seen as a virtue that takes its bearings from a view of human life, centered in attaining excellence in practical activities that are directed toward good ends. Both the Aristotelian idea that excellence is achieved in social practices and the accompanying claim that some activities are more productive of better lives and higher goods are basic to Ruskin's account of justice as a virtue.

How might justice, thus framed, mandate different treatments for currently more capable and currently less capable students? They may be treated differently, not as students being graded according to institutional procedures of fairness, but as students seeking knowledge and related goods as participants in the practices of learning. Setting aside the issue of grades and institutional rankings, comments on papers designed to help students improve will reflect their relative standing as measured against the purposes that the course and the assignment aim to achieve, which reflect in turn the governing ends, the internal goods, and the evaluative standards of the practice or "discipline" of which the course is a part and of which the teacher has been judged a "master," at least. A better student in the course may benefit from incisively critical comments that suggest to her, and possibly motivate her to attain, the higher levels opened up by her achievements to date. By contrast, hearty encouragement and clear direction in delimiting a paper topic may be what is due to the student who is a beginner. It is the master's job to give aid and praise, instruction and care, in the ways that will be "good for" different students. All the while expectations for every student can be held to the same grading standards. A paternalism of sorts thus combines with procedural fairness in balancing the goal of fostering excellence with the institutional mandate of nonpreferential treatment.

Michael Walzer helps clarify the strengths of Ruskin's idea of justice as a virtue and the limitations of his defining all justice as "desert." In *Spheres of Justice,* Walzer distinguishes three "distributive principles": free exchange, need, and desert. The principle of desert, he notes, "seems to require an especially close connection between particular goods and particular persons, whereas justice only sometimes requires a connection of that sort. . . . [Thus] we might insist that only artistically cultivated people, who deserve to have pictures, should actually have them."[26] That Walzer chose the arts as his example of the principle of desert suggests that he may have had Ruskin in mind. But unlike Ruskin, Walzer imagines that a politics of desert would entail the government's buying works of art and giving them to "artistically cultivated men and women." Ruskin proposes that the government buy the best works for public museums because the arts are so vital to everyone's development and the general welfare.

In this proposal for public purchases of art to serve every citizen's needs, Ruskin rejects the principle of "free exchange," and he elides the general category of "need" into the specific mandate of "desert." We have already seen his critique of "free exchange" in the art market as the abrogation of politics. Less obvious is his equation of "need" with "desert." Need has a more general connotation than desert; everyone has needs, many of which are common, such as the need for air, water, food, clothing, and shelter. Need is also a baseline principle; once a person's basics are met, "needs" give way to "wants." Moving above the baseline of need, we might think that distributions of goods in the space of "wants" are better served by "free exchange" because this principle leaves it to individuals to determine what exactly they are willing to trade in meeting their wants. But Ruskin resists the idea that needs are "general" and "basic" and the belief in free exchange as a mechanism of justice. These convictions reflect his "cathedral model" of a politics structured throughout by associations that have the characteristics of a social practice, namely, that there are mutually recognized ends to which all participants agree and that the praise and the aid required to pursue them are *due,* not in general as a matter of basic "need," but to particular people as a matter of acknowledged "desert."

We can now see why Ruskin's arguments for rights to public support are so forceful. For him people *deserve* to have their needs met—for education, shelter, food, clothing, health, rest, and so on—because, without these, they cannot develop their capacities and excellences at all and so contribute to and benefit from the goods shared in their associations and from the common good sustained by the polity as a whole. People *deserve* a range of goods from material necessities on up to the highest accomplishments that they might attain as individuals. Let me stress once again the "particularity" of the concept of desert. A just polity must have some mechanisms, Ruskin argues, for attending to the specific contexts of individuals' lives—recognizing that people face different obstacles, have more and less acute needs for public assistance, and, most importantly, deserve to have their particular obstacles and needs redressed to further their lives for their own good. His "cathedral model" of politics is designed to make practical this conception of justice as "desert." That is why he insists on paternal governance in identifying the ends of human life, directing individuals' desires and efforts and arranging economic and social conditions toward their attainment. As he looks around Victorian society, he sees that some people's legitimate demands for the basics, let alone for such "higher" goods as the arts, are denied, reinforcing his dualistic contention that the "death" of liberal institutions and their purported rules of fair play must be replaced by the "life" of cooperative associations and paternal governance.

Ruskin's Reforms

A good illustration of Ruskin's challenge to institutional procedures and rules of fair play is his criticism of his contemporary, Cambridge Professor of Political Economy Henry Fawcett. Fawcett presents the capitalist market as regulated by the fairness of free exchange, but his vocabulary reveals something else, Ruskin notes. Discussing the payments due for labor, land, and capital, Fawcett describes wages as paid in "portions," rents in "shares," and profits in "remunerations." The more well-heeled the word, the grander the payment its owner seems to deserve. Thus, Ruskin implies, appeals to rules of fair play are really ideological smokescreens designed to sneak back in claims of "desert." Fawcett's presumption of procedural fairness is belied by his unspoken recognition of social distinctions and power structures, and his language seeks to justify social patterns of power and privilege. In rejoinder to Fawcett's supposedly descriptive analysis, Ruskin proposes that such blinding subtleties of terminology are easily lost on

> the Image of Justice we used to set up in England, above insurance offices, and the like. Bandaged close about the eyes, our English Justice was wont to be, with a pair of grocers' scales in her hand, wherewith, doubtless, she was accustomed to weigh out accurately their shares to the landlords, and portions to the labourers, and remunerations to the capitalists. But Giotto's Justice has no bandage about her eyes . . . , and weighs, not with scales, but with her own hands; and weighs not merely the shares, or remunerations of men, but the *worth* of them; and finding them worth this or that, gives them what they *deserve.* (27.191–92; my emphasis)

Beyond being a characteristically evocative critique of his society, Ruskin's appeal to Giotto's portrait of justice exemplifies the centrality of individual desert to his politics and the degree to which his moralistic concerns with a hands-on cultivation of character and an all-encompassing vision of the good motivate his political reforms.

Ruskin proposes legal limits on "the properties and incomes of the upper classes" in an effort to lessen economic inequalities and promote good character. While the enterprising and the industrious deserve greater monetary rewards than the dull and the idle, at some point the life-long pursuit of wealth blinds people to its personal and social costs. Using accumulated riches to accrue further advantage for oneself denies opportunities for success to young people who have fewer means. This unceasing pursuit of monetary gain also distracts accomplished business leaders from worthier efforts, of which the "superintendence of public institutions" would put their managerial talents and entrepreneurial skills to better effect (17.321–22).[27]

Not only is it unfair that the wealthy can use their riches to their own advantage, but the risks and the costs of financial speculation, Ruskin observes, are unevenly distributed, too. The blind justice of financial markets strikes no balance between the gains "earned" and the losses inflicted through business speculation. When speculators succeed, the gains are all theirs, while the people put out of work are hidden from view. It is only when the speculators fail that all of the suffering, now inflicted on even more people, can be fully reckoned (as the recent spate of corporate disasters illustrates today). Speculation on government bonds is more nefarious, in Ruskin's judgment, because the interests at stake are public, not private. Citing the raging arms race with France and the burgeoning national debt, he charges that "the public," as always, is enlisted to support certain "shared" interests, but the only interests served in this case are those of people wealthy enough to live off of their "remunerations" from government bonds (17.389, 142). Speculation on public works is harmful, too, and Ruskin proposes making the construction of roads, harbor protections, and mines entirely public ventures (17.380). So too, he decries the "cast-iron cockades and zigzag cornices . . . 'supplied'" to the public as decorations for its railroad bridges and stations. These ill-designed "extras" pay handsomely in the higher cost of train tickets borne by the public without anyone's actually having "demanded" the art, such as it is.

In each of these cases, there is no governing vision to guide the "free exchange" of the market, leaving all sorts of bad characters at liberty to manipulate the rules of fair play for their own narrow interests. These are the real workings of supply and demand when used as the tools of public policy, Ruskin contends. They are anti-democratic, too, in denying improved assistance for and expanded consent by the people. Indeed, at no time were the people asked if they might prefer more schools and libraries, or possibly gardens, parks, and houses for the poor (17.389–90).

Ruskin does not embrace democratic forms of governance as the corrective to this lack of consent, however. It is not enough for him to excavate the hidden "social" elements of Victorian life. There can be no social justice, he often implies, apart from the consensus of a perfectly "organic" society. Again, he criticizes the refusal to regulate personal income and wealth, speculative business practices, and public works projects for leaving people bound by nothing more than the market exchanges and contractual relationships they "choose" to enter, if they had any choice at all. He concludes that electoral representation and individual rights are also incapable of fostering the shared agreements and ready cooperation that alone make for political legitimacy. That is why guild-like cooperatives predominate in his politics. He still supports state funding of decorations on public projects, as we have seen, but he insists that this art be produced by rising talents who are trained by well-regarded masters. Similarly, he favors the creation of guilds for every kind of useful product. These guilds would fix annual prices and wages and set quality standards, making all of this information public by opening the books of the associated businesses and marking their products with the guild's stamp of approval (17.384–87).

The associational character of Ruskin's reforms is further evidenced by his advice to the working classes to place their trust not in the Parliament, but in a parliament of their own. His concerns with political legitimacy and moral reform are obvious here. Workers should draw from their experience in forming plans for the "regulation of industry" and the "helpful discipline of [their] life" (17.327–28). Yet the implied independence for workers should not be exaggerated, for the egalitarian and the consensual always merge with the hierarchical and the paternal in Ruskin's politics, and he rejects out of hand workers' efforts to expand their "rights" against their "masters." "Rights" establish "an external mechanism of justice," a structure of laws as incapable as the laws of supply and demand of achieving the cooperation needed for a commonwealth (17.319–20, 27.147). Despite the democratic impulses of many of his reforms, he builds these reforms block by block into the cathedral model of his politics, leaving little room at all for the disagreements, differences, and conflicts mediated by liberal institutions.

The state still has work to do in his politics, granting pensions with dignity to the elderly, guaranteeing job training for the unemployed, and funding his ever-widening plans for public education. National trusts for the conservation of natural resources and historic treasures fall to the state, too, along with the public museums and cultural institutions already discussed. Although most political decisions and distributions would occur in associations, the state ensures the viability of this economic structure and guarantees the broader conditions of social justice. While many of Ruskin's proposals become hallmarks of the twentieth-century welfare state, some of the state's duties, as imagined by him, reflect the lengths to which he takes his belief that a just society must be organized as a perfect harmony of associations, bound not only internally among their members, but externally, too. For example, he gives new meaning to the "seven-year itch," urging the state to provide every eligible young couple with the same income for the first seven years of their marriage, with no recourse to family money or inheritance. Only if all households begin on a level playing field, he suggests, can the rules of "fair play" be truly just, for otherwise some families will gain undue advantage and strength from their associations to the detriment of basic justice (17.421).

Clearly the up-down structure of Ruskin's politics reinforces the urgency he ascribes to "shared agreements" about public ends and social responsibilities. It motivates as well his keen awareness of the economic exploitation, injuries, and losses suffered by those without the means to compete fairly with others in the conditions of Victorian capitalist society. Most importantly, it celebrates the social practices and intermediate associations of civil society as spaces where people can join together to enjoy the goods made available through their association and to work out cooperative commitments that extend their duties and enhance themselves as self-governing citizens. His analysis helps correct classically liberal models of society that reduce individual freedom and societal choices to the free play of self-interest. In the end, though, the grave defect of Ruskin's politics is his devotion to organic unity, seen most clearly in his denying any room for the "anarchy and competition" of liberty. A just polity must be structured *throughout* as a harmony of associations so as to produce a perfectly legitimate consensus about the common good and perfectly deserving judgments of everyone's due.

Paradoxically, in equating justice with "desert" alone, Ruskin frustrates a central aim of his politics—fostering a broader moral regard among citizens. In his cathedral model, although the members of a practice or association can judge what they each deserve given their relative position, talents, and accomplishments in a shared activity, how can they judge what outsiders are due? Indeed, Ruskin sets the standards of justice so high and makes them so particularistic that he ends up distrusting the abilities of ordinary citizens to meet the demands of justice without prescriptive guidance from the masters of their guilds and the overseers of their polity. This cathedral model is too perfect in its aspirations and arrangements. Its liabilities become fully clear in the governmental and familial structures he deems necessary to the united purposes and affections of a fully organic social life.

Nobility and Charity

Ruskin names the central letter of *Time and Tide,* his so-called "letters against anarchy," "Episcopacy and Dukedom." The titled figures of bishop, duke, king, queen, prince, lord, and lady all have their place in his "imaginary political arrangements" (17.409). No doubt we can read these character types as simply one more appeal to British culture, one more strategic use of "medievalism" in Victorian debates about the significance of the past. Unlike the other cultural appeals we have seen in Ruskin's criticism, however—such as his appeals to Gothic craftwork, iron's breath of life, Job's natural piety, the Mammon vespers of merchants, and Dante's Plutus and the sirens—Ruskin's appeals to dukes, bishops, queens, and the rest of his idealized aristocracy are backed by the concrete authority of legal arrangements for political offices and familial roles.

Ruskin is no apologist for the British aristocracy, as he declares their "fall" to be "wholly their own fault." But he still associates aristocratic virtue with self-sacrifice, public service, and good taste on behalf of the commonwealth. As he puts it starkly, "all government among good men [is] *the production and recognition of human worth,* and . . . the detection and extinction of human unworthiness" (17.446). In other words, his proposed institutions of government answer to the question, is it possible to preserve nobility in the emerging democracy of Victorian Britain? Both in *Time and Tide* and in his lecture on "War," Ruskin concludes that, in fact, the "martial virtue" of the old aristocracy must be thrown over in favor of more peaceful aims. Yet as he glances across the Atlantic, he sees "money-power" and "mob-violence" as the sole alternative energies of democracy, reflecting his fears of post–Civil War America and the limitations of his political vision (17.381; cf. 18.465–66).

In the letter on "Episcopacy and Dukedom," Ruskin finally breaks his silence over his declaration fifteen years earlier in "Modern Education" that guarantees of children's basic needs require a government with an undreamed-of "authority." His proposed political structure is so alarming that even he wonders if he should have continued to hold his tongue. He heralds an authority better described as a moral leadership than an official power. His dukes and bishops have their "offices" in the government and the church, but their authority resides in helping to make their subjects and flock "worthy."

These two offices localize the government's powers of provision and oversight. Dukes represent the executive arm charged with the tasks of developing people toward their potential, providing for the needy, and directing local projects for the community's well-being. But dukes can wield their powers justly only if they know, in detail, the lives of everyone in their locality. The task of recording what people do to deserve "honor" or "dishonor," reward or punishment, falls to the bishops as the biographers of their flock. Just as Ruskin plays on the etymology of the Greek term *"episkopos,"* or bishop, as the "overseer," he envisions the fruits of this political system as a community of "noble," or "known," characters, whose merits and demerits are duly recorded in "these honourable annals" (17.377–79). The intrusiveness of these "imaginary political arrangements" is sobering, even if, as Ruskin insists, these records would be made public and contestable, thus allowing for deliberation about communal commitments and priorities.[28]

Descending from the paternal governance of these instituted offices into the helpful hierarchies of the family, we arrive at the "true queenly power" of women. If dukes and bishops prompt their charges toward noble pursuits, sorting their talents and guiding their efforts from above, Ruskin's queens mold and mend their own and others' families, harmonizing the society throughout. In "Of Queens' Gardens" (1864), he describes the "natural" relations between men and women, and he calls for an innovative program of girls' education and women's leadership to make the most of the queenly virtue of charity.

Ruskin offers his clearest statement of the term "virtue" in his 1866 *Ethics of the Dust,* a work constructed as a dialogue between an old lecturer and the girls at a boarding school. "The very word 'virtue' means, not 'conduct,' but 'strength,' vital energy in the heart. Were you not reading about the group of words beginning with V,—vital, virtuous, vigorous, and so on,—in Max Müller, the other day Sibyl?"[29] Continuing his etymological musings, Ruskin refers to "virgin," not "virility," as a cognate term. Here Ruskin appears to be breaking the traditional masculine associations with "virtue." He presents a neutral sense of chaste restraint in the interests of present health and eventual blossoming as the source of virtue, or "a vital human strength, which instinctively, constantly, and without motive, does what is right" (18.288, 301). Despite this apparently gender-neutral portrait, an urgent question arises, both for this study and for today's proponents of a vocabulary of the virtues: can this language escape the privileging of "male" virtues and the gendering of roles that historically has been built into its usage? In Ruskin's case, despite recent efforts to reclaim "Of Queens' Gardens" as feminist inspired, there are intractable problems in its conceptual argument.[30]

"Of Queens' Gardens" is the second lecture collected as *Sesame and Lilies* (1865). In the first, "Of Kings' Treasuries," Ruskin advises his listeners on what to read to attain "calm, beneficent, and *therefore* kingly, power—

first, over ourselves, and, through ourselves, over all around us." The universalism of this language of "ourselves" and "us" must be qualified. While attaining the "kingly power" of books is the aim of all education, only a "special portion or kind of this royal authority . . . may rightly be possessed by women." That portion is determined by the "relations of the womanly to the manly nature," Ruskin claims in the second lecture, thus inserting the issue of men's and women's natural "spheres," "intellect," and "virtue" into a discussion of education that had specified no such restrictions for men as a class (18.110, 111).

The third and final lecture on "The Mystery of Life and Its Arts" (1868) clarifies that men have responsibilities of charity, too, in feeding, clothing, and sheltering the poor (18.184). But Ruskin singles out women as innately capable of charity, understood in the classical Christian sense of the virtue that most closely approximates the fully ordered vision of God's love. He calls women to individual acts of caring for and comforting those who suffer injury and loss in the competitive rounds of industrial capitalism. But his thesis is that women's character and visionary powers make them uniquely suited to arranging male powers and purposes and directing familial and social affections toward the "order, comfort and loveliness" of the home and the community (18.136).

Ruskin defines the "natural" division of men's and women's virtues as follows. The man is "the doer, the creator, the discover, the defender," while "the woman's power is for rule, not for battle,—and her intellect is not for invention or creation, but for sweet ordering, arrangement and decision." Ruskin names women's rule a "*guiding*, not a determining function." "Her great function is Praise: she enters into no contest, but infallibly judges the crown of contest."[31] The language of "battle" and "contest" is revealing. More clearly than before, we see the agonistic contestation that characterizes men's striving for individual excellence in the social practices and the economic and political associations that shape their lives. Men "by their nature," Ruskin claims, "are prone to fight . . . for any cause, or for none," which is why women must rule men toward peace, yet also why women cannot sustain men's powers for concentrated effort (18.121–22, 140).

In order to "guide" men, women need some understanding of the fields of male endeavor, and Ruskin includes natural science and physical training in what was then a fairly progressive curriculum for girls.[32] In his 1871 preface to *Sesame and Lilies*, however, Ruskin sums up the aim of this broad education in the lessons taught by music—that every girl should be able to "sustain a note of moderate compass in a concerted piece" by becoming a "clear-voiced little instrument . . . which other people can entirely depend upon for the note wanted" (18.123–27, 39). This image of harmony through self-sacrificial conformity to the good of others pins women into "relations and duties" they may not control. Certainly the ideal of Christian charity involves a transformation of love of self through God's love for all, a giving of oneself on others' behalf. But Ruskin identifies women's "nature" with charity. Even as he dignifies "women's work" as an arena of virtue or excellence, he makes this visionary power of self-sacrificial love *the* excellence achievable by women. Nowhere is this denial of the full range of excellent attainment and autonomous self-direction clearer than when he forbids the study of theology, "the one dangerous science for women." He declares, "Strange, in creatures born to be Love visible, that where they can know least, they will condemn first, and think to recommend themselves to their Master by scrambling up the steps of His judgment throne, to divide it with Him" (18.127–28). Considering Ruskin's readiness to appeal to God's providential order—to the ends of the "Maker of things and of men" (17.85)—theology would seem essential to women's visionary powers of charitable guidance.[33]

Recall here Ruskin's image of charity as the temple rising above the foundation of justice. Recall, too, Okin's criticisms of a communitarian politics rising above the conflicting claims of individual rights in the home in the interests of consensual agreements about mutually sought goods. Okin rightly notes that families and associations do not function as the idealized "family" of the happy home and the organic community of Ruskin's politics. Consensus about the good, the common good, good lives, and even the goods shared in families, practices, and associations is incomplete and often fleeting. Instituting a political structure premised on complementary roles and full agreement effectively subjects the groups with limited power to legal coercion and enforced self-sacrifice. Ruskin's opposition to the movement for women's rights justifies Okin's concerns. He declares, "We hear of the mission and of the rights of Woman, as if these could ever be separate from the mission and rights of Man;—as if she and her lord were creatures of *independent kind* and of *irreconcilable claim*" (18.111; my emphasis). The language of "lordship" might be excused as a historical oddity. Without established guarantees of property rights, political votes, divorce laws, and other freedoms protected by legal and political institutions, middle- and upper-class Victorian women were the de facto subjects of their "lords." But in Ruskin's denial of "independence" and "irreconcilability," we see a conceptual issue that outlasts the excuse of historical context and that cuts to the core of the perfect harmony of associations that is the premise of the cathedral model of his politics.

The critical offering of Ruskin's tradition of social thought is its attention to the "relationality" of politics—that politics consists in "the relations and duties of men to each other." By attending to social practices as arenas of individual excellence, to intermediate associations as spaces for cooperative self-governance, to public ends as measures of social responsibility, to power structures as obstacles to social justice, to social goods as shared possessions requiring fair distributions, Ruskin reminds his contemporaries of the folly and injustice of viewing themselves as the "unbound" individuals theorized in laissez-faire models and theologized in the reduction of the full range of the virtues to personal moral rectitude. But he also appears to exclude women from participating in much of this sphere of common life, reinforcing a barrier of "natural" virtue that should be opposed in the name of social justice. Here we must carefully distinguish between the "associational" and the "organic" in Ruskin's politics. At times he describes the makings of an *ethical interdependence* of ends, goods, virtues, and associations that participants work out together in activities of their own choosing. At other times he idealizes an *organic interdependence* of functional parts, granting to men paternal authority and the right to participate in social practices while demanding of women self-sacrificial charity in the home.

Ruskin argues as if there could be no society apart from a perfectly unified "social life." The "laws of life" are paternal "government and cooperation in all things"; "the laws of death" are liberal "anarchy and competition." Relying on free exchange, individual rights, and electoral politics to work out societal choices, arrangements, and distributions is no governance at all, he insists. In ruling out these institutional tools for mediating among individuals' *independent* and often *irreconcilable* claims, Ruskin refuses those mechanisms that historically have helped to carve out social spaces for self-assertion, for alternative visions of good lives and good societies, and for the associations and movements of people who agitated for women's and workers' rights.

The politics of medievalism found in Ruskin's corpus has its champions today, but I read in it a cautionary tale that today's communitarians would do well to heed. Before disposing of individual rights and liberal institutions for causing the incoherence of modern moral discourse, with its incommensurable conceptions of the good and irreconcilable conflicts about justice, we should explain how the injustices of Ruskin's politics can be overcome without the "battles" and "contests" that he allows only in the case of male striving.[34] Only women are to be "enduringly, incorruptibly good; infallibly wise—wise, not for self-development, but for self-renunciation" (18.123). Allowing room for battles and contests and admitting the individual and social costs of a too-perfect politics redirects us toward the fractures in his critical vision.

I argue in part 3 that Ruskin's ethics of consumption does not presuppose the same organic unity of purposes and affections that are won by loving deference to paternal governance and by women's stepping into the breach to make whatever self-sacrifice of the moment might be called of them. I close this chapter pointing the way ahead to his writings on consumption, where he takes more seriously the divisions and conflicts, the gains and losses, the command and toil, that he sees as inevitably arising in economic life. His cathedral model remains in the background, but he also accepts the need for institutional mechanisms like a money economy, however altered its use might be by an ethics where individual consumers choose to act on behalf of the public ends and shared goods advanced through just prices, fair distributions, decent work, and environmental protections.

Critical Fragments and Democratic Spaces

One difference between Ruskin's political theorizing and his ethics of consumption is that the latter is more a set of critical tools than an integrated framework for social life. These tools maintain the focus on character and vision that typifies his vocabulary of the virtues, but they do not presuppose the perfect agreement that underlies his dualism between associations and institutions. The best way to anticipate this looser, more divided social structure and the ad hoc, piecemeal style of his ethics of consumption is to observe that Ruskin shifts the locus of authority from the "masters" of his politics to "consumers" themselves. Ruskin does not explore the full implications of this reassignment of authority, but the shift takes his critical approach in more democratic directions and helps turn his entire tradition away from the unitary and exalted vision of the genius, poet, or hero toward the always-partial vision of individual consumers.

By "partial" I mean both narrow in scope and inclined toward oneself. In many ways the thrust of Ruskin's politics is to deny that such a partial, individuated perspective has moral standing. Abstracted from the cultural activities and everyday associations that inform and structure good lives, individuals will fail to promote these sources of excellence and flourishing and will succumb to mere self-deception or outright ideological self-justification in ignoring the networks of interdependence in which they participate. The cathedral model of Ruskin's politics is a forceful reminder of these broader "relations and duties." Yet too often he presents this politics as a beautiful edifice with no room for social conflicts and disagreements about the ultimate ordering of a community's ends.

Throughout part 2 I have argued that Ruskin's turn toward cultural critique disrupts his metaphysical sensibility. Although much of his politics is abstracted from Victorian culture, we do find some of the more fragmentary observations that are the gems of his criticism—his prophetic critique of the three versions of providence, his analysis of the irrationalities of the art market, and his rejoinder to Fawcett's "descriptive" analysis. In these nuggets of social criticism, Ruskin intervenes in the cultural productions, economic choices, and political decisions of Victorian life, seeking to jar his contemporaries out of the immediacy of their daily lives into a searching inquiry into the "relations and duties" that attend their chosen activities and associations and that attach to all of the praise and aid they may have received en route to attaining whatever social status, privilege, and authority they now enjoy.

Consider an example of his imaginative interventions in his contemporaries' lives and his efforts to convince them to abide by their professed commitments, not their narrow interests. In *Time and Tide* he advocates a "public education irrespective of class distinction." A universal public education for "education's sake" is right regardless of the social conflicts certain to follow from this political commitment to universal nobility (17.394, 396). But who, then, will stoop to doing the hard work required in any society, he imagines his well-heeled readers objecting. He responds sardonically, challenging the warring camps of "evangelicals" and "ritualists" to set aside their doctrinal battles and act on their shared profession of humility in making themselves over into society's "serviceable 'dust and ashes'" (17.406–7). They should do this hard work themselves.

Elsewhere we find Ruskin excoriating "speculative thefts" as inexcusable on grounds of "self-deception." When the powerful abuse "their good position and large knowledge of the world," he declares that their "betrayal of implicit trust" shows cunning "calculation." Then he rips his readers back to Golgotha, reminding them of the four figures standing in judgment before Pontius Pilate. In a highly compressed exegesis reminiscent of Augustine's analysis of his reasons for stealing pears, Ruskin proclaims that his contemporaries have inverted the rankings of theft and murder on the scale of human ills.[35] Murder has its reasons in passion, madness, or calamity, he observes, and the Gospels testify to these mitigating causes of murder in the freeing of the insurrectionist Barabbas. But, he continues,

> theft involving deliberative intellect, and absence of passion, is the purest type of wilful iniquity, in persons capable of doing right. Which being so, it seems to be fast becoming the practice of modern society to crucify its Christ indeed, as willingly as ever, in the persons of His poor; but by no means now to crucify its thieves beside Him! It elevates its thieves after another fashion; sets them upon an hill, that their light may shine before men, and that all may see their good works, and glorify their Father, in—the Opposite of Heaven. (17.391–92)

Ruskin argues here as a cultural critic, not a political theorist. Although the gist of the passage is consistent with his dichotomy between the perfect unity and cooperation of associations and the total separation and competition of institutions, this intervention into his contemporaries' cultural presuppositions does not require the premise of antithetical social visions. He simply contrasts popular attitudes about the severity of crimes with the biblical narratives and everyday prayers familiar to all Victorian Christians. Thus, Ruskin's argument gains force not as a portrait of the singular vision of the essential conditions required in any good society, but rather as a direct strike into the contradictions between widely held sources of moral judgment in the culture and apologetic justifications of a laissez-faire political order.

In these examples Ruskin seeks to persuade his audience of all that they do share, could share, and should share, were they to see across the moral distances opened up by the institutions of Victorian life. Again he *seeks* to *persuade,* recognizing that there will be battles, contests, and divisions, that the perfect coherence of his cathedral model is untenable. Arguments for social responsibility and social justice are not helped by organic appeals. The prevalence of the organic in Ruskin's tradition of social thought is a primary reason why secular appeals to progress and difference are so forceful and why, after Marxism, critiques of capitalism are so scarce today. But unlike today's communitarians, Ruskin develops a trenchant critique of economic injustice. His efforts to urge wealthy Victorians to recognize that their "relations and duties" transcend the family and social classes, his advocacy of rights to public support, his criticisms of arbitrary money-power, and his account of intermediate associations as arenas for enhancing people's individual excellences, social responsibilities, and civic participation reflect the lasting insights of his politics. There are also fractures in his critical vision, openings for institutions to carve out spaces of independence, arenas of conflict, means of mediating between individuals' lives that do not require the perfect agreement in purposes and affections presupposed in his cathedral model. Those fractures can be exploited most fully in his ethics of consumption.

PART THREE

The Ethics of Consumption

SIX

The Value of Virtues

The theme of consumption appears in various guises in Ruskin's criticism prior to his 1860 essays in the *Cornhill* magazine, published two years later as *Unto This Last.* As early as *Modern Painters* 2 (1846), he criticizes the "appetite of tasteful cruelty" for empty luxuries that consume the lives of untold millions (4.61). Insatiable desires for fanciful enjoyments and novelties deaden the senses to the "delights" of natural beauty and deny what he comes to call the "first of possessions, self-possession" (17.112). In 1849 he concludes *The Seven Lamps of Architecture* by remarking on his "strange notions" about whether the pleasures of jewelry compensate for the losses of life and power suffered by the workers who cut the gems (8.265). For the first time in "The Nature of Gothic" (1853), he puts his prohibition on the injuries caused by bad taste into practical guidelines governing the buying of art (10.197). But it is in *The Political Economy of Art* (1857) that these comments and injunctions about aesthetic taste assume the broader significance auguring his ethics of consumption. He declares, "Whenever we spend money, we of course set people to work: that is the meaning of spending of money . . . [and] by the way in which we spend it, we entirely direct the labour of those people during that given time. We become their masters or mistresses, and we compel them to produce, within a certain period, a certain article" (16.48–49).

In this passage Ruskin transfers the language of "mastership" from his politics onto every consumer and, with it, the responsibilities incurred by the master's privileged standing in a social practice. In other words, as consumption emerges as the "end" and, thus for Ruskin, the chief ethical determinant of economic life, he names the individual consumer the final authority directing the work of the people whose products he or she buys.

The ethics of consumption that he elaborates on this basis remains the most distinctive contribution of his criticism.

I approach Ruskin's ethics of consumption via the scheme I borrowed from M. H. Abrams in chapter 3. I argued that Ruskin's art criticism follows the trajectory of his growing attention to how people's "powers" of imagination shape works of art, both as made by the artist and as evaluated by the audience. Works of art stand at the center of a triangle surrounded by *nature, artist,* and *audience,* and the meanings of these works reflect the interpretations of artist and audience alike. Similarly, judgments of the value of any economic good must account for the product's relations to *nature, worker,* and *consumer.*[1]

NATURE

WORK/PRODUCT

ARTIST/WORKER AUDIENCE/CONSUMER

This modified scheme helps outline how the current chapter develops from the preceding ones in two ways.

First, as Ruskin moves toward the consumer's vantage point as the regulative perspective on economic life, that perspective can be seen as encompassing all of the moral relations at play in this scheme. In addition to the consumer's relation to the product itself, there are also the consumer's relations to the various workers employed in producing this good and to the natural world that provides the resources used to make it. Ruskin's ethics of consumption takes in all three relations, and consumers have ultimate responsibility for the claims attaching to each one. As such his ethics of consumption represents the apex of his social criticism in the sense that in it combine his earlier concerns with the duties to recognize the goodness of nature and the worth of human labor along with his newer mandate to practice good consumption.

Second, and building from the parallel in Ruskin's thinking between the authority of "masters" and the authority of consumers, the emergence of the consumer in place of the master marks a notable shift away from the immediate and hierarchical relations presumed in his politics. The shift from the master of a shared practice to the consumer of a product prompts Ruskin to admit greater difficulty in passing judgments on the value of the multitude of things that people buy and consume in the money economy of industrial capitalism. Not only are these products typically made by people completely unknown to the consumer, but consumers also have different desires and ends. Even as Ruskin acknowledges the distance between producers and consumers and allows for the diversity among consumers' interests, however, he still holds that acts of consumption incur obligations to all of the people involved and to the world more broadly still. Despite his turn from the master guiding the efforts of workers to the consumers appreciating the fruits of these labors, he retains his moralistic sense of the duties purchased by the authority that consumers wield.

Linda Austin has explored the connections between the themes of consumption and audience in Ruskin's later writings. She starts from his attempts to address new audiences over the course of his career, asking whether his thinking changes as he reaches past his upper- and middle-class readership to the lecture hall and magazine audiences he addresses in the late 1850s and 1860s and, finally, to the working-class readers he tries to cultivate through *Fors Clavigera* (1871–84). That Ruskin mostly wrote and spoke to people wealthy enough to enjoy discretion in their spending marks one way that his own awareness of audience may have led him to articulate an ethics of consumption. The wealthy are likely to put great stock in the "end" of wise consumption and the "duties" of cultivating good taste. A contrast can be drawn to Karl Marx and Friedrich Engels, whose most populist piece, "The Communist Manifesto" (1847), ignores both the dynamics of consumption and the responsibilities of individuals. Marx and Engels celebrate the unprecedented productivity of the industrial machine as an instrument for vanquishing the direct forms of oppression upheld by older social relations.[2] In Marx's theoretical writings, he largely dismisses consumption as irrelevant to the critique of capitalism, calling consumption the mere "finish" to production, not the "end" of economic life as Ruskin deems it (see chapter 7). Perhaps, then, an ethics of consumption only valorizes the privileged standing of the rich. Indeed, given the relative affluence of Ruskin and his audience, maybe his focus on consumption is more apologetic than critical because, by placing the chief ethical corrective to industrial capitalism in the hands of consumers and by charging them to spend wisely, he merely ratifies the economic inequalities prevailing at the time.

Yet Austin describes a remarkable spread of consumption across all classes in the period. In view of this continued expansion of consumer society, she argues persuasively that "the demands and tastes of a heterogeneous audience for books and the fine arts [begin] to guide meaning and determine value" in the more "populistic hermeneutics" of Ruskin's later writings. She cites *The Queen of the Air* (1869), in particular, where he proliferates the many meanings of Athena in tracing out the goddess's names, roles, and associations in the Greek mind. Ruskin's new readiness to offer myriad readings for his later audiences' consideration parallels his growing recognition of the conflicting preferences that consumers bring to economic goods and the impossibility of uniform standards of taste. As an example, Austin cites Ruskin's discussion of gold as an unreliable means of securing the currency.[3] Gold is a complex signifier, Ruskin observes, because its multiple functions as currency, commodity, and thing of beauty make people want it for competing reasons. Very different values attach to gold, depending on people's desires, needs, activities, and ends. As Ruskin the art conservator bemoans, the use of gold in paintings risks its being stripped and melted down for money by people unable, whether out of greed or desperation, to appreciate its "higher" uses in the arts (17.197–98).

Austin introduces how the reality of consumers' competing tastes and valuations opens up Ruskin's interpretive strategies and challenges what she sees as the unredeemably romantic assumptions and elitist assertions of his criticism. In her assessment, despite Ruskin's greater attention to the "mechanical system" of value creation that typifies the capitalist marketplace and transforms his own late writings, he ultimately offers nothing more in his portrait of good consumption than a "romantic solution" idealizing a "'natural' separation of classes." Ruskin the critic becomes the exemplar of good taste for his audiences of consumers to imitate to the best of their financial ability.

Although Austin is attentive to the limitations of Ruskin's writings, her verdict misconstrues his moral vocabulary and the range of its uses. When she criticizes his political economy for being based on "moral tenets like magnanimity, largesse and charity," she misses how these virtues-centered appeals rest on a conception of human activities and associations that unite their participants' commitments to shared goods and standards of excellence.[4] I have also criticized Ruskin's portraits of the magnanimous king and the charitable queen. The wise paternalism of the king reinforces the drive toward a singular vision of the good in Ruskin's politics. The self-sacrificing adjustment of the queen invites half of humanity to set their own ends aside when conflicts arise. But magnanimity and charity are not the sole virtues in Ruskin's ethics of consumption. More importantly, as he turns toward the vantage point of the consumer, the perspective of his criticism shifts, too. The question is no longer, how must the political order be structured to achieve a unified good? Rather the question is, how might consumers make intelligible judgments of things' value by looking beyond their immediate desires and ends to the complex ethical considerations at play in the uses of natural resources and other people's work?

In Ruskin's effort to enlist his audiences in imagining the moral contexts of economic life and the specific duties they incur as consumers, we see the constructive role of his vocabulary of the virtues. As he challenges the mechanical system of value creation in mainstream economic theory, he asks, how can consumers intervene ethically in economic exchanges, plumbing the value of commodities by looking past the surface measure of market price? He argues that things' goodness must be read in terms of how well any product meets the "intrinsic powers" of the natural or humanly made goods from which it was produced and how fully it expresses and develops the "virtues" of the laborers who made it and matches the "virtues" of the consumers who will use and enjoy it. This linkage of economic value with natural powers and cultivated virtues introduces the dual conception of value, as "intrinsic" and "effectual," that Ruskin works out in his ethics of consumption. What distinguishes my reading of this theory of value is that I give priority to the latter category—that is, to the need to develop people to be capable of the full range of intellectual, bodily, aesthetic, emotional, and social capacities required for a flourishing life. This focus reflects Ruskin's own commitment to developing people for good lives, and it reminds us of the great insight of his practical criticism, namely, that there are cultural spaces in the practices and activities that people choose to support and pursue where it is possible to make shared judgments of human worth and economic value. These shared judgments have their reasons in the ends and goods embraced by participants and the virtues they cultivate in pursuit of them. These judgments are also open to criticism and revision when individuals disagree.

Among Ruskin scholars Austin is not alone in overlooking his vocabulary of the virtues and the accompanying idea of a social practice, but her otherwise acute analysis helps diagnose that neglect.[5] Her dichotomy between the "mechanical" and the "romantic" repeats an antithesis often presupposed in our reception of nineteenth-century debates of subjects from art to economics. The choice is stark. On the one side are the mechanical systems that sift individuals' divergent desires and preferences through such liberal institutions as the market, electoral politics, and a free press. On the other side is the romantic insistence that true flourishing consists in a select set of higher goods and that only an organic social structure can bring these goods to fruition while allowing everyone his or her proper share in them. I present the contrast sharply, even crudely, because too often Ruskin's views on consumption have been identified with a "romantic" holism *as opposed to* a "mechanical" subjectivism. The assumption that these are the only alternatives clouds assessments of his contributions to ethical and critical thought.[6]

Here we return to the problem of "good consumption" I introduced at the beginning of this book. Besides art, it is difficult to think of an arena of life other than consumption where "subjective" taste is believed to operate legitimately apart from any regulative norms and duties. In consumption, as in art, the teleological structure of Ruskin's commitments to promoting good character, identifying shared goods, and advancing public ends bumps up against the empirical reality not only of diversity, but also of heterogeneity, in the desires, needs, and ends that individuals bring to buying, using, and enjoying the countless economic goods traded on the market. The challenge of part 3 is to answer two questions. Since the terms "ethics" and "consumption" seem oxymoronic when juxtaposed, how does Ruskin rework and apply his vocabulary of the virtues to the tasks of engaged reflection and social action on behalf of "good consumption"? As he holds to his teleological approach, are his moralistic arguments, with their intrusive scrutiny of desire, at odds with democratic commitments to liberty and difference as protected spheres of individual identity and social intercourse?

The current chapter addresses the first question, demonstrating the constructive role of Ruskin's vocabulary of the virtues in his dual conception of economic value as "intrinsic" and "effectual." I argue that the category of "effectual value" begins to free his criticism from the metaphysics that always shadows his normative arguments, and I demonstrate how his equation of economic value with human virtues anticipates what is now known as the "capabilities approach" to human development, most closely associated with Amartya Sen. In the next chapter I address the threat of paternalism in Ruskin's ethics of consumption. I show how his portrait of the proper workings of a money economy requires consumers skilled in the virtues of justice and piety and, thus, able to see past the limits of their own narrow visions of the good. The concluding chapter defends the very idea of an ethics of consumption as a practice of moral imagination, undertaken by individual consumers and directed toward visions of good lives that remain open to deliberation while seeking the cooperation and inclusion of democracy at its best.

Consumption in Economic Theory

By the mid-nineteenth century two basic assumptions structured the theory of classical political economy. First, the focal concern was production, not consumption, and second, the science was descriptive, not normative. Ruskin develops his own political economy in opposition to these assumptions. As James Sherburne pointed out several decades ago, "Ruskin's insistence on spending and consumption is the central theme of his economic criticism and his most important contribution to economic thought."[7] In addition, in the public essays that become *Unto This Last* (1860, 1862) and *Munera Pulveris* (1862–63, 1872), Ruskin challenges the theory's operational definitions for setting aside the central moral issues of character, culture, and community in his teleological criticism.

Beginning with the productivist bias of the classical theory, the main concern of theorists ranging from J. S. Mill back to David Ricardo was how to produce sufficient material goods under the conditions of scarcity. Consumers' needs outstripped available goods, requiring future growth in production and, more importantly, the steady increase in the capital stock necessary to advancing this economic growth. For the industrial economy to work and prosper, commodities must find buyers, of course. In the classical theory, however, this demand was simply assumed. The factors making up consumer demand—the desires, uses, and ends that consumers bring to their economic decisions—were extraneous to the production-driven theories. Production cost factors, not consumer preferences, were taken as determinative of the flow of producers in and out of the economy. Only with the rise of the marginal utility school of William Stanley Jevons and Alfred Marshall beginning in the 1870s did theorists accord a predictive role to consumer choices.[8]

In addition to placing production costs and capital accumulation at the center of his theory, Mill distinguished the *science* of political economy from the *art* of policy. The science is only a tool, a descriptive account of economic behavior distinct from the art of determining the ends of policy.[9] Ruskin, by contrast, insists that a science of "wealth" must focus on actual consumption, not capital accumulation. For him, "value" is not reducible to market price but is a complex qualitative measure. Thus, Ruskin disputes the operational definitions of wealth and value in Mill's *Principles of Political Economy* (1848), and the force of his argument builds through the four essays of *Unto This Last* to the claim that "consumption is the crown of production; and the wealth of a nation is only to be estimated by what it consumes." He adds that his consumption-driven inquiry introduces new complexities into political economy because "wise consumption is a far more difficult art than wise production" (17.98).

Mill's distinction between a "science" and an "art" contrasts with Ruskin's insistence that any science worthy of the name must keep in view the ends of good human lives and the arts, products, and wisdom that make for their proper arrangement, greatest achievement, and widest distribution. Later in the chapter I return to Ruskin's concern with the good life to explicate his definition of wealth and his theory of value. Important for now is simply marking the different approaches of Mill the theorist and Ruskin the moralist.

It must be said that Ruskin does not acknowledge the limits that Mill drew around his science, nor is he always fair or accurate in rebutting Mill's terms.[10] Partly this is due to Ruskin's different purposes as a moralist. He reads workers' efforts and consumers' choices in the flow of their lives—their seeking to satisfy needs, express desires, and meet obligations as purposive beings. By contrast, the theoretical models of classical political economy do not look to the commitments, relationships, and virtues that people develop over time; they begin from individuals' current preferences, the variety of available goods, and the market prices for them. Consumers' economic choices—from the prioritization of their preferences to the meanings that they attach to commodities—certainly reflect the broader goals and projects to which they commit their lives. But these purposes and values and the moral visions that sustain them are irrelevant in the marketplace, where efficient outcomes are the guiding concern. Theorists, like Mill, acknowledge the limits of these models. Apostles of market competition tend to claim much more. For the apologists, it is not only theoretically useful to focus on the snapshot picture of current prices and individual preferences provided by the market's calculations and adjustments. By abstracting out the goals, capacities, and activities that form people's lives, the market, it is claimed, guarantees the essential liberty that individuals need as economic agents so that they can enjoy self-determination in their lives.

Consumption in Ethical Context

In *Unto This Last* Ruskin criticizes both the theoretical assumptions of classical political economy and its ideological uses in equating industrial capitalism with freedom. He does not always separate these tasks carefully, one reason being that the theory itself and the ideology derived from it are both at odds with his teleological approach. Throughout the four essays of *Unto This Last,* he continually calls his readers' attention to the broader ethical contexts in which they make their choices as consumers. His task is to persuade them of the shared affections and common purposes, social trust and professional responsibilities, that make an economy run.

The genre of *Unto This Last* is not abstract theory. Ruskin makes frequent use of satire and symbolism, and even his definitions are characterized by wordplay. He is not constructing a theoretical framework to describe the machinations of the economy from moment to moment. Instead he seeks to draw readers directly into the subject by staging an assortment of scenes from economic life. Scenes they are indeed, for Ruskin is interested in the larger drama of a society as it is conducted in part through economic interactions. He is concerned with the play as a whole, too, and he refuses to abstract out any one scene as the model for every economic interaction. Most importantly, though, Ruskin presents these scenes to remind readers that no economy can operate without a great many actors, even if they are not all on stage at the same time. Purchases made in the market remove many of the participants from view and from moral consideration. For Ruskin, however, consumers' choices must be set in the context of the full range of moral relations and the other ethical circumstances pushed out of sight by the obscuring distances of a money economy.

The first two essays of *Unto This Last* take up this problem of moral distance, with the opening essay, "The Roots of Honour," beginning in the realm of business and the second essay, "The Veins of Wealth," extending Ruskin's argument beyond the relative "intimacy" of the relations between owners and workers and across the ever-widening gaps that separate producers from consumers. The force of Ruskin's rhetoric and the immediacy of his scenes have the unfortunate effect of obscuring his careful argumentation.

The readers of the *Cornhill* magazine, where *Unto This Last* was first published in a serialized form, must have had to catch their breath after the opening pages of "The Roots of Honour." Comparing the "the modern *soi-disant* science of political economy" to the pseudo-scientific "delusions" of "alchemy, astrology, witchcraft, and other such popular creeds," Ruskin dismisses "the idea that an advantageous code of social action may be determined irrespectively of the influence of social affection" (17.25). Consider just some of the rich imagery that tumbles forth in the cogent yet evocative few paragraphs that follow.

Calling *homo economicus* a "covetous machine," Ruskin equates the utility maximizer of economic theory to an ossified skeleton of a creature, soulless and bloodless in its relentless movements to acquire things of mere monetary value. Opposing the mathematical calculations of political economy to the complex chemistry of organic beings, he draws a parallel between the explosive dangers of a social policy based on self-interest and the folly of working even with *inorganic* elements, ignorant of the volatility of their gaseous compounds (17.25–26). I emphasize these appeals to the chemical and the inorganic as they speak to the fine line that Ruskin is walking between the mechanical and the romantic. There are complex and highly reactive dynamics at work in the cultivation of human character and the welfare of society that must be attended to in any ethics of economic life. Although this is true, a rhetoric of images, no matter how evocative, is no substitute for argument. Thus, while the readers of the *Cornhill* may not have grasped the sophistication of Ruskin's underlying argument, the shock of his imagery and the boldness of his apparent assertions gave them reasons to complain loudly, no doubt, and the editor of the *Cornhill* terminated the series after four essays (17.xxvii–xxix).

Ruskin's appeal to "honor" in the title of the first essay introduces his conviction that a working economy depends upon the circulation of what is now called "social capital." Business success, he contends, requires forms of mutual recognition for work well done and at least a degree of shared interest in a common endeavor. This insistence on joint purpose, regard, and trust contrasts with the exclusive focus on market pricing and market competition in the classical theory. The theory predicts that, although in the short term there may be pain for some people, material prosperity will be greatest in the long run where owners, workers, and consumers all pursue their interests of the moment. Challenging this assumption, Ruskin appeals to the "honor" of merchants and manufacturers. Should these business leaders seek praise from stockholders for the profits they generate or from the public for their honorable dealings with workers and consumers? This question looks to the realm of production, and not surprisingly, Ruskin borrows from his model of good labor in addressing it. Recall his argument in "The Nature of Gothic" that good work requires the existence of social practices where participants commit to shared ends, goods, and standards of excellence. Business "masters" must be as vigilant as the master of any craft in caring for the governing goals of their enterprises. Chief among these is that "what they sell [be] in the purest and cheapest forms" (17.26–27, 41).

In economic theory, competition is the surest means of producing high quality and low cost. If all participants aim to maximize economic gain for themselves, then the openness of the market to newcomers will of itself drive down prices and drive out faulty products. Large-scale commercial and industrial enterprises operate on an entirely different basis than Ruskin's model of craftwork. The concern in these enterprises is not the production of excellent art or the virtues necessary to these high achievements. And yet, he asks, what would happen if economic actors behaved exclusively on the basis of narrow self-interest? What if owners acted only with an eye to the balance sheet? It may be that high quality and low cost can be forced through an incentive structure of wage pressures on workers and profit margins for owners and investors, yet how much more might be achieved if workers committed to goals in common with their "masters." Where the operative interests are profits and wages, there will not exist even that minimal level of joint concern needed, Ruskin notes, to avoid the strikes that cripple the realization of these monetary goals, not to mention the other ends of industry.

This strategy of modeling every business as a practice is reminiscent of Ruskin's politics. There the good society is secured through a perfect harmony of cooperative associations that fixes everyone in a hierarchy of roles and duties. Although the paternalism of his politics carries forward here, too, he now admits forthrightly that "the varieties of circumstances which influence these reciprocal interests" are "endless." The interests of business owners and workers may converge or diverge for a great many reasons, making the scenes of economic life much more complicated than the theory of classical political economy allows. This exploding of the boundaries erected by economic theory is only a preliminary step in Ruskin's argument. His focal concern is with the contextuality of virtues-centered judgments, as becomes clear when he observes that "every man may know, and most of us do know, what is a just and unjust act" (17.28). Here Ruskin appeals to his readers' abilities to make nuanced assessments of what they owe to other people in the ever-changing scenes of economic life. The virtue of justice, though hard to define, is easily recognized by people skilled in its practice.

But is economic life really subject to such wide-ranging and context-sensitive judgments of what is due to other people? I return to Ruskin's account of the "just price" in chapter 7, but here in "The Roots of Honour" he seeks to convince his audience that the guaranteed salaries of professionals prove that his fellow Victorians are skilled judges who, unbeknownst to themselves, already accord dignity and reward to good work based on such ethical considerations as honorable and trustworthy service to the public.

The annual salaries of soldiers, pastors, doctors, and lawyers protect these workers from fluctuations in going wages. These four professional groups are insulated against the vagaries of market competition, he argues, because their services are recognized as promoting ends vital to the public good. Why then are merchants and manufacturers not given the honor of salaries? Ruskin answers that, as presently practiced, these occupations enjoy no such esteem because the merchants and manufacturers conduct their affairs within the limits of a commodity economy regulated entirely by monetary relations, thereby precluding the circulation of the trust, honor, and dignity that the public retains for its protectors, teachers, healers, and judges. To gain the public's accolades, a business leader must embrace some governing purpose, the abrogation of which would be dishonor. Discerning this purpose requires asking the question, "What is *his* 'due occasion' of death?" Just as the soldier must be ready to die for country, the doctor in times of plague, the teacher in the name of truth, the judge in the pursuit of justice, Ruskin claims that merchants would be honored if they were ready to make comparable sacrifices in providing for the nation, instead of simply seeking their own advantage in every transaction (17.38, 40).[11] That merchants are deemed less honorable than other professionals testifies, therefore, not to the irrelevance of normative evaluation in economic life, but to its unfortunate neglect in everyday practice.

If this argument begins to trace out the wider circulation of the social goods of honor, trust, and dignity throughout a whole economy, Ruskin's other argument in "The Roots of Honour" asks how these shared affections might be made to circulate within a business. Manufacturers, he argues, should guarantee their workers protections similar to those of the professional classes, offering workers fixed wages and guaranteed employment and assuming "responsibility for *the kind of life* they lead" (17.41; my emphasis). The intrusive moralism of this language of "kinds" of life captures well the "the distinctly paternal authority" that Ruskin assigns to business leaders. In his words, "the only means which the master has of doing justice to the men employed by him is to ask himself sternly whether he is dealing with such subordinate as he would with his own son" (17.42). The phrasing of this duty is troubling in valorizing the moral authority of one class over another. Nevertheless this paternalism should not entirely distract us from Ruskin's concerns with the welfare, health, and safety of workers and consumers. He is writing hard on the heels of the Factory Acts of 1833 and 1847, which regulated the employment and working hours of children, but only in the textile industry, making Ruskin's allusion to the employment of sons (he does not mention daughters) more chilling. Businesses today operate with a very different set of benefits, regulations, and laws—hard-won gains by unions and other social movements to secure the opportunities for good work and self-development at the heart of the ethical concerns of "The Roots of Honour."[12]

Ruskin does not call overt attention to this moral framework of ends, goods, and virtues, nor does he offer the systematic defense of his arguments needed to make them fully persuasive. His illustrations and appeals are more impressionistic, designed to bring into view for the reader a raft of moral issues shunted aside by the assumptions of economic theory. That same strategy structures the second essay of *Unto This Last,* too. If the profit motive already introduces a degree of moral distance between masters and workers, then monetary purchases of commodities by consumers seem to stretch ethical regard past the breaking point.

Theoretically the great power of money is to abstract out all evaluative concerns other than the consumer's given preferences and the relative prices of available goods. Yet Ruskin questions that view of economic exchange in "The Veins of Wealth." No longer confining his analysis to the model of businesses as shared practices, he introduces the function of "riches" as the ability to direct other people's labor from afar. Money is not a neutral medium of exchange as it is in political economy. Rather, for Ruskin, the "chief value and virtue of money consists in its *having power over human beings*" (17.54; my emphasis). Even a property with good soil, useful tools, and ample stores of food would soon become worthless to its owner without the commanding power of riches. Only by the rich man's possessing what others want can he acquire the labor needed to maintain the property and reap continued benefits from it.

Ruskin differentiates "riches" from "wealth." Although a relationship of comparative plenty and poverty defines all riches, wealth for him is a "real," not a relative, concept. The term "real estate" captures this sense of wealth's substantial worth in serving as a place of shelter, familiarity, and hospitality, some of the many goods available to people with actual homes. In addition to the goods that flow to the owners of wealth, Ruskin argues that the mechanisms by which an object of wealth is produced and purchased may add or detract from other people's well-being, too. As he puts it, the real value of "any given mass of acquired wealth . . . depends on the moral sign attached to it, just as sternly as that of a mathematical quantity depends on the algebraical sign attached to it" (17.52). If the commanding power of money produces greater harm than benefit, then the resulting "gains" are ill gotten, being, in Ruskin's memorable words, "illth" not wealth. The gravest form of "illth" comes from fostering disparities between rich and poor in order to command the poor's labor more readily and more cheaply. Those who are economically deprived can be made to work for less, yet if their deprivation is included in the balance sheets of wealth, it proves harmful both to themselves and to the larger community as well.

Once again Ruskin insists that moral concerns bear directly on economic life and on individual and social well-being. In setting the stage for his ethics of consumption, he reconfigures the interactions between owners and workers and consumers and producers as complex scenes that are incomprehensible apart from all that people bring to production and exchange. He does not stop at highlighting the moral complexity that economic theory obscures. He constructs an alternative conception of economic value that borrows from his model of good labor practices and his vocabulary of the virtues.

I have noted the problems with his language of mastership in "The Roots of Honour." Similarly, "The Veins of Wealth," with its organic metaphor of the "body economic," suggests that his definitions of wealth and value in the final essay of *Unto This Last* are predicated on a harmony of social roles within a functionalist hierarchy. Indeed, the transition from the internal authority of practices to the external operations of riches marks a movement outward, Ruskin notes, from the moral proximity and power of masters toward the more distant relations of the market, mediated as they are by the "always imperfect and doubtful" power of money (17.54). It might seem, then, that Ruskin has to lean even more heavily on an organic vision of a perfectly ordered society as he takes up the distant perspective of the consumer. But he closes the gaps of the money economy and the division of labor by approaching good consumption as a kind of social practice. As in other social practices, there are shared goods and standards, and consumers should commit themselves to these goods and standards, seeking excellence in their judgments about and their uses of the many things they buy. The close reasoning of Ruskin's argument will be missed if we neglect the emphasis on practical reason in his language of virtues and powers, the twin marks of good consumption.

Wealth, Value, and Virtues

Ruskin's elevation of consumption—a celebration of it in many ways—repeats the theme of abundance from *The Political Economy of Art*. In *Unto This Last* the abundant wealth of well-made things and well-made people that he imagines looks even more to the vitalism of his vocabulary of the virtues. In rejoinder to the utilitarian calculus of the "greatest happiness of the greatest number," he declares the upshot of the four essays to be that "THERE IS NO WEALTH BUT LIFE. Life, including all its powers of love, of joy, and of admiration. That country is the richest which nourishes the greatest number of noble and happy human beings. . . . But is the nobleness consistent with the number? Yes, not only consistent with it, but essential to it. The maximum of life can only be reached by the maximum of virtue" (17.105). In fact, this equation of wealth with an abundant quality of life looks more to virtues in the plural than to virtue in the singular, as Ruskin explains in *Munera Pulveris*. He names the "fortifying virtues" of prudence, justice, fortitude, and temperance the "greatest of economists." "These cardinal and sentinel virtues are not only the means of protecting and prolonging life itself, but they are the chief guards, or sources, of the material means of life, and the governing powers and princes of economy" (17.285). The effects of cultivating these virtues range from extending human life to increasing people's capacities for making the most of material goods. His concern is not with the quantity of things consumed but with the quality of life enjoyed, and he argues that the actual value of what we buy is inseparable from the virtues we bring to it.

The necessary relation that Ruskin charts between value and virtues aims at the two main errors that typify industrial capitalism for him. The first is the reduction of all value to market price. The other is the removal of virtues from economic interactions. Both errors are enabled by the distances that monetary exchange affords consumers in avoiding the people who help keep them alive. In relying on the abstract portrait of economic life supplied by the market, economic theory erases the moral contexts surrounding these fleeting exchange relations and so ignores the full value of commodities and the range of duties owed to other people and the world.

Central to Ruskin's understanding of economic value is his refusal to equate wealth with market price or "exchange-value." For him, wealth is "life"; wealth consists above all else in the abundant, noble, and happy lives of flourishing people. This language of "noble" and "happy" lives introduces the first question of Ruskin's political economy—namely, what constitutes a good life?[13] Only by inquiring into the activities, ends, virtues, and excellences that make for the best kinds of human lives can consumers determine what they should buy and in what proportions. As noted above, the concept of the good life has no bearing on classical political economy, and Ruskin criticizes the operational definition of "wealth" in Mill's *Principles* on these grounds. As recounted by Ruskin, Mill defines wealth as "all useful and agreeable objects which possess exchangeable value" (17.80). On the one hand, Mill remains agnostic about the good life, taking as the empirical basis of his theory whatever uses and enjoyments people find beneficial and agreeable at that time. On the other hand, it is only by having an exchange value, or a price on the market, that these useful and enjoyable objects can be measured as wealth.

For Ruskin, Mill's definition of wealth is two steps removed from the proper starting point of a science of "true" wealth. First, critical questions need to be asked about the goods that people find themselves desiring because an individual's current desires might not be conducive to a life of flourishing. Today this concern is called "preference deformation."[14] One thinks, for example, of the reduced expectations that some women have had about their education and careers. Allowed wider opportunities, some women might have developed new preferences and enjoyed a "fuller" life. Second, taking exchange value, or market price, as the measure of all value removes from consideration the uses that people make of things and, more importantly, their capacities for using them. To take one of Ruskin's examples, the decision to buy plows or bombs should be based on more than their relative prices. The real questions are, how will these things be used, by whom, and for what purposes? Only then can we judge whether plows and bombs are "wealth" or "illth."

Mill never responded to Ruskin and would likely have viewed his charges as irrelevant to the aims of the quantitative models of political economy. What makes these models remarkable is their power to translate the enormous complex of human desires, motivations, projects, and interactions into calculations and predictions of behavior under constrained situations. But as Ruskin displays through his rhetorical appeals and moral argumentation, the models cover only the patina glazing the top of the multidimensional character of economic life. Just as a disturbance at a frozen pond's bottom can disrupt the pond's surface, the comparative value of plows and bombs depends on more than the amount of money that people are willing pay for them. One must proceed from market price to actual consumption in order to judge what ends plows and bombs each serve and whether people might make better use of one or the other.

This scrutiny of *proper ends* and *good uses* underlies Ruskin's two-part conception of "value." In *Munera Pulveris* he writes that "wealth . . . consists in an *intrinsic value* developed by a *vital power*" (17.164; my emphasis). Intrinsic value reflects the ends of a thing, while vital powers are the capacities that people bring to a thing's use. He offers the same double definition in more vivid language in *Unto This Last*. Turning to etymology, his corrective for the "masked words" of political economy (18.65–66), he derives "value" from "*valorem*," and then, "*Valor*, from *valere*, to be well or strong . . . ;—strong, *in* life (if a man), or valiant; strong, *for* life (if a thing), or valuable." He continues, "To be 'valuable,' therefore, is to 'avail towards life.' A truly valuable or availing thing is that which leads to life with its whole strength. In proportion as it does not lead to life, or as its strength is broken, it is less valuable; in proportion as it leads away from life, it is unvaluable or malignant" (17.84). That Ruskin charts a connection between human flourishing and intrinsically valuable things is clear. While plows and bombs both have their uses, plows avail toward life, he claims, as bombs do not.

This appeal to "life" is a normative one, of course, and it therefore requires a moral argument to meet the objection, for example, that bombs also have their uses in protecting "life" and that there may be situations where it would be wise to buy bombs before plows. Ruskin does not supply such an argument, raising doubts about his normative account of value. Indeed, as intrinsic value is the leading concept in his dual notion of value and as this concept appears to rest on vague appeals to "life," can his account of value even get off the ground?

In the following two sections I argue that Ruskin's theory of value should be inverted. If we pay careful attention to the constructive role of his vocabulary of the virtues, it becomes clear that "effectual value" is the more critical concept. Before turning to this comparison of intrinsic and effectual value, however, let me stress that classical political economy avoids the problem of having to supply arguments about the "proper ends" and "good uses" of things. The mechanics of market exchange sift the preferences of a great many actors into aggregate statements of the relative "value" of every commodity, making irrelevant the actual goals and uses that consumers bring to their exchanges. Not everyone will agree about the comparative usefulness of plows and bombs, but a *working consensus* of sorts is reached by means of the market. This is why the market is such a marvel, theoretically at least. It serves to represent and prioritize a *society's choices about its "collective" ends and goods, without actually requiring any concerted efforts to agree in common about these societal ends and goods.* This point cannot be stressed enough, for it helps us understand why market competition is deemed not only an institutional mechanism for generating efficient outcomes but also an essential forum for legitimizing societal choices, even if no practical deliberation ever occurred.

Ruskin the moralist retorts, is this working consensus of the market good enough? Although it may be easier to build a theory of value from the structural elements of production costs and market prices, might it not be better if consumers actually asked themselves the difficult questions? What ends do they seek? What uses do they make of the things they buy? What valuable things and natural resources were expended in producing these goods? Do the activities in which the goods were made and where they will be used promote good lives for participants and for other people?

The more we recognize that the leading questions of Ruskin's ethics of consumption are corollary to his primary concern with good human lives, the more we see that it is his second category of value, "effectual value," that organizes and justifies his critical approach to good consumption. Instead of accepting the working consensus of the market, it is not only possible, but necessary, he argues, to deliberate with other people about which material goods and what human capacities are most productive of good lives. Admittedly, the "intrinsic value" of plows and bombs cannot be defended without a fuller analysis and argument than Ruskin gives. But as I read his account of value, its goal is more developmental, a matter of consumers educating their own capacities for ethical discernment in practices of good consumption. In other words, if there are reasons to think that it would be better to find ourselves in the situation of wanting to choose plows over bombs in every instance, then how might that moral judgment be brought not only to bear on our economic judgments but also to fruition in the rest of our lives? Ruskin offers his dual notion of value to advance this normative aim of fostering good character. As he works out his account of value, his use of the term "virtue" extends from a cultivated excellence in a practice of labor to a developed capacity for the use and enjoyment of things toward good ends for vitality's sake.

Intrinsic Value as a Foundational and Critical Concept

Ruskin's notion of "intrinsic value" fits his concern with acknowledging things' powers; his concept of "effectual value" expresses his commitment to developing people's vital powers. In taking up these twin parts of his idea of value, we should remember that he is moving away from his earlier concern with the kinds of work that are good for their participants to the far more open-ended task of evaluating the variety of goods sold as commodities. Assessments of good work might appeal to the standards of excellence shared within a practice by committed participants, but the domain of consumption is not so easily limited or subjected to ethical evaluation. Indeed, the difficulty in articulating an ethics consumption at all is our sense that individual taste is the only viable and acceptable standard in the realm of consumption.

Ruskin is aware of this challenge, more so than a production-driven theorist like Marx who replaces exchange-value with a labor theory of value as the sum total of labor expended in producing a commodity. Ruskin's multifaceted account of value is not restricted to human labor. Nor is value the product of consumer preferences as in the marginal utility school. In Ruskin's multifaceted schemes of value, the virtues of workers and consumers are both included along with the powers of the resources used in making things.

Ruskin's concept of "intrinsic value" applies to things' powers. Although he presents it as the foundational concept of his theory of value, I propose that we read it as a critical concept that calls into question key tenets of classical political economy. Ruskin's own definition of intrinsic value echoes with the metaphysics of the good dating all the way back to his early aesthetics. As he asserts in *Unto This Last,* "The value of a thing . . . is independent of opinion, and of quantity. Think what you will of it, gain how much you may of it, the value of the thing itself is neither greater nor less. For ever it avails, or avails not; no estimate can raise, no disdain repress, the power which it holds from the Maker of things and of men" (17.85). Taking this passage at face value and leaving aside Ruskin's transformation into a cultural critic, his insistence that all things have an unchanging intrinsic value is, as Sherburne puts it, "perversely unempirical."[15]

One reason is technological innovation. While Ruskin's ascription of intrinsic value to natural resources seems environmentally friendly, his pronouncement that material goods have a singular and fixed "power" conflicts with the great variety of human projects and purposes and with the many new uses of natural resources generated by the Industrial Revolution occurring in his day. In his 1858 lecture "The Work of Iron, in Nature, Art, and Policy," Ruskin himself details the wide range of uses for iron's properties, powers, or virtues. Although he declares in this lecture that iron's best uses are in nature, art, and policy and not in industry, it is willful blindness to reject out of hand, as he did, the technological advancements in railroads, building materials, and so on, occurring in this period. Or to take an example that would be more difficult for Ruskin to dispute, the virtues of iron make it useful for producing both plows and tractors. The gains in agricultural productivity over the past century offer strong reasons to view fuel-fired machines as "availing toward life," to use his words, even with their environmental costs. At the very least these changes belie any essential connection between the "fixed" powers of things like iron and their "proper" uses.

This appeal also conflicts with Ruskin's portrait of natural limits in "The Work of Iron." As I argued in chapter 3, he relocates iron's "natural" limits from the inherent powers of things in God's eternal order to the relational limits found in ecological systems. While there are some natural limits like iron's chemical tendency to rust, debating how iron avails toward or away from "life" requires a searching inquiry into its myriad roles in the natural world, an inquiry as flexible and open as the dynamically replenishing systems of ecology. All told, claiming that intrinsic value is dictated by "the Maker of things" overreaches both in restricting the range of the uses of any given resource and in defining natural limits as inhering in resources themselves.

Ruskin's appeal to things' inherent "powers," fixed and arranged by the "Maker" of life, repeats Richard Hooker's image of all things' striving toward their God-given perfections (see chapter 1). To the degree that people recognize the "perfect" ends of natural resources, they will discern the intrinsic value of these things and, in so doing, accumulate real wealth. The language of availing toward or away from life conveys the same upward movement of flourishing along a single pathway that leads toward wealth if pursued assiduously, or toward "illth" if not. There is no evaluation here of the complex decisions along the way or the potential benefits and costs of economic tradeoffs. Favoring plows over bombs may be a relatively straightforward choice, but a preference for many labor-intensive plows over one resource-intensive tractor is hardly persuasive.

Despite these holdovers from Ruskin's early metaphysics, his concept of intrinsic value does not reduce to the dictates of God as "Maker." Rather than look to this final appeal, we do better to concentrate on the claim that "the value of a thing . . . is independent of *opinion*, and of *quantity*." It does not matter how much we have or what we think of some material substance. In Ruskin's words, "we know, that no force of fantasy, will make stones nourishing, or poison innocent; but it is less apparent in things affecting the mind" (17.85, 164). Two points follow from this passage. First, Ruskin is staking a modest claim about "human nature," namely, that rocks and poisons are harmful to creatures like us. But the force of this claim is limited, even if arguments for certain basic needs might be advanced by noting that creatures like us cannot exist without food and water and other necessities.[16] The second point moves in a different direction toward the cultural standards of evaluation and the distributive mechanisms of capitalist economies that are the real targets of Ruskin's critical concept of things' intrinsic value.

Jewelry is one of Ruskin's favorite examples of how "opinion" and "quantity" cloud consumers' evaluations of economic goods. The properties of gold and gems have their uses in promoting good ends, he allows, but their ascribed market value has nothing to do with them. The prices paid for jewelry are inflated by jewelry's being a mark of social status (opinion) and by the scarcity of gold and gemstones (quantity). Yet the theory of political economy simply accepts individuals' preferences and market conditions as they are. By treating wealth as nothing more than "all useful and agreeable objects which possess exchangeable value," political economists fail to address how "opinion" and "quantity" distort judgments of economic value, leaving these theorists incapable of fathoming a great many things, Ruskin charges. The limited quantities of precious metals and stones might result from monopolistic practices designed to inflate prices. The difficulties in mining these resources—and the brutal and oppressive forms of labor often used in extracting them—might require a reassessment of whether jewelry is really an "agreeable" object, making its market price all the more ridiculous as a measure of its value as wealth. Of course, jewelry's capacity to buy its wearers social status and power depends on its costliness. The social valuation of jewelry functions as all "riches" do; if everyone could afford magnificent adornments, they would no longer signify the gap between plenty and poverty that lends luster to the luxury.

Ruskin does not offer a countervailing list of all of the best uses of precious metals and gems, and this silence counts against his presumption of a metaphysics of things' inherent powers. It also underscores, however, that his appeals to "intrinsic value" are critical, not foundational. His aim is to cast doubt on the dictates of market pricing and the premises of political economy. Thus he calls consumers to question their "opinions" about the value of things. What contributed to their desires? Are they the product of their own tastes or enculturated wants? Again these questions about character formation and the cultural influences on people's desires are foreign to classical political economy with its focus on existing preferences. That said, Ruskin's questions sometimes seem to miss their mark because, as a "descriptive" science, political economy leaves such normative considerations to individuals. Consumers' preferences certainly reflect their visions of the good, their commitments to family, and their place in the community, but these considerations fall outside the theory's purview. Political economists do not teach a science of "true" wealth, nor would their advice be welcomed by others.

If we move onto the issue of "quantity" and the history of economic thought, however, the line between descriptive theory and normative inquiry becomes less clear-cut. The premise of Ruskin's ethics of consumption is abundance. The world's limited, though bountiful, resources and people's creative and imaginative powers promise an abundance of well-made things and well-made people, provided that the most is made of them. The premise of the classical theory, by contrast, is scarcity.[17] If Ruskin's explicit normative goal is a wealth of the best goods shared among fully developed people, then political economy posits a world beset by a lack of wealth and a constant struggle toward increase because there is never enough. That is partly why nineteenth-century political economists like Mill reject the "physiocratic" sensibility that carries forward in Ruskin's idea and examples of intrinsic value. Like the eighteenth-century physiocrats, Ruskin always returns to land, agriculture, and food as the "natural" basis for all wealth.[18] Mill, by contrast, stresses industrial productivity, and he makes capital (not land or labor) the driving force toward greater prosperity. The priority Mill ascribes to capital increase is foundational to his theoretical distinction between the two types of consumption. For him only "productive consumption" uses things up in order to increase the capital stock; all other kinds of consumption are, in his words, "unproductive consumption."

Both the physiocratic overtones and the normative thrust of Ruskin's concept of intrinsic value figure in his rejoinder to Mill's distinction. Iron and silver both have their powers for life, Ruskin claims, and regardless of anyone's "opinion," these properties are rightly applied "to ploughs, but not to bayonets; and to forks, but not to filigree" (17.80). In his favoring plows and forks, we see the priority he ascribes to agriculture and food as the basis of "life" and, thus, the fundamental source of "wealth," or well-being. In his ranking plows and forks as equally good uses of these metals, he takes direct aim at Mill's distinction. For Mill, making a plow is "productive consumption," while manufacturing forks would be "unproductive" because it goes no further, or so Ruskin would put it disparagingly, than the feeding of mouths. No addition is made to the nation's stock of capital, but only to the nourishment and health of people.

Mill did not discount ordinary consumption, despite the pejorative connotations of his terminology.[19] But Ruskin is not just scoring a rhetorical victory either. His point is to highlight the normative assumptions built into Mill's production-driven political economy. Most importantly, for Mill, scarcity makes growing the capital stock the first priority of any nation. Moreover, Ruskin's ascription of intrinsic value to silver forks challenges another assumption of Mill's *Principles.* Mill's theory answers to his sense that consumers do, in fact, overvalue certain items due, it would seem, to their opinions about luxuries and to the rarity of a set of silver. Thus normative commitments creep back into the empirical science of political economy, not through a metaphysics of things' powers, but through a valorization of production itself.

Ruskin's challenge to classical political economy cannot be written off as the complaints of a Victorian sage deriding a "descriptive" science in the interests of foisting his tastes on the public. The science answers to normative concerns, too, including the importance that Mill ascribes to the liberty of choice and the democratic potential of industrialization in gaining power for workers and challenging established structures of privilege. No doubt Ruskin's idea of intrinsic value warrants scrutiny because his metaphysical sensibility so often stands in tension with democratic individuality. But he uses his concept of intrinsic value in ways that are more complex than his rhetorical tendency toward dualism suggests. In his formulation of intrinsic value, he implies that, if a full reading of the value of things answers neither to "opinion" nor to "quantity," then the real basis of all wealth must *therefore* be the "Maker of things and of men." Yet to leap from the mechanical subjectivism of political economy that Ruskin rightly criticizes to a romantic holism transferred onto God's natural order is to deny the intervening layers of the human making of culture and character that move increasingly to the center of his criticism over the course of the 1850s, as demonstrated in part 2.

Effectual Value and Good Character

To separate Ruskin's concept of intrinsic value from his metaphysics and, therefore, to set his consumption-driven challenge to classical political economy on firmer ground, we must turn to his category of "effectual value." With this concept he introduces human character into his scheme of valuation. As with the growing interest in people's powers of imagination that redirects his art criticism in the 1850s, his notion of effectual value reflects his conviction that the realization of things' "powers for life" depends on their users' capacities, their excellences, or, in a word, their virtues. "*The production of effectual value . . . always involves two needs: first, the production of a thing essentially useful; then the production of the capacity to use it.*" As stated here, both aspects of effectual value depend on human powers of making, first, an "essentially useful" good and, second, the "acceptant capacity" for using it well. Ruskin's ethics of consumption occupies this territory between well-made goods and well-made people (17.154).

Two points warrant emphasis. First, in defining effectual value, Ruskin allows for the possibility that what is "essentially useful" might not be dictated by God's purposes as "Maker" but is subject to the shifting understandings of good lives that people work out for themselves. He does not develop this line of argument in *Unto This Last,* though hints of it appear in *Munera Pulveris.* Second, and more important for now, Ruskin proposes an approach to assessing use-value by locating it, in part, in the vital powers or capacities that consumers bring to everything they buy.

As noted earlier, classical political economy dispenses with the concept of "use-value." The uses of goods are so various and so subjective that it would be practically impossible to measure the relative value of these many uses apart from the market's translation of use-value into exchange-value. People buy goods with certain uses in mind, and the degree of desire in wanting to make some use of a particular good is reflected in the price that consumers are willing to pay for this good relative to all others, each of which may have its own anticipated uses. This collapsing of use-value into exchange-value is one of the defining features of capitalist exchange that political economists from Mill to Marx accept as given.

Yet Ruskin questions the ease of that translation by interrogating Mill's definitions once again. "'To be wealthy,' says Mr. Mill, 'is to have a large stock of useful articles.'" For Ruskin, however, someone *has* something only to the degree that it is *useful* to him or her. As he puts it, "possession, or 'having,' is not an absolute power, but a gradated power; and consists not only in the quantity or nature of the thing possessed, but also (and in a greater degree) in its suitableness to the person possessing it and in his vital power to use it." For example, a farmer has a plow to plant more crops, but the plow will have "effectual value" only if the farmer knows how to make the plow useful, which requires knowledge, skill, and judgment in the practices of farming. Ruskin condenses his argument in a single sentence: "For wealth, instead of depending merely on a 'have,' is . . . seen to depend on a 'can'" (17.87). Plows are relatively useless in the wrong people's hands, no matter what intrinsic value a plow might have. Likewise, "A horse is no wealth to us if we cannot ride, nor a picture if we cannot see, *nor can any noble thing be wealth, except to a noble person*" (17.154). The term "nobleness" recalls the emphasis on excellence in Ruskin's politics. It signifies here the role of virtues in his ethics of consumption and the need to educate people's capacities for good use in specific practices as well as their judgments about which activities, uses, and enjoyments are best to pursue in a good life.

An intriguing footnote helps to clarify the direction of Ruskin's argument. Criticizing the concept of "demand" in political economy, he draws a larger lesson about how the meanings of this term might be judged in the economy of language as a whole. Political economists, he writes, use the term "demand" to mean "'the quantity of a thing sold.' I mean by it 'the force of the buyer's capable intention to buy.' In good English, a person's 'demand' signifies, not what he gets, but what he asks for" (17.84n). In this brief and seemingly simple distinction, Ruskin shifts attention away from the amount of a product supplied to consumers toward the actual demands that consumers make and, more importantly, the various capacities they bring to their "asking for" things. This placing the consumer's *asking for* in the active voice reorients the focus of political economy from the passing needs and desires satisfied through commodity exchange to the developed abilities and adopted aims that inform a person's independent judgment about the best things to demand. This *asking for* elevates the proposed uses and the user's fitness to the desired ends. Thus, in Ruskin's own explication of the word "demand," he contends that in the exchange of words—in the economy of language—he deserves higher regard than his opponents for his "powers" of judging the meaning of the word "demand" and using it well in the practice of good English.

The implicit claim is that "we"—the community of English speakers—can distinguish between good and faulty English usage. More broadly, though, Ruskin is raising the question of whether "we"—the community of consumers—are capable of distinguishing between good and faulty consumption. Good consumption entails the "good usage" of natural resources and the talents and capacities of workers and consumers, while faulty consumption takes stock of none of these factors directly, relying instead on market outcomes to determine what each person shall get for his or her pains.

Ruskin's challenge can be stated more broadly still: how can we best assess the quality of life produced, distributed, and enjoyed in an economy? For Ruskin the standard of living must account for all three factors at work in the value of any good—things' intrinsic powers and workers' and consumers' virtues, though human virtues clearly come first in his idea of well-being. Economic theorists, by contrast, tend to privilege one of two standard measures of the quality of life—"income" or "utility." The income approach equates well-being with *aggregate income or goods possessed in a society,* as Mill does in privileging productive over unproductive consumption in order to increase prosperity in the form of more economic goods. The second approach measures well-being in terms of *aggregate utility or preference satisfaction,* as the marginal school does in privileging the relative achievement of greater satisfaction through the different combinations of purchases that consumers might choose to make. These two approaches to the standard of living have been criticized in recent decades by economists, underscoring the continued relevance of Ruskin's critique of political economy.

Virtues and Capabilities

In rejecting both "quantity" (income) and "opinion" (utility) as insufficient grounds for assessing the quality of life, Ruskin advances a critical insight into the limitations of the classical theory. He does not develop an alternative theoretical model in any systematic way, and he begins his critique from a notion of intrinsic value that has its flaws. Nevertheless, although Ruskin has not been recognized as a source of the "capabilities approach," his concept of "effectual value" and his equation of "wealth" with well-made people anticipate the focus on human development and positive freedom in this more recent approach.[20]

Detailing the conceptual affinities between Ruskin's virtues-centered approach to good consumption and Amartya Sen's capabilities approach extends beyond the purposes of this book. I draw only a few comparisons between their vocabularies to indicate the critical significance of Ruskin's insights, while acknowledging the different purposes motivating the two thinkers. By putting Ruskin into conversation with Sen, I aim to clarify the breadth of Ruskin's ideal of the full development of good character as well as the complex dynamic at work in his dual scheme of value. Sen's language of "capabilities" indicates the directions and implications of Ruskin's moral vocabulary, even as Ruskin would resist the ethical strictures that Sen places around his approach.

In Sen's early essay "The Living Standard," he echoes Ruskin's criticisms of the usual economic measurements of welfare. Neither the perspective of "utility" nor the perspective of "opulence" (or "income") captures what is of fundamental concern to people's quality of life—in Sen's words, their "freedom" (in the positive sense of the term), or their "*capability* to live well." In distinguishing the perspectives of utility, opulence, and freedom, Sen discusses four ways that the act of consuming bread might be judged to contribute to a person's standard of living. "There is the notion of a *good* (bread); *characteristic* of a good (calories and other nutrients); that of *functioning of a person* (the person living without calorie deficiency); that of *utility* (the pleasure or desire fulfillment from eating bread or from being well nourished)." Proponents of measuring the standard of living in terms of opulence, income, or goods possessed would look to the first of these features—how much bread one has. Advocates of satisfaction or utility would look to the last—how much pleasure or fulfillment results from eating the bread. It is worth noting that the second item on Sen's list—the "characteristics" of bread that sustain human life—repeats Ruskin's concerns with the "powers for life" of material goods, though again the metaphysical constraints that Ruskin imposes on his category of intrinsic value are too narrow.[21]

The term "functionings" marks Sen's contribution to the debate. For him, functionings are what a person does and achieves. In later writings he has expanded this notion to include a person's "doings" and "beings." A person's functionings consist not only in what he or she does, but in being well nourished, for example, so as to be free to read or to engage in the other activities included in this person's range of functionings. By attending to functionings, Sen seeks to overcome the one-sidedness of the other two standard approaches to the quality of life. Knowing that someone has enough income to buy a certain amount of bread is insufficient to judge that person's standard of living, for he or she may have caloric needs far greater than the average person. Nor is the issue simply the satisfaction or utility that a person derives from eating food or from being well nourished. Food is good not only because it gives pleasure and satisfies a need, but more importantly because it allows a person to function in life without being ravaged by the ill effects of hunger or, perhaps, by the loneliness that comes from not being able to entertain guests over dinner.[22]

The emphasis in all of Sen's examples, as in Ruskin's, is on economic *activity*—on the overall goal of living well and the specific goods, including health, education, dignity, equality, companionship, hospitality, and so on, that are the real aims of economic exchange. Individuals will pursue different paths and choose different means toward these goals, but Ruskin and Sen both argue that measures of the quality of life must somehow account for these ends of well-being. Although their approaches are very different in detail, both Ruskin and Sen employ a classical notion of human activity that bases judgments of the quality of life, not on quantity or opinion, income or utility, but on the personal capacities and social conditions required for participating in what Sen calls "valued activities."[23]

Let me turn now to the concept of "capabilities." People will be free to participate in valued activities only if they *can* attain the requisite "beings" and "doings." As Sen puts it, "A functioning is an achievement, whereas a capability is the ability to achieve." A person cannot read without being literate. Or to use another of Sen's examples, a person cannot appear in public without shame if he or she is unable to afford the kinds of clothing deemed minimally acceptable in a culture. As Sen notes, Adam Smith recognized this relative component of the standard of living, arguing that a linen shirt was not a luxury but a necessity for working-class people of his day.[24] Thus a functioning like "having dignity" involves both the possession of goods and the enjoyment of using them. But the main consideration is not income or utility; it is what a person is capable of "doing" and "being," where that is a matter of judgments about the contents of human achievement or flourishing.

To translate Sen's language into Ruskin's moral vocabulary, the "having" (income) and "enjoying" (utility) of material goods always depends on a "can" (capability). If a person lacks the "vital powers" required to possess a thing and to use or enjoy it fully, then his or her quality of life will suffer. For Ruskin, then, the concept of "effectual value" reinforces his mandate to his audiences of merchants, manufacturers, and consumers that they devote themselves to the cultivation of a good and full character, not only for themselves, but for all of the people touched by the long reach of their economic decisions.

Sen signals the normative concerns of his theory by locating assessments of a person's standard of living in "the nature of the life the person leads" or in "the goodness of the life one can lead." If people's happiness reflects the "nature" and "goodness" of their lives, then some corrective must be made when people are so deprived in their experiences and capabilities as to accept the current life they have as being adequate, despite clear evidence to most everyone else of their deprivation. Sen's appeals to the "nature" and "goodness" of a life recall Ruskin's charge to business "masters" to take responsibility for "the kind of life" their workers lead, as if these workers were their sons. Yet Sen's notion of capabilities assiduously avoids this paternalism for two reasons. First, capabilities are not functionings. The mandate of Sen's approach is only that people *can* achieve, not that they *must* achieve in ways valued, in this case, by the "master." Second, individuals will differ over both the "valued activities" required for good lives and the specific capacities and means for participating in them. That is why Sen describes capabilities as sets. Capabilities are not isolated abilities to do this or to be that; they come bundled together in distinct combinations with tradeoffs between the ensembles. Because each available set of capabilities allows for a different kind of life, for Sen, enhancing the quality of life entails not only making people more capable of specific valued functionings, but making available a range of lives, or "capability sets," from which individuals may choose.[25] For Sen, choosing and pursuing one's own idea of a good life and, thus, one's preferred set of capabilities is itself a vital human functioning. So even as he argues that there are different "kinds" of human lives and that some of these lives can be judged as better than others, he remains agnostic about which activities and which ends constitute the good life itself.

Here we see a crucial difference between Ruskin's vocabulary of the virtues and Sen's terminology of capability sets. Both critics locate the quality of life in the valued activities that a person is capable of, and both emphasize how the various functionings or excellences a person achieves come together in particular kinds of lives. But Ruskin insists that evaluating the quality of life is a matter of practical reason. The ability to know what is "noble," to make judgments about the goodness of different kinds of life, depends, first, on a person's embracing not just any "valued activities" but the best activities well ordered into a good life. In addition, evaluating the quality of life requires cultivating the virtues appropriate to those activities, without which judgments about the relative goodness of different kinds of life could not be made. Once again we see the circularity in Ruskin's teleological ethics between the development of good character and the exercise of moral vision. Thus we return to the organizing questions of his ethics of consumption: what is the good life, and which activities, desires, ends, capacities, and excellences are most conducive to flourishing lives?

Sen resists these questions because he rejects a uniform conception of the good life as a limitation on individuals' freedom. Ruskin's challenge to Sen, however, would be whether the goal of improving the quality of life for destitute people, and for their "masters," can be realized apart from a more general commitment to a clearly articulated conception of a good life—that specific activities and related capabilities need to be guaranteed for all, at least up to a minimal threshold of well-being that is recognizably human.[26] This challenge is not merely philosophical. In Ruskin's writings, it assumes great urgency as he calls his contemporaries to assess the full value of the goods they buy, not only in terms of the effectual value that consumers can derive from the goods they purchase, but also in terms of the lives enjoyed or not by the workers who made them. This task requires consumers to develop their capacities for moral imagination. It requires their searching out how their purchases contribute to or detract from their own and other people's capabilities for pursuing, enjoying, and choosing a flourishing life.

The Practice of Moral Imagination

Ruskin develops his account of value in the years following his 1858 lecture "The Work of Iron, in Nature, Art, and Policy." Already this lecture anticipates his argument for equating the value of economic goods with things' powers and people's virtues. More importantly, it exemplifies the interpretive practice of good consumption that he seeks to teach to his audience of consumers. His strategy is to take iron as a symbol of how people in Victorian Britain see and use the goods of their world. He charges his contemporaries that they value iron solely for its role in building the vast machine of productivity that dominates their lives. Yet this narrow vision of iron's value ignores the many meanings attaching to iron in the uses and purposes it serves in a range of human activities that are threatened by industrialization. In the lecture he reads this wealth of iron's meanings, arguing that his contemporaries are blind to its many powers for life and lacking in the virtues required to make good use of them.

I have already explored in chapter 3 how the term "virtue" figures in Ruskin's portrait of the "work of iron in nature." Iron itself has specific virtues or properties, the most important of which is, surprisingly enough, its tendency to rust. Inviting his audience to consider the stains on the fountains of their beloved Tunbridge Wells, he writes, "it struck me that you might not be unwilling, to-night, to think a little over the full significance of that saffron stain, and of the power, in other ways and other functions, of the steelly element to which so many here owe returning strength and life;—chief as it has been always, and is yet more and more markedly so day by day, among the precious gifts of the earth." The "power" for "strength and life" of this "markedly" "precious gift" lodges primarily in iron's oxidized forms (16.376). The residents of this spa town should know that iron's virtues make it fit for a range of uses and enjoyments other than those of the industrial economy. The town's economy is in no small part based on the healing properties of its mineral springs. Broken-down forms of iron also play essential nourishing functions in the soil and in blood. Finally, there are all of the ways that iron colors the earth in various shades of reds, oranges, and purples.

As Ruskin details iron's many roles in nature in the first part of the lecture, he proceeds in a manner consistent with his notion of "intrinsic value." Material goods have powers for life, and this natural ordering of things' goodness is the first priority, it seems. But his account of the work of iron in nature makes other appeals that look not to the all-encompassing good of God's Creation but to a moral argument that details the component parts of good human lives. Iron's tendency to rust is its chief virtue because its oxidized forms contribute to people's nourishment and health along with another vital aspect of any good life, as Ruskin sees it, the capacity for wonder before the world's beauty. This delight in nature's splendor is not simply a matter of the natural world's intrinsic value. A person's delight must be made *effectual* by his or her choosing to participate in those activities that develop the requisite virtues or capabilities needed to judge things well—in this case, a natural piety and the observational acuity of a practiced sketcher, as detailed in chapter 3. The more that Ruskin's argument leans on the idea of a good life, the more that his appeals to intrinsic value give way to the goal of cultivating people's vital powers.

It might be objected, however, that the rhetorical structure of the lecture actually grounds his vision of good lives in a metaphysics of the good. He begins from the work of iron in nature, and he equates iron's tendency to rust with its affinity for the creator's "breath of life." While it may be unobjectionable that health and nourishment are "essential" to good human lives, people differ in their conceptions of and paths to these ends. Still more questionable, does "delight" in the world's beauty warrant the same primacy and universality accorded to the goods of health and nourishment? Ruskin appeals to the earth mother's wisdom here; she places the delightfully colored iron oxides in clays and slates near the earth's surface where everyone can enjoy them equally, for "Nature paints for all the world, poor and rich, together" (16.383). This common treasury of vivid color brushed across the landscape is a greater source of wealth, he contends, than all of the riches of gold and gems that must be mined underground and then are hoarded by the powerful. These intuitive appeals suggest that the practice of good consumption modeled in this lecture amounts to nothing more than an authoritative account of iron's intrinsic value and its place in a good life that Ruskin's readers must simply accept.

Reading farther into "The Work of Iron," however, we see Ruskin shifting his attention more emphatically from things' powers to human virtues. The movement of the lecture clarifies the centrality of human activity to his account of value. His discussions of iron in art and policy focus directly on his contemporaries' "work," that is, on the activities they currently value. But he asks more critically, what personal capacities and societal conditions are needed to participate in the activities that should be valued as making for good human lives?

That Ruskin cares about human virtues more than things' virtues becomes obvious in his imaginative reading of the iron fences of Victorian Britain in the second section on the "work of iron in art." As before, he begins his argument from iron's virtues—its properties of ductility and tenacity. These virtues make iron well suited, artistically speaking, for the crafting of intricately designed fences, but the fences purchased by his contemporaries are a monotonous succession of menacing spikes.

This misuse of iron might be seen as a failure to discern iron's inherent powers for life as fixed by God's Creation. Yet Ruskin looks elsewhere in disparaging these fences. He writes, "Consider every other kind of fence or defence, and you will find some virtue in it; but in the iron railing, none." Fences of brick, stone, and hedge all express particular virtues. Brick walls, for example, show more "modesty" than "unkindness." They allow their owners to escape the observance of neighbors, and they have the advantage of sheltering ripening fruit trees. Low stone dykes signify the industry required to farm a stony field, while hedges of brambles and berry bushes speak of cultivating a delight in the world's bounty (16.388–389). Here we see the importance of a range of virtues to Ruskin's vision of good lives, and something else, too. Clearly he does not object to all fences. Boundaries are integral to the institution of private property, which he supported, and to the freedom to choose some activities over others.[27] Thus he includes privacy and autonomy as components of a good life, but he sets limits on them.

Consumers should not be free to erect impregnable boundaries around their lives, refusing to acknowledge the ethical entailments of the commodities they buy and the activities they choose to support with their purchases. Ruskin does not fix these limits by mere appeals to the "natural" properties of iron. He focuses instead on human activity. Simply put, Ruskin formulates his sense of the limits of privacy and autonomy by asking the question, how do the many uses of iron and other things correspond to the activities, virtues, vices, and societal conditions that all figure in a constructed cultural landscape where one lives not alone but with others?

The connection between activities and virtues is clear in Ruskin's preceding examples. Different activities foster different virtues. But whether people are free to participate in the activities best suited to the cultivation of their vital powers depends on societal conditions and economic relations, too. When he writes that the iron fences of Victorian Britain have no virtue in them, he means that these fences testify to the deficiencies in the character of the people living on both sides of them. The exchanges between rich and poor transpire across the distances of the money economy, and the wealthy give no consideration to the kinds of lives purchased for the people who live outside their gates.

Thus Ruskin traces the deficiencies in his contemporaries' character to the injustice of existing societal structures, declaring that there are only two possible meanings to this "police force of iron bars" that divides the built landscape of Victorian Britain. "Either, observe, that you are living in the midst of such bad characters that you must keep them out by main force of bar, or that you are yourself of a character requiring to be kept inside in the same manner. Your iron railing always means thieves outside, or Bedlam inside; it *can* mean nothing else than that" (16.390). Ruskin is calling attention to the social ills created by an economic system that operates without regard for the kinds of character that people are "free" to develop, including not only their moral virtues but all of their vital powers, excellences, and capabilities.

Why call these ills "social"? First and foremost, for Ruskin, class divisions reflect the refusal, mainly by the rich, to acknowledge the growing interdependence of economic life. Even if iron bars have their uses in keeping the poor away from the fabulous "wealth" possessed and enjoyed within these walls, the riches of the industrial elite depend upon the efforts of many workers and the choices of an even wider circle of consumers. This expanding interdependence generates more extensive social ties and imposes broader social obligations in economic life than presently observed.

Another reason to call these ills "social" has to do with Ruskin's insights into the cultural formations of desire. The desire for an iron fence of mass-produced railings and bars is vicious, he contends, not simply because individual consumers show their poor judgment in choosing this kind of fence. Ruskin reads the motives and consequences of these individual choices as social in nature because they reflect the kind of character and community chosen by the members of this society. For Ruskin, people's desires are not subjective, either in their origins or in their effects. Nor are people's ends uniquely formulated for each and every one of their actions. Instead they follow the cultural patterns that define "ideal" lives, however varied the means taken toward these ends may be.

Ruskin's attention to the connections among consumer choice, cultural patterns, and societal structures suggests how many social ills proceed from failures of human development. To use his words, the "thieves outside" are the people whose lives are so deprived that a life of crime may become preferable. Indeed, the refusal to countenance other people's need to develop their capabilities is not just a one-time injury. It can hinder their independent judgment about the good and their active pursuit of flourishing. As Ruskin observes, however, most of the people outside the fences do not choose a life of crime. To these people the "insolent" fences call attention to the wealth within and tell passersby to "depart in humiliation" (16.390, 391).

Here we see another social ill caused by the lack of access to such social goods as respect and recognition and such valued activities as art and education. Too often these activities and their corresponding excellences circulate within narrow circles of social privilege, with insiders trading favors and connections, ensuring that they remain the beneficiaries of these higher goods, which, while readily shared among themselves, stand as barriers to other people's participation in a truly "social life." For the people outside the fences, the difficulties of judging the best kinds of lives are compounded by structures of entrenched power and privilege that keep the activities that might help these outsiders cultivate their ideas, imagination, and pleasures off-limits to all but an elite.

The final social ill signified by Ruskin's fences looks not to the people outside, but to the residents within. Here we see how his interests in the cultural components of and barriers to good lives intersect with his arguments that income and utility are poor measures of the quality of life. Even as these iron fences signify the "quantity" of their owners' enviable "income" and possessions, their moneyed estimates of their own wealth are false. Nor do these people living on the inside in Bedlam enjoy the full satisfaction or "utility" that might be derived from all their possessions, even if in their "opinion" their life is complete. So vital is a well-developed character, meaning a person's intellectual, bodily, aesthetic, emotional, social, and practical capacities, that if the wealthy fail to develop their vital powers, they will never achieve well-being, no matter how many other people they command as rich consumers.

Ruskin reads the built environment of Victorian Britain as proof that consumer practices aimed at satisfying immediate desires, in as thrifty a fashion as possible, cannot produce a high quality of life, either for oneself or for others. If instead his contemporaries bought fences that made more of the builders and themselves, too, their estimates of the quality of life would be improved. Human development is necessary to the kind of moral evaluation that Ruskin models in this lecture. In judging the best products to buy and, thus, the best forms of work to support, consumers have to seek out the kinds of labor that are valued by workers because the activities enhance their lives. In the process consumers can gain an appreciation for these activities, too. They might learn to discern, for example, which crafted flowers required the most creativity and how the crafted form of a vine is an accurate rendering of yet another of the amazing designs found in the natural world. As Ruskin counsels his listeners, it is "in your power to turn all your police force of iron bars . . . into drawing masters, and natural historians. . . . The main question is only—what is worth doing and having" (16.391–92). This passage is the nexus of the lecture. It joins his pleas to respect natural beauty and promote social justice with his conviction that an ethics of consumption begins with the task of imagining a good life for oneself and for others.

Certainly Ruskin appeals to iron's "natural" powers and to the intrinsic value of "natural" beauty, but as he insists here, the main question is, "what is worth doing and having," a question that his contemporaries can answer only by reading the cultural landscape of Victorian Britain, seeking out the social practices and other activities that foster the vital powers of consumers and workers alike. Cultural activities and effectual value thus emerge to the fore in his full account of value. Together they provide a sufficient basis for the normative evaluation at the center of his ethics of consumption.

Good lives consist in valued activities and the virtues or capabilities needed to engage in them. Yet the good life is not simply a matter of achieving excellence in particular activities. Excellence is an afterthought if more basic needs go unmet. It is in the third section on "the work of iron in policy" that this concern moves to the fore. Ruskin cites three "typical" uses of iron in policy: the plow, the fetter, and the sword. These uses reflect iron's "power of bearing a pull, and receiving an edge." He spends most of his time on the plow because food production is the first of all labors, and "nearly all our misery and crime result from . . . one misapprehension. The law of nature is, that a certain quantity of work is necessary to produce a certain quantity of good, of any kind whatever." Or to put it in Ruskin's graphic language, if your work is not as necessary as the growing of food, then you are, "in plain Saxon, STEALING," another person's labor. The only "way of taking our hands off the plough handle [is to bind] another's upon it." So if one guides neither the plow, or the "feminine plough," the needle, then one's work must answer to an equally good purpose, always respecting the priority of food and clothing as human needs (16.396, 402).

Ruskin is issuing two challenges here, both answering to his mandate to imagine good lives. First, he tells his audience to look to their own work. If it is to be judged as necessary as the growing of food or the making of clothing, then it must contribute to people's possibilities for developing the virtues and capabilities requisite to good lives. Second, he warns his listeners to consider whether or not the prices they pay for their own essentials afford the same possibilities for sustenance and self-development to the people who grow their food and sew their clothing. If not, then they are denying these workers the basic capabilities of being well nourished and well clothed and, thus, the freedom to cultivate the other capabilities and excellences that make for human flourishing.

Ruskin comes full circle in tracing out the lessons taught by "The Work of Iron." Iron's goodness starts from its tendency to rust—its affinity for the "breath of life"—for life would not be possible apart from the roles it plays in the "circles of vitality" of nature's economy. In art, iron is good for the crafting of decorative fences because such work serves to develop the virtues of its makers in a way that mass-produced fences and, more generally, the whole system of factory production and market exchange do not. Finally, in aiding the growing of food and the sewing of clothing, iron enforces the need to extend concern to other people that they be able to develop a full complement of capabilities, beginning with being well nourished and well clothed so as not to be prevented from participating in a life of valued activities due to poor health or a lack of dignity. All told, Ruskin models an integrated practice of moral imagination combining delight in the natural world, respect for human excellence, and fairness in providing for basic needs.

Virtues, Practices, and Good Lives

Clearly, for Ruskin, virtue and value are inseparable. His critical interest in the place of the virtues in economic life and in human flourishing more generally encompasses moral virtues as well as a great many other human excellences and basic capabilities. It is difficult, however, to conceptualize this multifaceted understanding of character and to make it morally compelling. That is why Ruskin takes a different approach, the approach of a social critic, not a philosopher. He constructs his scenes of economic life in *Unto This Last,* and he reads his contemporaries' cultural activities in "The Work of Iron." He situates the consumption of things in the context of people's activities, enjoyments, delights, and commitments, always returning to the cultivation of character and the development of human capabilities, the missing elements in classical political economy that, in Ruskin's judgment, vitiate its conclusions. We do not need to follow him so far as to deny the uses of economic theory or to reject the normative aims of a theorist like Mill. But we should also learn from Ruskin's method of reading a culture's activities for the component parts of good human lives. We should also recognize that his cultural approach requires every consumer to undertake the same imaginative efforts, for it is only in the context of a developing and self-directed life, the substance of which is a person's vital powers, that the good doing, having, and enjoying and the wise judging and just relating of an ethics of consumption can be practiced.

No commentator on Ruskin's writings on consumption has related his account of value to his vocabulary of the virtues, and as a result, his ethics of consumption has not received its due. Take, for instance, Austin's criticism of Ruskin's concept of intrinsic value. In her judgment he makes the same mistake in his account of good consumption that he does in his early theory of beauty. Initially "Ruskin tries to formulate innate properties of beauty," she writes, "but in the process describes it as a phenomenon of perception. His use of economic principles places him in a similar dilemma: in defining intrinsic value, Ruskin ends up describing value-in-use or value in the eyes of a certain group of consumers."[28] Austin's criticism builds from the complaints about Ruskin's purported refusal to admit "subjectivity" into individuals' judgments of beauty. As argued in chapter 1, however, this theory of beauty answers to ethical, not epistemological, concerns. His early aesthetics aimed at "community" in taste because Ruskin took beauty itself to be instructive of God's created order and, thus, the chief guide in people's development of their "perfections" and performance of their appointed "function." The teleological framework of his criticism has shifted away from God's virtue and the metaphysics of the good in *Modern Painters* 2 to the centrality of people's virtues and cultural practices in his later writings. So when Austin writes that after beginning from intrinsic value Ruskin "ends up" at "value in the eyes of a certain group of consumers," she accurately charts the path of his argument, but she discounts how his critical interests in the virtues of good character and the cultural activities that form them direct our attention to groups of reflective people who can, through the cultivation of their vital powers, have good reasons for judging things' value in common.

On my reading, Ruskin is arguing that it is possible for consumers to arrive together at shared judgments of the value of commodities that will differ from the valuation assigned by market pricing, by hierarchies of social status, and by their own "subjective" preferences. That is the goal of his vocabulary of the virtues. He is attempting to articulate a social practice of good consumption in which individual consumers, by reflecting on their vision of good lives and the activities constituting them, commit with others to meet the moral obligations attaching to their purchases. Clearly there is a movement from intrinsic value to "value-in-use or value in the eyes of a certain group of consumers" in "The Work of Iron." Ruskin's claims about iron's "powers" are instrumental to his argument that certain activities should be valued more highly for the ways that they develop their participants' excellences and capabilities. Iron's properties allow for certain "intrinsically" valuable uses and enjoyments, but to recognize them, consumers need some exposure to and, better yet, direct experience of the shared goods and self-development made available in and through those endeavors. These judgments are not strictly subjective, nor need they be metaphysically sanctioned or coercively enforced.

My reading of Ruskin prompts a reconsideration of his definitions of value. Instead of grounding "effectual value" in "intrinsic value" as he appears to do, a better and, indeed, a more accurate reading of his ethics of consumption takes "effectual value" as the regulative concept. This reformulation makes "intrinsic value" a matter of the considered judgments of individuals actively seeking out good lives for themselves and others through certain cultural activities. It fits Ruskin's awareness of how social practices develop people's virtues and capabilities. Finally, it suggests a revision of his idea of intrinsic value that clears it of metaphysical pretensions, while still prompting the moral commitment to observe the physical limits of the earth's natural resources.

John Fain also stresses the "reciprocal action" between the intrinsic and effectual aspects of Ruskin's concept of value. For Fain there is no metaphysical basis of value in Ruskin's theory; there is only the claim that economic goods must have some utility in themselves. But the goods have value only if, in addition to being useful, there are capable people who can use them. Fain's position captures the "embedded" quality of Ruskin's appeals to intrinsic value.[29] If we factor in Ruskin's turn toward cultural activities as the locus of human action, development, and judgment, then we see that his concepts of intrinsic and effectual value must be related to the virtues, vices, ends, goods, practices, and commitments pursued by some group of people. Thus, for Ruskin, value does not inhere in human labor, consumer demand, or natural powers. Evaluating the full worth of things requires a broader cultural inquiry into the social logics of valuation operative in a society and the social costs and benefits of existing patterns of production and consumption.

Consider how my proposal responds to Sherburne, who, with Austin, is another astute critic of Ruskin's account of value. Once again, Sherburne dismisses intrinsic value as "perversely unempirical," and he adds that a "concern for spiritual qualities becomes obvious" in the concept of effectual value. I agree that, if Ruskin's idea of intrinsic value answers to the fixed powers for life set by the "Maker of things," then the concept is too inflexible to be helpful. But it is more complex in Ruskin's usage of the term. He challenges his audience to consider the myriad uses of iron, not just its roles in industry that so dominate his contemporaries' minds. He urges his listeners to acknowledge that there are some insurmountable limits to using this resource. More importantly, he calls them to observe the interdependence of ecological systems in learning to make more of the natural world, examining all of the possible uses and enjoyments of iron and other resources in light of current and future environmental costs.

In addition to challenging his contemporaries to examine the effects of their consumption on the health of the environment, Ruskin employs his idea of intrinsic value as a placeholder for a vision of abundant wealth that stands in contrast to the premise of scarcity in production-driven political economies. He achieves two things by doing so. On the one hand, he reminds his audience that judgments of economic value are subject to the distorting effects of "quantity" and "opinion" and that consumers always need to step back and consider which desires and what ends are best for them and others. On the other hand, he also exposes the normative aims of the "descriptive" science of political economy, which in Mill's case, privileges capital accumulation and largely unconstrained choice in the interests of a vision of the good life aimed at enhancing democratic individuality.

Challenging his fellow Victorians to seek out the limits of the world's bounty and the limits of classical political economy are only two of Ruskin's goals, however. To appreciate the force of his arguments and the promise of his ethics of consumption, we must take seriously his concept of effectual value. The crucial connection between his vocabulary of the virtues and his interests in practical activity puts this concept in its proper context. Virtue and value depend on developing people. Unlike Sherburne, I accept Ruskin's claim that individuals can develop vital powers and so derive more value from the goods they buy. We expend great effort in educating and training our minds, bodies, tastes, emotions, and pleasures, precisely to gain more value out of things. We also know that certain types of work leave people incapable of effective use and enjoyment of almost anything.

Sherburne contrasts Ruskin's account of value with those of Aristotle and Aquinas, for whom value in use, in Sherburne's words, "is as much subjective as objective; it is dependent on man's wants and needs." Once again, the language of subjectivity and objectivity is unhelpful because it distracts attention away from Aristotle's, Aquinas's, and Ruskin's practical interests in how the virtues, desires, needs, pleasures, ends, and goods that people take on in their activities form their abilities to use and judge things. It is puzzling therefore that Sherburne calls Ruskin's concerns with human "capacities" and "nobleness" mere "spiritual qualities" that carry no more weight than Ruskin's asserting that they are worthy of esteem because, presumably, they reveal something of the human spirit or the divine itself. While such an appeal would be at home in Ruskin's reading of the Gothic, his turn toward Victorian culture directs his appeals elsewhere. When Sherburne writes that, for Ruskin, the "spiritual qualities of an object . . . can only be grasped by a 'genial' man like himself," he calls our attention to the classist problems in Ruskin's account of value.[30] But Sherburne neglects the developmental thrust of Ruskin's arguments and the democratic commitments to expanding people's capabilities. He also misses the ways that Ruskin's precise conceptual vocabulary of specific virtues, not vague "spiritual qualities," can sustain reasonable claims subject to debate and deliberation.

Ruskin's account of value looks to things, asking whether or not they "avail toward life." But wealth for Ruskin consists less in things than in people. Again, in his words, "That country is the richest which nourishes the greatest number of noble and happy human beings; that man is richest who, having perfected the functions of his own life to the utmost, has also the widest helpful influence, both personal, and by means of his possessions, over the lives of others" (17.105). This idea that wealth is primarily a matter of well-developed people is a hallmark of the "capabilities approach." The judgment that the good economy is "person-centered," not "thing-centered," is echoed by a great many religious critics of capitalism from Mohandas Gandhi to Martin Luther King Jr.[31]

For Ruskin, judging wealth, value, and the quality of life begins with a cultural reading of human activity. I noted earlier in this chapter that *Unto This Last* begins in the realm of social practices. "The Roots of Honour" harkens back to Ruskin's architectural studies and his politics because once again he praises those forms of labor that are good for workers because internal goods and opportunities for individual excellence and social recognition are shared within. But clearly an ethics of consumption must move beyond the confines of social practices and direct associations as Ruskin acknowledges, too. Thus, while he still celebrates certain practices like wrought iron work, sketching, and natural history, his ethics of consumption is more open to the varieties of activities and associations that people choose. Of course, the more we open up his ethics of consumption to the diversity of human endeavor and to the widely varying uses and enjoyments, competing desires, and contrasting lives of individual consumers, the question becomes: can we maintain Ruskin's character-based conviction that people should uphold shared judgments of better and worse enjoyments, uses, and desires and that consumers can articulate and defend their reasons by appealing to the ordering of ends and the cultivation of character in good lives?

Common Spaces of Moral Vision

I am arguing for a middle space of ethical evaluation and cultural critique in economic life that refuses both the metaphysics of the good and the hierarchy of classes found in Ruskin's corpus and the merely mechanical calculations of income, utility, and exchange-value relied on in classical political economy. We can learn from Ruskin's account of value so long as we heed the constructive developments in his vocabulary of the virtues and his turn toward cultural critique. No doubt when he claims that things avail toward or away from life, he seems to appeal to a natural ordering of things' powers, which does appear, at best, to be "perversely unempirical" and, at worst, subject to political abuse. But I read the appeal to things' "availing toward life" not against the backdrop of an imagined natural order, but in the context of Ruskin's analysis of the cultural landscape of Victorian Britain. Reading fences is only the start of things, and Ruskin is just one critic inviting others to a public practice of moral imagination.

The outstanding question is whether it is still possible to arrive at intelligible and shared judgments of things' value once a great many people undertake this endeavor. If we focus on the virtues and activities that do or do not promote personal and communal well-being, then we can begin to see past the diverse uses and enjoyments that people make of things to a narrower set of ends of good human lives. That is why, I take it, that Sen also stresses capabilities and valued activities in working out his approach to the standard of living. People consume with heterogeneous uses, pleasures, and tastes in mind, which is why the market's "working consensus" is so attractive. Nevertheless it is not that hard to imagine a usual set of human desires and ends and, still more clearly, the typical valued activities and capabilities that go with them. Ruskin trods the same path, though he does so with greater ethical urgency and evocative argumentation. People build fences for privacy to be free to choose the activities that they like best, and yet they will include efforts at nourishment and health, imagination and delight, companionship and play, expression and independence, solitude and rest. Other activities take people outside of their homes, and all of them transpire in a cultural landscape that shapes consumers' choices and judgments. Ruskin's questions about the ends that we and others pursue, about the sources and effects of our desires, about the vital powers we and others cultivate (or not), and about the properties of things and their limited uses, always revolve around his concern with the cultural activities that individuals choose for themselves and others. This practical and cultural focus opens up these concerns to critical reflection and engaged debate. It takes imaginative effort to set standards in the use of resources, the employment of people, and the capacities of consumers, but through the banding together of reflective consumers and the hard work of persuasive argumentation, it is possible to make some standards customary in a way that parallels the "good usage" of a language. We can work toward a "grammar" of good consumption that shows in the best practices.

"The Work of Iron" constructs an exemplary reading of iron designed to inspire Ruskin's audience to imagine for themselves the full significance of the many goods in their lives. The complexity he achieves in his symbolic rendering of iron is stunning, and the intricate portrait of good character he elaborates on this basis is central to his ethics of consumption. I have focused on the issue of character in this chapter, reserving the trickier question of moral vision until the next chapter, but here, too, we must appreciate the interplay between moral vision and cultural endeavor.

Ruskin makes religious appeals at the start and at the end of this lecture in support of his own vision of the good life. Echoing the appeal to the creator's "breath of life," he concludes by hurling the Psalms and Proverbs at his listeners. "The Bible hardly ever talks about neglect of the poor. It always talks of oppression of the poor—a very different matter." "You know it is rather singular language, this!—rather strong language, we might, perhaps, call it—hearing it for the first time." As Ruskin's co-religionists in the audience would know, the Church of England stipulated that these books be read through once each month. Their moral content should not be unfamiliar to his listeners. They should have heard it, even if they chose not to heed it. Indeed, this failure to "hear" the shared liturgy of the Church of England suggests that his contemporaries' failure to imagine how their consumption oppresses the poor is, in fact, a willful misreading of the value of things that takes market price—because it is convenient—as the last word on value. If market price signifies a cacophony of competing interests and desires, abstracted from the wider ethical implications of economic choices, then equating it with true value licenses the rich to set their eyes, not simply "*away* from [but] *against* the poor," which, Ruskin declares, is "the main point I want to fix your attention upon" (16.398–399).

Ruskin's religious appeals to iron's "breath of life" and the "law of nature" that one reaps as one sows certainly echo his metaphysics of the good. At times the distance between his ethics of consumption and the "Divine Corporation ethics" of his early aesthetics is all too slim. But what is profoundly new is his naming individual consumers the authority in economic life and his calling them to envision and pursue good lives for themselves and others. By reading the cultural landscape of Victorian Britain, just as Ruskin reads its fences, consumers are to select those activities and associations that make for the best uses of things and the fullest development of people. He appeals to the common liturgy of the Church of England as part of that cultural landscape; in another place and time, new arguments will be necessary. Likewise, the vision of the good life that Ruskin constructs in "The Work of Iron" is only one account, and perhaps no one in his audience agreed with it entirely, indeed if any one of them had ever stopped to consider what makes for good human lives.

That is why Ruskin gives the lecture. He aims to invite his listeners to an engaged ethics of consumption that only works by moving back and forth between a searching effort to envision good lives and a participatory commitment to supporting and joining in the activities integral to the vision one imagines. The great value of his vocabulary of the virtues, as it gets applied in his ethics of consumption, is that it directs all of us consumers to scrutinize the cultural landscape of the activities supported by our economic choices. What hierarchies of values, what societal conditions and relations, what opportunities for development, and how much access to them are bought by our purchasing decisions?

Ruskin does not always allow sufficient space for the inevitable disagreements among reflective of consumers, but just as his focal concerns with "effectual value" help recast his appeals to "intrinsic value," so too in naming the individual consumer the primary authority in economic life, he begins to point the way beyond the limits of his vision of good consumption and the metaphysical appeals to organic form and social unity in his politics. I have discussed "The Work of Iron" at length because it so clearly illustrates Ruskin's virtues-centered approach to consumption and his public attempts to instruct others in the critical uses of this vocabulary. "The Work of Iron" is finally an educative endeavor, and its success rests on inspiring others to follow Ruskin's lead, assessing where his vision is persuasive and where it falters. If the response is a self-satisfied indifference or a slavish devotion to Ruskin's vision, then the virtues-centered argument of the lecture fails. Its goal is the development of people's vital powers, including the capacity for undertaking an expansive inquiry into the makings of an abundant quality of life and the fostering of human virtues and capabilities through commitments to activities that reach beyond oneself to others, with whom one must engage openly and critically in working toward shared judgments of the value of economic goods.

SEVEN

Is Good Consumption Possible?

The focus of the previous chapter is Ruskin's argument that consumers can strive to discern the full value of the many things they use and enjoy. In his public lectures and essays, Ruskin endeavors to teach his audiences to practice good consumption by learning to read the "powers" of natural resources and the "virtues" of workers and consumers. Once we step back to imagine the setting of a lecture like "The Work of Iron," questions arise, however. Who was Ruskin's audience? How representative were they? Were these people already inclined to accept his reading of iron's value and the priority he assigns to the beauty of nature and art over the productivity of the industrial machine? While his integrated portrait of the virtues necessary to human flourishing might have been compelling on a first hearing in a lecture hall, how well did it translate into everyday economic decisions? The lecture hall comes with its own conventions and style of consumption. The audience chooses to attend whether to be edified, entertained, or simply to be seen. The culture and the confines of the lecture hall are important reminders that an ethics of consumption is not merely a matter of one's own moral imagination. That vision must be put into practice across an actual economy.

As argued throughout this book, Ruskin develops his virtues-centered approach to social criticism in his architectural studies. The connection between human virtues and social practices that he first works out in "The Nature of Gothic" is pivotal to his evolving discussions of nature, religion, politics, and economics. In his portraits of Gothic craftwork, Ruskin imagines these craftsmen producing highly personal and distinctive work, but only because they have committed to the shared goods and standards internal to their practices. The benefits for the participants are many: the cultivation of their virtues, excellences, and capabilities; the justly given aid and praise from other members of the practice; the enjoyment of goods in common with these other people; and the sense of fellowship and purpose that arises from their willing cooperation and sacrifice in a cooperative endeavor to which the participants freely assent. The promise of Ruskin's ethics of consumption is that these same commitments to mutual self-development, the common good, distributive justice, and communal flourishing might be extended across a whole economy. But is it really plausible to think that all work could be done in social practices, let alone to imagine that there could be a single practice of good consumption?

In the closing pages of *Unto This Last,* Ruskin tells his readers that they must consider in all their consumption, "first, what condition of existence you cause in the producers of what you buy; secondly, whether the sum you have paid is just to the producer, and in due proportion, lodged in his hands; thirdly, to how much clear use, for food, knowledge, or joy, this that you have bought can be put; and fourthly, to whom and in what way it can be most speedily and serviceably distributed" (17.113). This call for an almost omniscient practice of good consumption conjures an image of a Gothic "master" craftsman guiding and cultivating the efforts of his charges and distributing praise and aid according to their due. Practically speaking, however, can consumers actually attain the critical perspective needed to judge the far-reaching effects of their choices across the distances of the division of labor and a market economy? Morally speaking, should consumers be asked to regulate their tastes, preferences, and desires in promoting distributive justice and the welfare of other people, or is this not too grave an infringement on democratic individuality?

Before considering these two questions—the core challenges of Karl Marx and J. S. Mill to Ruskin's ethics of consumption—let me acknowledge a third objection: the creed that an ever-increasing rate of consumption is the engine of growth on which today's economy depends more and more. This objection, by itself, does not offer moral reasons to reject Ruskin's argument. It may be inconvenient and downright painful to wean ourselves from the economic growth that fuels everything from job creation to pension plans, from international development to welfare programs, but refusing to think critically about how best to conduct and arrange our economic lives, simply on the grounds of inconvenience or immediate pain, is insufficient. Repeating the mantra of growth is to refuse the hard work of an ethics of consumption.

Marx raises the problem of the impracticality of an ethics of consumption when he names consumption the "finish," not the "end," of production. For Marx, consumption is a mere finish because, although consumers have specific uses and ends in view when they buy commodities, these ethical considerations are irrelevant to the operations and ends of capitalism. As he puts it, "The product only obtains its 'last *finish*' in consumption." Consumption matters because it closes the circle of industrial productivity, earning the returns on capital that drive the whole economy. It is impractical, therefore, to expect people to grasp the full implications of other people's work or their own consumption because no one can fathom industrial capitalism's operations.

For Marx, consumption is a mere "finish" in another sense, too. Different cultures apply their own finish to consumption in the distinctive manners and styles they exhibit. Every society requires status symbols and social hierarchies to maintain the relations of its economic base. In Marx's words, "Production . . . [also] gives consumption its specificity, its character, its finish." The relations of production in a historical period shape the manner in which people consume.[1] Here Marx's analysis suggests that Ruskin may be less a critic of capitalism than an apologist for an economic system that serves his interests quite well and would serve them even better if he could persuade more consumers to demand the excellent craftwork that he desires. Viewed from this perspective, Ruskin is that rare consumer whose public authority as an art critic was so great that he helped produce the symbols, values, and hierarchies necessary to the operations of industrial capitalism.[2] Marx's advice to Ruskin's readers would be caveat emptor: buyer beware this ethics of consumption dressed up in the language of virtues, moral duty, and self-sacrifice. The only vision of "good" consumption attainable under the conditions of nineteenth-century industrial capitalism is an ideological vision that reifies existing class divisions and gender roles.[3]

Even setting aside Marx's critique of ideology, we might think that Ruskin's admirable commitments to expanded human development, a higher quality of life, and the wider distribution of both might be met only through activism in the realms of politics and production, not in the diffuse arena of consumer choice. Consumers lack the vision and power to change the economy. Consumers cannot control their desires. These beliefs mirror Marx's conviction that people are, or at least they could become, creators in the sphere of production, but they are creatures in the realm of consumption. The "productivist bias" in Marx's social thought—that people are agents as "makers," but not as readers of goods—still influences scholarship in consumption studies and economic ethics, and it should be shaken off. Consumers are not passive creatures buying into whatever the culture creators have in stock for them.

In my judgment it is Mill's objection about democratic individuality that poses the deeper challenge to Ruskin's ethics of consumption. Perhaps the normative work that Ruskin calls for does not belong in the realm of consumption, which is an arena rightly answering to nothing other than individual tastes. In drawing this connection between consumer liberty and individuality, I am not supposing that, for Mill, having countless choices among consumer goods is essential to his goal of a greater cultivation and expression of individuality. I have in mind instead his fuller defense of democratic individuality in *On Liberty* (1859), published one year prior to *Unto This Last.* It is striking to note that when Mill turns to "Applications" of his liberty principle, most of his examples of undue encroachment on individuality focus on legislation in the areas of religion and consumption.

On Liberty argues for distinguishing between that area of a person's life that affects the interests of other people and another area that affects one's own interests alone. How, Mill asks his fellow Britons, would they react if, living in a Muslim country, they were prevented by law from eating pork? Anticipating his audience's strong opposition to the justice of such a law, he reminds his readers that consuming this "unclean beast" is so offensive to Muslims that they would have compelling reasons to think it necessary to prevent all members of their society from engaging in such an abominable practice. Nor is this a case of denying the religious liberty of a minority. While Christianity does not prohibit the eating of pork, neither does this or any other religion require it. Thus, Mill concludes, "The only tenable ground of condemnation [of this law] would be that with the personal tastes and self-regarding concerns of individuals the public has no business to interfere."[4] He draws a similar conclusion in rejecting attempts to legislate bans on entertainment and alcohol, along with efforts to impose fixed wage rates for labor done by members of the same trade.[5]

In each of these instances, Mill rejects legal strictures on consumers, even as he allows for "public control" over businesses where the health and safety of workers or the general public are subject to injury. When individuals consume intoxicants that harm no one but themselves, however, this choice falls within the sphere of liberty, and few restrictions and no prohibition may be imposed on the purveyors or the consumers of these goods. Thus, Mill opposed laws advocated by the leaders of the Temperance Movement.[6] He also condemned the Chinese government's prohibition of the import of opium in the midst of the second "Opium War" (1856–60), during which Britain and France sought to impose treaties reopening Chinese ports and legalizing the use of this drug there.[7] Although these two examples are very different—in light of the relative degree of harm posed by alcohol and opium and in light of Britain's readiness to use its imperial might to protect its commercial and political interests in China—for Mill the same principle holds in both cases. When individuals harm only themselves, no interference with personal tastes is permissible.

Mill's principle and his examples raise two interrelated challenges for Ruskin's virtues-centered ethics of consumption. First, Mill's examples of improper restrictions on consumers' choice involve attempts to mold moral character. The very name of the Temperance Movement declares a goal of promoting virtue and preventing vice. For Mill, there is no legal justification for efforts to regulate individuals' buying decisions so as to make them more virtuous, whether the virtue is temperance (in the drinking of alcohol), piety (in the eating of pork), or prudence (in the taking of drugs). Second, Mill judges this intrusion on people's tastes and character to be paternalistic, meaning the imposition on others of what one deems to be good for them. But where harm is strictly individual, and even where personal tastes begin to harm others, as in the case of a father's drinking up his family's income, Mill refuses societal and legal measures that regulate individuals' desires.

Although Ruskin's culinary preferences would have led him to agree with Mill, we can see why the example of a religious prohibition on pork issues a direct challenge to Ruskin's virtues-centered ethics of consumption. For Muslims, refusing to eat pork is a first step toward making culinary practices pious. It is a first step in cultivating the virtue of piety, and it allows one to participate in the activity of eating well. A refusal to eat pork makes sense, therefore, given the vision of the good life that strict Muslims are to adopt in submitting to the authority of their tradition. The prohibition, the virtue, the practice, the vision, and the tradition are intrinsic to making oneself a good Muslim. The same concern with making good people runs throughout Ruskin's corpus. Indeed, his moralistic mode of argumentation seeks not only to persuade other people of his views, but also to transform their very character, tastes, and desires so that they can grasp the wisdom of those views.

For my purposes the issue of the legitimacy of a legal prohibition against pork is beside the point. This illustration is a useful reminder that Ruskin also argues that virtues, practices, and visions of good lives interrelate in a similarly self-defining way. The problem with this style of argumentation is that it seems to place the lecturer and the audience on an unequal footing, and Ruskin's ethics of consumption appears to do the same. Consumers are to adopt the virtues and practices authorized by the vision of the good life and the good society commended by the "wise" who already have the requisite virtues and benefit from the "best" practices. To put the issue bluntly, is Ruskin inviting his audience to embrace a practice of good consumption of which he himself is the "master"? Is there finally only one legitimate vision of the good for consumers to adopt, as is implied by Ruskin's appeals to the laws of nature, the dictates of God's Creation, and the binding practices of a vital culture and community? Throughout this study and in the chapter on Ruskin's politics in particular, I have demonstrated the linkages between his drive for a singular conception of the good and his affirmation of social hierarchies, gender roles, and paternal governance. Indeed, considering the anti-democratic tendencies of this politics, perhaps we should also resist his moralistic insistence that an ethics of consumption begins from an integrated vision of the virtues and the practices that together enable good lives.

An important contrast can be drawn here to Mill's principled moral philosophy. Ruskin appeals to virtues, whereas Mill builds from principles. These contrasting styles offer two very different portraits of the moral considerations attaching to consumption. Mill's principle of individuality draws boundaries around people's indifferent tastes—lines of non-interference that protect these preferences from outside scrutiny and legal sanction. The governing image is one of division and independence. It reflects a democratic suspicion of any social conformity that cuts to the core of a person's desires. It champions a vibrant culture and the free exchange of ideas. So vital are these principled lines of non-interference around personal tastes that Mill is prepared to use force, if necessary, to preserve the bounded spaces of individual choice opened up by free trade and the capitalist marketplace, even in the disturbing case of opium sales in China.

Ruskin's virtues-centered approach, by contrast, refuses these insurmountable boundaries around individual desire and choice. His concern is to draw connections. A person's desires reflect the broader culture and the activities in which he or she participates. Choices of consumer goods are votes for certain societal arrangements and economic conditions. Always in Ruskin's criticism there is this drive to trace out an integrated vision of the "whole" economy that people choose for themselves *and* impose on others. Grounding an ethics in principles alone forecloses, he would argue, the imaginative reach needed to discern how one's tastes affect other people, not just in the direct injuries caused by paying too little money for some purchase, but much more so in the sapping of the energies, capacities, and excellences that might have furthered other people's well-being, where the accent falls on their very *being* itself.

I have raised the issues of the practicality and the desirability of Ruskin's ethics of consumption. We can sort out the potential paternalism and anti-democratic implications of that ethics by examining how he puts his scenes of economic life into operation in an actual economy. I am thinking of his theory of money, and in returning to it (see chapter 4), I shift from his critique of the idolatry of capitalism to his account of the proper workings of a money economy. I ask whether, for Ruskin, a market economy creates the insuperable barriers to a vision of good consumption that Marx claims. I also consider whether Ruskin's virtues-centered approach can sustain the ethical judgments that he demands of individual consumers, while still allowing for the spaces of democratic individuality that Mill rightly defends.

Wealth, Wisdom, and Paternalism

In the last chapter I observed that *Unto This Last* begins in the realm of production. Only in "The Veins of Wealth" does Ruskin begin tracing out a practice of good consumption that spans the distances opened up by the "always imperfect and doubtful" power of money in market exchanges (17.46). In this second essay there is a movement beyond the cooperative efforts of social practices. Ruskin offers examples of a rich man needing others to cultivate his land and then of two sailors stranded on a desert island before he takes up the practical difficulties of calculating and paying a "just price" in all transactions in his third essay, "Qui Judicatis Terram."

As Ruskin proceeds to translate his scenes of economic life into an alternative "theory" of political economy, he holds to his equation of value and virtues. The "true science of Political Economy," he declares, recognizes the necessity of developing "manly character to deal with material value" because "while the manly character and material value only form wealth by their conjunction, they have nevertheless a mutually destructive operation on each other." In the ideal economy described by the classical theory, he continues, we have "a community regulated only by laws of demand and supply, but protected from open violence." In such a society, "the persons who become rich are, generally speaking, industrious, resolute, proud, covetous, prompt, methodical, sensible, unimaginative, insensitive, and ignorant. The persons who remain poor are the entirely foolish, the entirely wise, the idle, the reckless, the humble, the thoughtful, the dull, the imaginative, the sensitive, the well-informed, the improvident, the irregularly and impulsively wicked, the clumsy knave, the open thief, and the entirely merciful, just, and godly person" (17.89–90). Clearly Ruskin places the *thoroughly* wicked person, the *clever* knave, and the *stealthy* thief on the side of the wealthy, but he finds virtues and vices on both sides of the dividing line between rich and poor.

One wonders how these moralistic generalizations were received by his audience. No doubt passages like this one contributed to the uproar against *Unto This Last* and *Munera Pulveris* that led to their early termination in the *Cornhill* and *Fraser's* magazines. They also undermined Ruskin's claims to be articulating a "theory" of political economy. A theorist like Mill begins from assumptions about individuals as rational utility maximizers who calculate their economic opportunities within a competitive framework of prices for capital, rent, and wages. Generalizations made on that basis aim for predictive power about empirical, not moral, behavior. As detailed in the last chapter, Ruskin builds his analysis from various scenes of economic life, always dwelling on the character of the people found there. His questions are less about the "rationality" of people's actions than the goodness or badness of them. But he also constructs something of a theory of economic life, and his scheme of the virtues supplies the critical basis for his "calculations" of the irrational effects of individuals' buying decisions on the public welfare.

We can approach Ruskin's argument that his contemporaries irrationally privilege value over virtue, capital accumulation over human development, by beginning from one of his scenes in *Munera Pulveris.* In an imagined community of farmers living on the banks of a river, only one saves stores of food and builds levees around his land in the good times. When the river floods, he becomes the "master" over all the others when they come to him for aid after the disaster. Ruskin presents this scene as an imagined portrait of the historical origins of money economies. Instead of bartering goods for goods, this accidental master trades goods for his neighbors' promises that they will return an equivalent amount of goods in the future. Here we see the two functions that Ruskin reads in the use of money—the acknowledging of debt to others and the commanding of others' labor. The foolish farmers are indebted to the prudent farmer, and he now has the authority to command their labor by cashing in on their promises of a return of goods and the labor required to produce them. The critical question for Ruskin is, how will he exercise this newfound power of command? (17.265–66).

While recovering the goods and labor lent to his neighbors, the new "master" can guide his neighbors to become more prudent, devoting some of their efforts to protecting their farms and storing food while also returning to him what they owe. In this case the master renders the others his equal "in worldly matters." Alternatively, he can claim their land as repayment for the debt, make them tenants, and require them to work to improve his farm and house. "In one part of the district, we should have unhealthy land, miserable dwellings, and half-starved poor; in another, a well-ordered estate, well-fed servants, and refined conditions of highly educated and luxurious life." After observing that "all the relations of society are but the expansion of these two typical sequences of conduct and result," Ruskin allows that the latter circumstance may be preferable in some ways (17.267, 268). "Servants, and artists, and splendour of habitation and retinue, have all their use, propriety, and office. But," he continues, "I am determined that the reader shall understand clearly what they cost; and see that the condition of having them is the subjection to us of a certain number of imprudent and unfortunate persons (or, it may be, more fortunate than their masters), over whose destinies we exercise a boundless control. 'Riches' mean eternally and essentially this. . . . Every operative you employ is your true servant: distant or near, subject to your immediate orders or widely communicated caprice" (17.268).

This imaginary scenario actually outlines three options facing rich consumers. Making others one's equal "in worldly matters" is preferable to keeping others in a state of deprivation to take advantage of them. But consumers might also choose to purchase better lives not only for themselves, but possibly even more so for the people they hire, by funding projects employing artists, architects, and other craftspeople to develop their own excellences in ways that the rich are too busy, insensitive, or unimaginative to pursue for themselves.

This example is instructive for several reasons. It introduces Ruskin's two functions of money—acknowledging debt and commanding labor. It also demonstrates the continuing hold of his hierarchical language of master and servant. What appears here more subtly, too, is Ruskin's broad understanding of the virtues, both moral virtues and the many other excellences of a fully developed character. In the case where the master makes his neighbors his equal, they gain in prudence, thrift, and diligence. In the case where the master employs other people as artisans and musicians, he displays a more exalted wisdom in cultivating a wider range of excellences in the people touched by his buying decisions. In the latter case, the moral virtues go to the master, while the aesthetic, practical, intellectual, emotional, and bodily excellences go to everyone else. There is a division of labor and of virtue here that actually reverses the usual doubly damning conjunction of hard work and low status.[8] The "wise" master does the hard work, ruling over others for their benefit and sacrificing those desires that require the exploitation of his neighbors. Although the workers in his employ are clearly subordinate to him, they do not suffer the added injury of brutal toil.

This division of virtue among different social classes is both antidemocratic (though in a somewhat unexpected way) and contrary to Ruskin's broader argument. I will come back to this second point later in the chapter. More important for now, we can see what Ruskin means by "manly character." It consists in the wisdom required to use the power of money well. And this takes self-possession to exercise this power not in meeting one's own immediate desires or in seeking further advantage, but in promoting other people's self-development and, thus, greater individual flourishing and societal abundance for everyone, oneself included.

To use that power properly, instead of worshipping it idolatrously, one must use the power of money by spending it. Indeed, Ruskin was no ascetic, and his call for consumer spending should lead us to think differently about other religious, particularly Christian, figures who also imagine an earthly abundance of well-made goods, well-made people, and a continuous exchange of joy, admiration, and gratitude as the true end of economic life.[9] Ruskin himself derides the hoarding of money, that odd preference for being "curators, not possessors, of wealth." Asking why people salt their money away instead of spending it, he answers, most "men, it appears, dislike the sight of their fortunes going out into service again," praying rather "let a merciful death save me from being a witness of [other people's] satisfaction; and . . . let no good come of any of this money of mine before my eyes." For those with "just tastes and worthy passions," Ruskin encourages liberal spending, not outright generosity. If a person lacks taste, or if the amassed fortune exceeds his or her ability to consume well, then it should be put into circulation in some other way, such as through philanthropic ventures. In either case the "true ambition as an economist should be, to die, not as rich, but as poor, as possible" (17.168,

276). Always the best use of money is to keep it moving along. If spent wisely, money will fund the increase of material goods and, more importantly, other people's self-development, thereby furthering the overall wealth of those goods because there are such good people to make, use, and enjoy them.

This vision of abundant consumption rejects hoarded accumulations of money in the form of riches. It does not, however, reject inequality. Indeed, Ruskin's examples and language justify social inequalities on moral grounds. Here as elsewhere in his writings, he assumes that inequalities are inevitable, including differences in economic, political, and social standing and disparities among individuals' talents and virtues. The rich are often not the most talented, in fact, which is why they find themselves in jobs that require such virtues as diligence and thrift rather than imagination and sensitivity. But for Ruskin the rich must be the wisest because the overall quality of life enjoyed in a society depends on whether the wealthy exercise the "boundless control" of their money wisely or capriciously. As Ruskin portrays the workings of "riches" in the long passage above, the only options appear to be the wisdom of "immediate orders" or the injuries of a "widely communicated caprice." It is as if good consumption could be exerted only through the direct relations of an economy of masters and servants. As presented here, the distant relations mediated by the money economy of industrial capitalism make wise expenditure impossible because those distances excuse the wealthy from assuming responsibility for the lives of workers, as if these people were servants living under their own roof.

Ruskin's awareness of the power of the rich is acute and apt, but replacing the moral distances of a money economy with the "immediate orders" of a "wise" master to a "loving" servant only valorizes paternalism and deference in class relations. Mill's *Principles of Political Economy* and his other writings pose a fundamental challenge here. Although Mill subordinates the science of political economy to the art of policy, he embraces the classical theory partly for normative reasons. As discussed in the last chapter, he adopts its production-driven framework for promising greater material prosperity in overcoming scarcities. He also embraces the theory as proof of the relatively progressive influence of the industrial class in nineteenth-century Britain as contrasted with the conservative tendencies of the largely aristocratic landowners. On this contest between "capital" and "rent" hang, in the words of Mill's famous chapter, the "Probable Futurity of the Labouring Classes."

For Mill, rent is a conservative force because, unlike the drive to increase capital that is essential to industrial production and progress, landlords have economic incentives not to build more housing or improve their properties because rents are higher and thus profits are greater where the housing stock is kept artificially low and relatively unimproved. Ruskin agrees with this part of Mill's analysis and praises Mill's argument that rents are morally legitimate to the extent that landlords improve their properties "consistent with the public good." But he also remarks on a single sentence slipped into Mill's larger argument, an apparent defense of the right of slumlords to charge whatever the market may bear. In Mill's words, again as quoted by Ruskin, the "rents or profits which [a landlord] can obtain from [land] are his, and only his," no matter what condition the property may be in (17.443). What can explain this apparent contradiction between Mill's sense that rents are legitimate to the extent that landlords improve their properties and his claim that rents—obtained in whatever amounts—are a landlord's lawful due?

The key word is "lawful."[10] The legal framework that protects private property rights and market competition is one of the institutional supports required, in Mill's judgment, for increased societal prosperity and democratic individuality. A competitive market sends signals, sometimes in the form of exorbitant rents, that opportunities exist for making profits. Over the long run, in theory at least, new landlords will enter the market, build additional housing, and so drive down rents and increase the quantity and quality of available shelter. All of this transpires, moreover, without infringing on the property rights of landlords or requiring tenants to beg for fairer rents and better living conditions.

It is interesting to compare Ruskin's response to unjust rents and poor housing. In *Time and Tide* (1867) where he criticizes Mill on rent, Ruskin proposes a salaried aristocracy. Instead of allowing the landed aristocracy to live off rents from their properties, they should be made public servants paid and entrusted to preserve Britain's natural and historical treasures. The idea here, as in the first essay of *Unto This Last* (see chapter 6), is that professionals enjoy their secure annual salaries because the public recognizes that the professions contribute to the public good. If the rent market exerts pressures against the maintenance and improvement of Britain's land and other common treasures, then a government response is needed to stave off both problems. Putting the aristocracy to work by institutionalizing their presumed loyalties to "place"—to the land, its beauty and history—removes one cause of expropriative rents while creating something like a national trust for parks, monuments, and other public treasures (17.439). In Ruskin's personal affairs he took a different course of action, lending his capital to two model tenement projects spearheaded by the pioneering reformer Octavia Hill (1838–1912). This initiative paid Ruskin rents pegged below market rates and allowed residents the chance to govern themselves and to buy out the leases on their residences (17.437).[11]

This brief foray into the economics and politics of rent, as approached by Ruskin and Mill, underscores their theoretical differences. Ruskin's argument that "manly character" is essential to the handling of "material wealth" structures his policy recommendation of institutionalizing a public-minded aristocracy along with his personal intervention in an exploitative market for rent. Mill, by contrast, affirms not only his theoretical commitments to giving an empirical description of the legal and commercial framework of capitalist economies, but also his ethical commitments to the liberal institutions that he deems best suited to the clearing away of patronage relationships and to the expansion of democratic individuality.

Mill's conviction that capital, not rent, promises improved lives for the poor and working classes helps structure his theoretical argument in the *Principles of Political Economy.* Again the descriptive and the normative interrelate in Mill's *Principles,* as can be seen in two of his core tenets, the complementary theories of the "wages fund" and the "natural rate of wages" (or, as it is also known, the "iron law of wages"). The theory of the "wages fund" pins the improvement of the lot of laborers on a steady growth of capital.[12] If overall wage increases outpace capital accumulation in an economy, then industrial growth will be stifled to the detriment of those workers who would otherwise escape from the grasp of the landowners' patronage and power. The "natural rate of wages" justifies low wages for another reason. If wages rise too quickly, then workers will dissipate their gains through having larger families and more mouths to feed. With such dreary protections as capital growth, on the one hand, and wage restriction, on the other, it is little wonder that Thomas Carlyle dubbed political economy the "Dismal Science."

While unfair to Mill's intent, a strong impression is left by his *Principles* that laborers lack agency, kicked about as they are in the contest between industrialists and landowners. Nevertheless, given the overt paternalism of Carlyle, Ruskin, and other Tory radicals, Mill's argument for a "reservoir" or "pool" of capital as the best guarantor of the increasing independence of laborers is a fundamental challenge to their tradition. For Mill, industrial capitalism, in tandem with the expansion of democracy, education, and press freedoms, signals the death knell of the "theory of dependence" championed by these defenders of a dying social order.[13] Ruskin's language of mastership and his examples of direct relations between protector and protected reflect the theory of dependence that Mill criticizes so powerfully in his *Principles, On Liberty,* and *The Subjection of Women* (1869).

In Ruskin and Mill we have two visions of what is best for those excluded and injured by the current economic, political, and social conditions of Victorian Britain. Given the historical developments since their day, Mill is right to claim that a mixture of liberal institutions has aided in the dismantling of paternal relations and the opening up of opportunities for women, workers, and excluded minority groups. He is too blithe, however, in predicting inevitable improvements through capital accumulation alone. A great many public initiatives, including the rent controls and national trusts advocated by Ruskin, have been used to redistribute the flow of wealth and to secure goods shared in common—public initiatives that inevitably involve the curtailment of some liberties and even the reform of individuals' desires toward common ends, social relations, and economic conditions that are "good for" the people themselves.

What is jarring in some of Ruskin's arguments is his professed support for aristocratic birth and station as legitimate means of institutionalizing "common" commitments to a stock of national symbols in Britain's history, traditions, community, and culture. The same conviction that one's place in the social order is the ideal training ground for one's talents carries over into his readiness to stake the quality of life in any society on the combination of wealth, wisdom, and paternalism.[14] Ruskin's insistence on social roles and duties and a perfect harmony of associative relations as the essential checks on individual desire—and the teachers of good character and moral vision—reminds us of the fundamental dichotomy in his cathedral model of politics. The "anarchy and competition" of liberal institutions can be corrected only by the paternal "government and cooperation" of a society structured throughout by intermediate associations and social practices (7.207). This dichotomy shadows his theory of money, too, as when he describes the ideal workings of riches as the "melodious inequalities of concurrent power." As a believer in natural inequality, Ruskin doubted that the earth would be worth the meek's inheriting if they were not first protected and directed by the wise in cultivating its promise. Without wise spending toward a harmony of interests, there can only be the "rugged system of subjection and success" (17.48).

Ruskin's imagery of the good economy disdains the deep waters of

Mill's "reservoirs" of capital accumulation in favor of cascading streams of wealth flowing to everyone as abundant consumption. In Ruskin's judgment the universal influence of these streams requires the most capable to manage them for the common good instead of siphoning off their healthful flows into "pools" and "eddies" of "dead water" called "illth" (17.89).[15] There is realism in this call for the rich to assume the responsibilities of their power. There are further attractions in this image of a wider distribution of wealth and of broader commitments to improving the societal conditions and developing the personal capacities required for better lives. Certainly Ruskin is right to argue for public initiatives to redistribute a great many resources, to preserve shared goods, to guarantee access to the means and opportunities required for societal participation, and even to educate people into making the most of themselves. He is also correct to illustrate the limits and, indeed, the incoherence of classically liberal models of institutions joined by nothing more than the free play of individual interests, with no attention to the individual virtues, the social trust, the economic networks, the cultural norms, and the public symbols that sustain their operations. Nevertheless, given his embrace of "paternal" wisdom in the realm of politics and here in the spending of money, can his moralistic criticism help us articulate an ethics of consumption?

Before proceeding to argue that Ruskin's complete theory of money corrects against the paternalism written into his imagery of "The Veins of Wealth," let me reiterate that even in his "descriptive" theorizing, Mill's empirical account reflects his own normative aims. Blurring the lines between moralism and theory, between the normative and the descriptive, moral principles and virtues, is critical to understanding the lasting value of Ruskin's approach. In his critique of industrial capitalism, he begins as a moralist, charging individuals to observe the duties attaching to their consumption. In his construction of a broader "theory," as we shall see, he systematizes his scenes of economic life by tracing out how the flows of money in a society may be directed toward wealth or "illth." Specifically, he highlights the exploitation enabled by an economic system that legitimizes capital and autonomy at the expense of capabilities and interdependence. Mill, by contrast, starts as a theorist, describing how the historical retooling of an industrializing economy, aided by the power of capital over the power of rent, is a force of progress. Although his focus is on empirical behavior within a competitive price structure, elements of his theoretical account reflect his sense of the democratic possibilities opened up by the unraveling of older patronage relations through the growth of industrial capitalism. Thus the moralist and the theorist each borrow the other's tools, with Ruskin developing a theory of political economy to condemn economic exploitation and with Mill advocating economic growth to promote an ethics of democratic individuality.

Is there an impasse in the approaches and concerns of these two thinkers? Must we side with Mill for his recognition of the new possibilities for women, workers, and other relatively powerless groups signaled by the breakup of a social order harkening back to feudal rankings and noblesse oblige? Can Ruskin's virtues-centered conception of the quality of life and the duties of consumers be disentangled from the paternalism of the "theory of dependence"? This final question is crucial because an ethics of consumption that relies on a vocabulary of the virtues and the idea of social practices is committed to appeals to visions of good lives, the common good, and shared goods. Yet are such visions practical given the ever-widening distances of global capitalism? Are such visions too grave an infringement on democratic individuality and the spaces of personal liberty and social disagreement carved out by liberal institutions like the capitalist market?

Putting Practice into Theory: The Just Price

One of the clearest illustrations of Ruskin's moralism is his argument that money is not the neutral medium of exchange theorized by classical political economists. Money has two functions for Ruskin—commanding labor and acknowledging debt. These two functions can only be construed in moral terms. By this I mean that commanding labor and acknowledging debt are moral actions, even if market exchange is remarkably good at masking the ethical implications of spending money. Ruskin's purpose in his theory of money is twofold—to provoke ethical reflection about the working conditions, power structures, societal choices, and networks of interdependence that both structure and are sustained by market transactions and to describe the social, cultural, and psychological factors always in the background of a money economy.

In *Unto This Last* Ruskin names the function of commanding labor the "chief value and virtue of money." This power of command is implicit in the relative terms "rich" and "poor," a necessary relationship that is lost, he claims, on ordinary political (or what he calls "mercantile") economists. "Men nearly always speak and write as if riches were absolute. . . . Whereas riches are a power like that of electricity, acting only through inequalities or negations of itself. The force of the guinea in your pocket depends wholly on the default of a guinea in your neighbour's pocket. If he did not want it, it would be of no use to you; . . . and the art of making yourself rich, in the ordinary mercantile economist's sense, is therefore equally and necessarily the art of keeping your neighbour poor" (17.44). In the quantitative models of political economy, the circulation of goods through an economy is facilitated by money's capacity to translate the value of each commodity into the single abstract equivalent of cash. Money is little more than a lubricant that brings the clashing cogs of self-interest and individual tastes into a working system of market exchange.

In chapter 4 I described how money, conceived as a neutral medium of exchange, simply marks the relative value of all commodities by enabling a continual adjustment in prices based on a great many variables in supply and demand. In this view of money, money serves as the eyes of the whole economy, affording an overarching perspective on the complex dynamics of economic interactions otherwise unavailable to any single participant. Ruskin agrees that money does signify the wealth and vitality of a whole economy, but a just and abundant economy is possible only if consumers recognize the moral signs attaching to all of their spending. His comparison of money to electricity offers a very different picture of the operations of a money economy. Always acting across the differential of relative surplus and deficit, money is used to hire—or, to put it in his moralized language, to "command"—another person's labor. For the most part, Ruskin charges, the rich are well aware of this power and take full advantage of it in building up their holdings of cash and capital at the expense of paying just prices and wages. The production-driven theory of political economy legitimizes these actions, too, in describing the outcomes of market exchange as a neutral sorting of individuals' aggregate desires. But money functions poorly as the eyes of an economy if participants turn a blind eye to its moral operations.

Ruskin argues that money's power of command must be met by the moral counterweight of the "just price," his focus in the third essay of *Unto This Last.* Two years later in his new 1862 preface to the book, he regrets structuring the four essays so that the most inflammatory and, as judged by his critics, the most ludicrous of his proposals entered the first essay (17.18). Recall from chapter 6 that he proposes that an "equality of wages" be honored within each branch of labor—trade or profession—regardless of the quality of the work done. As noted earlier in this chapter, Mill rejects a similar proposal the year before in *On Liberty* as an infringement on the liberty of consumers and on the workers who are most skilled at their trades. Ruskin counters that a standard wage for every type of work is the only way to prevent the misappropriation of laborers' just due for their work. Salaried professionals receive guaranteed pay, but in the realm of wage labor, competition pits workers against each other, driving down the price paid to all (17.34).

In the third essay Ruskin returns to set this equal wage proposal in the context of his broader analysis of money, which though needed from the start was impossible in the monthly format in which *Unto This Last* was originally published. Once again the four essays proceed from the internal relations of a social practice to the external relations of monetary exchange. The idea of a standard wage—in place of market competition—does appear to infringe on consumer choice and to be unfair to skilled workers, as Mill contends. Here the one-on-one relations that typify Ruskin's scenes of economic life only compound these worries, which is why the parable of the penny paid to all of the workers hired at different hours of the day—even "unto this last"—seems so unjust (Matt. 20.1–16).[16] In fact, Ruskin's own definition of the "just price" is at odds with his equal wage proposal, too. As he defines it, the "right or just payment" consists in one-for-one trades of equivalent labor, "giving time for time, strength for strength, and skill for skill" (17.65).

To grasp the reasons behind his wage proposal, we must proceed beyond the face-to-face relations that Ruskin takes as his starting point and examine how he puts his practical examples into a broader theoretical perspective. His idea of the "just price" straddles this line between the focus on practices in his social criticism and the actual workings of money economies. As he notes, it is not easy to measure an equivalence of labor in any case. Once we move past labor time to consider strength, skill, and the many other factors involved in the quality and worth of labor, these calculations of "equivalent" work become exceedingly complex even in the confines of a social practice. But Ruskin claims that these difficulties are secondary when calculating a just price. The complications that he emphasizes are not these challenges of practical judgment, but the societal realities of the deflationary tendency of money and the power relations between classes.

I examine Ruskin's analysis of the fluctuations in money's value in the next section. Very briefly, the reason that money deflates in value, according to him, is that the amount of money in circulation tends to increase relative to a society's holdings of material goods or its actual wealth. The desire for money becomes more intense as its power of command appears to reach farther and farther. Paradoxically, as people want money more, its value decreases because there are fewer products out there relative to each unit of the currency. Given this deflationary tendency of money, Ruskin declares that although the just price "consists in absolute exchange; or, if there be any respect to the stations of the parties, it will not be in favour of the employer: there is certainly no equitable reason in a man's being poor, that if he give me a pound of bread to-day, I should return him less than a pound of bread to-morrow" (17.65). If someone performs a job for another person, then the payment must suffice for the worker to purchase a return amount of labor needed to produce a similar quantity of good whenever that is desired. Since labor time, strength, and skill do not deflate over time as money does, consumers should actually give more than is immediately due.

While this point anticipates Ruskin's debt analysis of money, his main argument for the just price concerns the power differentials between economic actors and their distorting effects on the pricing of goods and services. He offers an example of a consumer who needs to hire a worker. Laws of supply and demand suggest that the consumer bid two (or more) workers against each other, using the less skilled one to force down the other's asking price. If the consumer succeeds in hiring the good worker for only half the full worth of his labor, then this first worker is paid the "asking price," but only half of the due wage. Although this injustice might seem limited to an isolated scene, Ruskin the theorist is describing an occurrence that repeats many times daily with vast implications. In a competitive environment of systematically lowered wages, the same consumer can hire the second worker—or even better, another skilled one—to do additional work for him with the remaining half of the just price. If instead the first skilled worker got what he deserved, then he could turn around and hire someone else—also at a just price—to meet his demands (17.68–69).

What distinguishes these two scenarios? In both cases two people are employed for the money owed to the first worker. But in the first case, one man enjoys the labor of two workers, while in the second, the two people work for two different consumers. Thus,

> The difference between the just and unjust procedure does not lie in the number of men hired, but in the price paid to them, and the *persons by whom* it is paid . . . the influence being carried forward by justice, and arrested by injustice. The universal and constant action of justice in this

> matter is therefore to diminish the power of wealth, in the hands of one individual, over masses of men, and to distribute it through a chain of men. . . . [B]y the just procedure, [a man] is permitted to touch the nearest only, through whom, with diminished force, modified by new minds, the energy of the wealth passes on to others, and so till it exhausts itself. (17.69–70)

What appeared as a restriction on consumer choice and an unfairness to skilled workers looks rather different here. The difference is that Ruskin has recast the issue of justice-in-exchange by approaching it through a broader framework of distributive and social justice. It is the disparities in economic power that make market pricing and, indeed, all merely face-to-face measures of the "just price" seem woefully inadequate. Rich consumers have many options, while poor workers do not. If market competition is made the de facto measure of just pricing, then stark imbalances like these go unchallenged. Ruskin's proposal of standard wages in the trades and consequent limits on consumer choice are not so unwise or unjustified, in fact, especially given the lack of union power in securing good wages and of government regulation in protecting workers during his period.

This passage introduces a different picture of the flow of wealth and power throughout an economy. Justice means giving others their due in the relations of daily life. For consumers this means that justice-in-exchange has to look beyond two-party agreements, however noncoercive they may appear. Justice-in-exchange also requires seeing where power is exerted unjustly in restricting or stopping the flow of wealth throughout a society. Paying the just price keeps the power of money moving throughout the body economic, ensuring that every participant can enjoy the power of choice as a consumer in commanding other people's labor in turn. Here there is no division of virtue between "wise" masters and dependent laborers.

This extension of power and choice to all workers puts the paternalism of Ruskin's image of the "melodious inequalities of concurrent power" in a new light. In his scene of the prudent farmer who guides his neighbors, inequalities of wisdom and authority are inevitable, and they are justified by Ruskin's ascription of moral virtue to this farmer and to the wise "masters" of every good enterprise. But now his emphasis shifts from these "melodious inequalities" to the "concurrent flows" of power. His electrical imagery helps make the point. Concurrent flows of money power continuously cycle back and forth as does the "alternating current" of electrical circuitry. People occupy, or at least they should occupy, the roles of consumer and worker in turn. In any economy there must be some such trading of roles for money to circulate. In Ruskin's political economy those who presently lack turns as consumer would get them more frequently, while others who currently take too many turns would lose some. Even in the best economy, however, the relationship between "consumer" and "worker" is shot through with power, he contends. Money always entails command by the consumer. And here we see the importance of the closing lines of the previous passage. The power of money should "touch the nearest only, through whom, with diminished force, *modified by new minds*, the energy of the wealth passes on to others, and so till it exhausts itself." Ruskin's account of the just price undercuts the paternalistic wisdom he accords to the well-off and the well-placed in many of his examples and scenes of economic life. Paying just prices redistributes power and choice by directing them away from protected professionals with their guaranteed salaries toward unprotected laborers with their competitive wages. It does not validate anyone as "master" but proposes the extension of good consumption that would come about if all workers were granted their due wages so that they might choose how to meet their wants and needs, while developing their capabilities and excellences as they see fit.

This rereading of Ruskin's imagery begins to show how the resources of his ethics of consumption help to overcome the paternalism of his politics. But while his arguments indicate the need for union efforts and public legislation to lessen economic power imbalances, there remain the practical difficulties of calculating the "just price" in actual exchanges. Although market competition is no substitute for full justice, maybe it is just enough. Considering Ruskin's claim that just pricing must account for both quantities of labor time *and* qualities of strength and skill, perhaps a retreat to the market's means for divining prices is the only logical course.

Once again it is important to see that Ruskin seeks to meet this challenge at a theoretical level. Claiming that his notion of the just price is a more "practically serviceable approximation" than the abstract calculations of exchange-value adopted in classical political economy, he writes that there is not "so much difficulty or chance in determining [the just due of labor], as in determining the ordinary maxima and minima of vulgar political economy. . . . It is easier to determine scientifically what a man ought to have for his work, than what his necessities will compel him to take for it. His necessities can only be ascertained by empirical, but his due by analytical, investigation" (17.68). What is striking in Ruskin's language is his meaning of the terms "scientific" and "analytical." Unlike Mill he sees no reason to consider a strictly empirical analysis of market outcomes as in any way "scientific." Again this is to abstract out the "accidental" circumstances of the amounts of power and money and the actual desires, whether good or bad, that people bring to economic exchanges. What would make political economy "analytical," Ruskin argues, is ethical reflection about the makings of good lives and a good society for everyone. But as discussed in chapter 6, is it possible to envision those ends, activities, and capabilities that are basic to any human life and to judge the full value of things and the just prices due for them? Here the concern is not so much paternalism as it is the problem of a unitary conception of the human good.

One final feature of Ruskin's idea of the "just price" enters here. Even as he holds that there is a duty to compensate others for their labor time, strength, and skill, he acknowledges an insurmountable obstacle to paying others justly. All human labor acquires a certain priceless sanctity in being the "'quantity of toil which we die in'. . . . it cannot be bought, nor sold. Everything else is bought and sold for Labour, but labour itself cannot be bought nor sold for anything, being priceless" (17.183). In Ruskin's view, not every form of work is "toil" alone, but all work involves some "toil." The just price for another person's labor must account, therefore, not only for the time, strength, and skill that people expend in producing some good, but also for the degree of suffering that different kinds of work inflict.

Making the "just price" practicable introduces a great many difficult calculations. How, for example, do the skill and suffering of growing food compare with the skill and suffering of writing a book? Perhaps Ruskin deems labor to be ultimately priceless because translating such qualitative judgments into monetary terms presents far too many problems. Linda Austin claims as much when she charges that Ruskin's appeal to Genesis in equating toil with suffering reflects the biblical "labor theory of value" that ultimately serves as the basis of his ethics of consumption.[17] Thus, it seems, once Ruskin sets economic life in motion, moving beyond his isolated scenes and endeavoring to impose his ethical concerns on the ceaseless rounds of market exchange, he must grab for some seemingly solid measure of value. But Ruskin does not, in fact, have a singular conception of value. Unlike Marx, who adopts the singular measure of labor time as the basis of his theory of value, Ruskin factors in the strength, skill, excellence, and suffering of people's work. But this ethical complexity only reinforces the objection that just exchange, as Ruskin imagines it, requires a God's-eye view of economic life. Does his ethics of consumption reduce in the end to a metaphysics of the good, as first seen in his early theory of beauty in *Modern Painters* 2 and reverberating throughout his ideal medievalist polity?

This conclusion, which is echoed by other commentators, misreads Ruskin's ethics. The claim that labor is finally "priceless" does not govern his account of value, which includes other factors than labor, as discussed in chapter 6. His claim about the pricelessness of labor concerns his account of pricing, and its purpose is to set moral limits on monetary compensation. Simply put, if money is all that consumers give for the things they buy, then their payment will always be insufficient and therefore unjust. Once again the connection that Ruskin draws between virtues—in this case the virtue of justice—and practices is crucial. Although he is in earnest about paying just prices, the full calculations of labor's "due" go beyond the abstractions of monetary payment and labor time. His fuller model of justice-in-exchange is that of the "justice of praise" discussed in chapter 5. Like an art critic evaluating the excellence of a painting, consumers are to undertake an imaginative effort of assessing other people's work on terms that are germane to the activities in which the workers participate, whether out of choice or out of necessity. In judging the skill another person displays in "good kinds" of labor, the consumer will have to look to the goods and standards of the practices in which that work is done, giving the worker his or her due in light of the degree of excellence attained. Or if the work is performed in conditions that afford no room for workers' self-development, then compensation for arduous toil becomes the more immediate practical consideration (though efforts on behalf of societal transformation should follow not too far behind).

I read these imaginative efforts as interventions in the market. Completely replacing the scheme of market pricing with one based entirely on such ethical considerations would require knowing how exactly farming and writing and all of the other activities in which people participate might be judged, not on their own terms, but on some overall scale of calibrating their part in the human good. If this metaphysical hope is all that Ruskin offers, then his ethics of consumption is impractical. I read a different goal in his ethics, though. What is most significant about his ideal of the just price is how it motivates attempts to cross over into other people's lives and endeavors, asking how their work should be judged in light of the activities they have chosen or, possibly, the suffering they experience as a result of having limited capabilities and few opportunities.

For Ruskin the spending of money always entails the power of command by consumers and the suffering of toil by workers—roles, which we have already seen, are interchangeable, or at least would be in a just economy. This moralized language of command and toil is essential to two lessons of his ethics of consumption, and these lessons help to unsettle the hold of Ruskin's paternalism and his unitary vision of the good over the other parts of his corpus.

First, in economic life there will always be command and toil and, with them, inequalities of power among individuals. While these inequalities may be lessened by trying to ensure that everyone takes turns as consumers and workers, Ruskin's language of command and toil, power and suffering, is an important reminder of the need to consider who gains and who loses in economic exchanges. Unlike his politics, where he envisions a perfectly cooperative structure of social practices and paternal governance, his ethics of consumption focuses on individuals. Who has power, and how do they use or abuse it? Who works and who toils, and are the compensations adequate to their contributions and sufferings? Here it is not the master or the magnanimous king who rules on these questions; it is individual consumers whenever they command other people's labor. Thus, the language of Ruskin's ethics of consumption highlights the powers and privileges, the abuses and injuries, of specific individuals. Elevating the importance of individual consumers, and their vantage point on and responsibilities within an economy, helps to defuse the paternalism and the defense of social hierarchies so prominent in his politics.

Second, and following from this first point, for Ruskin economic life is always subject to conflict. Conflicts inevitably arise among individual economic actors when some consumer and some worker do not, in fact, see eye-to-eye about the ends and desires they each bring to an economic transaction. Even as Ruskin calls consumers to cross over into other people's lives, there must be room for interpretive gaps, for differences between consumers and workers over how to read things given their respective desires and purposes. He admits as much himself when he writes that the flow of money through a good economy will be "modified by new minds." If we accept Ruskin's claim that assessments of value depend on the characters that people have developed in their cultural activities, then clearly there will be disagreements. It is impossible for any one consumer to "master" the range of goods and excellences that might be pursued and enjoyed in the many kinds of work and endeavor from which he or she derives sustenance in maintaining and enriching his or her life. Full justice of this sort would require the command of a benevolent despot who sees the "human good" in all its variety and harmony and directs everyone, according to his or her talents and needs, toward their due contributions and rewards in a perfectly cooperative endeavor akin to a Divine Corporation (see chapter 1).

This "ideal" polity is the basis of Ruskin's politics. His ideal of the just price, by contrast, urges consumers to seek out what full justice would demand in every purchase, even as it stipulates the impossibility of completely just compensation. The "pricelessness" of labor is both a reminder of the duty to imagine all that is owed to others and a caution against the belief that consumers can prescribe another person's good. Instead of presuming, as Ruskin does in his rhetoric, that there is only one ideal type of character and only one perfect set of practices, we do better to pay attention to the places where he allows that individuals do possess and pursue different virtues, activities, and visions of good lives.

The paradox of Ruskin's ethics of consumption is that his appeals to "masters" and their vaunted authority mandate moral efforts to guarantee power and choice to everyone who works and spends. Every consumer plays the role of "master" whenever purchasing goods and services, dictating how others spend their time, their strength, their skill, their life. Ruskin's imagery of flowing streams of wealth is transformed by his account of the just price. The task of directing these streams is not the privilege or duty of the rich alone. It does not fall solely to the wise expenditure of these few to foster a common good for all. Each consumer is charged with imagining other people's lives and labors, asking what a given product cost workers in making it and what all they should gain in return. Here Ruskin's streams of wealth are not governed by any one person or, more importantly, by any one vision of the good. They are cascading flows that prevent everyone from drinking unduly from them.[18]

Putting Practice into Theory: Money as Debt

Ruskin's account of the just price introduces the wider reaches of his alternative "theory" of political economy. To trace them out more fully, we have to proceed to the other function he reads in money—the acknowledgment of debt. Ruskin's "debt-analysis" of money is the most persuasive part of his theory, judged both as an astute piece of criticism and as an empirically predictive account of the cultural and psychological factors at work in the social trust that people have to invest in a currency.[19]

Again Ruskin rejects the political economists' idea of money as a neutral meeting place of exchange. He points out, quite rightly, the continual fluctuations in the value of money in people's eyes, and he disparages the "gold standard" upheld by the classical theorists of his day. Currency markets today confirm Ruskin's awareness of money's variability, the very thing that a gold standard is designed to protect against. As James Sherburne notes, Ruskin was "nonchalant for a Victorian" in dismissing the need for a gold standard. Few laws and regulations existed to protect against currency panics, making a promised exchange of gold for money the main pillar of the public's trust.[20] Yet Ruskin questions gold's stability in arguing that the value of money should not "rest on a basis of imagination," certainly not an imagination as flighty as the craving for gold (17.199).

Ruskin's nonchalance about doing away with gold as a fixed measure of money's worth is an important reminder of the different basis of his political economy. Ruskin the moralist argues that judgments of economic value should look to "shared agreements" about which ends, goods, activities, excellences, and capabilities make for the best kinds of lives. Ruskin the theorist describes the alternative. Gold may seem like a sound alternative to cash when currency panics strike, but its buffering is chimerical. The value of gold is susceptible to the whims of people's imagination, whether these are conditioned by a culturally constructed desire for the glitter of gold or by the reactions of speculators imagining the best or the worst about a whole economy. Observe that these judgments about gold are predicated on cultural patterns of value ascription, on the one hand, and advantage-seeking estimates of economic health, on the other.

Contrary to classical political economy's description of the market as a neutral meeting place of exchange, relying on money to measure value does not remove, as Ruskin observes, the need for some sort of shared agreements in economic life. In claiming that an economy should not "rest on a basis of imagination," he is not thinking of individuals' "subjective" tastes and preferences. He is highlighting the shared assumptions behind his contemporaries' confidence in money as the supreme measure of value—namely, the cultural and psychological factors that buttress the worth of gold. As long as everyone knows that gold is a mark of social status, its value will remain stable. If most people assume that an economy is on the skids, then gold's value will assuredly increase. But why should cultural and psychological attitudes be allowed to replace ethical reflection as the source of the "shared agreements" that secure public confidence in money-based judgments of value?

Ruskin's frequent criticisms of the finery of jewelry and the speculations of financiers frame a central question about the capitalist system of market pricing that he never poses quite so directly. Is it wise to base a whole scheme of valuation on unexamined cultural and psychological attitudes and the underlying social relations that they entail? Consider how the cultural agreement that gold is a mark of status involves everyone, both those who do and those who do not wear it, in a hierarchy of social esteem. That hierarchy honors even the people who purchase jewelry bought by unjust wages and brutal toil and mined in environmentally destructive ways. Similarly, a nervous panic in the face of an economic downturn only heightens the sense that an economy is out of control and completely mysterious for all but those wealthy enough to make every swing in the collective mood pay richly indeed.

For Ruskin, money's value is never constant. Therefore money cannot be a neutral sign, a mere medium of exchange, as money is portrayed in classical political economy. Where these theorists see only the abstract equivalent of cash, Ruskin views money as an ethical sign, and the value of money, he argues, is necessarily contingent on something else. It may be contingent on unexamined cultural symbols and passing psychological trends, or its value can rest in something more substantial.

I have concentrated on money's power of commanding labor, but Ruskin defines money in terms of its primary function of acknowledging debt. As he puts it with emphasis, "*The currency of any country consists of every document acknowledging debt, which is transferable in the country,*" and every currency depends "ultimately *always on the existence of substantial means of meeting its demand*" (17.194). Money is worthless if it cannot buy things. If no one believes that money can be trusted to purchase goods and services, then a currency will have no value. This need to back the currency with something is recognized even by political economists in their support of the gold standard. Ruskin, however, proposes a different guarantor of a national currency, a basket of the actual goods—food, clothing, and other necessities (he lists "bread, iron, or silk")—required to maintain people's lives. If a government wanted to stabilize its currency, then a guaranteed basket of such means would be more stable and more useful than gold. But such a basket of goods would only be a "provisional" standard, he argues, first, because its components would have to be to agreed to (presumably by members of the community, given their cultural sense of the "basics") and, second, because the only sure guarantee of a currency is the sum total of the "substantial means" or actual wealth held in a society at any time (17.199–200).

Ruskin names this sum total of existing wealth the "national store." At the abstract level of theory, money represents a debt held against this national store. When consumers use money to buy goods and services, they signal their debt with the money they give. The seller who takes the money receives a credit. In other words, the recipient of cash is promised a return amount of goods and services whenever and wherever he or she wants, an amount equivalent, or so Ruskin presumes, to the labor expended in producing the goods and services initially sold. No money economy could operate, however, if this credit could be cashed in only against the consumer who bought the seller's wares in the first place. Enter the currency. A currency generalizes the debt; it literally makes the credit circulate, allowing individuals to claim whatever goods and services they choose and can afford to buy from the "national store."

Ruskin canvasses a number of practical implications of this theory of money. He stresses the "debt" that money represents. As an outstanding claim on the national store, money signifies a *deficiency* insofar as the goods and services it can claim have not been purchased. Consider once more Ruskin's example of the prudent farmer. Following the floods that ruin his neighbors, he receives the power to command their labor as a result of the debts that they incur because of his assistance. Now this new master might put his neighbors' debts, or the "money" he receives from them, to good use, paying each of them sufficiently so that the community at large returns to prosperity while he recoups what he lent. Even in such an ideal situation, the introduction of money into the society marks the "establishment of mercantile wealth"—the holding of money instead of actual wealth—and therefore "signifies a political diminution of the real wealth" of the community as a whole. If the floods had not come, then the national store would still contain the goods saved by the prudent master and all of the other wealth that his neighbors had possessed (17.51).

For Ruskin, this version of the story reflects the best possible use of money. In this case money is a "means" to renewed prosperity by facilitating a just distribution of goods and a fuller development of people in the community. As discussed in chapter 4, however, people often treat money as an "end," not a "means," seeking to increase their holdings of "mercantile wealth" by paying other people as little as possible and leaving them destitute of financial and personal resources. Thus, "the art of becoming 'rich'" nearly always entails "the art of establishing the maximum inequality in our own favour" (17.46). Instead of moral opprobrium, such arts attract imitation. Not only do the rich practice this art, but bargain shoppers are also guilty of putting the "mercantile wealth" of money ahead of "real wealth" for themselves and other people, too. Disdaining the "present rage for cheapness" in Victorian consumer society (or in Wal-Mart aisles today), Ruskin declares the quest for bargains to be either "a rage for badness of all commodities, or . . . an attempt to find persons whose necessities force them to let you have more than you should for your money . . . and your boasted cheapness is thus merely a measure of the extent of your national [and, I would add, global] distress" (17.185n). Here, too, the theme of deficiency or the absence of wealth characterizes his debt analysis of money. These arguments tie in as well with his two core criticisms of classical political economy—the theory's inability to address either the issue of distributive justice or the need for character development, including the excellences and capabilities that constitute Ruskin's full sense of that term.

If we add back in Ruskin's arguments against the gold standard, we can now see why he deems the theory of classical political economy to be bankrupt. In his judgment the calculations of political economists are as unstable as the currency on which they are based. In the classical theory it is possible to calculate the value of commodities and the community's wealth because both are translatable into money terms through market pricing. But what if the value of money is as utterly contingent as Ruskin claims it to be?

Ruskin freely admits that evaluating the actual wealth of a society, and thus knowing the current value of money, is an enormously complex interpretive task. In his words, the "working power or worth of the currency is founded on the entire sum of the relative estimates formed by the population of its possessions" (17.189). As already noted, the value of money depends on "the existence of substantial means of meeting its demand," but in practice, what really matters are the judgments of the many consumers who trust that they will be able to purchase what they want from the national store. Here we move onto the character of these individuals, for "the sum of the wealth held by the nation, instead of being constant, or calculable, varies hourly, nay, momentarily, with the number and character of its holders!" (17.170). For Ruskin, character determines what individuals consider to be wealth and also what the total wealth of a society is. On the one hand, good character makes for accurate judgments of those well-made products that are "real" wealth. On the other hand, the more well-developed people there are to produce, exchange, and enjoy this material abundance, the greater the "effectual value" of that wealth will be. All told, where character is lacking, money's value will have only a tenuous connection to the actual wealth held by the national store.

A recent example illustrates the contingent relationships among individuals' estimates of their society's wealth, the character of the people (especially their leaders), and the variability of monetary measures of value. When the United States stock market "bubble" burst in 2000, two things quickly became clear. First, many people had placed far too much faith in the market value of the companies traded on the various stock exchanges. Second, this "irrational exuberance" was due in part to deceptive and fraudulent accounting practices engineered by unscrupulous executives who set immediate gains in stock price above all other commitments they had to shareholders and other stakeholders. If we factor in the quasi-religious performance and edicts of the chairman of the Federal Reserve System in calming market jitters and instilling confidence in the U.S. economy, then Ruskin's analysis of the "idolatry" of money (see chapter 4) looks rather insightful.

At the heart of Ruskin's critique of the idolatry of money is his dichotomy between God and Mammon or, as he also puts it, between "true imagination" and "false idolatry." With his full theory of money now in view, it is clear why he insists that imagination, whether true or false, is inescapable in money economies. Although Ruskin rejects the gold standard, for him, money's value always "rests on a basis of imagination." His debate in the *Times of London* with the political economist J. E. Cairnes is a good illustration of Ruskin's practical contrast between a true imagination and a false one. The difference is scope of vision. Debating the recent causes of inflation in Britain, Ruskin challenges Cairnes's claim that the gold rushes in Australia and California have a "direct" deflationary effect on the British pound. For Cairnes, the currency's worth and power are a direct function of gold. Ruskin does not deny this deflationary effect, but he counters that other factors, like the "destruction of property in the American [Civil] war and our European amusements in the manufacture of monster guns . . . lower the value of money far more surely and fatally than an increased supply of bullion" (17.490).[21] Understanding the value of money requires a broad and exacting assessment of all of the shared agreements that guide the society's choices about where to invest its efforts, commitments, and hopes.

For Ruskin, classical political economy is predicated on the false imagination of Victorian capitalism. This imagination is falsified by the exclusive focus on mere monetary considerations at the expense of the many political, social, environmental, and characterological factors that determine a currency's actual worth. In the classical theory it is possible to calculate the value of commodities and the wealth of a society because both are translatable into money terms through the all-important concept of exchange-value, or market price. Yet Ruskin's argument against the gold standard calls into question the confidence vested in these calculations and in the image of the market as ruled by nothing more than the free play of individual preferences. He contends that the play of the imagination—whether ruled by status symbols and estimates of economic trends or by reflective judgments about the basic necessities, full capabilities, best activities, and ordered goods of human lives—always determines money's value. Noting the historical abandonment of "substances of intrinsic value as the materials of a currency," Ruskin predicts that the need for a gold standard will also cease in "proportion to the extension of civilization, and increase of trustworthiness in Governments" (17.159). Although his prediction has proven prescient, the utterly contingent variability of the currency poses a challenge to his own attempt to construct an alternative theory able to offer any intelligible lessons.

While Ruskin admits the impossibility of a snapshot reading of the currency at any given time, his theory of money recommends a specific course of action. It is important to remember where we are in his argument. The moralist is now the theorist, constructing a theory of money to explain the irrationalities of industrial capitalism, as its institutions are described by classical political economy. Ruskin's theory argues that political economists should not merely seek to stabilize the currency in order to instill confidence in the market's operations. Instead of making more money—the end of capitalism—the better aim is to make more *of* money—to increase money's power to command labor, goods, and services and, so, to enhance people's consumption. Investing in people—because "persons themselves *are* the wealth"—is the surest way to secure a currency, promote justice, and enhance flourishing for all (17.55).

If the value of money reflects the community's current wealth of material goods and human excellences, then fully developing people to produce more well-made things augments money's power of command. We have already seen that for Ruskin the fastest route to developing people's "vital powers" and improving the qualities of their strength and skill is to pay just prices. Only then will all workers enjoy the initiative and choice to develop themselves as they see fit. This vision of the growing worth of money drives his theoretical analysis. His image of the currency as an ever-circulating power steering useful and enjoyable goods to people, while enhancing the community's overall wealth and individuals' self-development, joins his notion of the just price with his ideal of the abundance promised by good consumption. That vision of communal wealth and the enhanced consumption achievable through acknowledging debts to other people is, finally, why he proposes the just price as a more "practically serviceable approximation" of the money owed to others than the market prices dictated by supply and demand. For Ruskin, the real value of money reflects the existing wealth of well-made things and well-developed people, and prudence alone counsels heeding these ethical considerations and joining in efforts to meet them so as to increase the power of money and the quality of life that consumers may purchase with it.

Putting this theoretical vision into practice takes more than prudence. Alongside justice, consumers must also cultivate piety. Again, for Ruskin, money represents an "acknowledgment of debt." At the level of theory, money is an acknowledgment of debt in being a promissory note held against the national store. Money, however, is made to circulate in a society. Money gets spent, and it is in the consumer's spending of money that the act of "*acknowledging debt*" occurs. In practice, then, money signifies an acknowledgment of debt *by someone* for goods and services rendered *by another person.* Thus money rightly calls forth an acknowledgment of indebtedness to other people when, as consumers, we command them to do our bidding. Somehow this sense of indebtedness has to be fostered in the everyday acts of spending money.

It is here at the practical level of moral imagination that we see the dynamic interaction between the two cardinal virtues of an ethics of consumption, justice and piety. When spending money, consumers should strive to compensate other people for their labors, avoiding undue gain for themselves and undue losses for other people. But acknowledging one's full indebtedness as a consumer goes beyond the concerns of justice. Justice asks, how much time, skill, strength, and suffering did other people expend in making something? Piety asks, how much good does one derive from these efforts as a consumer, and more importantly, how does that good relate to the good sought by the makers of these things?

I can clarify the dynamic between justice and piety by returning to Ruskin's reading of Dante's Plutus and his followers from chapter 4. As the symbol of "Evil commerce," Plutus is unjust in failing to pay due wages and to secure decent and healthful working conditions. He is impious in refusing to countenance much more—what Ruskin typically calls the "life" or vitality displayed (or not) by people, their culture and community, and the world around them. I use the word "countenance" deliberately. Quoting Dante, Ruskin writes that Plutus "'makes all men strangers;' his speech is therefore unintelligible, and no single soul of all those ruined by him *has recognizable features*" (17.210). In hell Plutus rages incoherently, and his followers look nothing as they did in life. Having foresworn the claims of the members of their community—as if they were strangers—not one of these figures would now be acknowledged by those who once knew them. What would it take, Ruskin asks his audiences of consumers, to acknowledge the extent of their own indebtedness? How can consumers put a "face" on economic transactions, even across the distances of a money economy?

Justice alone is insufficient in meeting this challenge. For Ruskin, consumers must also cultivate piety. By "piety" I do not mean the performance of worship through formulaic ritual, as is suggested by a superficial reading of this chapter's opening example of Muslims' honoring their tradition's prohibition against eating pork. For Ruskin's favorite philosopher Plato, piety means knowing what is owed to the gods, but it is hard to know how to repay debts to the givers of life.[22] There are some debts that finally cannot be repaid, as Ruskin claims in declaring labor to be "priceless." Such debts require acknowledging, not just what we take from others when we buy things, but what they sought in making these things—these gifts—that sustain our lives.

This critical question is motivated and framed by the teleological structure of Ruskin's ethics as it gets recast by the changes in his virtues-centered approach. Piety toward God or the gods answers to divine purposes and inspires obedience. Not eating pork, for strict Muslims, respects the limits imposed by Allah's gifts, instilling virtues, purifying activities, and guiding "the believers" to the dignity and community ordained for human beings. This is not formulaic ritual, but the performance of "binding practices" that are recognized as the source and substance of good lives. We saw in "Modern Education" (1853) that Ruskin reconceives religion as the "binding" practices of a people, counseling his readers to ask whether they "had better consult the Bible, Koran, or Council of Trent" for these practices (11.259). So significant is this cultural reconception of religion that he shifts the focus of his criticism from the "moral perception" of God's purposes as seen in the beauty of the Creation (see chapter 1) to the moral imagination that people practice, in part, through their cultural "invention of material symbols which may lead us to contemplate the character and nature of gods, spirits, or abstract virtues and powers, without in the least implying the actual presence of such Beings among us, or even their possession, in reality, of the forms we attribute to them" (20.242).

If piety toward the gods answers to divine purpose, then as a full-fledged virtue, piety fosters a searching reverence for all of the givers of life. Over the course of his criticism, Ruskin expands his sense of who is included among the givers of life, but always the issue of purpose is pivotal. As discussed in chapter 3, by the 1870s he names the teaching of piety toward the natural world as one of the primary goals of his criticism. In consuming natural resources as we must, our existence is sustained by the world not once or occasionally, but with every breath. How can consumers fully acknowledge these gifts? In Ruskin's way of thinking, consumers are to imagine nature's purposes and the intricate ways that the earth's "circles of vitality" are ordered toward them. Thus he appeals to organic form, the breath of life, and the earth Mother to give credence to the purposes he reads in the "natural order." And yet the trajectory of his virtues-centered criticism makes over all such appeals as cultural offerings. It is only by participating in the activities of one's culture that individuals cultivate their virtues, commit with other people to certain goods and standards, and so begin to recognize which purposes are rightly "binding" on their common judgments of things' beauty and worth.

Ruskin's debt analysis of money stretches the reach of piety yet again. He calls for piety toward the makers of the many things we buy. Dante's punishments indicate how plutocrats cut themselves off from the other members of their community. They see everyone else's labors solely in terms of their own good, refusing to acknowledge how their very existence and their own contributions always depend on deriving good from other people. This piety toward other people complicates Ruskin's ethics still further, for the question is not, how are nature's purposes known through our activities, but what different purposes might consumers and workers seek?

A conversational model of good consumption presses to the fore here. Just as the virtue of justice requires a crossing over into other people's lives to see what is owed for their labors, the virtue of piety requires a crossing over to see what they sought for themselves. If market pricing were the sole consideration of economic justice, then consumers could rest secure in the dictates of classical political economy. If our own good were the sole consideration in judging a product's value, then there would be no need to attend to the meaning and purpose that workers invest in what they make. For Ruskin, the evaluative task of assessing the just price requires an imaginative effort of judging other people's labor in the hopes of establishing "equivalence" in exchange. The evaluative task of acknowledging debts is better characterized as a "translation," for the good that we take from the things we consume may often have little to do with the good that other people sought in producing them.

If money is an acknowledgment of debt, it is insufficient to give only the just price that the recipient needs to buy an equivalent amount of whatever good he or she needs or desires. The punishment imposed on Plutus and his followers would then be restricted to poverty and deprivation, not the denial of all exchange—all communication—with others in their community. For Ruskin, the debt incurred in spending money commits consumers to appreciate what is good for that person and how the pursuit of that good is invested in the work performed. Consumers must therefore move from a blind and uncritical pursuit of whatever vision of the good life they hold, however vaguely they might have formulated one for themselves. They must also embark on a searching effort to fathom what the work they take from others signifies in the light of other people's conceptions of what it is to live well. Only in this manner is it possible to appreciate the full significance of the gifts of other people's labor. Thus the problems of paternalism and the unitary conception of the good that dog Ruskin's corpus are further unsettled by this call to piety in consumption.

For Ruskin, money is not a neutral meeting place of exchange. Spending money involves consumers in an ethical encounter. There are two temptations to avoid in the ethical encounters of a money economy. The first is to ignore the moral functions of money in commanding labor and acknowledging debt, opting instead for an uncritical acceptance of the creed that society as a whole prospers best when consumers take their "individual" tastes to be the only practical and legitimate norm in the realm of consumption. The other temptation is the one to which Ruskin falls prey whenever he presumes that there can be only one vision of good consumption. Cultivating piety corrects against both temptations. The meeting place of a money economy calls forth the imaginative effort of acknowledging one's indebtedness even as it reminds one of the moral distances between commanding consumers and toiling laborers. As a consumer it is impious to refuse to countenance one's debts to other people for helping to keep one alive. It is also impious to remake the meaning and purpose of other people's work entirely in the image of one's own "imagined good." Recognizing indebtedness in economic life requires this balancing act of facing up to all that we receive from others and accepting that these people bring their own visions of good lives to their chosen endeavors.

A "Mixed Economy" of Good Consumption

Ruskin's theory of money mitigates his tendencies toward paternalism and a sovereign conception of the good, but it does not eliminate them. Building from his fundamental dualism between liberal "anarchy and competition" and paternal "government and cooperation," he rejects industrial capitalism as irredeemably beholden to Mammon worship. In chapter 4 I cited Ruskin's dualism between the Eidolon, or "phantasm, or imagination of Good," at work in the money economy of industrial capitalism and the "eternal goodness" of all things "which [God] is said to have 'seen good' in creating" (17.287). This metaphysics of the good stands in here as the sole grounds for the "true imagination" needed to counter the "false idolatry" of industrial capitalism.

If we set aside this dualism and concentrate instead on the term "imagination," a more productive line of argument emerges. For Ruskin the operations of money depend on the existence of some sort of social trust, on some vision of the "whole" of economic life—of the "imagined good" that an economy generates for oneself and for others—without which there would be no confidence in the currency nor any willing participation in economic transactions. What he obscures in his appeal to a metaphysics of God's Creation is that *every* vision of the "whole" of economic life is an "imagined good."

In Ruskin's ideal economy consumers would strive to imagine what good things should be made, to what uses they should be put, to whom they should be distributed, and what excellences must be developed for individuals to achieve societal abundance and individual flourishing. As he admits in his theory of money, it would be impossible for any one person to take stock of this dizzying array of moral considerations in pricing all that one buys, but an ethics of consumption requires this imaginative effort. It is equally impossible, of course, for anyone to calculate the price dictated by all of the variables at work in the supply and demand of commodities, which is why the market wins accolades even from its critics. But individuals participate and cooperate in the capitalist market not simply because it offers a practical mechanism for setting prices. In Ruskin's way of thinking, money is always an ethical sign; it has to answer to some informing vision of an "imagined good." And for him the "imagined good" motivating his contemporaries' participation in the money economy of industrial capitalism reflects an entirely misguided faith that this institutional mechanism not only accurately marks the value of all things in money terms but, more importantly, directs the flows of money toward the achievement of the greatest possible societal good.

In assessing the strengths and weaknesses of Ruskin's theory of money, we should recall the interplay between the descriptive and the normative in Mill's political economy. Mill equates value with exchange-value and the increase of wealth with the growth of capital because this seems to describe how industrial capitalism works *and* because he views this set of institutions as preferable to the economic and social order it is replacing. The theoretical and the ethical are intertwined. The theory is responsive to a *set of goals*—which for Mill center around the democratizing of Victorian Britain through the expansion of industrial production in tandem with the extension of other liberal institutions of press freedoms, electoral representation, and individual rights. Mill's goals are no less normative than the ends that Ruskin champions.

Simply rejecting Mill's political economy as amoral in theory and immoral in its practical effects on Victorian society, as Ruskin does, is to fail to heed the central lesson of Ruskin's own analysis. As he makes clear in his theory of money, a currency requires some grounds for social trust. The grounds may be irrational as in the reliance on gold, backed as it is by the hierarchies of status and the hedging of bets that influence the shifts in its market value. Or the grounds may be rational if individual consumers, business leaders, and governments choose, produce, and support a wealth of well-made things and, more importantly, of well-made people. Imagining this wealth and the conditions for abundance is the tricky part. Ruskin's own either/or of either a morally bankrupt political economy and anarchic liberal institutions, on the one hand, or a "true science of Political Economy" and perfectly harmonious practices, on the other, is insufficient. There are more options than just these two.

Too often critics of capitalism refuse to acknowledge the moral reasons people have for their ready cooperation in market transactions. I do not mean here the "self-interested" meeting of desires, wants, or needs or the acquiring of "external goods" such as wealth and power, though these can be moral reasons, too. I mean something more like Mill's conviction that a system of market exchange is itself good in increasing material prosperity while enhancing the liberty of participants as they fashion their preferences and pursue their goals and projects. Mill's defense of liberty argues that one of the mainstays of a money economy is a "shared *moral* agreement" among participants that liberty is a great good. Institutions that help cultivate liberty warrant political support *and* ethical commitment.

While Ruskin is correct to criticize classical political economy for failing to address issues of distributive justice and character development, he ignores the normative force of the arguments for liberty. The capitalist market and other liberal institutions help protect social spaces for disagreements about the good. Based on his rhetoric, Ruskin is unable to grasp why any room for disagreement, why spaces of liberty for one's "personal tastes and self-regarding desires," warrant respect on *moral grounds.* He paints all of these arguments with the broad brushstroke of the anarchy of liberalism and the covetousness of Mammon worship. Yet Ruskin's acceptance of the need for a money economy shows why this categorical dismissal of industrial capitalism and market competition needs reconsideration.

Ruskin offers two ways of thinking about an ethics of consumption. The first parallels the medievalist ideal of a perfect social harmony found in his politics. The other takes stock of the power differentials always operative in a money economy. These two models, the cathedral structure of his politics and the electrical circuitry of economic exchange, sustain two different moral languages in his criticism.

The moral vision at work in the cathedral model is one of authority and sacrifice. Here people cooperate in pursuit of the shared goods of social practices, and consumers join in support of the ends and excellences pursued by workers and even sacrifice some of their desires in the interests of furthering those goods. Thus, these goods are shared, and they are "authoritative." They reflect agreements made across the distances that separate workers from consumers, so the "sacrifices" that consumers make are a matter of assent. Despite the risks of using a language of authority and sacrifice, I agree that as consumers we need to decide what goods and ends should govern our consumption and what sacrifices those commitments require.

In addition to this cathedral model, Ruskin clearly accepts the need for a money economy and, with it, the exercise of power by commanding consumers and the suffering of loss by toiling workers. On this other conception of economic life, the power differentials of electrical circuitry are unavoidable. A second moral language of "power" and "loss" emerges to the fore here, one that looks beyond the encircling relationships of Ruskin's cathedral model to individuals' actual efforts, goals, and development and to the particular conflicts and harms that inevitably arise. The ethical concerns here are whether individuals' power is well used or abused and whether individuals' injuries are acknowledged or forgotten.

In some ways these two conceptual models and their moral languages of authority and sacrifice, and power and loss, are compatible. In chapter 5 I noted how the cathedral structure of Ruskin's politics has both an upward and a downward movement. The upward movement puts the focus on common goods and the authoritative judgments (and paternal governance) that they uphold. The downward movement inquires into the harms suffered by those in the lower orders of society when their masters fail to accord them due consideration, praise, and aid. But Ruskin's analysis of the operations of a money economy disrupts the integrated structure of his politics.

To see how, we need to make a crucial distinction, one that exploits the developments in Ruskin's vocabulary of the virtues away from the metaphysics of his early aesthetics toward the "endeavours in description" of his later criticism, focused as they are on the cultural practices of his fellow Victorians. Throughout this study I have traced this gradual, if somewhat halting, transformation in his criticism away from a theological conception of the good toward a cultural conception of the norms, ideals, and standards upheld in the activities that individuals support. The following distinction captures the tensions in Ruskin's ethics. He frames his appeals to the good in culturally contingent terms when his aim is to advocate for more social practices productive of *goods shared among interested people.* He makes metaphysical appeals when he envisions the whole of life as a perfect harmony where *everyone's activities contribute directly to a unified good.* To return to the cathedral analogy, at times it would seem sufficient for the participants in a Gothic craft or even just a few innovators in a social practice to judge a person's work as excellent. Ruskin tends not to stop there, however. A person's contribution can finally be declared good only in light of the cathedral's "whole" beauty.

It is difficult to tease apart the places in Ruskin's criticism where he appeals to shared agreements among interested people and where he argues for a consensus in everyone's tastes. Consider how the force of his critique of capitalism reflects his broad construal of consumers' complicity. Consumers are responsible for imagining their way into other people's lives, looking to whether those labors make for excellent and healthy work. As if this responsibility did not extend moral obligations in the economic realm far enough, consumers are also responsible for developing good taste, which involves desiring only those things that can sustain a good society and a good life for everyone.

I agree with Ruskin that an ethics of consumption requires something like this zeal in consumers—the moralist's sense of the magnitude of one's economic choices and the refusal to see one's tastes as indifferent in their effects on other people and the world. As Marx's analysis of the "finish" of consumption makes abundantly clear, the hurdles to attaining a moral vision of one's consumption are very high, but they are not insurmountable. Indeed, wealthy consumers can exert such commanding power over others that there must be institutionalized checks on the imposition of one's "imagined good," one's vision of the "whole" of economic life, on other people, as Mill's liberty principle insists. What is needed, then, is a "mixed economy" of social practices and mediating institutions.

Ruskin's virtues-centered teleological approach points us to the importance of social practices as cooperative activities that develop people's character and promote shared judgments. Vital to any ethics of consumption is the creation and preservation of these social spaces where individuals can join with others to train their desires, cultivate the virtues of justice and piety, and commit to shared goods and standards of excellence that take them beyond their own preferences as they currently stand. Ruskin describes various practices that afford consumers opportunities to exert control over their desires and band together with other people to change the course of their economy. His "endeavours in description" are incomplete, of course, because he focuses on Victorian culture and because the vision he constructs reaches only so far. The most valuable of the practices he presents, in fact, is his own social criticism. His offerings of his vocabulary of the virtues, his concerns with authority and sacrifice and power and loss, and his imaginative reworking of cultural norms, symbols, and ideals must not only be embraced and put into practice by his audience of consumers, but must *also* be scrutinized and reworked by them, too, if his aim of advancing an ethics of consumption is to be met.

This need to allow room for a response, for critical differences with Ruskin, is paralleled in the need to allow for distances between commanding consumers and toiling workers. Ruskin argues that command is always present in consumption, even if—and this is a big "if"—workers are not coerced into producing the things they make. Still there will always be disagreements over the purpose, meaning, and value of the goods bought and sold in a money economy. That is why "external goods" like money are useful, along with the mediating institutions in which they work. Money has no intrinsic connection to any social practice; it can be put to different, even contrary, ends.[23] This leads to an important moral implicit in Ruskin's account of the functions of money, though he does not draw it himself. Justice and piety demand a searching vision of the harmful effects of one's spending *as well as* a recognition of the limitations of that vision.

Every estimate of the wealth of one's society and the vital powers of other people to use that wealth well will be as "provisional" as Ruskin's proposed basket of the means of life. It must be subject to debate and discussion. He is right to engage the moral imagination of wealthy consumers in seeing how far their own power and debts reach. He is right to agitate for reforms designed to secure more just prices for wage work and to develop and enhance the excellences, capabilities, and choices of every worker. Only then can the conversational model of good consumption that he envisions come to fruition because only then will each participant be able to articulate and act on his or her sense of the good that might be achieved in an economy. Ruskin's cathedral model of the ideal society, with its harmony of cooperative practices, cannot accommodate the distances and conflicts in moral vision that are inescapable in a money economy and a conversational ethics of consumption. There must be room for differences over tastes, preferences, goods, and ends. A market economy helps carve out the institutionally established boundaries that enable interested individuals to forge agreements among each other without requiring a perfect consensus across the community. The mediating institution of market exchange opens up these spaces of disagreement and protects the liberty required to make the activities and agreements that committed consumers work out among themselves matters of free assent.

Ruskin aims to provoke individual consumers to reflect on their choices and to intervene in market exchanges aware of the moral operations of money and their responsibilities to other people and the world around them. In putting his theoretical vision into practice, he proposes a more mixed economy of practices and institutions than his dualism between God and Mammon—between a perfect harmony of associations and the competitive anarchy of liberalism—seems to allow. For example, when he proposes government-run factories and trades for producing goods and services of a certain quality at a just wage, he encourages private businesses to compete, too. Consumers are free to choose whose products to buy and which labor arrangements to support. Ruskin does not propose getting rid of market competition here. Rather, this intervention in the market has the aim of ensuring the reliable information about product quality and the higher pay for workers that consumers need to be able to make and act on moral choices. Here government activism assists, but does not dictate, individuals' ethical decisions.

This particular mix of institutional aids to good consumption is also provisional, of course. Historically other measures have proven better at striking a balance between promoting shared commitments to better wages and public goods and allowing room for consumer choice. They include government regulations of product safety and environmental safeguards, legal protections for union activity and workers' rights, consumer cooperatives, and so on, all of which can help make an ethics of consumption more practical given the limitations of individuals' moral vision in a money economy.

Ruskin's "theory" of money reminds us of the original meaning of that term. A theory offers a systematic view of some whole, whether a field of knowledge or an arena of human life. The theory of classical political economy begins from a set of premises about economic actors and describes the role of money in producing a workable and predictable system of market pricing. Ruskin's counter-theory questions the boundaries of a theory of economic life that accepts individuals' preferences as they are and views the juggling of these preferences through market competition as the best means of achieving the greatest good for all. His approach challenges the calculations based on these assumptions as the cause of the various ills of industrial capitalism. His attention to the brutal working conditions and the deadening work of nineteenth-century industry, his criticism of reducing the value of goods and people to money terms, his scrutiny of the poor's lack of liberty before the power of the rich, and his rejection of continued growth in production without regard to its environmental and human costs—all of these concerns take on broader significance as he traces out how the flows of money might be directed toward wealth or toward "illth."

Relating Mill's theory of political economy to his normative defense of liberty helps us see the dangers in Ruskin's teleological approach to good consumption. If there are no instituted boundaries of indifference around individuals' personal tastes and preferences, then there can be no room for the plural visions of good lives that Mill is right to protect. Mandating that every consumer adopt Ruskin's magisterial vision of good consumption—buying things made in the crafts that he praises and forming their desires and character as he dictates—is coercive to the core—akin to legislating a ban on pork in the interests of cultivating virtues, purifying activities, and making good lives for individuals without their consent. As stated in the Qur'an, "There is no compulsion in religion."[24] Unlike religion, there can be some compulsion in regulating consumption, for example, when consumers are compelled to buy cars with higher fuel efficiency standards. Other factors may convince consumers to reform their tastes, too, including their coming to see the goods and excellences in certain practices, such as local farmers' markets or vegetarian cooking. But even here this compulsion should not require submission to an "imagined good" for which one has been given no good reasons.

Ruskin's moralistic vocabulary of the virtues can still serve us in articulating an ethics of consumption precisely because he traces out so clearly the integral connections among people's chosen activities, their character, culture, and community, and the visions of the good lives informing their preferences as they currently stand. Abstracting out these features of the moral life from empirical accounts of market exchange does not imply their removal in practice. Likewise, while Mill rejects legal measures to promote distributive justice and good character through the shaping of individuals' desires, he allows for moral suasion. It is fine, on his argument, to criticize a father for drinking up his family's resources. But given Mill's strictly principled defense of liberty, what moral vocabulary is to be used? More importantly, if we think that an ethics of consumption is a worthy goal, how can consumers trace out the effects of their desires on other people's lives and life possibilities, their culture and their character?

We can place Mill's and Ruskin's ethical concerns on a spectrum of injury. Mill limits injuries to direct harms to another person's interests. Ruskin extends this concept of injury to include the obstacles to and the depletions of other people's vital powers, or their very well-*being*. Ruskin's criticism provides a moral language—in fact, a set of moral concerns—to help us see beyond our current preferences and across the distances of a money economy. His moral vocabulary of the virtues, tamed by a mixed economy of social practices and liberal institutions, is a resource that has been neglected for too long. The more Ruskin turns to the perspective of individual consumers having to make day-to-day decisions, the more the democratic possibilities of his ethics of consumption unsettle his organic metaphors of the proper workings of riches, the paternalism of the wise, and any singular conception of good consumption. The more he focuses on the practices of good consumption that individuals commit to with others, the less plausible it is to think that there can be one ideal of good taste. Making an ethics of consumption practical requires these cooperative commitments to activities that shape people's desires, judgments, and visions. It requires institutional means as well, for guaranteeing minimum wages, managing public goods, and protecting individual liberties. The mix of these practices and institutions will always be a matter of debate, a debate that is well served by making more explicit the integral connections among character, culture, and community at the center of Ruskin's criticism and reflecting more carefully on the "imagined good" that we seek in our economic lives, whether by design or by default. Ruskin's vocabulary of the virtues can serve us well, maintaining its critical force while leaving room for imagined conceptions of shared goods, good lives, and the common good that are always plural and revisable.

CONCLUSION

Moral Vision in Religion, Culture, and Consumption

This book is structured in three parts, and one way to read the movement of the argument is from religion to culture to consumption. Similarly, the main chapters address, in turn, art, architecture, nature, religion, politics, value, and money. But we cannot divvy up Ruskin's career or his criticism into three distinct periods or seven separate topics. That would ignore the drive toward an integrated moral vision that makes him one of those writers who provoke a decided response in readers. He inspires strong reactions because he is such an integral thinker, and I have sought to give a conceptual accounting of how his moral vocabulary enables him to make powerful connections designed to provoke his audiences into a clearer and fuller vision of their lives and society.

Ruskin offers his account of good consumption, an abundant quality of life, a vibrant culture, and a just community as a religious critic. Although scholars continue to debate the course of his religious affiliation and beliefs, he retains a "religious sensibility" throughout his writings. In ascribing a "religious sensibility" to him, I mean that for him societies, communities, or groups of people have "binding" practices and commitments that form participants in the virtues and moral vision necessary to the best kinds of lives. Those "binding" ties may be patterned in helpful or harmful ways, but Ruskin's appreciative recognition of their formative authority in people's lives distinguishes his religious criticism from the secular theories of figures like Marx and Mill. His insistent search for the "binding" ties of economic life is also basic to his working out an ethics of consumption.

Ruskin's religious sensibility persists, above all else, in his awareness of the vulnerability and the interdependence in human life. That is why he appeals to religions in describing the "gifted" character of shared goods and social exchange and the blighting injuries at their absence. From early on in his writings, he also develops a moral vocabulary that construes his fellow Victorians as desiring subjects who pursue ends that bind them into a community, knowingly or not. Ruskin derives this vocabulary mainly from Augustinian strands of Christianity, though he extends its critical possibilities as he examines the activities and relationships of contemporary life. As he turns toward Victorian culture, he rejects the theological conviction of his youth that God alone dictates the structure of the good. Nevertheless, his religious training in Evangelical practices of daily Bible memorization and typological exegesis hone his excellences as a biblical exegete and a symbolic interpreter, and these virtues carry forward into his interpretive skills as a culture-analyst and a culture-maker. Finally, as he looks to traditions other than Evangelical Anglicanism, not only do these religions become historical repositories of different visions of the good for him, but more importantly, they model the need for an integrated set of practices to make these visions "real" for adherents.

Ruskin's development as a practical critic complicates the history of religious ethics if we take seriously his cultural conception of religions. On Ruskin's cultural model, religious identity is more practical than theological. As a result, it makes little sense to narrow the scope of the field of Christian ethics to theologians and church officials, leaving figures like Ruskin outside the canon and omitting the religious resources he offers for an ethics of economic life. His sensibility as a religious critic is also more eclectic than uniform. It should not be a mark against him that his critical vision extended into so many spheres of culture or that he drew widely in his innovative readings of Christianity and other religions. To be a religious thinker, one does not have to start from first principles derived from a religious tradition that then get applied to the cultural mix. Instead, a culturally engaged religious critic finds affinities among the practices of various religious traditions and between these practices and the other activities of a culture. All the while, he or she offers the lessons at hand to other people and invites them to put their own hands, and minds, to work in imagining the "binding" ties and commitments that should organize their lives. A theological tradition cordoned off from cultural engagement loses the insights gained from Ruskin's descriptive ethical criticism. More worrisome, it fails to take responsibility for the historical views of a major religious critic whose moral arguments join a trenchant critique of industrial capitalism with a defense of hierarchy that appeals partly to Christianity.

In assessing Ruskin's religious sensibility and its place in his ethics of consumption, a comment by Christopher Lasch is instructive. Remarking on recent calls for consumers to discipline their spending, Lasch notes that "progressives" tend to reject appeals for self-restraint as a privilege of the well-off. Instead, social justice first requires unchecked economic growth to ensure a minimally decent standard of living for all. "The trouble with this argument," Lasch writes, "is that political pressure for a more equitable distribution of wealth can come only from movements fired with religious purpose and a lofty conception of life. . . . If the many now enjoy some of the comforts formerly restricted to the few, it is because they have won them through their own political efforts, not because the wealthy have freely surrendered their privileges or because the market automatically assures abundance for all."[1] This claim that reform movements require a vision of "religious purpose and a lofty conception of life" seems partly right in view of the history of social change (one thinks of the Abolitionists and the Civil Rights Movement in the United States) and partly disturbing in light of that same history, too (one thinks of justifications of slavery and opposition to women's rights). I mention Lasch to put a similarly ambivalent spotlight on Ruskin's moralism as it relates to his religious sensibility that, in every society, there will be "binding" practices and that matters of distributive justice and the goals of human well-being should be addressed in reference to them.

"Character" and "vision" interrelate in any teleological ethics. In order to develop one's character well, one must see how certain activities and excellences have their point in the good. In order to envision the good, one must cultivate the character needed to pursue key aspects of it. If we apply this circular dynamic to Lasch's example, it would appear that movements for social change demand more than a sense of "religious purpose and a lofty conception of life." They also demand people who have the formative experiences and the character traits to see the point of this vision and the more meaningful life and the better society that might be achieved.

This suggestion that insiders can imagine moral possibilities that outsiders cannot puts into sharp relief the issues raised by Ruskin's insistent search for a formative moral vision in his teleological ethics. As he puts it in "Modern Education" (1853), religion teaches "Where [a man] is going," and he thinks every nation and community must take this question seriously (11.258). But here is the dilemma. The more that ethical reflection proceeds from a vision of the good reflecting a particular religious identity or social location, the less likely it seems that this normative approach can help us decide where "we" are going together, given democratic commitments to individual liberties, heterogeneous tastes, and rational public discourse.

Teleological Ethics and Democratic Consent

Consider an illustration of this problem taken from Ruskin's 1858 lecture "The Work of Iron, in Nature, Art, and Policy." This lecture offers the fullest portrait of his ideal economy and the "imagined good" that would make for justice and abundance. I have already explored the appeal to iron's affinity for the "breath of life" and its "natural" binding with oxygen as a typical example of the religious appeals in Ruskin's social criticism, offered as they are in a spirit of revivifying the metaphors and ideals of Victorian culture. I passed over his symbolic renderings of the "sword" and the "fetter" in the lecture's final pages.

The sword represents the honor and courage of martial virtue, and Ruskin challenges his listeners to apply these ideals to their own lives. They should honor soldiers, by educating them instead of simply sacrificing them and by guaranteeing that they have to fight only for just aims. Courage is required in the populace, too, specifically, the courage to work for a just peace at home. Criticizing the empty religious practices of his contemporaries, Ruskin writes, do not buy "your peace, with silenced consciences, . . . broken vows, . . . lying words, . . . base connivances, . . . smiling at your serene hearths, lisping comfortable prayers evening and morning, and counting your pretty Protestant beads (which are flat, and of gold, instead of round, and of ebony, as the monks' ones were)" (16.409–10). Ruskin's icon of the "fetter" also applies to his audience, for it symbolizes "the typical instrument of the restraint or subjection necessary in a nation—either literally, for its evil-doers, or figuratively, in accepted laws, for its wise and good men." In this, the briefest part of "The Work of Iron," he declares his usual antipathy for liberty as always baser than restraint. And then he turns right around, admitting the folly of reasoning from "abstraction, for both liberty and restraint are good when they are nobly chosen, and both are bad when they are basely chosen" (16.407–8). As always, questions of character and purpose, desires and ends, lead the way in Ruskin's argumentation, which is why he insists that deliberating about good lives and the common good comes first.

What is disturbing here and in philosophical arguments for rational subjection to the good more generally is that, right at the point where "deliberation" is called for, it seems foreclosed. There are two argumentative styles at work in this section on the sword and the fetter. On the one hand, Ruskin loves provocation, and he often sets up his audience's expectations (for a paean to the virtue of warriors) only to draw a surprising conclusion—that today's heroes oppose unjust wars abroad and economic injustice at home. On the other hand, he loves dualism, and lining up his favorite dualisms—life versus death, paternal governance versus liberal anarchy, true worship versus false idolatry—reminds us of the opposition between "obedience" and "liberty" that repeats throughout his social criticism. Here in "The Work of Iron," it appears that the members of his audience are asked to obey his vision of the good, for only then will they gain the practical knowledge and develop the virtues required in good consumers.

To state the issue more sharply, if teleological approaches to ethics work only when the members of a populace first submit themselves to the authoritative arrangement of the virtues and excellences, roles and duties, goods and ends, that are rightly "binding" on their individual tastes and desires, their economic choices and social relationships, and their reasoned moral judgments, then we have powerful democratic reasons for resisting Ruskin's criticism and his religious sensibility.

In this study I have argued against this assessment, and I have detailed how Ruskin's conceptual adjustments as a practical critic help make his arguments compatible with democratic commitments. The most important of these adjustments are, first, his movement beyond the Christian "theoria" of his early aesthetics as he develops into a practical critic; second, his broader turn toward culture as an arena of common life where people must learn to "recognize" what is good in their shared inheritance while imaginatively "making" it anew; and finally, his reconception of religions as part of this cultural mix. In concluding, I discuss how theoretical and practical reason, recognition and making, and religion and politics relate in Ruskin's mature criticism to show that democracy is served by the kind of searching vision of the good that remains a central feature of his reflections on consumption, culture, and religion.

Ethics and Economics, Practical and Theoretical Reason

In chapter 1 I compared Ruskin's early writings to J. B. Schneewind's model of "Divine Corporation ethics." In this teleological framework God ordains the duties and ends attaching to every station in the great hierarchy of life, and God brings the perfections of each participant into a harmony of mutual flourishing.[2] Ruskin's criticisms of classical political economy as being incapable of meeting the challenges of distributive justice and character formation map neatly onto this framework. For Ruskin, every individual's contributions, excellences, and toil would ideally be measured and compensated in light of his or her role in this corporate body of life. Likewise every person would ideally receive the aid and opportunities needed to develop his or her virtues, excellences, capabilities, and talents to their fullest.

Ruskin charges consumers to make these ideals a reality when he asks, for example, what is the "real politico-economical significance" of the dresses that ladies wear to high society balls? He answers

> that you have had a certain number of people put for a certain number of days wholly under your authority, by the sternest of slave-masters,—hunger and cold; and you have said to them, "I will feed you, indeed, and clothe you, and give you fuel for so many days; but during those days you shall work for me only: your little brothers need clothes . . . your sick friend needs clothes, but you shall make none for [them]: you yourself will soon need another and a warmer dress, but you shall make none for yourself. You shall make nothing but lace and roses for me; for this fortnight to come, you shall work at the patterns and petals, and then I will crush and consume them away in an hour." (16.50)

Both the imaginative reach of this example and the potent sense of moral complicity that Ruskin brings to it reflect his conviction that it is possible and desirable to attain an overall vision of the good served by an economy. He departs from the Divine Corporation model, however, because he throws off the creaturely limitations on human knowledge of the good and on individual responsibility for the whole enterprise. No longer must people cling to their stations to chasten their fallen desires; rather they must make their own desires good.

This comparison of Divine Corporation ethics to Ruskin's ethics of consumption teaches an important lesson. Every ethics of consumption requires broad judgments about desire; some desires are better than others, and they are better not only for oneself but for other people, too. In evaluating one's desires as a consumer, desires that lead to buying choices, reflective consumers (especially those with the most money) choose not only what vision of the good life to purchase for themselves, but also what activities, capabilities, and excellences other people should be "free" to seek out and develop. This means that prescriptive judgments about how to make other people's lives good are unavoidable in an ethics of consumption. Consuming well means refusing to accept current individual preferences and existing societal conditions, imagining instead an economy that produces greater well-being, as one envisions it, for everyone affected by one's choices.

Progressives can get queasy when discussions of desire move beyond critical suspicion to constructive argument. Ruskin insists that both tasks are necessary. He certainly recognizes that Victorian desires are constructed within structures of power, and he denounces at nearly every turn the culture of individualism he sees being produced by industrial capitalism and liberal institutions. This idea that cultures are humanly made products and that they constitute individuals to the very core of their desires is familiar. Cultural analysis, critique, and resistance are hallmarks of today's academic discussions from art history and political theory to consumption studies and ethics. What Ruskin adds to this picture is his inquiry into cultural activities and the character that people develop within them. Thus his moralistic scrutiny of his contemporaries' character reflects his conviction that their ethical, aesthetic, and economic judgments are culturally constructed, but—and this is a crucial point and the promise of his criticism—in ways that can be made practically intelligible and therefore subjected to reasoned critique and moral reform. Today's analysts of consumer desire typically reject Ruskin's language of virtues, ends, good lives, and the common good in favor of theoretical accounts of desire's construction. But relying on theory alone limits the critical resources available to us and lessens the likelihood of building broad public support for collective goals and social responsibility.

One of the most important lessons Ruskin teaches is that his virtues-centered critique of capitalism and the descriptive models of political economy differ in how they relate theory to practice. Ruskin draws this contrast sharply because, on the one hand, he shows that classical political economy relies on a normally unacknowledged whole vision of economic life and because, on the other hand, he endeavors to articulate an alternative approach to arriving at such a theoretical vision. The key point is this: classical political economy and Ruskin's alternative both treat theory as an aid to practical reason, but they conceive theoretical and practical reason very differently. Clarifying these interactions between theoretical and practical reason shows the limitations of moral and political arguments that rely exclusively on the theoretical frameworks that have displaced Ruskin's teleological approach.

Ruskin's conception of practical reason starts from an idea of people as desiring subjects who are always having to choose how to arrange the ends and goods they seek. He sees these practical choices as *developmental,* not *instrumental.* Although at any point in a person's life we might isolate a set of preferences, wants, and needs, these desires have both a personal and a cultural history. In other words, people's desires reflect past decisions, both their own and others', most notably about the activities that already do, or ideally would, make up their lives. The constant cycling in a person's selection of specific endeavors that shape his or her character is the central dynamic in Ruskin's model of practical reason. These choices are not a strictly "individual" affair—nor are they merely "subjective" preferences—because the activities give a cultural shape to participants' desires. It is this cultural shaping through social practices and human activity more generally that occupies Ruskin as he moves past his early art criticism.

Although Ruskin updates this character-based account of human activity and practical reason, it has a history. While he exhibits the sage's typical reluctance to cite past influences, he acknowledges Plato, Aristotle, Richard Hooker, and other "guides." For each of them, practical questions about the ends, goods, and virtues that should steer a person's life are integrally related to theoretical reflection about the good. Here we see how practical reason and theoretical reason interact for Ruskin. Theory aids practical reason by offering a vision of how best to order people's goals, endeavors, and relationships so as to make for a good life and contribute to the common good. Even acknowledging that the proponents of this approach disagree about whether such a "theoretical vision" is attainable and how it might be discerned, there are clear differences between this teleological approach to ethics and the empirical models of economics.

In describing the conception of practical reason operative in economics, the most relevant place to look is the discipline's model of individuals' buying behavior. The type of practical reason modeled here is *instrumental,* not *developmental.* The model does not examine how people come to choose certain ends, goods, and activities over time, defining their desires and character in the process. It simply starts with existing preferences and seeks to maximize utility. Certainly it is acknowledged that individuals' economic choices—from the prioritization of their preferences to the meanings that they attach to commodities—reflect the broader purposes and values to which they commit themselves and the associations into which they enter. But these purposes, meanings, and values and the associations and the conceptions of the good that sustain them can all be set aside because they have no direct bearing on the marketplace. What matters in this arena is the empirical question of how individuals will act given their current schedule of preferences and the existing structure of market prices for commodities.

The task of practical reason in economic life is now much narrower. Most importantly, this modest portrait of economic choice appears self-contained in a way that allows us to omit the contentious issue of having to debate and articulate any "theoretical vision" of the good. The functions of economic theory seem similarly modest, even as the theory has descriptive power. Consider how the theory describes the operation of market competition. The collective buying choices of consumers, along with the constant entry of sellers into profitable opportunities and their exit from failing enterprises, maintain the market's short-term efficiency by continually adjusting to "Pareto Optimal" equilibria. It is a mistake to conclude, however, that the practical decisions modeled here are unaided by a theoretical vision. In my judgment this is one of the most telling insights of Ruskin's social criticism.

Economic models seem to offer only a descriptive account of the workings of the market. But the market itself provides a "theoretical vision" of the complex whole of a great many individuals' efforts, preferences, choices, and interactions. What market exchange achieves, in theory, is a continual adjustment to the aggregate preferences and choices of many individuals, and this gets expressed in the accurate pricing of every commodity. The practical decisions that individuals make are therefore aided by the market's capacity to provide a vision of the whole economy unavailable to any one participant. Thus theory still affords a vision of the whole, but it does so now by tracing out people's behavior at the empirical level without any explicit attention to how people order their lives around particular goods, ends, and activities, generating and pursuing broader meanings in the things they make, use, and enjoy.

These two different conceptions of practical reason reflect and rely upon distinct ideas of theoretical reason. As already noted, there are legitimate reasons to be wary of Ruskin's critical efforts to envision the good for all. The great achievement of the classical models of economics seems, then, to be their helping to make *historically effective* a reconception of theoretical reason that avoids these pitfalls. It appears that democracy is served by jettisoning concerted efforts at moral imagination about the good. No one has to be instructed in the makings of good lives; no one has to be taught which cultural activities are better and worse. Instead, individuals are at liberty to consume as they choose, and the aggregated choices of the market contribute to the governance of society without requiring people to cultivate certain excellences, to embrace shared standards, or to adopt a common vision before they are eligible to pass moral judgments on "where we should be going."

Insofar as ethics sets aside critical reflection about the ends, goods, and virtues we pursue in our practical activities, it accepts two things. First, it accepts a theoretical basis for its work that limits moral debate and social cooperation to a system of fair play and principled boundaries that tend to narrow obligations and insulate individuals' desires from scrutiny. This way of framing ethical reflection and modern societies does valuable service in liberal polities, which Ruskin simply failed to appreciate. It is not just that we cannot achieve greater agreement about good lives and good societies, making this "compromise" solution the best we can do. Rather, these self-directed ways of thinking and the institutions that help sustain independent spaces of social conflict, moral disagreement, and public debate serve to make our lives our own to shape, and this liberty is crucial to their being "good."

Second, there is, however, a problem in taking theoretical accounts of our common life as a full description of it. Ironically this narrowing of our moral vision prevents us from arguing that liberal institutions were created and continue to receive support because we agree that good lives include liberty as one of their components. This narrowing of moral vision also has the pernicious effect of circumscribing efforts to shape good lives as demanding nothing more than "subjective" preferences mediated through a structure of institutions that become, by default, the sole means of arriving at societal "agreements." This circumscription of the moral imagination degrades and excuses a noble task. I use the Ruskinian language of nobility and degradation intentionally, even though it echoes with his fondness for hierarchical structures that make some people "nobles" while grading all others according to "natural" characteristics such as birth, talent, or sex. While I reject the aristocratic and gendered implications of Ruskin's restricting certain virtues to specific kinds of people, I commend his reflection on the virtues for elevating concerns with the distinctive excellences that make people dignified and with the public ends that make societies just.

Ruskin's criticism teaches that theory cannot do away with the need for moral vision. Theory stands in for practical reflection about the good, offering an abstract vision of "where we are" and "where we are going." We see these limitations in Marx's overreliance on theoretical accounts that strip human agency by denying grounds for normative reflection and in Mill's principled protections of individual liberty that narrowly construe the injuries inflicted and suffered in economic life. Theory has its uses, of course, as do the liberal institutions it describes, more appreciatively in Mill's writings and more critically in Marx's. When Ruskin retreats to his dichotomy between "restraint" versus "liberty," he simply fails to ask when liberty is good and when it is nobly chosen. In order to answer such questions, we must also recognize, as Ruskin did not, how liberal institutions protect certain freedoms that allow people to cultivate their desires in activities of their own choosing and toward projects of their own design. Always an appreciative "recognition" of our cultural, political, economic, social, and religious inheritance is necessary to an imaginative "making" of better lives. In other words, we need to explore both paths at the crossroads of nineteenth-century critical thought, combining the critical insights of Mill's and Marx's theories with the moral vocabulary of Ruskin's teleological ethics.

A shorthand way to sum up the differences between these three figures is that Ruskin is more enamored of the aesthetic and the religious, the two domains of culture that summon forth the heartfelt and absorbing responses he associates with good character and moral vision. In this matrix of ethical concerns, we see why his effort to envision the "whole" of life, the "imagined good" of an economy, is a strong tendency throughout his writings. Likewise, we have good reasons to challenge those places in his criticism where the aesthetic and the religious become mysterious sources of intuited wisdom. Far better are his more tentative, partial, culturally contingent, and audience-exposed ways of trying to convince readers of their moral capacities for imagining what they do or should hold in common with other people and how their ethical reflection and practical goals might be directed toward individual excellence, communal abundance, and social justice.

Aesthetic Agreement and Good Consumption

Ruskin is a moralist, much more so than the secular theorists Marx and Mill. Ruskin cut his interpreter's lens in an art criticism informed by his early theological conception of the good and his didactic tendencies. His ethics of consumption builds from his evolving teleological approach and his devotion to aesthetic interpretation. A remark by Stanley Cavell on the limits of explanation in matters of aesthetic judgment helps make sense of Ruskin's vehemence in urging his audiences to become better consumers. At some point, Cavell notes, aesthetic judgments call for reasons like, "don't you see, don't you hear, don't you dig?" If such reasons fail to move you, then the critic can "start training and instructing you and preaching at you" because explanation is limited if one does not already "see *something.*" Cavell continues, "A critic like Ruskin can be a bit eager in seizing this direction, but it is a measure of his honesty, and his devotion to art, never to shrink from it; as it is part of the permanence of his writing to exemplify that moral passion which is a *natural* extension of the critical task."[3] As we have seen, Ruskin does not restrict his moralism to the subject of art. He intrudes himself upon people's character and desires, goals and vision, in all of the cultural spheres he analyzes from art and architecture to natural history and religion to politics and economics.

The arguments, examples, and language of Ruskin's ethics of consumption are meant to provoke a response in his audiences. Often he constructs a set of scenes that when held side by side provide evidence in the form of a shock of recognition, of "something" seen anew, which vitiates accepted practices and arrangements. The scenes he paints—the competitive bidding of wage workers to drive down the prices paid to all, the "origins" of money in the debts acquired by a prudent farmer and now "accidental master," the consumption of a dressmaker's life for a few hours of fashionable pleasures—are meant to convince his audience that they already do "see something," in fact, many things. They recognize that the virtues of justice and piety are worthy, even if they do not fully understand them or practice them well. They also recognize the images of beauty manufactured by current styles and the hierarchies of status signaled by the accoutrements of high fashion. All of Ruskin's redescriptions of economic life work by substituting in a changed interpretive backdrop that highlights the cultural and evaluative nature of all consumption while calling into question the judgments his contemporaries typically make.

Thus he puzzles over the fascination with "excrescences of shell-fish . . . and pieces of blue and red stone" as things that depend on scarcity rather than abundance in people's estimate of their worth (17.85). On the subject of the peculiar power of what he calls the "pluses" of profits in dispelling concern over the human costs, or "minuses," involved in getting them, he writes more sweepingly; "the pluses, make a very positive and venerable appearance in the world, so that every one is eager to learn the science which produces results so magnificent; whereas the minuses have, on the other hand, a tendency to retire into back streets, and other places of shade—or even to get themselves wholly and finally put out of sight in graves: which renders the algebra of this science peculiar, and difficultly legible" (17.91–92). The responses he seeks are once again of the "don't you see, don't you hear, don't you dig" sort. If not, then consider iron's affinity for the "breath of life" and all that follows from recognizing its "gifted" character. Most notably, like Nabal and Dives in the Bible, the wealthy refuse to look across class boundaries. As the Bible states, with their eyes "set *against*" not "merely set *away* from the poor," the powerful willfully deny the debts and dependences that can be seen only by striving to imagine the whole intercourse of economic life (16.399).

Each of these examples is meant to persuade a Victorian audience that their taste for jewels and desire for profits put a stranglehold on their imaginations. Unless they learn to recognize what is most valuable in their cultural activities and inheritance, they will not be able to imagine the better lives they might create and enjoy together.

The challenge confronting Ruskin can be summed up in the cliché, given authority in the Latin phrasing, that there is no disputing about taste: *De gustibus non est disputandum.* Typically this dictum gets invoked to carve out a space of freedom around the "subjectivity" of tastes, but there is another way to read its meaning. It is impossible to dispute matters of individual taste because it is so difficult to fathom how taste is formed to begin with and, more importantly, how those formations of desire "bind" us culturally and socially. Taste appears to be a narrow concept, dealing with little more than such supposedly "indifferent" matters as the arts. But insofar as tastes steer desires toward certain ends, as in all consumption, an uncritical acceptance of merely subjective tastes becomes untenable. Although tastes for some goods are indifferent matters, Ruskin teaches us not only to work toward shared agreements about good consumption, but also to recognize all that currently binds individual desires and public tastes.

Beginning with his earliest art criticism, Ruskin clings to this conviction about the inseparability of taste and ethics because he senses that his fellow Victorians hold more in common than they allow. The idea that individuals have purely subjective tastes, free of the formative influences of character, culture, and community, makes no sense to him. Desires are teleological; they point to the goods and the ends that are sought and the patterns of cultural significance and the structures of economic interdependence through which people evaluate and strive to obtain, use, and enjoy what they want. Consumption is thus both a perplexity and an opportunity for him. In the realm of consumption, the task of imagining and committing with others to common ends and shared goods is both so difficult and so urgent because in "our" theory, rhetoric, and self-conception, we see ourselves as "unbound" individuals.

The workings of aesthetic judgment give the lie to the notion of purely subjective tastes in the realm of art—people must already "see something." As we move onto consumption, the critical task of searching out and evaluating the prevailing agreements in economic life is more complex due to the expanses of economic life and the sheer variety from which consumers have to choose. The more occasional and piecemeal arguments of Ruskin's social criticism reflect this complexity. As he moves to meet the interpretive and rhetorical challenges introduced by this more wide-ranging and culturally engaged criticism, he works as an imaginative critic, reading the contemporary landscape of practical activity, aiming to provoke a broader vision of economic life in a way that exposes people's moral complicity and self-deception while remaining subject to his audience's critical responses.[4] As Ruskin puts his own moral imagination into practice in his ethics of consumption, he invites his contemporaries to "see" what he sees, while leaving them to imagine the implications for themselves.

Consider how his critique of industrial capitalism and his evocative vision of good lives can call forth an appreciative, though critical, response. Ruskin's argument about the lack of "virtue" in iron fences prescribes a clear-cut preference for wrought ironwork over fences of iron spikes. Consumers should buy wrought iron fences because the workers who craft them deserve to have their products purchased because this work fosters their excellences. But what should be done for the factory workers who mass-produce iron railings and bars? In light of Ruskin's account of the "just price," these workers would seem to deserve an even higher price due to their suffering toil. In "The Work of Iron," however, their labors deserve no support at all because this work is not good for workers or consumers. Ruskin's insistence that workers be bound to the social practices and excellences that he deems best for them is paternalistic. Very quickly, then, the admirable commitments of character ethics to human development, individual excellence, creative work, and common goods run into the problem of paternalism when the imperious critic or consumer imposes a vision of the good life on everyone affected by his or her choices.

For Ruskin consumption is simply too important to leave to individual taste, which is why he places at the center of his ethics of consumption the educative endeavor of cultivating his contemporaries' virtues. Indeed, we must not forget that he chose to construct this ethics in public lectures, essays, and letters. These occasional forms of direct appeal suit him well because he so readily adopts an authorial tone of voice and so keenly understands the arts of persuasion. A tension exists, however, between his authorial manner of address and his turn toward individual consumers as the authorities on economic life. Too often he acts as the ideal consumer, not as a critic crafting his own innovative uses of a vocabulary of the virtues and coining imaginative cultural readings in order to provoke others to do the same. That is not to make the same choices in their consumption, but to become practical critics in their own right.

Crucial here is the distinction between *a practice* of good consumption and *practices* of good consumption. What Ruskin finds most objectionable about the iron fences dividing Britain is that they cut off intercourse between their owners and everyone outside. Other fences do not erect the same insurmountable barriers, even if they offer spaces of independence—arenas for choosing one's activities and commitments—separate, yet not entirely removed, from shared spaces of moral regard and societal interdependence. Ruskin's call for decorative iron fences splits this difference between consumer sovereignty and uniform taste. In consumers' buying excellent craftwork, they do more than support forms of labor that are "good for" workers. They engage with the activity to the extent that they recognize why other people might choose the work. That is, they cross over the barrier separating workers and consumers, making possible shared judgments of things' goodness. Moreover, in buying and erecting iron fences crafted with an eye to the formal beauty of grasses, leaves, and vines, consumers offer passersby opportunities to learn the value and meaning that these fences have for committed practitioners who are knowledgeable in natural history and formal design. Once again a boundary is crossed freely, even as in choosing to cross that boundary one subjects one's taste and judgments to external reform.

These fences and the moral imagination and shared judgments they help to form represent a public space for ethical reflection in economic life, a space centered in the activities that people choose to support or join. This boundary crossing, this recognition of the goods attainable through other people's creative reworking of culture, adds to the economic exchange of ordinary things the "gifts" of an abundant life. At the same time, the meeting place of a wrought iron fence sits within a money economy that preserves spaces for competing visions of good lives and, thus, the refusal of unwanted "gifts." In sum, Ruskin's crafted fences point to the restructuring of economic exchange as an ethical encounter to the extent that people band together in practices of good consumption of their own design. These fences—well made, well chosen, and well used—allow different people—workers, consumers, and passersby—a space of mutual recognition, common purpose, and shared judgments of the value and meaning of economic goods along with the more independent spaces needed to choose which activities and commitments fit one's vision of good lives and a good society and, so, become enriching of and binding on one's consumption.

This part of Ruskin's ethics of consumption—his call to his fellow Victorians to engage their moral imaginations in seeking out the activities best able to develop people's virtues and capabilities, to fashion cultural ideals and standards, and to promote broader judgments about and common commitments to goods that reach beyond one's own current preferences—does not, in itself, mandate any single practice of good consumption nor any singular conception of the good. The attempt to imagine a broader vision of the "whole" of economic life is inescapable in any ethics where consumers have to account for the moral claims attaching to all that they buy, but if we follow out Ruskin's turn toward culture and the myriad activities constituting contemporary life, then the normative visions that consumers bring to their buying will reflect their choices about the best activities to participate in and support. There will be diversity of vision, therefore, even as there will be spaces where reflective consumers can forge agreements about how to consume well. Although the spatial metaphor of an iron fence is located in a specific place, these practices of good consumption can join people far away from each other.

Since Ruskin's day there are many examples of people banding together in practices of good consumption and seeking to persuade other people to join in. Just as his vocabulary of the virtues can be an invaluable resource, these other initiatives have fashioned their own appeals in articulating their concerns, commitments, and goals. There are many ways of talking about all that attaches to our consumption—buying locally and buying black, choosing green products and supporting the arts, boycotting unfair employers and checking for "No Sweat" labels, and paying for environmental cleanups and safeguards. We also recognize the shameful costs of our consumption—averting eyes from garbage collectors who ply our streets only to get from us what we would rather not acknowledge, almost as much as we would rather not acknowledge them. Or, take an easier instance because the distances ensure that we have to face only ourselves. Maybe we wonder what the tag "Made in China" reveals about that pair of running shoes that fits so well. What level of inequity is at stake: cowed labor or only non-union labor? It helps to have a range of options to sort through, even if the best option is unacceptable. Not knowing for sure how bad things are can be as good as not knowing for sure that they are bad. So many difficulties and excuses stand in the way of a clear moral vision of good consumption that mostly we deny its importance, putting our faith in one theory or another.

Ruskin calls individual consumers to a searching vision of their own sense of good lives, the common good, shared goods, and the "binding" practices requisite to them—a vision that if acted upon deliberately can find and persuade other people of its wisdom, thereby fostering the ethical exchanges, shared judgments, common commitments, *and* public debate that are finally the substance of the educative efforts, political action, and societal reform needed to make an ethics of consumption practical and desirable. Apart from the social spaces of a great many practices of good consumption, it is difficult to see how the imaginative vision of an ethics of economic life can gain any purchase on the sweep of a global economy that mirrors far too closely the theoretical premises of classical political economy and its inability to address the aims of distributive justice and human development.

Religion, Authority, and Argument in Public Life

Religion, and its conceptual equivalent, "tradition," have become emblematic of "something" in recent debates about modern liberalism. How much agreement in our visions of the good is possible and desirable in liberal democracies? Where should our efforts at agreement and our responsibilities to each other focus—on the means or the ends of good lives? Among left-leaning intellectuals, the debate is about the relationship between solidarity and freedom. For those who criticize the minimalist arrangements of liberal institutions, moral discourse and mutual concern are impossible apart from the formative practices and harmonious ends of a community united in its vision of the good. For those who reject the ideological effects of appeals to a communal consensus about the ends that "we all" desire, democratic arrangements and public deliberation must be conducted on the basis of universally acceptable reasons that do not privilege any one vision of the good.

Ruskin also "sees something" in the gestures of worship, the symbols of divine gifts, and the stories of common life in religious traditions. He suggests that if these visionary resources are put into practice by imaginatively critical people, then they can help turn a society's organizing ends and institutional structures and its schemes of economic valuation and social regard toward good. To the extent that Ruskin heeds his own recognition of the culturally contingent grounds of his religious appeals and the need to make his arguments persuasive to people who are free to debate and dispute his claims, he shows the way beyond the limitations of his teleological ethics. The example of his criticism also demonstrates the importance of religious reasons in public deliberations along with the independent spaces of judgment and critique that liberal institutions preserve.

We find two types of religious appeal scattered throughout Ruskin's criticism. There are the appeals that presuppose a metaphysics of the good, a prophetic intuition of God's own moral purposes. A typical example of these appeals is his definition of "intrinsic value" as the "power [a thing] holds from the Maker of things and of men." Here the singular purpose of a resource is independent of human judgment about the uses and ends of things (17.84). Such appeals to a "whole" vision of life's perfection—intuited by the great seer and not at all subject to his audiences' imaginative response—warrant critical scrutiny.

The other type of religious appeal reflects Ruskin's growing appreciation of human "making" in every cultural sphere, religion included. I traced these transformations out in part 2. In chapter 3 we saw Ruskin appealing to the biblical Job as needing to learn a natural piety. This appeal directs his readers to attend to the natural world but leaves it to them to draw the specific moral taught by their practical pursuits and imaginative readings of nature's intricate beauty and awesome might. In chapter 4 I noted Ruskin's metaphorical readings of the economic sins that Dante associates with Plutus and the sirens. The same two characters populate Victorian society, Ruskin charges, prompting his readers to consider how closely their own character matches either type and what they might do to avoid these failures of moral vision. In chapter 5 I ended with Ruskin's allusion to the thieves crucified at Golgotha as the best illustration of how the religious appeals of his social criticism typically work. Here he juxtaposes Victorian practices and priorities with a starkly different scene of the moral life incumbent on his fellow Christians, even if they have forgotten the shock of recognizing "something" in their heritage that they had better not have neglected.

The difference between these types of religious appeal highlights the two different modes of Ruskin's moral vision. On the one hand, he paints miniature canvases of human activity and association, both past and present, to provoke his audience to see their society's failings more clearly. In the manner of his art criticism, as described by Cavell, Ruskin locates readers in a scene that cannot but spark some kind of identification, some moral regard, some broader purpose, leading readers to exercise their independent judgment while also prompting a recognition of shared cultural norms. On the other hand, sometimes his efforts to provoke other people's moral imagination aim at conversion to his singular conception of the good. That is, he circumscribes the canvases of his criticism within an idealized composition of a perfectly unified, harmonious whole of paternal "government and cooperation," the sole alternative to which is the "anarchy and competition" of modern liberalism. Simply put, Ruskin's religious appeals sometimes rely on a perfectly beautiful vision of the "whole," an aestheticized vision of social life, not at all provisional or open to deliberation.

These two different types of appeal have everything to do with how religion, authority, and argument interact in Ruskin's corpus. Recall that he moves away from a belief-centered conception of religions as he comes to see religions as part of the cultural mix. In chapters 1 through 4, we saw him reorient his teleological approach from a theological conception of the good to a culturally located telos, with practices of religious worship serving as one, but only one, of the arenas in which people imagine the good by performing the stories, symbols, rituals, and ideals of their traditions. No longer does he hold to the belief-centered view of religion presumed in his early aesthetics. Although he never claimed that the "pure in heart" had only to align their inward beliefs with a saving truth, his early theory of beauty set aside human excellences and cultural practices. It narrowly construed the ascent to God's perfect ordering of life as a matter of intuiting the metaphysical structure of nature's beauty. By Ruskin's late writings, the doctrinal insularity of this portrait of the religious life is intolerable and unintelligible for him—intolerable because the inwardly turned religiosity he now associates with "modern Protestantism" distracts his fellow Christians from the sufferings of the people around them and unintelligible because he no longer sees how there can be any worship apart from the practices of historical traditions and the enlivening imagination of individuals.

If we adopt the belief-centered conception of religion in Ruskin's early writings, then the question of religion—"Where [one] is going"—is a question about which beliefs are essential to the final destination. If the public lectures and essays of Ruskin's social criticism presuppose this same conception of religion, then his audience must already share or readily submit to the requisite beliefs for his arguments to have any authority for them. On this view, a doctrinal consensus about the good is essential to the critic's success in marshalling public support for social change. If this describes the necessary conditions for public reflection about good lives and the common good, then public intellectuals who make such appeals are unlikely to generate more than a short-lived following of ardent believers.

In chapters 3 and 4 I argued, however, that "Modern Education" marks the start of the practice-centered conception of religion that Ruskin works out over the rest of his career. On this view, religious traditions encompass a range of practices, and these practices bear family resemblances to other cultural activities instead of being qualitatively distinct as in Ruskin's early aesthetics. What joins a person's commitments is not the singular vision of the good organizing the common beliefs of a group of devotees, but the ensemble of activities that individuals choose to participate in or support and the extent to which they engage themselves with the goods, ends, excellences, and standards of those practices. Here knowing "where [one] is going" and, more importantly, convincing others to share in that vision are very different matters. They require the exercise of a moral imagination capable of taking in the wide variety of activities constituting a culture, the signs of virtue and vitality in some people's endeavors and interactions, the ends and excellences they seek, and the prospects for extending this flourishing to other people with the greatest benefit and the least cost. As Ruskin also comes to recognize, these imaginative efforts can be made "real" only through the active "help" of the audience's responses.

Prophetic authority is one thing; prophetic voice is another. Ruskin's image of journeying toward a common destination through the "binding" ties of religions clarifies this distinction. The critic who speaks with prophetic authority—"Thus saith the Lord"—imagines the telos on the model of a necessary, perfect, and final set of ends, the truth of which is intuited by those with the right beliefs. In this belief-centered approach, the role of religions in public discourse has two typical expressions. On the one hand, an embattled encampment of wanderers in the wilderness must protect against idolatrous enemies, both inside and outside of its small group. On the other hand, an exiled people who have at last returned to the promised land insist on reinstituting the religious, social, and familial institutions that served their ancestors so well when the faith was common and pure. These narratives of aliens in a foreign land and of decline from a harmonious past are with us still. In both cases the necessary condition for social justice and communal abundance is a faithful agreement among the people to submit to a common belief in a singular vision of the good. Let me stress the priority of this faithful agreement; the people must first be "made" to obey that formative vision, and the prophetic word is Gospel.

In the case of prophetic voice, however, although there is a common destination in view and the critic tries to articulate a core set of ends for good human lives, the focus is on the existing activities of a culture. The difference is not just scope of vision, but location of vision. When the critic looks to the current arrangements of human activity in a culture, different avenues may be taken toward the same goal, and this opens up various argumentative inroads for the critic. Delight may be an essential component of the best human lives, for example, but the cultural forms and expressions of delight can vary from a fascination with the intricacy of living beings to a recurrent joy at a familiar hymn to an unexpected turn in a conversation to a new mechanical solution. The challenge is to convince an audience to care about the makings of good lives by offering glimpses of better and worse activities in which to realize them. After prompting the audience to recognize what is best and worst in the contemporary cultural landscape, then the critic must inspire the audience to take stock of their ethical commitments and apply their imaginations to the effort of envisioning and debating where they wish to go as a society. A prophetic voice adds urgency to the effort, but it does not prescribe a settled vision of the good for the audience. If this describes the cultural context for public reflection about "where [we are] going," then the critic still needs to appeal to those goods, ends, excellences, and standards that have a formative authority over people, but now as participants in a range of activities, religious and otherwise. Listeners need not be true believers—committed insiders—to see the point of those appeals and follow them out or dispute them as practical critics in their own right.

To the extent that Ruskin's public arguments remain open to these deliberative possibilities, his moralistic scrutiny of individual desires and cultural ends have a vital role to play in a democratic polity. Indeed, moral vision is a problem not only when it is imposed on people without their consent. The very difficulty of getting clear in one's moral vision is a problem, too, and it is a challenge that is cultural in nature. Just as no one can build a cathedral alone, no one can envision all that is worth caring about or its proper arrangement in good lives and a good society without drawing on the inherited resources of a culture even as one imagines them anew. I entitled this section "Religion, Authority, and Argument in *Public Life*," not "Public Reason," because I am persuaded that democratic deliberation must be open to the visionary aspects of people's ideals and aspirations that give meaning and purpose to their choices, relationships, and endeavors.

Without subscribing to this view, Jeffrey Stout has described the conditions for a democratic discourse that allows people to argue for public policies and priorities based on their religious convictions so long as they expose their religious premises and reasons to others' scrutiny to the extent that they can. Important for my purposes are Stout's attention to the "democratic virtues of speech" and his expectation "that different improvisations and different immanent criticisms—indeed, different vocabularies—might well be called for in response to each interlocutor." One of these democratic virtues is the "charity" of assuming that another person's religious arguments are backed by premises and reasons that can be made intelligible to people with different religious or secular outlooks. If we approach Ruskin's arguments with charity, it is clear that he meets this standard of reason giving as he weaves his arguments from religious grounds into the tapestry of his many-sided criticism. A charitable response to another person's religious arguments does not entail, however, deference to a set of beliefs one does not share. For Stout, respect is displayed by assuming one's interlocutor is a lover of justice and truth who will therefore give reasons and listen to criticisms of his or her argument that draw on the premises, norms, and examples of his or her tradition. I have brought this kind of immanent criticism to Ruskin's moralism. On the one hand, I have demonstrated the troubling ties between his drive for a unified moral vision and his defense of "natural" social hierarchies. On the other hand, I have shown the implausibility of this metaphysical certitude or even a singular vision of the good, given his own cultural conception of religions.

Stout also helpfully observes that today's communitarian critics and contractarian defenders of democratic liberalism invert each other's arguments about the conditions for rational discourse. Both camps base their hopes for a good society on "a single comprehensive normative vision," which in the case of John Rawls's followers becomes "a sort of all-purpose, abstract fairness," the mirror image of the communitarians' call for a consensus agreement to a substantive good. The problem, for Stout, is that neither group can "imagine ethical or political discourse *dialogically*."[5] Ruskin's aestheticized mode of argumentation and his anti-liberal politics seem to put him in the company of those who argue today that good lives and the good society are possible only where the members of a community are bound by the formative authority of a single religious tradition, a perfectly ordered arrangement of practices, and a comprehensive conception of the good. Yet Ruskin's critique of political economy, his analysis of Victorian culture, and his arguments for shared goods are not contingent on a finished telos and the beliefs essential to its pursuit. They are contingent on his descriptive ethical criticism of Victorian practices and institutions, presented anew through the fragmentary miniatures and the shocking connections of his public arguments. It is a style of criticism that unsettles standard arguments for and against liberalism. It is a style of normative reflection that deserves its due in the history of religious ethics. It is a style of engaged ethics that can assist us in finding new creative responses to global capitalism today.

Ruskin's practice-centered idea of religions fits our need for a public discourse rich enough to account for and contest our sociality—both the commitments we have to ensuring each other access to the means of life and the readiness we have to join together in activities in pursuit of shared ends. By contrast, the assumption that we cannot enter into reasoned exchanges that cross the boundaries of religious traditions or substantive accounts of good lives mimics the belief-centered conception of religion that shadows Ruskin's metaphysical appeals. Ruskin's wide-ranging practical criticism offers a model of an engaged ethics that is not bound by any final arrangement of divinely appointed ends and the religious beliefs necessary to their discernment. Instead of the prophetic authority he invokes at times, we should heed his prophetic voice. We need to imagine the ends we want to pursue together and to analyze the cultural activities that may or may not get us there. This combined ends-talk and cultural analysis remains a valuable model for any ethics dedicated to engaging people's moral imaginations as an ethics of consumption must.

Indeed, the realm of consumption is ideally suited to a recovery of Ruskin's teleological criticism. The strong presumption in favor of accepting the sovereignty of consumer tastes as the sole norm of economic life testifies to two key secular liberal convictions that, although they have merit, cannot serve us well if they are held unreflectively. The first conviction is that the freedom to form one's vision of life's meaning and purpose is so essential that the liberty of choice is put at a premium in aesthetic and economic matters where tastes and preferences seem so indisputably tied to personal vision. The second conviction is that theoretical accounts of institutional mechanisms like the market supply all that we need to know about individuals' behavior without having to intrude on people's actual desires and ends to argue about which ones are better or worse. These two convictions reflect legitimate qualms about presuming too much about people's character and desires, ends and vision. But we are already so driven by images of happiness, of visions of flourishing, that shape our very desires as consumers that we curtail our own and others' freedom when we fail to analyze and dispute our tastes and preferences. If we recognize the fact of constructed desires but allow theory to stand in for reflective deliberation about good lives and a good society, then we fail to imagine and deliberate about the people and society we wish to become.

Ruskin's moralistic criticism deserves a renewed hearing, especially among democratic liberals. At their best, democratic liberals have sought to acknowledge diversity and champion inclusion, but as a normative ideal, "inclusion" implies that there is something worth being included in. The liberty of choice, though necessary to making our lives good, is insufficient to the moral task of working out meaningful and dignified lives and ensuring that others may do so, too. Ruskin's awareness of the range of harms done to other people through the individual choices and power relationships of economic life is a reminder that democracy must be social and economic, not just political. Ruskin's normative concerns, his mastery of moral language, his imaginative appeals, his evocative scenes, and his readings of culture should be mined as critical resources for an ethics that refuses to stop at theoretical accounts of the cultural construction desire and at principled defenses of sovereignty over one's desires. Theoretical analysis and resistant subjectivity are insufficient tools and commitments for an engaged ethics or a democratic politics. Democratic liberals should also imagine and debate visions of good lives, the common good, shared goods, and the activities and practices needed to sustain them. The current deficit of moral vision on the left has to be addressed if we want to revive public and moral deliberation about a good society and the requirements of social responsibility. It is possible to moralize as Ruskin does and to accept the partiality of one's imaginative efforts. Progressives would do well to heed that lesson, while recognizing that the cultural resources for shared agreements today differ from the cultural mix that Ruskin found in Victorian life.

I offer one final religious appeal from *Unto This Last* to clarify the balancing act at the center of Ruskin's ethics of consumption. He cites "two most remarkable passages" from the Book of Proverbs:

> The rich and the poor have met. God is their maker. (Prov. 22.12)
>
> The rich and the poor have met. God is their light. (Prov. 29.14)

Ruskin continues, the hope for an ethical encounter in economic life "depends on both rich and poor knowing that God is their light; that in the mystery of human life, there is no other light than this by which they can *see each other's faces, and live*" (17.58–59; my emphasis). These passages reflect the understanding of the moral imagination that Ruskin works out over the course of his writings. The word "maker" reminds us of the transition in his criticism away from a purposive scheme of creaturely life, in which all striving is after God's perfect ends, toward a purposive scheme of human activity, in which people continually "make" their character, culture, and community and, in the process, fashion and arrange the desires, ends, and attitudes that give meaning to all that they produce, use, and consume. Here in this passage, though, Ruskin names God *the* "maker" and *the* "light" by which *the* telos of human flourishing must be seen.

Ruskin always walks this line. On the one hand, he becomes more of a cultural critic who takes people's activities as the source and substance of the norms, ideals, and standards to which his own normative arguments must appeal. On the other hand, he holds to his conviction that his contemporaries can deliberate well about their chosen ends and the personal capacities and societal conditions needed to pursue them only if they are fired with the "religious purpose" that there is but one "lofty conception of life" to which their own and others' efforts should be directed. This balance is difficult to strike, which is why a democratic polity, able to sustain the multiple lights of reflective consumers who are dedicated to making good lives through cooperative practices and institutionally mediated interactions, is a vital check on the limitations of Ruskin's criticism.

In the end a religious sensibility, aware of its practical sources and imaginative riches, helps overcome the aestheticizing tendencies we find in Ruskin's writings. A biblical caution is called for in response to his pronouncement of the "sun of justice" as the only light by which rich and poor "can see each other's faces and live." After the wandering Hebrews break their new covenant and the prohibition on idolatry, God declares to Moses that no more shall anyone be able to see God's face, "for man shall not see me and live." This chapter in Exodus begins with God's directive to resume the path to the promised land, and it comes with an admonition: "Go up to a land flowing with milk and honey; but I will not go up among you, lest I consume you in the way, for you are a stiff-necked people" (Exod. 33.20, 3). The theme of journeying is an apt reminder that the telos is never reached; nor can it be specified in perfect detail by anyone, whether a far-seeing critic like Ruskin or even the "wisest" consumer.

A perfect vision of the good, backed by divine authority, will consume a stiff-necked people. Democracy demands both imaginative efforts to envision and participate in an enriching public life along with the stiff-necked people who are capable of the task. Retreating to small encampments of the like-minded and instituting law and policy on the basis of a presumed core set of beliefs are two of the temptations that accompany the central conviction of a teleological ethics—namely, that *moral vision* must be brought to bear on our public discussions and personal choices. Redirecting the focus of contemporary ethics toward the often unacknowledged agreements and harms that prevail in a vast global economy, while accepting the inevitable variety in reflective consumers' visions of good lives, will enhance democratic commitments to individuality and fairness, participation and freedom.

The Hebrews' idolatry can be interpreted as the sin of failing to submit to a set of commanded beliefs, without which people are divided and directionless. Or their idolatry can be read as a reminder of the thin line between idolatry and imagination in a cultural conception of religion. As Ruskin puts it, our efforts to envision "where we are going," to imagine the ideals, activities, standards, commitments, and obligations that properly bind us, require us to read our inherited cultural landscape and invent those "material symbols which may lead us to contemplate the nature of the gods, spirits, or abstract virtues and powers," all the while striving to "see something" and to "'*make something* trustworthy by passionate desire that it should be so' . . . [as do all] religious persons of the present day, who are kindly and sincere" (20.242, 258; my emphasis). It takes a stiff-necked person to generate the light needed for a moral vision of an abundant economy, imagining reasons to persuade others of those ends and supporting or joining in the activities that sustain them.

Ruskin is right that we are morally bound as consumers. In consuming we shape each other's lives to the core of our character and vision and command others to do our bidding every time we buy things. For this reason we must also be wary of the temptation to make our own settled vision of the good the sole possibility for other people. Consumers cannot act imperiously, as if they could see the faces of everyone, upon whom they depend, from a God's-eye point of view. That would be to consume other people's lives in a way that adds the denial of liberty to the suffering of toil. Somehow the moralistic urgency of an ethics of consumption must be maintained in our active efforts to find and create practices of good consumption. At the same time, the agreements worked out within these cultural spaces remind us of the need to recognize what is good in the moral distances of economic life insofar as they afford liberties and differences, disagreements and debates, that we do well to cherish, too. The conflicting moral visions of consumers and producers are not served by binding up the distances required for a more boundless abundance than Ruskin could imagine all by himself. Finally it is not his own integrated vision of the good life, but the many critical tools he develops in arguing for it, that stand as his lasting contribution to the history of ethics.

Notes

All references to John Ruskin's writings are to the multivolume library edition of *The Works of John Ruskin*, edited by E. T. Cook and Alexander Wedderburn. I list references parenthetically in the standard form of the volume number followed by a period and the page number(s). Like all Ruskin scholars, I am indebted to Cook and Wedderburn's efforts.

Introduction

1. Rorty, "Historiography of Philosophy," 49–56.

2. I take the term "productivist bias" from Colin Campbell, though he uses it for different purposes. The relevant point for me is his observation about the lack of attention to consumption in nineteenth-century thought. Campbell, *Romantic Ethic*, 7. For an excellent overview of nineteenth-century figures, from political economists to poets, who addressed the theme of consumption prior to Ruskin, see Sherburne, *Ambiguities of Abundance*, esp. 149–50.

3. Agnew, "Coming Up for Air," 20, 30.

4. Consider one example where Marx sets consumption outside the scope of his political economy. In the *Grundrisse* he writes, "consumption, which is conceived not only as a terminal point but also as an end-in-itself, actually belongs outside economics except insofar as it reacts in turn upon the point of departure and initiates the whole process anew." Marx, *Grundrisse*, 89.

5. Terry Eagleton describes the folly of a politics of resistance through consumer reinvention: "Capitalism has always pitched diverse forms of life promiscuously together—a fact which should give pause to those unwary postmodernists for whom diversity, astonishingly, is somehow a virtue in itself." Eagleton, *After Theory*, 49.

6. J. S. Mill allows that society may intervene in the areas of production and commerce, regulating, for example, conditions in the workplace and sales of fraudulent goods. But Mill objects to restrictions on the individual liberty of consumers. In his words, "with the personal tastes and self-regarding concerns of individuals

the public has no business to interfere." Mill, *On Liberty,* 94–95, 83. I return to these issues in chapter 7.

7. Agnew, "Coming Up for Air," 33.

8. The labels "Romantic prophet" and "Victorian sage" are reminiscent of Friedrich Engels's dismissive epithet "true socialist," which he applied to Romantics and utopians alike. Marx and Engels, *Collected Works,* 5.455–57, 540–81.

9. The details of Ruskin's biography have been pored over by scholars. I discuss only those parts of his biography that relate directly to the themes of this book. The most notorious biographical details that I omit are Ruskin's annulled marriage to Euphemia Gray (1828–97) and his love for Rose la Touche (1848–75), whom he met when she was a girl and to whom he proposed when she turned sixteen. While relevant to Ruskin's views on women (see chapter 5), I set these events aside because excellent scholarship already exists and because the popular accounts of these relationships tend to excuse the need for reflective engagement with most of Ruskin's writings. Just as I do not want to retrace debates about his biography, I also find that much of the fascination with his life, especially its oddities, serves mostly to confirm us in the opinion that he has nothing to offer today. This gives us one more reason not to take his work seriously if his writings disturb us because of his tone, vocabulary, or demands. I hope that my reconstruction of his vocabulary of the virtues and my recovery of his ethics of consumption will disprove that easy assumption.

10. Tim Hilton identifies Ruskin's political views, his religious convictions, and his relations with women as three areas that Ruskin's editors neglected in the library edition of his *Works.* T. Hilton, *Early Years,* xii.

11. See Stoddart, *Ruskin's Culture Wars;* Weltman, *Ruskin's Mythic Queen;* Birch, *Ruskin and the Dawn;* Birch and O'Gorman, *Ruskin and Gender.* Stoddart, in particular, appreciates Ruskin's self-consciously historicized approach to culture in his late writings. In this she refutes the kind of argument made, for example, by Hilary Fraser (based mainly on the first decade of Ruskin's writings) that Ruskin sought to erect an "absolute and a-historical" value system and that he refused to accept his own historical conditioning. Fraser, *Beauty and Belief,* 108, 111.

12. John Rosenberg notes the constructive significance of Ruskin's interest in practical activity. Citing John Robertson's 1927 lament that Ruskin "is always seeking to graft moral or religious issues upon aesthetic" matters, Rosenberg describes the challenge of appreciating Ruskin's integrated vision as an effort "to build the broadest possible bridge between the perception of art and the activities of life." In this book I draw the conceptual blueprint of that bridge, showing how Ruskin's focus on activity helps us recover the connections between judgment and practice, individual perception and cultural activities, at the core of an ethics of character. Rosenberg, *Darkening Glass,* 21.

13. Sherburne, *Ambiguities of Abundance,* 106.

14. Landow, *Aesthetic and Critical Theories,* 243, 261. Landow concludes that allegory becomes the new mode of argumentation that Ruskin uses to sustain his aesthetic interpretations (p. 457).

15. J. S. Mill, *Subjection of Women,* 42, 20–21.

16. See, for example, J. S. Mill, *Utilitarianism,* in Mill and Bentham, *Utilitarianism and Other Essays,* 277–82.

17. I discuss Marx's analysis of commodity fetishism and his critique of religion in chapter 4.

18. Cornel West connects the critique of religion and the disregard for culture in twentieth-century Marxist thought in "Religion and the Left," 13.

19. In using the image of a nineteenth-century crossroads between religious and secular critical thought, I am influenced by Charles Taylor's account of Hegel's "expressivism." Taylor contrasts a premodern view of the subject as finding meaning and purpose in the cosmic order of things with a modern view of the subject as "self-defining." My discussion in chapters 3 and 4 of the tension that emerges in Ruskin's writings between the "recognition" of things' goodness and the "making" of things on one's own terms builds from Taylor's contrast. Ruskin does not resolve this tension as Hegel does, however. Taylor, *Hegel,* 6–11.

20. J. S. Mill, "Of the Stationary State," *Principles of Political Economy,* 111–17.

21. For a reading of Mill that moves beyond the procedures of institutions to the associations that cultivate liberal virtues, see Berkowitz, *Virtue and the Making of Modern Liberalism,* chap. 4.

22. Williams, *Culture and Society,* 138–40, 148. See Thompson, *William Morris,* 196–202. Building from E. P. Thompson's admission that there is more British radicalism and romanticism in Morris than there is strict Marxism, P. D. Anthony claims that Morris is primarily indebted to Ruskin for his critique of capitalism, but that Ruskin, in the words of J. A. Hobson, remains "more definitely moral and more practical" than Morris. I echo this emphasis on the moral and the practical. Anthony, *Ruskin's Labour,* 194–200.

23. From Clement Attlee's report of the findings of a questionnaire given to the first twenty-nine Members of Parliament from the Labour Party. For an extended discussion of this survey and the use of Ruskin's books in working-class education, see Goldman, "Ruskin, Oxford, and the British Labour Movement," 58.

24. MacIntyre, *After Virtue,* chaps. 6 and 2, esp. p. 72.

25. MacIntyre acknowledges Ruskin in passing in *After Virtue,* 72. Earlier in his career, MacIntyre cites Ruskin as the critic of Victorian capitalism closest to Marx and Engels in wanting to "close the gap between the industrial and the aesthetic." But MacIntyre is right that Ruskin did not appreciate sufficiently the transformative effects of industrialization. MacIntyre, *Marxism and Christianity,* 133–34.

26. MacIntyre, *After Virtue,* 243.

27. MacIntyre rejects the "communitarian" label, for example, in "Politics, Philosophy and the Common Good," 235, 243–46. Here MacIntyre argues that communitarians highlight the deficiencies of liberalism without escaping from the strategic coalitions and market manipulations of liberal politics. MacIntyre calls for an entirely different politics, a "kind of community of political learning and enquiry participation in which it is necessary for individuals to discover what their in-

dividual and common goods are." This politics fits Ruskin's social vision rather closely. And that is why MacIntyre along with those who do wear the communitarian label should reconsider their critiques of modern liberalism in light of the problems with Ruskin's politics (see chapter 5).

28. McGowan, "New Tory Radicals," 482, 478.

29. I thank an anonymous reviewer for encouraging me to clarify how this cultural conception of religion shapes my reading of Ruskin's intellectual development and indicates the continuing relevance of his public arguments and his engaged ethics for today.

30. Ruskin is absent from Reinhold Niebuhr's account of British socialism, where he advances J. S. Mill as the representative figure "who turned in his later years from individualistic to collectivistic political ideas." R. Niebuhr, *Moral Man and Immoral Society,* 204–5. H. Richard Niebuhr concludes his discussion of "Christ the Transformer of Culture" with F. D. Maurice, who admittedly matches Niebuhr's ideal of a socially engaged *theologian* better than Ruskin. But the consequence of elevating Maurice is that Ruskin's more trenchant critique of economic injustice is lost, adding to the sense that theological critics of capitalism must look to Marx for nineteenth-century resources. H. R. Niebuhr, *Christ and Culture,* 220–29. It makes more sense that a liberation theologian like Gustavo Gutierrez overlooks nineteenth-century Christian critics of capitalism like Ruskin, as Ruskin offers no concerted analysis of European imperialism. Gutierrez does acknowledge J. A. Hobson, the most important economist to champion Ruskin, suggesting that there are neglected critical resources in Ruskin's writings. Gutierrez, *Theology of Liberation,* 85.

31. Collini, *Public Moralists,* 58; and Eagleton, *After Theory,* 143, 124–25.

32. Eagleton, *After Theory,* 32; and Collini, *Public Moralists,* 100.

ONE The Duty of Delight

1. Valcanover and Pignatti, *Tintoretto,* 112–13.

2. Williams, *Culture and Society,* 325, 139.

3. Landow, *Aesthetic and Critical Theories,* 179. Among the scholars who follow Landow in criticizing Ruskin's supposed claims to "objectivity" in aesthetic meaning and economic value are Hewison, *Argument of the Eye,* 55–57, and Austin, *Practical Ruskin,* 90.

4. Wihl, *Rhetoric of Infallibility,* 2–4. Cf. Rorty, *Philosophy and the Mirror of Nature,* 6–7. See Rorty, "World Well Lost," 3–18.

5. I cannot emphasize enough how much the scholarly projection of epistemological problems onto Ruskin's criticism has blinded us to his normative concerns, his teleological framework, his moral vocabulary, and the reasonableness of his style of argumentation. To take one extreme example, Hilary Fraser reads Ruskin as so torn between the objective and the subjective that Ruskin is certain of nature's divinity in his earliest writings but becomes obsessed by "the question of the self in aesthetics and religion." Thus, Fraser concludes, "when Ruskin could no longer feel with any certainty the divine meaning of nature, he had neither the inner resources

nor the philosophical resources to sustain him, and was obliged to turn his main critical effort away from aesthetic concerns to social questions." This suggestion that Ruskin's social criticism results from a loss of personal reserves and critical acumen misrepresents both the efforts he invested in his critique of Victorian society and the conceptual clarity he brings to his analysis of political economy. It also distorts the continuity in Ruskin's concerns, not with the self, but with character. Fraser, *Beauty and Belief,* 111, 113.

6. Ruskin adds many misleading notes to the 1883 revision of *Modern Painters* 2 that bracket nearly every hint of his Evangelical Anglican upbringing as a distortion of his meaning. Stephen Finley is right that "Ruskin is unjust, and in the deepest sense unkind to himself, when his late fulminations upon rabid Protestantism conceal the consistent and self-critical engagement of the young Ruskin with the resources of his theological tradition and immediate religious environment." Finley, *Nature's Covenant,* 3.

7. Ruskin distinguishes purity from "sinlessness" or "spotlessness." He defines purity instead by analogy with the "purity of matter . . . the vital and energetic connection among its particles." He adds that "we illustrate [moral] virtues by the desirableness of material purity" (4.131–32). The "purity of the heart" is therefore best thought of as the proper arrangement of the moral virtues that makes for an active character and that fits one for vital relationships with other people and the world's creatures. Although I depart from James Sherburne's "romanticized" reading of Ruskin's idea of purity, he rightly notes that Ruskin does not escape the associations of purity with sinlessness, as when he bemoans the terrible lack of "vital beauty in man"—notably, the "evil diversity and various degradation" that must be overcome to "restore to the spirit the purity, and to the intellect the grasp, that they had in Paradise" (4.176, 177). Sherburne, *Ambiguities of Abundance,* chap. 1, esp. 5–6, 9.

8. While making final revisions to the book, I learned that George Pattison has also recognized the concern with character at the heart of *Modern Painters* 2. He writes that the sense for beauty, "as Ruskin repeatedly emphasizes, depends on a proper moral disposition" and "the cultivation of the full Christian character." There is much to learn from Pattison's discussion. Pattison, *Art, Modernity and Faith,* 62. I thank Frank Burch Brown for this reference.

9. Landow, *Aesthetic and Critical Theories,* 101–9, 69–74, 92–94. In arguing that Ruskin has to admit individual associations into his theory of beauty, Landow cites a long passage from *The Seven Lamps of Architecture* (p. 106). But at the center of this passage we find, not the language of emotion, but a particular set of "associations," namely Ruskin's sympathy for the "deep colours of human endurance, valour, and *virtue*" (8.224; my emphasis). Keeping the focus on Ruskin's vocabulary of the virtues helps clarify the precise shifts in his aesthetics, from God's virtue to human virtues and from God's ends in the Creation to the human ends of historical cultures.

10. Landow also looks past nineteenth-century associationist and romantic aesthetics to the place of character in Ruskin's teleological criticism. Landow cites this key passage from Ruskin's 1864 lecture on "Traffic": "What we like determines what

we are, and is the sign of what we are; and to teach taste is inevitably to form character" (18.436). Then he adds that "Ruskin, in other words, says of art what Plato says of philosophy: that it leads us toward the Good." Landow, *Aesthetic and Critical Theories,* 66.

11. Once again Landow's careful grappling with Ruskin's vocabulary clarifies how difficult it is for us to fathom the terms of his teleological approach. Puzzling over Ruskin's description of the perception of beauty as "moral," Landow observes that eighteenth-century thinkers did not separate moral philosophy and psychology into disparate fields as we do. Then he concludes, "Ruskin could use the term 'moral' to mean simultaneously 'ethical' and 'referring to all mental processes.'" Ibid., 157. But the empiricist psychology of a subject who perceives the world through "mental processes" is always misplaced in Ruskin's case. To put it paradoxically, he does not have "the mental" in mind when he discusses the deficiencies in people's perceptions of the beautiful. Consider a simple illustration: while writing this note, I stopped to dress my younger daughter who afterward asked me if I liked the picture of the setting sun and the sparkles on her outfit. But I hadn't noticed them because I was, we might say, "morally" distracted, not because I made any missteps in my "mental processes." It was not my "mind," but my "attitude," that misled me. My feelings of the moment—caring more about this book than my daughter's joy in wearing her new clothes—kept me from seeing what was right before my eyes—that my daughter's happiness and perception of things answer to the goods she loves and the activities she pursues. Unlike inner "subjective" emotions or "mental processes," we can make our loves and aspirations intelligible to others. We can also judge them morally and reform ourselves and our attitudes when they are found lacking as mine were. Similarly, Ruskin argues in *Modern Painters* 2 that nature's beauty can be grasped only by people whose worshipful reverence, gratitude, and admiration (and other appropriate feelings or attitudes) make them capable of a full "moral perception" of these things in light of the ends that God's creatures do and should seek. This is not an "emotionalist" aesthetics at all, but a teleological one that describes the orientation of moral perception through one's loves toward the ends one pursues. Nicholas Shrimpton also explores Ruskin's "ambiguous" use of the term "moral" and the "patchwork of conflicting views" that allows him to claim in the Inaugural Address to the Cambridge Art School that "you must not follow Art without pleasure, nor must you follow it for the sake of pleasure" (16.197). But on Ruskin's teleological approach, there is no contradiction between celebrating the pleasures of beauty and insisting that such pleasures can only be known if people have well-trained desires for the ends that beautiful things serve. That is not to defend Ruskin's teleological account of beauty, but to explain its consistency. Shrimpton, "Ruskin and the Aesthetes," 149.

12. In the 1883 edition of *Modern Painters* 2, Ruskin adds to his sense of indebtedness to Aristotle, though misleadingly. Referring to a passage from the *Nicomachean Ethics* that he used as the postscript to his discussion of "typical beauty,"

Ruskin declares that this one passage goes well beyond what he had attempted to say in the whole volume (4.145n).

13. Aristotle, *Nicomachean Ethics,* 253.

14. Ibid., 254.

15. Burke, *Sublime and Beautiful,* 16.

16. Aristotle, *Nicomachean Ethics,* 260.

17. Landow, *Aesthetic and Critical Theories,* 162–66, 92.

18. James Sherburne is right in cautioning, "When one tries to discover the real sources of Ruskin's sociological aesthetic, one is surprised to find him referring as much to eighteenth-century or earlier figures as to Romantics. Indeed, Ruskin's eclecticism is an excellent antidote to the temptation to accept the usual categories of scholarly interpretation." But although Sherburne cites Aristotle and Hooker as influences on Ruskin, he stresses the romantic "organicism" in Ruskin's criticism and then faults Ruskin for lacking Coleridge's appreciation of "organic growth." Sherburne, *Ambiguities of Abundance,* 29, 10–12, 30.

19. Hewison, *Argument of the Eye,* 55.

20. Burke, *Sublime and Beautiful,* 91; my emphasis. Reinforcing the sense of beauty's inherent attraction instead of its objectivity, Burke describes beauty in terms nearly identical to those used by Ruskin in his original definition of "ideas of beauty" in *Modern Painters* 1 (3.109). Burke writes, "It is not by the force of long attention and enquiry that we find any object to be beautiful; beauty demands no assistance from our reasoning; even the will is unconcerned; the appearance of beauty as effectually causes some degree of love in us, as the application of ice or fire produces the ideas of heat or cold." Burke, *Sublime and Beautiful,* 92.

21. Michael Wheeler also notes the lack of attention to Richard Hooker's influence on *Modern Painters* 2, claiming that "Ruskin comes closer to a mainstream Anglican position [in this volume] than at any other time" in his writings. Wheeler canvasses the passages where Ruskin quotes from Hooker, and he cites an 1844 letter from Ruskin's tutor Osborne Gordon asking Ruskin, "if the cultivation of taste be a proper 'ergon' [work] of a man's life"? Wheeler does not, however, connect the teleological language of cultivation and "ergon" with Aristotelian themes of character development and good human functioning. Nor does he relate Ruskin's theory of beauty to Hooker's metaphysics of God's "participation" in the world and creaturely "participation" in God. Wheeler, *Ruskin's God,* 53, 56, 57–58, 61. For authors who limit Hooker's influence mainly to Ruskin's style, see Landow, *Aesthetic and Critical Theories,* 145; and Hewison, *Argument of the Eye,* 54. See Ruskin's comments on Hooker's style: 4.334, 18.32, 27.168, 35.414.

22. Ross, "Ruskin, Hooker and 'the Christian Theoria,'" 284. Ross shows how Ruskin's borrowings from Hooker distinguish his theory of beauty from "evangelical pietism and romantic pantheism."

23. Hooker, *Laws of Ecclesiastical Polity,* 66–67 (I.5.1–2). Parenthetical references to Hooker give book, chapter, and paragraph numbers.

24. George Landow recognized the importance of typological readings in Ruskin's religious upbringing and his art and social criticism. Landow, *Aesthetic and Critical Theories*, chap. 5. Other scholars who discuss Ruskin's use of typology and its influence on his contemporaries include: Sussman, *Fact into Figure;* Sawyer, *Ruskin's Poetic Argument;* and Finley, *Nature's Covenant.* See also Landow, *Victorian Types.*

25. Hooker, *Laws of Ecclesiastical Polity*, 63 (I.3.4).

26. In 1883, acknowledging a decisive change in his intellectual development, Ruskin retracts his initial formulation of God's relating to the created world as a kind of "participation." He shifts to a notion of the divine as an informing and enlivening "Intelligence" (4.46n, 47).

27. Hooker, *Laws of Ecclesiastical Polity*, 63 (I.3.5).

28. Gary Wihl identifies the central question in Ruskin's type of "unity," namely, how is the great variety seen in the world's creatures structured into "unified 'perfect' complexes"? But Wihl concludes that Ruskin's "distinction between variety for its own sake and variety that contributes to difference turns out . . . to have little relevance to the human grasp of the divine harmony that permeates creation." Wihl's conclusion overlooks Hooker's claim that we perceive divine harmonies only by moving from the imperfect variety of creatures on their own to their more perfect unity with other creatures. Once again Ruskin's arguments make sense if we accept the lineage he claims for his teleological criticism, even if he and we ultimately reject Hooker's metaphysics. Wihl, *Rhetoric of Infallibility*, 48–49, 51.

29. Not surprisingly for a Victorian, Ruskin rules out one characteristic as antithetical to all "high beauty" in natural creatures, namely, the vice of sloth. In his 1883 revision, he italicizes this assertion (4.157).

30. I take the term "logic" from Michael Walzer's theory of distributive justice. He identifies "social goods" with different spheres of distribution, e.g., money and market exchange, power and political office. Walzer's discussion of the distribution of God's grace looks nothing like the "logic" of vital beauty, but his approach suggested this line of analysis to me. Walzer, *Spheres of Justice.*

31. Hooker, *Laws of Ecclesiastical Polity*, 56 (I.2.4).

32. Ibid., 67 (I.5.2).

33. Ruskin comments in an 1883 footnote to *Modern Painters* 2 that Burke's "essay on the Sublime and Beautiful is, like all his writing, extremely rational and forcible; and deserves most careful and reverent reading." This praise is appended, however, to a criticism of Burke for denying that "proportion" has any measure in beauty. For Burke the proportions of beautiful creatures are too varied to think that proportion is a cause of beauty. In defending proportion as having a role in beauty, Ruskin argues that the varied forms of different species are beautiful, but not to the same degree. As Ruskin puts it, "while we find in all animals such proportion and harmony of form as *gift them* with positive agreeableness consistent with the station and dignity of each, we perceive, also, a better proportion in some (as the horse, eagle, lion, and man, for instance), expressing the nobler functions and more ex-

alted powers of the animal" (4.109n, 109–10; my emphasis). God's charity in *gifting* things with their perfections and natural functions is once again seen as the basis of Ruskin's theory of beauty. Gary Wihl cites this same passage, but he dismisses Ruskin's chain-of-being hierarchy of form as a "poor judgment, standing as it does midway between Alison's denial of the inherent meaning of form and the radical Darwinian separation of the appearance of livings forms from a divine teleology. A symbolism of form that depends upon proportional value within a divinely sanctioned scheme collapses when the scheme does." Wihl's verdict is true enough; Ruskin's later criticism requires a very different conception of the telos. But in dismissing the teleological structure of Ruskin's criticism because it does not conform to other theories of the day, Wihl commits the error that my reconstructive efforts in this chapter aim to correct. We must first reconstruct Ruskin's vocabulary as representative of a normative approach at odds with, and to a large extent displaced by, other emerging theoretical structures. Only then can we make Ruskin's critical arguments intelligible, and only then can we evaluate where they may still prove useful to us. Wihl, *Rhetoric of Infallibility,* 60–61.

34. We see Ruskin's distrust of "custom" in *Modern Painters* 1 when he makes it his task is "to raise, as far as possible, the deceptive veil of imaginary light through which we are accustomed to gaze upon the patriarchal work" of past artists (3.83). In volume 2 he rails against the deadening accretions of "custom" and false "authority or fashion" of "ignorant masters" (4.36, 58).

35. Christopher Lasch actually distinguishes Carlyle from "the tradition of Burke, Ruskin, and Continental sociology." A preference for custom over vitalism is the sin of Burke, which is how Lasch also portrays Ruskin's love of art (an odd reading of the early volumes of *Modern Painters,* at least). According to Lasch, the error that separates Ruskin most directly from Carlyle is paternalism, which no doubt applies to Ruskin, though equally to Carlyle. Lasch, *True and Only Heaven,* 239, 226–27, 231.

36. Ibid., 233–34.

37. Ruskin notes in a June 6, 1841, diary entry that he read "some of Carlyle's lectures [on heroes]. Bombast I think: altogether approves of Mohamet, and talks like a girl of his 'black eyes.'" Quoted in Spear, *Dreams of an English Eden,* 86.

38. Lasch, *True and Only Heaven,* 235, 239.

39. Thoreau, *Journal, vol. 10,* 69, 147.

40. Schneewind, "Divine Corporation," 176–77.

41. Coleridge, *Constitution of Church and State,* chaps. 5 and 6.

42. See J. S. Mill, "Bentham," in Mill and Bentham, *Utilitarianism and Other Essays,* 173–74.

43. Defending the claim that Ruskin's early aesthetics allows no independent room for artistic creativity takes me beyond the theory of beauty to the idea of "imagination" that Ruskin also develops in volume 2. I discuss this initial idea of the imagination in chapter 3.

44. Burke, *Sublime and Beautiful,* 77. Linda Austin also cites Ruskin's connec-

tion between "excellence" in a work of art and a "great power" that overcomes some "difficulty." This confirms for her Ruskin's commitment to a biblicized Ricardian labor theory of value, where the measure of labor is not time but suffering. This reading misses Ruskin's gloss that recognizing excellence requires "practice and knowledge" in the art. Austin, *Practical Ruskin,* 61. I discuss the differences between Ruskin's and Marx's views of labor, power, and value in chapters 2, 4, and 6.

45. Burke, *Sublime and Beautiful,* 46, 36–37.

46. On the topic of the sublime's "greatness," Burke writes: "A great beautiful thing, is a manner of expression scarcely ever used; but that of a great ugly thing, is very common. There is a wide difference between admiration and love. The sublime, which is the cause of the former, always dwells on great objects, and terrible; the latter on small ones, and pleasing; we submit to what we admire, but we love what submits to us; in one case we are forced, in the other we are flattered into compliance." Ibid., 113.

TWO The Spirit of Labor

1. Benhabib, *Critique, Norm, and Utopia,* 10.

2. Cornel West finds the "ethical dimension" of Marx's thought in a "radical historicist" approach to ethics that denies universal foundations for moral principles in favor of the "*contingent, community-specific* agreements people make in relation to particular norms, aims, goals, and objectives." I argue that Ruskin's account of practical labor lends itself to the engaged analysis, rhetorical persuasion, and shared cultural agreements that West is calling for, more so than does Marx's theoretical account of labor. West, *Ethical Dimensions of Marxist Thought,* 1.

3. I thank George Landow for informing me that Ruskin's criticisms of faceted jewelry coincided with the Castellani family's revival of Etruscan jewelry. See *Castellani and Italian Archeological Jewelry,* ed. Susan Weber Soros and Stefanie Walker (New Haven: Yale University Press, 2004). It should be noted that Ruskin's later criticism of luxury consumption often falls hardest on women, with his sternest words directed against jewelry, dresses, and other bodily adornments. I discuss Ruskin's views on women in chapter 5.

4. I follow Alasdair MacIntyre, who argues that the Greek term *aretê* is better translated as "excellence" than as "virtue." Today we tend to limit virtues to moral traits. Excellence captures the wider range of human capacities—moral, practical, aesthetic, intellectual, bodily, and so forth—that Ruskin has in mind when he uses the term "virtue." MacIntyre, *After Virtue,* 122. For MacIntyre's account of a "social practice," see esp. chaps. 12, 14, and 15.

5. Ruskin's opposition between architectural decoration and a building's utility is less odd if we note that his definition of architecture downplays the importance of technical expertise and redirects personal thrift toward public purpose. On the latter point, aware that advocating lavish decor in churches might seem uncharitable or "Romanist" to his fellow Protestants, Ruskin argues that individual devotion to utility and thrift are more immediate obstacles to a vital Christian faith. "The

question is not between God's house and His poor [lack of charity]: it is not between God's house and His Gospel [threat of Romanism]. It is between God's house and ours" (8.37). Ruskin was never one for austerity, but he linked abundance to public spiritedness rather than private expenditure.

6. Benhabib, *Critique, Norm, and Utopia,* 49.

7. The moments of "externalization" and "appropriation" proceed as follows. First, Spirit establishes the object as its own object, as distinct from itself. In so doing, Spirit defines the object's properties by embodying in the object potentialities that were only ideally internal to Spirit. Second, as the object—now determined by Spirit's act of self-externalization—is made real by Spirit, Spirit eventually comes to recognize itself, its own potential, realized in the object. Thus, Spirit overcomes the false nature of the object as "given" by reappropriating the transformed object, still including its prior forms. This self-articulation of inner potential through intelligible expression out in the world is Hegel's "expressivism." Benhabib takes this term from Taylor, *Hegel,* 13–18.

8. Benhabib, *Critique, Norm, and Utopia,* 84.

9. Ibid., 87.

10. Marx and Engels, *Collected Works,* 3.332–33.

11. Ibid., 5.42, 44.

12. "Naturalism," as I mean the term here, is the view that human motives and intentions proceed from desires, instincts, and impulses that can be fully accounted for apart from the authority of social goods. Charles Taylor discusses this "naturalism" as it figures in utilitarianism and Marxism and in what he calls "neo-Nietzschean" criticism. Taylor, *Sources of the Self,* esp. chap. 1. 5.

13. Marx and Engels, *Collected Works,* 3.276.

14. Marx, *Capital,* 284.

15. Marx and Engels, *Collected Works,* 3.275, 277.

16. Benhabib, *Critique, Norm, and Utopia,* 64, 62.

17. Marx and Engels, *Collected Works,* 5.218.

18. In this merging of machine production and Spirit's labor, there is a sense in which Marx's analysis of capitalism translates the workings of Schneewind's "Divine Corporation" into a historical process. People's duties and roles are not dictated by a good known only to God, the chief executive of the Corporation. Rather the good awaits the end of history, but workers feel equally in the dark until that time. See chapter 1 for my discussion of "Divine Corporation ethics."

19. Benhabib argues that Marx's concern with concrete human needs can be stretched to incorporate the needs for and the cultural possibilities of self-expression and mutual recognition. Marx's idea of working oneself out can be corrected by adding in the need to work things out with and for other people; thus the drive toward radical self-creation is mediated by the cultural shape of human needs. Benhabib, *Critique, Norm, and Utopia,* 60.

20. Marx and Engels, *Collected Works,* 5.47.

21. Ibid., 5.394.

22. I draw Marx's views on art from *The 1844 Manuscripts, The German Ideology,* and the introduction to the *Grundrisse.* None of these texts was published during Marx's lifetime, and the introduction is notoriously suspect because little of it survived in *Capital* for which the *Grundrisse* is the "outline." I am also relying on M. Rose, *Marx's Lost Aesthetic.*

23. Margaret Rose traces the transformational aspect of Marx's view of art to the "productivist aesthetic" he develops from Heinrich Heine and Saint-Simon. M. Rose, *Marx's Lost Aesthetic,* 12–13.

24. Carlyle, *Past and Present,* 189, 163.

25. In the 1892 preface to the Kelmscott edition of "The Nature Gothic," William Morris called this chapter "one of the very few necessary and inevitable utterances of the century." Quoted in Rosenberg, *Darkening Glass,* 101. For Ruskin's influence on Morris, see Spear, *Dreams of an English Eden,* chap. 4, and Boris, *Art and Labor,* 3–12.

26. A striking example of the errors caused by neglecting Ruskin's vocabulary of the virtues is John Unrau's suggestion that Ruskin's praise of Gothic "savageness" implies that its builders were "inspired savages." Unrau wonders how Ruskin can describe these builders' skill and calculations as "primitive" when he calls the Gothic style the only "rational architecture." Instead of Unrau's odd inference about "savages," it is clear that Ruskin celebrates the rough-hewn creativity of the Gothic style as an "excellence" shared by everyone who reworked its characteristic forms and elements, from the designers to the carvers. Ruskin exaggerates the "freedom" enjoyed by ordinary workers, no doubt, but his imaginative portrait makes conceptual sense if we heed the consistency of his moral language. Unrau, "Ruskin, the Workman and the Savageness of Gothic," 36, 42.

27. Commenting on Ruskin's Oxford lectures in the 1870s, Linda Austin notes that Ruskin expands on Aristotle's *Nicomachean Ethics* by bringing the artisan into the sphere of human excellence. Aristotle argued that "production" aims at an end other than excellence in the action itself. For Ruskin, by contrast, excellences or virtues can be achieved in many different activities. His distinction between "art" and "manufacture" repeats Aristotle's concern with cultivating character, but Ruskin increases the range of human excellences and the types of people who can achieve them. Austin, *Practical Ruskin,* 58–59.

28. MacIntyre, *After Virtue,* 187.

29. Richards, *Commodity Culture of Victorian England,* 23.

30. In *Cultivating Victorians* David Thomas places Ruskin alongside nineteenth-century liberals seeking to create a conception of moral agency that accepts the limitations of the culturally situated self but that allows for a transcending aesthetic vision leading to a better self. Ruskin is a promising source for this effort to find non-ideological uses for aesthetic appeals. But Thomas does not address how the theme of "cultivation" intersects with Ruskin's vocabulary of the virtues, despite focusing on the chapter on the "Ducal Palace." Thomas overlooks the detailed account of the virtues there, falling back instead on the epistemological preoccupa-

tions of Ruskin studies and Ruskin's supposed need to project his subjectivity onto the objects he is interpreting. Thomas, *Cultivating Victorians*, 51, 57–71.

31. In an 1853 letter to his father, Ruskin describes his changed attitude toward Aristotle. After ranking the *Nicomachean Ethics* above all other philosophy and memorizing half of it, Ruskin began to doubt the entire system so that, by *Stones* 2, he criticizes the *Ethics* as "so false, so forced, and so confused, that the study of it at our universities is quite enough to occasion the utter want of accurate habits of thought. . . . In a word, Aristotle mistakes the Prudence or Temperance which must regulate the operation of the virtues, for the essence of the virtues themselves." Ruskin rejects both Aristotle and Cicero for treating the four cardinal virtues as the summit of ethics, not as the restraints on a moral life that is properly directed toward and by "Heavenly Wisdom" and the "nobler law of love" (10.374n, 371–74).

32. MacIntyre, *After Virtue*, 204. Michael Wheeler's reading of Ruskin as a "Victorian Solomon" affirms "unity" as a dominant principle in Ruskin's social order and his own life. Wheeler traces out the appeals to the biblical Solomon throughout Ruskin's corpus, including his role in the combined types of "King and Prophet" in *The Bible of Amiens* (1884). Wheeler's attention to Ruskin's late works supports his thesis that Ruskin remains more of a religious thinker and more committed to a feudal society ordered by prophetic judgment and monarchical rule than other scholars allow. While I agree that Ruskin remains a creative religious thinker, I read him primarily as a critic of human cultures, not of God's culture, as Wheeler emphasizes. Ruskin's eclectic interests in the complexities of culture, religion included, blunt those parts of his critical vision—his metaphysical proclamations and his medievalist social order—that are dangerously apologetic for the anti-democratic and hierarchical tendencies in his tradition. Wheeler, *Ruskin's God*, 259, 277–78.

33. Williams, *Culture and Society*, 133–48, esp. 139–40. Williams, "John Ruskin," 234–35.

34. The phrase "endeavour in description" comes from an 1847 letter of Ruskin's cited in Bloom, "Ruskin as Literary Critic," 177.

THREE The Nature of Imagination

1. For scholars who mention Ruskin's tract on "Modern Education," see Fain, *Ruskin and the Economists*, 29–31; Sherburne, *Ambiguities of Abundance*, 69–70; Spear, *Dreams of an English Eden*, 55; and T. Hilton, *Early Years*, 161.

2. As "Modern Education" is Ruskin's critique of the classical education at British universities, it makes sense that he focuses on men here. He turns to female education in the 1860s. His curriculum for girls is "progressive" in including natural science and physical activity. As I discuss in chapter 5, however, these curricular reforms are not egalitarian, as boys' and girls' educations must conform to the "natural" virtues of their sexes.

3. Oakeshott, "Rational Conduct," in *Rationalism in Politics*, 97–100.

4. James Sherburne notes, by way of criticism, Ruskin's "circular" argument that great art requires "morally 'whole' individuals" to make it even as it helps form

such individuals and a "healthy social environment," too. This circularity is less damning if we take seriously the connections between virtues, activities, good lives, and good societies. Sherburne, *Ambiguities of Abundance,* 28.

5. Chadwick, *Victorian Church,* 1. 167–211.

6. For scholars who equate the subtitle "Of Many Things" with a transitional haphazardness in Ruskin's thought, see Landow, *Aesthetic and Critical Theories,* 29; Hewison, *Argument of the Eye,* 128; and Abse, *Passionate Moralist,* 149.

7. Hooker, *Laws of Ecclesiastical Polity,* 55 (I.2.2); my emphasis.

8. Ibid., 56 (I.2.4).

9. George Landow makes the most persuasive case that Ruskin adopts a more fully "expressive" aesthetics during the 1850s. He reads *Modern Painters* 3 as the work that culminates Ruskin's movement toward a romantic aesthetics focused on "the nature of the artist, the importance of external nature, and the role of the imagination, emotion, and detail in art." Although Landow describes Ruskin's theory of the imagination as an "eclectic" mixture of eighteenth-century views of "the imagination as maker of images" and the romantic notion of "the imagination as creator of emotional states or sympathies," he argues that the artist's expression of emotion is the vital center of Ruskin's mature theory. The term "emotional states" is better than emotion all by itself. It conveys Ruskin's sense that the artist's character—that is, the arrangement of his virtues and emotions toward an ordered set of ends and goods—is what shapes the meaning and worth of an artwork. Landow does not draw out these teleological elements of Ruskin's criticism as I do, though he has an eye for the importance of Ruskin's vocabulary of the virtues, as he cites passages from Ruskin on the "virtue of the Imagination" and its "virtue of originality" (4.284, 253). Landow also quotes with approval Ruskin's claim that "the art of any county *is the exponent of its social and political virtues*" (20.39) and notes that, for Ruskin, "As all lovely art is rooted in virtue, so it bears fruit of virtue" (19.394). I share Landow's appreciation of Ruskin's eclecticism, but I argue that it is Ruskin's interests in human virtues, goods, and ends, not a romantic appeal to emotion, that sustain the creative tensions, justify the central arguments, and motivate the conceptual innovations of his criticism. Landow, *Aesthetic and Critical Theories,* 29, 74, 72, 56, 68. Rosenberg describes Ruskin's aesthetics as romantic from the start. Rosenberg, *Darkening Glass,* 14–18.

10. Two studies deserve special mention for resisting the thesis that Ruskin adopts a romantic aesthetics of the imagination and thus fails to take seriously the "subjectivity" of taste and perception. Both studies hint at the importance of developing good character in perceiving things well. Elizabeth Helsinger contrasts Ruskin's criticisms of the romantic ideal of the creative genius with his own stress on the beholder's "visual habits" and their continual improvement. Helsinger, *Ruskin and the Art of the Beholder,* 4. Paul Sawyer's reading of *Modern Painters* 1 and 2 is noteworthy for his argument that Ruskin resists the "subject-object distinction" in favor of a "vitalistic Aristotelianism." Sawyer, *Ruskin's Poetic Argument,* 37.

11. Abrams, *Mirror and the Lamp,* 6–7.

12. Ruskin rejects the metaphor of the "mirror" in other passages from *Modern Painters* 3. He describes bad art as art "produced by men who do not feel at all, but who reproduce, though ever so accurately, yet coldly, like human mirrors, the scenes before their eyes." He adds elsewhere that people who demand realism in their paintings seem to think the "only valuable paintings would indeed be *mirrors*, reflecting permanently the images of the things in which they took delight." Perhaps Ruskin never saw any value in the image of the mind as mirror, raising questions about my account of the "linear model" of his early aesthetics. Nevertheless his turn from God's Creation to human creativity complicates his aesthetics. For Ruskin "great art" is distinguished by the "nobleness of the end to which the effort of the painter is addressed" (5.32, 39, 42). The clear difference between his early and later aesthetics is that, at first, great art mirrors God's purposes, but increasingly he accepts that imaginative artists bring their own ends to their representations of things and that these ends reflect the existing cultural practices.

13. Ruskin reports that one time in the Alps when his imaginative powers had been spent, he "had not mind enough to give to" any Alp, "and none were of any value. The conclusion which would have been formed, upon this, by a German philosopher, would have been that the Mont Blanc *was* of no value; that he and his imagination only were of value" (5.184). This humorous suggestion that Mont Blanc can have value only in someone's eyes anticipates Ruskin's later claims that nature has "intrinsic value" and that consumers' "opinions" are not the source of economic value.

14. George Pattison stresses that his reading of the "subjective" aspects of Ruskin's theology of art is phenomenological, that is, having to do with the "existential commitments" that make for one's being in the world in a particular way. He denies that Ruskin's aesthetics relies on "objective doctrinal truth," and he focuses instead on the formations of character as I do. Pattison emphasizes, in particular, "the requirements of Christian conversion and discipleship" and the "passions of the Christian soul." Unlike Pattison, I read Ruskin's mature account of the character needed for moral imagination as cultural, not existential, in the sense that a great many activities and practices can help form the attitudes and commitments needed to imagine things fully and well. Christian theologians frequently separate questions of the self from concerns about society. We should appreciate how Ruskin's cultural approach integrates issues of character and community. Pattison, *Art, Modernity and Faith,* 75–77.

15. In introducing the "pathetic fallacy," Ruskin mentions the "fallacy of wilful fancy." In the latter case a person is not overwhelmed by an "excited state of feelings, making [him or her], for the time, more or less rational." Instead people who commit this fallacy actively misrepresent things to bend other people to their own ends (5.205). In Ruskin's later writings the pathetic fallacy and this ethical fallacy become the two forms of "idolatry" that he discusses in his analysis of money. See chapter 4.

16. George Landow argues that Ruskin continues to view the imagination as "prophetic" after *Modern Painters* 2 and relies on its dictates to correct against the

problems of subjectivity in romantic aesthetics. I read in Ruskin's arguments against the pathetic fallacy a new effort to make the cultivated excellences, mastered passions, and proper ends of the good man, or here the ideal artist, a new model of a truthful or moral imagination, which has its own practical reasons and does not need supplementing from "prophetic" appeals. Landow, *Aesthetic and Critical Theories*, 373–75, 379–80.

17. Shrimpton, "'Rust and Dust': Ruskin's Pivotal Work," 60.

18. I developed this reading of Ruskin's turn from natural theology to natural piety as a student of Jeff Stout's. Stout defines piety in general as "the proper acknowledgment of the sources of our existence and progress through life." His recent work demonstrates how disagreements about the scope of this virtue and its obligations have been central to debates about democracy, religion, and culture, from the nineteenth century to today. Stout, *Democracy and Tradition*, 9, and chap. 1.

19. Hewison, *Argument of the Eye*, 58.

20. For a discussion of Ruskin and William Buckland, see Spear, *Dreams of an English Eden*, 43–45. For Ruskin's own use of Charles Bell, see 4.103–5n, 159.

21. For two different discussions of Wordsworth's influence on the early Ruskin, see Hewison, *Argument of the Eye*, 16–19; and Finley, *Nature's Covenant*, 118–34.

22. Ruskin makes some disparaging remarks about Darwinism, but in *The Queen of the Air* (1869), he notes that the "facts" he plans to discuss "are in nowise antagonistic to the theories which Mr. Darwin's unwearied and unerring investigations are every day rendering more probable" (19.358n). Sharon Aronofsky Weltman quotes this passage and canvasses Ruskin's divergent comments about Darwinism and Darwin in "Myth and Gender in Ruskin's Science," 161–62.

23. In an 1878 *Fors Clavigera* letter, Ruskin contrasts the "moral species" of virtuous cultivation with the natural species of scientific observation. He names wisdom, justice, judgment, and equity four "species," the origins of "which you have not only to *per*ceive, but to *re*ceive. And the species of these four things, and the origin of their species,—you know them, doubtless well,—in these scientific days?" (29.375). Quoted in Wheeler, *Ruskin's God*, 239.

24. Sharon Aronofsky Weltman contrasts the moral "telos" governing Ruskin's works on natural history and "the moral significance of each natural form" with "Darwin's metaphor of fitness," which "implies a teleology without moral significance." I do not read Darwin's theory of natural selection as teleological at all, but Weltman is perceptive in describing Darwin as an exemplar of "what Ruskin demands from scientists: a meticulous observer who loves the profusion of nature without exploiting it, who records resemblances in richly metaphorical language." Weltman, "Myth and Gender in Ruskin's Science," 164, 161–62.

25. For an example of Darwin's naturalized use of such terms as "character," "habits," and "constitution," consider this passage: "Natural selection . . . leads to divergence of character; for more living beings can be supported on the same area the more they diverge in structure, habits, and constitution, of which we see proof

by looking to the inhabitants of any small spot or to naturalised productions." Darwin, *Origin of Species,* 105.

26. Francis O'Gorman notes Ruskin's "general desire to teach a science which was human centred, moral in the broadest but most fundamental of terms, [a] pedagogic project aimed to produce specific mental attitudes and forms of ethical behaviour from his students." He also cites Ruskin's 1884 declaration that "The laws of virtue and honour are . . . to be taught compulsorily to all men" (29.499). These observations support my reading of Ruskin's practice-centered conception of the sciences and other cultural activities and the shared attitudes and common goals produced through instruction in them. O'Gorman, "Ruskin's Science of the 1870's," 47–48.

27. For Ruskin's relations with Friedrich Max Müller and his interests in comparative mythology, see Fitch, *Poison Sky,* 271–72, 538–41; and Birch, *Ruskin's Myths,* 40–42, 102–17.

FOUR The Vision of Religion

1. Wilson, *God's Funeral,* 268.

2. Two decades after *Stones* 1, Ruskin criticizes the destruction of religious art by some of the Protestant reformers. He cites the commandment, "'Thou shalt not bow down to them, nor worship them.' 'Assuredly no,' we answered once, in our pride; and through porch and aisle, broke down the carved work thereof, with axes and hammers" (20.270).

3. For Ruskin's reponses to the positions taken by Evangelicals, High Churchmen, and Catholics in the early 1850s, see Wheeler, *Ruskin's God,* 74–77, 79–81, 82–83, 84–86. See Chadwick, *Victorian Church,* 1. 271–90, esp. 273, 290.

4. Gary Wihl's is the most extensive discussion of Ruskin's concept of "idolatry," but he subordinates the sins of economic idolatry to the idolatry of false artistic representation. I do not read Ruskin's reflections on idolatry as chiefly concerned with epistemology (how people know things' value) but rather with ethics (how people should judge things' value). That is why I read Ruskin's discussions of the idolatry of modern art as complementary to his argument that piety is the virtue due to others in economic life. Wihl, *Rhetoric of Infallibity,* 126.

5. Sharpe, *Comparative Religion,* 38–40, 42.

6. Both Dinah Birch and Sharon Aronofsky Weltman explore Ruskin's borrowings and departures from Müller's largely dismissive reading of myth. See Birch, *Ruskin's Myths,* 40–43, 99–100, 104–15; and Weltman, *Ruskin's Mythic Queen,* 13.

7. Barbour, *Versions of Deconversion,* chap. 4, esp. 56–57. Ruskin describes his 1858 "un-conversion" first in *Fors Clavigera* in 1877 and then in a significantly revised version in *Praeterita* in 1888. Michael Wheeler challenges Ruskin's memory of this period and argues that Ruskin's Christian "belief in divine wisdom and a God of peace" permeates his writings and unifies his life. Wheeler, *Ruskin's God,* xv, chap. 6, esp. pp. 148–51. For an overview of Ruskin's religious wanderings, see Landow, *Aesthetic and Critical Theories,* 243–317.

8. Ruskin endorses the invention of cultural myths in *Fors Clavigera.* Imagining that Cincinnatus never existed, he continues, "if Cincinnatus never was so found, nor ever existed at all in flesh and blood; but the great Roman nation, in its strength of conviction that manual labour in tilling the ground was good and honourable, invented a quite bodiless Cincinnatus . . . ; *this* fable, which has no foundation;—this precious coinage of the brain and conscience of a mighty people, you and I—believe me—had better read, and know, and take to heart, diligently" (27.357–58). Quoted in Landow, *Aesthetic and Critical Theories,* 417.

9. Feuerbach, *Essence of Christianity.* Van Harvey discusses the problems with Eliot's choice of "projection" to translate a number of terms. Harvey, *Feuerbach,* 32.

10. Harvey, *Feuerbach,* 10.

11. Marx and Engels, *Collected Works,* 3.175; my emphasis.

12. Ibid., 3.175–76.

13. Ibid., 5.4.

14. Ibid., 5.46.

15. Ibid., 5.4.

16. Ibid., 5.36, 4.

17. A good example of Marx's reliance on "scientific analysis" in place of normative argumentation occurs in his discussion of the "surplus labor" extracted through capitalist production. Marx writes that "the daily sustenance of labour-power costs only half a day's labour, while . . . the very same labour-power can remain effective, can work, during a whole day, and consequently the value which its use during one day creates is double what the capitalist pays for that use; this circumstance is a piece of good luck for the buyer, *but by no means an injustice towards the seller [of that labour].*" The force of the passage suggests that these subsistence wages are unjust, but no moral argument is given. Marx, *Capital,* 301; my emphasis.

18. Ibid., 171.

19. Ibid., 163–64.

20. Ibid., 164–65. Writing in 1863, four years before the publication of *Capital* and nearly two decades before its English translation, Ruskin names the commodification of human labor the key transformation wrought by industrial capitalist production. "The idea that [labour] is a commodity to be bought or sold, is the alpha and omega of Politico-Economic fallacy" (17.183).

21. Marx, *Capital,* 270.

22. Ibid., 136.

23. Ibid., 128.

24. Ibid., 152.

25. Ibid., 167.

26. Ibid., 170–73.

27. Quoted in Austin, *Practical Ruskin,* 138–39.

28. Before analyzing Dante's "types" of the Plutus and the sirens, Ruskin writes, "It is a strange habit of wise humanity to speak in enigmas only, so that the highest truths and usefullest laws must be hunted through whole picture-galleries of

dreams, which to the vulgar seem dreams only." Among the "wise" who follow are Homer, Plato, Dante, Goethe, and Spenser. When Ruskin comments in a later footnote, however, that his mythic rendering of these authors' images "is of more value than any other part of the book," one wonders whose wise enigmas he is referring to here (17.208).

29. For a reading of *Aratra Pentelici* and *Fors Clavigera* that also emphasizes Ruskin's efforts to "make" and "make-believe" the public symbols governing Victorian life, see Stoddart, *Ruskin's Culture Wars,* 117–25. This study is an invaluable antidote to scholarly tendencies to ignore Ruskin's self-conscious turn toward culture and to discount as the signs of his impending madness the more risky, experimental, and culturally contingent arguments of his late writings. Both tendencies are exhibited in Rosenberg, *Darkening Glass,* chap. 9, esp. 151–52.

30. Mill, *Subjection of Women,* 9–10.

31. Ruskin's practical interest in religion shows in his reaction to the growing interest in German philosophy in Britain in the 1850s. There are two ways to inquire into the "grounds of religion," Ruskin writes. The way of "scholarly men, who have leisure" to devote years to reading Immanuel Kant and D. F. Strauss, is of no interest to him because it is impractical for his intended audience, readers who lack leisure time. It is impractical, moreover, because these people "have been brought up as Christians" and can learn the truth or falsity of their tradition only by taking the Sermon on the Mount (Matt. 5–7) and giving it a "fair practical trial" in their daily lives (5.425–26).

32. Chadwick, *Victorian Church,* 1. 545, 547–48; and 2.83–84.

33. Quoted in Finley, *Nature's Covenant,* 121–22. David Bromwich has also discussed what he calls the "egotistical sublime" in Wordsworth's poetry. In his words, "Wordsworth, chastened by the reign of terror in France, and returning to swell the war-whoop in England, came to exemplify all that Hazlitt most distrusted about 'poetic versatility' and the imagination's affinity for power." Bromwich, *Hazlitt,* 150.

34. Marx and Engels, *Collected Works,* 3.304.

FIVE The Politics of Medievalism

1. Harris, "Ruskin and Social Reform," 8. Harris cites Ruskin as the coiner of the phrase "*social* welfare," and she provides an overview of his policy proposals (10–11).

2. Boos, introduction to *History and Community,* xi.

3. Dellheim, "Interpreting Victorian Medievalism," 39, 44–53. Dellheim also claims that William Morris's "medievalism" is "progressive" as Ruskin's is not (46). See Waters, "Marxism, Medievalism and Popular Culture," 140–41.

4. Aristotle, *Nicomachean Ethics,* 1–2.

5. McGowan, "New Tory Radicals," 482.

6. Ryan, introduction to *Utilitarianism and Other Essays,* 36, 44, 45.

7. Alasdair MacIntyre never directly states that social practices cannot coexist with the institutions of modern liberalism, but this seems to be the consequence of

his arguments in *After Virtue.* John Milbank does claim that social practices cannot survive capitalism, and he cites Ruskin as the figure who recognized this incompatibility. See *Theology and Social Theory,* 197; and "On Complex Space," in *The Word Made Strange,* esp. 274–78. For a critical discussion of Milbank's reading of Ruskin, see Craig, "Naves and Nukes." For Milbank's response, see Milbank, "The Invocation of Clio," 36–40.

8. Emerson, introduction to Carlyle, *Past and Present,* xiii.

9. Carlyle, *Past and Present,* 65, 5–6, 163, 141.

10. Ibid., 33–34.

11. Ibid., 88, 80.

12. Ibid., 23.

13. Burke, "Speech on Moving His Resolutions for Conciliation with the Colonies," in *Selected Writings,* 158–62.

14. Burke, "Thoughts on the Cause of the Present Discontents . . . ," in *Selected Writings,* 109 (my emphasis).

15. Addams, "Subjective Necessity of Social Settlements," 29–32.

16. Michael Wheeler notes that Ruskin's parents chose not to attend the chapel of the popular, "extremist" preacher Edward Irving. For "all Margaret's [Ruskin's mother's] more extreme views, the Ruskins would not have associated themselves with the pre-millenialist, pentecostal, adventist and revivalist Irvingites." Wheeler, *Ruskin's God,* 8–9.

17. Hilton, *Age of Atonement,* 10, 13, 15–17.

18. Cf. three commentators with very different political views: Schneewind, *Sidgwick's Ethics,* 6; Thompson, *Making of the English Working Class,* 37–46; Waterman, *Economics, Revolution and Religion,* 5–7.

19. John Fain rightly criticizes the assumption that classical political economists were doctrinaire proponents of laissez-faire. Fain, *Ruskin and the Economists,* 64–65. James Sherburne stresses Mill's readiness to set such doctrines aside in practice. Sherburne, *Ambiguities of Abundance,* 111–17.

20. For a reading of *The Political Economy of Art* that focuses on the Solomonic wisdom of proverbs, not the classical idea of politics that I emphasize, see Wheeler, *Ruskin's God,* 161–64. Wheeler's claim on p. 179 that "Solomon's 'maxims' . . . provide Ruskin with . . . the main ethical source for his own writing on political economy" discounts the varied sources that Ruskin cites and his acute conceptual analysis.

21. Okin, *Justice, Gender, and the Family,* 30–31, 28.

22. Ibid., 101.

23. J. B. Schneewind notes that one reason social justice becomes a concern in the nineteenth century is that the prosperity gained through industrialization meant that overcoming poverty and securing an adequate quality of life for everyove were real possibilities for the first time in history. This made economic inequalities seem that much starker and that much more morally objectionable. Schneewind, "Philosophical Ideas of Charity," 68–69.

24. I am influenced in my discussion of social justice by Hollenbach, *Common Good and Christian Ethics*, 201–3.

25. Hyde, *Gift*, see chaps. 2 and 3. Ruskin's influence on theorists of gift economies, from Marcel Mauss to Lewis Hyde, is a matter of speculation, but Jose Harris traces a direct line from Ruskin to Richard Titmuss, "the leading creator of the academic discipline of 'social administration'" and author of *The Gift Relationship: From Human Blood to Social Policy* (London: Allen & Unwin, 1970). See Harris, "Ruskin and Social Reform," 7, 30.

26. Walzer, *Spheres of Justice*, 24.

27. Although the American steel magnate Andrew Carnegie surely rejected Ruskin's critique of industrial capitalism, his *Gospel of Wealth* (1886) repeats Ruskin's advice that the wealthy put their managerial virtues to the "furtherance of public advantage" through philanthropic work (17.322). Carnegie's support for inheritance taxes, what he called the "death duties" owed if the wealthy fail to give philanthropically while alive, repeats Ruskin's view that the true economist dies, not as rich, but as poor, as possible. Carnegie, *Gospel of Wealth*, 6.

28. Harris softens the authoritarian implications of Ruskin's proposed moral surveillance by noting that Hubert Llewellyn Smith, who "in 1893 became a head of the newly constituted Labour department in the Board Trade, . . . set about fulfilling Ruskin's dictum that the collection of detailed knowledge about its citizens was one of the first duties of good government." She adds that, in general, British socialists of the 1890s and 1900s overlooked Ruskin's tendency to valorize authority in favor of "his support for public welfare schemes, his idealization of the independent master craftsman, and his ethics of public service." Harris, "Ruskin and Social Reform," 21, 27.

29. Quoted in Birch, *Ruskin's Myths*, 107–8.

30. An important development in Ruskin studies is the recent effort to recover Ruskin as a proponent of broader education and public roles for women. Linda Peterson argues that "Of Queens' Gardens" should be read as an effort to promote the educational and occupational goals of a group of Victorian feminists centered around Anna Jameson. Peterson, "Feminist Origins of 'Of Queens' Gardens,'" 86–106. Dinah Birch discusses Ruskin's support for women's education and self-development, more generally, in Birch, "'What Teachers Do You Give Your Girls?'" 121–36. Sharon Aronofsky Weltman paves the way for these claims by arguing that, in his 1860s writings about and for women—"Of Queens' Gardens," *The Ethics of Dust*, and *The Queen of the Air*—Ruskin writes as a "myth-maker," who, in mythologizing women as Victoria's queens, girls as crystals, and Athena as language herself, actually "disrupts both conventional gender categories and his own implication in them [by] creating through mythic discourse an alternative to bipolar oppositions." Weltman, *Ruskin's Mythic Queen*, 21. As I focus on Ruskin's vocabulary of the virtues, which he invokes in support of his arguments for distinct, but complementary, roles for men and women, I find his idealizations of women's "natural" virtues more stubborn than do these other commentators.

31. While acknowledging the deficiencies of Ruskin's "Of Queens' Gardens" when compared to Mill's *On the Subjection of Women,* Dinah Birch notes that Ruskin's acumen as a critic fits the traits that he assigns to women more than the traits that he assigns to men. When Ruskin embarked on his career, he set aside his "creative" talents as a painter in order to judge and praise other men's work. He wrote about art and other subjects deemed womanly by his peers. As Birch reads "Of Queens' Gardens," "Ruskin is writing across gender, and he is writing of himself." She adds that his vitrolic criticisms of women are really directed at his own perceived shortcomings. Birch, "Ruskin's 'Womanly Mind' (1988)," 111.

32. Commenting on Ruskin's female audience and the "meticulous but passive observation of nature" he teaches in his scientific works, Sharon Aronofsky Weltman argues that Ruskin "feminizes" science and so "subverts the masculine/feminine hierarchy that partly constitutes Victorian scientific culture." Reading Ruskin as a precursor to eco-feminism, Weltman finds a fluidity of "natural" categories in his studies of natural history that belie his rhetoric of women's "natural" virtues and spheres. These themes fit nicely with Ruskin's attention to moral interdependence and circulating cultural power. I question, however, Ruskin's and Weltman's tendency to privilege interdependence and flux as "female" and division and assertion as "male," thereby reifying the "natural" divisions in "Of Queens' Gardens." Weltman, "Myth and Gender in Ruskin's Science," 156–60.

33. Dinah Birch reads Ruskin's scornful rejection of theology as a field for women in light of his frustrated love for Rose la Touche, whose ardent religiosity contributed, he felt, to her refusal of his marriage offer and her increasing decline into mental illness. Birch, "'What Teachers Do You Give Your Girls?'" 122.

34. The most influential exemplar of a politics of medievalism today is Alasdair MacIntyre, though John Milbank is more explicit in his defense of a "medievalist" social order. These critics do not talk of "natural" differences between men and women. But Ruskin's misgivings about "irreconcilable claims" anticipate their complaints against liberal institutions for structuring social relationships through the clashing claims of individual rights and for requiring little more than tolerance for competing conceptions of the good.

35. Augustine, *Confessions,* 30 (Book 2.6.11).

SIX The Value of Virtues

1. Abrams, *The Mirror and the Lamp,* 6–7.
2. Marx and Engels, *Collected Works,* 6.487.
3. Austin, *Practical Ruskin,* 106, 91–99, 64.
4. Ibid., 17, 89.
5. David Bromwich's remark that *Unto This Last* "contains a chapter relating value intimately to virtue" first sparked my interest in the connection between these two terms and made me pay closer attention to Ruskin's discussions of the virtues throughout his corpus. Bromwich, "Victoria's Secret," 30. John Milbank also notes

that "value" and "virtue" relate in Ruskin's social criticism. Milbank, *Theology and Social Theory,* 198–99.

6. Judith Stoddart's recent book is remarkable for arguing that Ruskin rejects these oppositions between romanticism and empiricism, between high-brow culture and consumerist entertainment, and between "Wordsworthian imagination" and "disinterested observation." She interprets his late writing in *Fors Clavigera* as the work of a critic who accepts the historicist insight that individual agency, social practices, and rational argument are always structured by the productions of the "cultural moment." Challenging the long-standing scholarly critique of Ruskin for projecting his own "subjectivity" onto all that he reads, Stoddart notes that for him "our opinions, our sensual perceptions, our conceptions of ourselves—[are] in fact dependent upon this larger cultural conversation." Thus in her felicitous phrasing, the critic does not aspire to Matthew Arnold's standard of "disinterestedness." Rather the critic practices a "disinterested interest." Because one's reading of things reflects one's present commitments, the critical task is to evaluate those interests disinterestedly, seeking a wider vision of the effects of one's judgments and choices on other people with whom one is tied as members of an interdependent community, sharing and contesting a common, if highly complex, culture. My analysis of the increasingly cultural shape of Ruskin's vocabulary of the virtues complements Stoddart's portrait of the late Ruskin, while showing how his conclusions emerge out of the teleological structure of his whole corpus. Stoddart, *Ruskin's Culture Wars,* 16, 19, 20, 54, 63, 81, 115.

7. Sherburne, *Ambiguities of Abundance,* 148.

8. J. A. Hobson lists the "doctrine of the social utility of unlimited saving, the assumptions that industry is limited by capital, and that the demand for commodities is not demand for labour" as tenets of classical political economy "successfully exploded by Mr. Ruskin in various skilful analytic passages." Quoted in Goldman, "Ruskin, Oxford, and the British Labour Movement," 71. While scrupulously reserved in his assessment of Ruskin as an economic theorist, James Sherburne adds to the impressive list of Ruskin's criticisms that have "been incorporated into the fabric of professional economics. They include his emphasis on demand as a determinant of price; his awareness of psychological factors in changing currency values; his rejection of the gold standard; and his view of currency as an instrument to be 'managed' for prosperity." Sherburne, *Ambiguities of Abundance,* 124. For an assessment of Ruskin's influence on later economists, see Henderson, *Ruskin's Political Economy,* 27–28, 37–40.

9. De Marchi, "The Success of Mill's Principles."

10. For Ruskin's misrepresentations of J. S. Mill's *Principles of Political Economy,* see Fain, *Ruskin and the Economists,* chap. 5.

11. Mohandas Gandhi described reading *Unto This Last* as a moment of awakening. The dual meaning of Gandhi's term *sarvodaya* as the "welfare of all" and the "awakening of all" reflects Ruskin's profound influence on Gandhi. Among the at-

tractions for Gandhi were Ruskin's ethics of honor in the professions and his critique of market competition as a waste of energies. Ruskin's image of distinct professions, all performing some vital public good, mirrors Gandhi's idealized portrait of the caste system. Stripped of the accretion of "untouchability" and the error of different levels of dignity for different castes, the Indian caste system represented for Gandhi a truth about "human nature" that Hinduism simply reduced to a "science." In his words, "Varnashrama [the combination of caste and stages of life] is self-restraint and conservation of economy of energy." For Gandhi, renunciation of the desire to change one's inherited occupation serves as a brake on economic and social competition. The problem with this defense of caste is that fixed social categories always become, in practice, fixed hierarchies of unequal dignity, opportunity, and reward. Gandhi's and Ruskin's calls for self-restraint and sacrifice in the public interest have their merits, but the close connections between the moral language of "honor" and "worthiness" and socially reinforced hierarchies must be attended to very carefully. Gandhi, *Selected Writings of Mahatma Gandhi,* 174–75.

12. Since Ruskin's day workplace reforms have proceeded through government regulations and through the extension of benefits. Although Ruskin would have welcomed laws setting limits on hours and ensuring workers' health and safety, as these fit with his own reform efforts, it is unlikely that he would have welcomed the legal machinery of rights and regulations that goes with them (see chapter 5; 27.147). He preferred that masters see to their workers' needs as a parent looks out for children. This is an area where we must push beyond Ruskin's paternalism.

13. James Sherburne remarks that Ruskin's attitude toward wealth is shaped by "Greek philosophers" for whom "wealth is neither an end in itself nor a means to the insatiable pursuit of pleasure. It is a means to the 'good life' or 'living in accordance with the virtues.'" Sherburne does not develop the role of the virtues in Ruskin's social criticism except to question the wisdom of approaching economics from the standpoint of ethics. Sherburne, *Ambiguities of Abundance,* 154. Willie Henderson analyzes Ruskin's debts to Xenophon and Plato in giving an instructive reading of Ruskin's rhetorical construction of a new model of economic agency—referring specifically to Plato's account of *techné,* the equivalent of "social practices." When Henderson turns to Ruskin's language of "manly character," however, he writes of "associated subjectivities" and, slightly better, "ethical and emotional capacities," once again obscuring Ruskin's vocabulary of the virtues. Henderson, *Ruskin's Political Economy,* chap. 3, esp. 53, 58, 62.

14. My reading of Ruskin's concerns about "preference deformation" is influenced by the work of Amartya Sen and Martha Nussbaum; see esp. Nussbaum, *Women and Human Development,* 112–15. Nussbaum might categorize Ruskin's account of "good desires" under her category of "platonism," which argues for an objectively good set of desires with no regard for what individual human beings actually prefer in their lives. In his more metaphysical moments, Ruskin can be seen as asserting an objective set of preferences with little or no regard for what his contemporaries want. Yet the more he focuses on his contemporaries' activities, as he

does in his ethics of consumption, the more democratic he becomes in his arguments. For Nussbaum on "platonism," see p. 117.

15. Sherburne, *Ambiguities of Abundance,* 127.

16. Terry Eagleton makes modest appeals to "human nature" to remind advocates of social justice to address basic human needs and not simply reconstruct culture. Eagleton, *After Theory,* 115–22.

17. Although James Sherburne cites a number of critics of classical political economy's "scarcity" premise, he names Ruskin "the most important nineteenth-century precursor of Simon Patten [the first professional economist to presuppose abundance] and twentieth-century abundance thinking." No scholar has taught us more about the theme of abundance in Ruskin's criticism than has James Sherburne. Sherburne, *Ambiguities of Abundance,* 86, 139–40.

18. Galbraith, *Economics in Perspective,* 48–52.

19. For a discussion of Mill's distinction between productive and unproductive consumption, see Fain, *Ruskin and the Economists,* 135–39. For a discussion of Ruskin's critique of capital accumulation, see Sherburne, *Ambiguities of Abundance,* 146–47.

20. In "The Living Standard" Sen writes that, in addition to Adam Smith, "[t]he possibility of judging advantage in terms of the extent of freedom also has been discussed by Karl Marx and John Stuart Mill." Yet Ruskin is the nineteenth-century figure who shares Sen's criticisms of the standard economic measurements of the quality of life and an explicit concern with the specific capabilities that people need to function well. Sen, "Living Standard," 293. For an excellent discussion of the capabilities approach in relation to twentieth-century Christian ethics, see Hicks, *Inequality and Christian Ethics.*

21. Sen, "Living Standard," 291, 293, 294.

22. Sen, *Standard of Living,* 29, 37; and "Living Standard," 294–295.

23. Sen, "Capability and Well-Being," 47.

24. Sen, *Standard of Living,* 36; and "Living Standard," 292.

25. Sen, *Standard of Living,* 8, 25; and "Capability and Well-Being," 30, 38–40.

26. Martha Nussbaum has argued that Sen must adopt an "objectivist approach" to the good life to advance the normative aims of his theory. Nussbaum, "Nature, Function, and Capability," 176. For Sen's response to her proposal, see Sen, "Capability and Well-Being," 46–47. Although Nussbaum defends forms of "paternalism" that increase people's choices by "underwrit[ing] central values, on an equal basis," she would distance herself from Ruskin's paternalism. Nussbaum, *Women and Human Development,* 51–55.

27. Ruskin's five categories of "property" and their accompanying "rights" clarify his own vision of the good life. He cites two kinds of "property necessary to life." The first kind includes water, air, and land, those goods that cannot be produced by human labor. Rights to these goods (or, in place of land, an equivalent amount of "wages and privileges") are inalienable. The remaining necessities of life are made through human effort, and "no person capable of doing the work necessary for

[their] production has a right to it until he has done that work." These duties to work are matched by rights to due compensation. The next two kinds of property center on pleasures—the "bodily pleasures and conveniences" that do not "directly . . . sustain life" and the "intellectual or emotional pleasure" that one takes from parks and wilderness, "books, works of art and objects of natural history." Ruskin accords the latter pleasures far greater value, going so far as to equate "well-being" with these intellectual and emotional goods—calling them the only "real property" because they are the only kind that gives continual and shared pleasures without being used up. As he puts it, food gives "being," but not "well-being." The fifth type of property is "representative property," which includes money and other documentary forms of property (16.129–35).

28. Austin, *Practical Ruskin*, 90.

29. Fain, *Ruskin and the Economists*, 80–81.

30. Although Sherburne dismisses the "spiritual qualities" of effectual value, he highlights the parallels between Ruskin's, Xenophon's, and Aristotle's interest in human capacities. Sherburne, *Ambiguities of Abundance*, 127–29.

31. Mohandas Gandhi not only echoes Ruskin's equation of "wealth" with well-developed people, but he also translated the entirety of *Unto This Last* into Gujarati. In 1967 Martin Luther King Jr. declares, "We must rapidly begin the shift from a 'thing-oriented' society to a 'person-oriented' society." King, "Time to Break Silence," 148.

SEVEN Is Good Consumption Possible?

1. For Marx, the "finish" of consumption shows most clearly in enjoyment of the arts: "The need which consumption feels for the object is created by the perception of it. The object of art—like every other product—creates a public which is sensitive to art and enjoys beauty. Production thus not only creates an object for the subject, but also a subject for the object." Here Marx recognizes the cultural character of consumption, but again production determines how people consume, thus denying them the independent judgment and agency at the heart of Ruskin's ethics of consumption. Marx, *Grundrisse*, 91–92.

2. In view of Marx's analysis of the contradictions between "overproduction" and "underconsumption" in industrial capitalism, getting wealthy consumers to prefer expensive and labor-intensive craftwork would be one way to decrease output and absorb some of the surplus value extracted through factory production. Marx, *Capital*, 264.

3. Time and again, Marx rules out consumption as a defining moment in economic life, as when he ridicules Anastasius Grün for proposing that production and consumption could be brought into a "unity" if only people consumed in a "human" way. Marx cites Grün's comment, "'It is believed that the enjoyment of coffee, sugar, etc., is mere consumption; but is this enjoyment not, in fact, production in the colonies?' [Grün] might just as well have asked," Marx continues poignantly, "Does not this enjoyment imply that Negro slaves enjoy the lash and that floggings

are produced in the colonies? One can see that the outcome of such exuberance as this is simply an apology for existing conditions." Marx and Engels, *Collected Works,* 5.515–16.

4. Mill, *On Liberty,* 83.

5. Ibid., 84–87.

6. As noted in chapter 5, Ruskin was no proponent of the Temperance Movement either, and his wariness reminds us of what he meant by a well-developed character and what he saw as the primary obstacles to it. On the rare occasions when he narrows his sights to moral virtues, he typically urges the rich and the powerful to learn temperance, for example, not the poor upon whom a meager living is strictly enforced.

7. Among the interferences that are "objectionable, not as infringements on the liberty of the producer or seller, but on that of the buyer," Mill includes the "prohibition of the importation of opium into China." Mill, *On Liberty,* 94–95.

8. Walzer discusses the "negative good" of "hard work" and its distribution "to degraded people" in *Spheres of Justice,* 165.

9. A recent example of a Christian ethicist who draws on a vision of earthly abundance is Nash, "On the Subversive Virtue," 416–36. For historical examples of the theme of an abundant life with roots in various strands of Christianity, see Shi, *Simple Life.* For a critic who reduces Christian ethics of consumption to asceticism, see Schudson, "Delectable Materialism," 253–55. Although Ruskin criticizes luxury, he was no proponent of austerity, as is suggested by John Rosenberg's claim that the "cardinal virtue" of Ruskin's ethics is "self-denial." Rosenberg, *Darkening Glass,* 112.

10. The paragraph on rent that Ruskin quotes from Mill's *Principles* actually states that "with regard to the land, in everything which [the landlord] abstains from doing, he is morally bound, and should whenever the case admits, be *legally compelled* to make his interest and pleasure consistent with the public good" (17.443; my emphasis). Thus Mill is open to legal measures against slumlords, but he does not specify them here.

11. For Ruskin's financial support of Octavia Hill's housing initiative (over £10,000), his proposals for "gardens, nurseries, playgrounds, summer outings, and communal Christmas and May-day festivities," and the eventual public dispute between Ruskin and Hill, see Harris, "Ruskin and Social Reform," 17–19.

12. Mill recanted the "wages fund" theory in 1869. James Sherburne notes the various formulations of this theory in classical political economy. He describes Mill's version as "harmless," suggesting that Mill may have recanted the theory for political, not theoretical, reasons. Sherburne, *Ambiguities of Abundance,* 156–57, 160.

13. Mill, *Collected Works,* 3.749–50, 759.

14. On Ruskin's proposals to professionalize aristocratic virtue, Lawrence Goldman quotes T. W. Price, a working-class supporter of Ruskin's "swift but accurate analysis" in *Unto This Last,* who nevertheless criticized "the fantastic provisions of Ruskin's scheme of land reform, with the landed gentry retained as national orna-

ments at a fixed salary." Goldman, "Ruskin, Oxford, and the British Labour Movement," 80–81.

15. James Sherburne cites various sources in the history of economic thought for Ruskin's "streams" and "flows" of wealth. Sherburne, *Ambiguities of Abundance,* 92–93. Willie Henderson notes that Mill's economic "rhetoric" championed "growth," while Ruskin's envisioned "development." Henderson, *Ruskin's Political Economy,* 40.

16. The title *Unto This Last* lends biblical support to Ruskin's proposal for a standard wage in every trade. Just as the vineyard owner paid the same penny to the workers hired at different hours of the day—even "unto this last"—Ruskin calls for standard wages regardless of the work's quality. Only then, he argues, will competition be kept out of the trades as it is in the professions. Thomas Aquinas's exegesis of this parable suggests another intriguing source for Ruskin's title. Aquinas writes that "equal reward is given for all the works of virtue; because it is written (Matt. 20.10) that all who labor in the vineyard *received every man a penny.*" If Aquinas was somehow a source for Ruskin, then my interpretation of the centrality of the "virtues" to Ruskin's ethics of consumption gains further strength. St. Thomas Aquinas, *Summa Theologica,* 1. 609 (Pt. I–II Q. 5 Art. 2).

17. Austin, *Practical Ruskin,* 8.

18. Although Ruskin was no democrat politically speaking, his ethics of consumption advocates "economic democracy." If democracy grants power to "the people" to decide the present shape and future course of their society, then Ruskin's arguments for the just price and a pious acknowledgment of one's economic indebtedness are democratic. He mistakenly believed that fairer distributions of decision-making power were simply a matter of economic justice, not political reform. Douglas Lummis names Ruskin's ethics a cornerstone of "economic democracy." Lummis, *Radical Democracy,* 70–71.

19. I take the term "debt analysis of money" from John Fain, who notes that Ruskin's view of money is "in its essentials . . . the currently accepted view." Fain, *Ruskin and the Economists,* 123.

20. Sherburne, *Ambiguities of Abundance,* 140.

21. Quoted in Fain, *Ruskin and the Economists,* 130–32.

22. Plato's classic statement on piety as a species of justice is his "Euthyphro." Socrates practices piety in his service to his *daemon* in the "Apology." Plato, *Five Dialogues,* esp. 27–29.

23. In chapter 2 I introduced Alasdair MacIntyre's distinction between "internal" and "external goods." A similar distinction between the distributive mechanisms of practices and institutions is basic to Ruskin's critique of classical political economy. MacIntyre allows that practices always sit within a framework of institutions, though he also appears to reject modern liberal institutions for producing an unsustainable moral language of rights and utility. MacIntyre, *After Virtue,* 194–95.

24. Pickthall, *Glorious Koran,* Surah 2.256.

Conclusion

1. Lasch, *True and Only Heaven,* 80.
2. Schneewind, "Divine Corporation," 177–78.
3. Cavell, *Must We Mean What We Say?* 93.
4. For an excellent analysis of Ruskin's rhetorical efforts to build commonality with his audience, before shocking them with the contradictions in Victorian public life, see George Landow's discussion of Ruskin's 1864 lecture "Traffic": Landow, "Ruskin as Victorian Sage."
5. Stout, *Democracy and Tradition,* 34, 80, 73–74.

Bibliography

Abrams, M. H. *The Mirror and the Lamp: Romantic Theory and the Critical Tradition.* New York: Oxford University Press, 1953.

Abse, Joan. *John Ruskin, the Passionate Moralist.* New York: Knopf, 1981.

Addams, Jane. "The Subjective Necessity for Social Settlements." In *The Social Thought of Jane Addams,* ed. Christopher Lasch. Indianapolis: Bobbs-Merrill, 1965.

Agnew, Jean-Christophe. "Coming Up for Air: Consumer Culture in Historical Perspective." In *Consumption and the World of Goods,* ed. John Brewer and Roy Porter. London: Routledge, 1993.

Anthony, P. D. *John Ruskin's Labour: A Study of Ruskin's Social Theory.* Cambridge: Cambridge University Press, 1983.

Aquinas, St. Thomas. *Summa Theologica.* First complete American ed., vol. 1. Trans. Fathers of the English Dominican Province. New York: Benziger Brothers, 1947.

Aristotle. *The Nichomachean Ethics.* Trans. David Ross. Oxford: Oxford University Press, 1980.

Arnold, Matthew. *Culture and Anarchy.* Ed. J. Dover Wilson. Cambridge: Cambridge University Press, 1988.

Augustine. *Confessions.* Trans. Henry Chadwick. Oxford: Oxford University Press, 1991.

Austin, Linda M. *The Practical Ruskin: Economics and Audience in the Late Work.* Baltimore: Johns Hopkins University Press, 1991.

Barbour, John D. *Versions of Deconversion: Autobiography and the Loss of Faith.* Charlottesville: University Press of Virginia, 1994.

Benhabib, Seyla. *Critique, Norm, and Utopia: A Study of the Foundations of Critical Theory.* New York: Columbia University Press, 1986.

Berkowitz, Peter. *Virtue and the Making of Modern Liberalism.* Princeton, NJ: Princeton University Press, 1999.

Birch, Dinah, ed. *Ruskin and the Dawn of the Modern.* Oxford: Oxford University Press, 1999.

———. *Ruskin's Myths.* Oxford: Clarendon Press, 1988.

———. "Ruskin's 'Womanly Mind' (1988)." In *Ruskin and Gender,* ed. Dinah Birch and Francis O'Gorman. New York: Palgrave, 2002.

———. "'What Teachers Do You Give Your Girls?' Ruskin and Women's Education." In *Ruskin and Gender,* ed. Dinah Birch and Francis O'Gorman. New York: Palgrave, 2002.

Birch, Dinah, and Francis O'Gorman. *Ruskin and Gender.* New York: Palgrave, 2002.

Bloom, Harold. "Ruskin as Literary Critic." In *The Ringers in the Tower: Studies in Romantic Tradition,* 169–83. Chicago: University of Chicago Press, 1971.

Boos, Florence S., ed. *History and Community: Essays in Victorian Medievalism.* New York: Garland, 1992.

Boris, Eileen. *Art and Labor: Ruskin, Morris, and the Craftsman Ideal in America.* Philadelphia, Temple University Press, 1986.

Brewer, John, and Roy Porter, eds. *Consumption and the World of Goods.* London: Routledge, 1993.

Bromwich, David. *Hazlitt: The Mind of a Critic.* New York: Oxford University Press, 1983.

———. "Victoria's Secret." *New Republic,* May 15, 1995, 28–35.

Burke, Edmund. *A Philosophical Inquiry into the Origin of Our Ideas of the Sublime and Beautiful.* Ed. J. T. Boulton. London: Routledge & Kegan Paul, 1958.

———. *Selected Writings and Speeches.* Ed. Peter J. Stanlis. Washington, DC: Regnery Gateway, 1963.

Campbell, Colin. *The Romantic Ethic and the Spirit of Modern Consumerism.* Oxford: Blackwell, 1987.

Carlyle, Thomas. *A Carlyle Reader: Selections from the Writings of Thomas Carlyle.* Ed. G. B. Tennyson. Cambridge: Cambridge University Press, 1984.

———. *On Heroes, Hero-Worship and the Heroic in History.* Ed. Carl Niemeyer. Lincoln: University of Nebraska Press, 1966.

———. *Past and Present.* London: J. M. Dent, 1947.

———. *Sartor Resartus.* In *A Carlyle Reader: Selections from the Writings of Thomas Carlyle,* ed. G. B. Tennyson. Cambridge: Cambridge University Press, 1984.

Carnegie, Andrew. *The Gospel of Wealth.* Indianapolis: Indiana University Center on Philanthropy, 1993.

Cavell, Stanley. *Must We Mean What We Say? A Book of Essays.* Cambridge: Cambridge University Press, 1976.

Chadwick, Owen. *The Victorian Church.* 2 vols. London: Adam and Charles Black, 1966, 1970.

Coleridge, Samuel Taylor. *Biographia Literaria; or, Biographical Sketches of My Literary Life and Opinions.* Collected Works of Samuel Taylor Coleridge, vols. 7 and 8, ed. James Engell and W. Jackson Bate. Princeton, NJ: Princeton University Press, 1983.

———. *On Politics and Society.* Ed. John Morrow. Princeton, NJ: Princeton University Press, 1990.

———. *On the Constitution of Church and State, according to the Idea of Each.* Collected Works of Samuel Taylor Coleridge, vol. 10, ed. John Colmer. Princeton, NJ: Princeton University Press, 1983.

———. "The Statesman's Manual; or The Bible the Best Guide to Political Skill and Foresight: A Lay Sermon." *Lay Sermons.* Collected Works of Samuel Taylor Coleridge, vol. 6, ed. R. J. White. Princeton, NJ: Princeton University Press, 1972.

Collini, Stefan. *Public Moralists: Political Thought and Intellectual Life in Britain, 1850–1930.* Oxford: Clarendon Press, 1991.

Craig, David M. "Naves and Nukes: John Ruskin as 'Augustinian' Social Theorist?" *Journal of Religious Ethics* 32, no. 2 (Summer 2004): 325–56.

———. "The Virtues and Limits of Good Consumption: John Ruskin's 'Work of Iron.'" *Soundings: An Interdisciplinary Journal* 84, no. 3–4 (Fall/Winter 2001): 337–63.

Crocker, David A., and Toby Linden, eds. *Ethics of Consumption: The Good Life, Justice, and Global Stewardship.* Lanham, MD: Rowman and Littlefield, 1998.

Darwin, Charles. *The Origin of Species.* Ed. Gillian Beer. Oxford: Oxford University Press, 1996.

Dellheim, Charles. "Interpreting Victorian Medievalism." In *History and Community: Essays in Victorian Medievalism,* ed. Florence S. Boos. New York: Garland, 1992.

de Marchi, Neil B. "The Success of Mill's Principles." *History of Political Economy* 6, no. 2 (Summer 1974): 119–57.

Eagleton, Terry. *After Theory.* New York: Basic Books, 2003.

Elster, Jon. *An Introduction to Karl Marx.* Cambridge: Cambridge University Press, 1986.

Emerson, Ralph Waldo. Introduction to *Past and Present,* by Thomas Carlyle. London: J. M. Dent, 1947.

Fain, John Tyree. *Ruskin and the Economists.* Nashville, TN: Vanderbilt University Press, 1956.

Feuerbach, Ludwig. *The Essence of Christianity.* Trans. George Eliot. New York: Harper & Row, 1957.

Finley, C. Stephen. *Nature's Covenant: Figures of Landscape in Ruskin.* University Park: Pennsylvania State University Press, 1992.

Fitch, Raymond E. *The Poison Sky: Myth and Apocalypse in Ruskin.* Athens: Ohio University Press, 1982.

Fraser, Hilary. *Beauty and Belief: Aesthetics and Religion in Victorian Literature.* Cambridge: Cambridge University Press, 1986.

Galbraith, John Kenneth. *Economics in Perspective: A Critical History.* Boston: Houghton Mifflin, 1987.

Gandhi, Mohandas. *Selected Writings of Mahatma Gandhi.* Ed. Ronald Duncan. London: Faber & Faber, 1973.

Goetz, Sister Mary Dorothea, O.S.F. *A Study of Ruskin's Concept of the Imagination.* Washington, DC: Catholic University of America, 1947.

Goldman, Lawrence. "Ruskin, Oxford, and the British Labour Movement, 1880–1914." In *Ruskin and the Dawn of the Modern,* ed. Dinah Birch. Oxford: Oxford University Press, 1999.

Goodchild, Philip. *Religion and Capitalism: The Price of Piety.* London: Routledge, 2002.

Gutierrez, Gustavo. *A Theology of Liberation: History, Politics and Salvation.* Ed. and trans. Sister Caridad Inda and John Eagleson. Maryknoll, NY: Orbis, 1973.

Harris, Jose. "Ruskin and Social Reform." In *Ruskin and the Dawn of the Modern,* ed. Dinah Birch. Oxford: Oxford University Press, 1999.

Harvey, Van. *Feuerbach and the Interpretation of Religion.* Cambridge: Cambridge University Press, 1995.

Helsinger, Elizabeth K. *Ruskin and the Art of the Beholder.* Cambridge, MA: Harvard University Press, 1982.

Henderson, Willie. *Ruskin's Political Economy.* London: Routledge, 2000.

Hewison, Robert. *John Ruskin: The Argument of the Eye.* Princeton, NJ: Princeton University Press, 1976.

Hewison, Robert, ed. *New Approaches to Ruskin: Thirteen Essays.* London: Routledge & Kegan Paul, 1981.

Hicks, Douglas A. *Inequality and Christian Ethics.* Cambridge: Cambridge University Press, 2000.

Hilton, Boyd. *The Age of Atonement: The Influence of Evangelicalism on Social and Economic Thought, 1785–1865.* Oxford: Clarendon Press, 1991.

Hilton, Tim. *John Ruskin: The Early Years, 1819–1859.* New Haven, CT: Yale University Press, 1985.

———. *John Ruskin: The Later Years.* New Haven, CT: Yale University Press, 2000.

Himmelfarb, Gertrude. *The De-Moralization of Society: From Victorian Virtues to Modern Values.* New York: Alfred A. Knopf, 1995.

Hirschman, A. O. *The Passions and the Interests.* Princeton, NJ: Princeton University Press, 1977.

Hobson, John A. *John Ruskin, Social Reformer.* Boston: D. Estes, 1898.

Hollenbach, David. S.J. *The Common Good and Christian Ethics.* Cambridge: Cambridge University Press, 2002.

Hooker, Richard. *Of the Laws of Ecclesiastical Polity: Preface, Book I, Book VIII.* Ed. Arthur Stephen McGrade. Cambridge: Cambridge University Press, 1989.

Hyde, Lewis. *The Gift: Imagination and the Erotic Life of Property.* New York: Vintage Books, 1979.

Jay, Elisabeth, and Richard Jay, eds. *Critics of Capitalism: Victorian Reactions to "Political Economy."* Cambridge: Cambridge University Press, 1986.

King, Martin Luther, Jr. "A Time to Break Silence." In *I Have a Dream: Writings and Speeches That Changed the World,* ed. James Melvin Washington. San Francisco: HarperSan Francisco, 1992.

Kirchhoff, Frederick. "A Science against Sciences: Ruskin's Floral Mythology." In

Nature and the Victorian Imagination, ed. U. C. Knoepflmacher and G. B. Tennyson. Berkeley: University of California Press, 1977.

Landow, George P. *The Aesthetic and Critical Theories of John Ruskin*. Princeton, NJ: Princeton University Press, 1971.

———. *Ruskin*. New York: Oxford University Press, 1985.

———. "Ruskin as Victorian Sage: The Example of 'Traffic.'" In *New Approaches to Ruskin*, ed. Robert Hewison, 89–110. London: Routledge & Kegan Paul, 1981.

———. *Victorian Types, Victorian Shadows: Biblical Typology in Victorian Literature, Art, and Thought*. Boston: Routledge & Kegan Paul, 1980.

Lasch, Christopher. *The True and Only Heaven: Progress and Its Critics*. New York: W. W. Norton, 1991.

Le Quesne, A. L. *Carlyle*. In *Victorian Thinkers: Carlyle, Ruskin, Arnold, Morris*. Oxford: Oxford University Press, 1993.

Locke, John. *An Essay concerning Human Understanding*. Vol. 2. New York: Dover, 1959.

Long, D. Stephen. *The Divine Economy: Theology and the Market*. London: Routledge, 2000.

Lummis, C. Douglas. *Radical Democracy*. Ithaca, NY: Cornell University Press, 1996.

MacIntyre, Alasdair. *After Virtue*. 2d ed. Notre Dame: University of Notre Dame Press, 1984.

———. *Marxism and Christianity*. London: Duckworth, 1968.

———. "Politics, Philosophy and the Common Good." In *The MacIntyre Reader*, ed. Kelvin Knight. Notre Dame, IN: University of Notre Dame Press, 1998.

———. *Whose Justice? Which Rationality?* Notre Dame, IN: University of Notre Dame Press, 1988.

Malthus, Thomas. *An Essay on the Principle of Population; or, A View of Its Past and Present Effects on Human Happiness*. Cambridge: Cambridge University Press, 1992.

Marx, Karl. *Capital*. Vol. 1, trans. Ben Fowkes. London: Penguin Books, 1990.

———. *Grundrisse: Foundations of the Critique of Political Economy (Rough Draft)*. Trans. Martin Nicolaus. London: Penguin Books, 1973.

Marx, Karl, and Friedrich Engels. *Collected Works*. Trans. Richard Dixon et al. 50 vols. London: Lawrence and Wishart; New York: International, 1975–2001.

Maurice, Frederick Denison. *Reconstructing Christian Ethics: Selected Writings*. Ed. Ellen Wondra. Louisville, KY: John Knox Westminster Press, 1995.

Mauss, Marcel. *The Gift: The Form and Reason for Exchange in Archaic Societies*. Trans. W. D. Halls. New York: W. W. Norton, 1990.

McGowan, John. "The New Tory Radicals." *Soundings: An Interdisciplinary Journal* 72, no. 2–3 (Summer/Fall 1989): 477–500.

McKendrick, Neil, John Brewer, and J. H. Plumb. *The Birth of a Consumer Society: The Commercialization of Eighteenth-Century England*. Bloomington: Indiana University Press, 1982.

McLaughlin, Elizabeth T. *Ruskin and Gandhi.* Lewisburg, PA: Bucknell University Press, 1974.

Milbank, John. "The Invocation of Clio." *Journal of Religious Ethics* 33, no. 1 (March 2005): 36–40.

———. *Theology and Social Theory: Beyond Secular Reason.* Oxford: Blackwell, 1990.

———. *The Word Made Strange: Theology, Language, and Culture.* Cambridge: Blackwell, 1997.

Mill, John Stuart. *The Collected Works of John Stuart Mill.* Ed. J. M. Robson. Toronto: University of Toronto Press, 1965.

———. *On Liberty.* Ed. Elizabeth Rappaport. Indianapolis, IN: Hackett, 1978.

———. *Principles of Political Economy with Some of Their Applications to Social Philosophy, Books IV and V.* Ed. Donald Winch. London: Penguin Books, 1985.

———. *The Subjection of Women.* New York: Greenwood Press, 1969.

Mill, John Stuart, and Jeremy Bentham. *Utilitarianism and Other Essays.* Ed. Alan Ryan. Harmondsworth, Middlesex, UK: Penguin Books, 1987.

Miller, Daniel, ed. *Acknowledging Consumption: A Review of New Studies.* London: Routledge, 1995.

Millett, Kate. "The Debate over Women: Ruskin versus Mill." *Victorian Studies* 14, no. 3 (1970): 63–82.

Morris, William. *News from Nowhere and Other Writings.* Ed. Clive Wilmer. London: Penguin Books, 1993.

Müller, F. Max. *The Science of Language.* New York: AMS Press, 1978.

Murdoch, Iris. *The Sovereignty of Good.* London: Routledge, 1970.

Nash, James A. "On the Subversive Virtue: Frugality." In *Ethics of Consumption: The Good Life, Justice, and Global Stewardship,* ed. David A. Crocker and Toby Linden. Lanham, MD: Rowman and Littlefield, 1998. Originally published as "Toward a Revival and Reform of the Subversive Virtue: Frugality," in *The Annual of the Society of Christian Ethics* (1995).

Niebuhr, H. Richard. *Christ and Culture.* New York: Harper & Brothers, 1951.

Niebuhr, Reinhold. *Moral Man and Immoral Society: A Study in Ethics and Politics.* New York: Charles Scribner's Sons, 1941.

Nord, Deborah Epstein. "Mill and Ruskin on the Woman Question Revisited." In *Teaching Literature: What Is Needed Now,* ed. James Engell and David Perkins. Cambridge, MA: Harvard University Press, 1988.

Norman, Edward. *The Victorian Christian Socialists.* Cambridge: Cambridge University Press, 1987.

Nussbaum, Martha C. "The Good as Discipline, the Good as Freedom." In *Ethics of Consumption: The Good Life, Justice, and Global Stewardship,* ed. David A. Crocker and Toby Linden. Lanham, MD: Rowman & Littlefield, 1998.

———. "Nature, Function, and Capability: Aristotle on Political Distribution." *Oxford Studies in Ancient Philosophy* suppl. vol. (1988): 145–84.

———. *Women and Human Development: The Capabilities Approach.* Cambridge: Cambridge University Press, 2000.

Nussbaum, Martha C., and Amartya Sen, eds. *The Quality of Life.* Oxford: Clarendon Press, 1993.

Oakeshott, Michael. *Rationalism in Politics and Other Essays.* New York: Basic Books, 1962.

O'Gorman, Francis. *Late Ruskin: New Contexts.* Aldershot, UK: Ashgate, 2001.

———. "Ruskin's Science of the 1870's: Science, Education, and the Nation." In *Ruskin and the Dawn of the Modern,* ed. Dinah Birch. Oxford: Oxford University Press, 1999.

Okin, Susan Moller. *Justice, Gender, and the Family.* New York: Basic Books, 1989.

Pattison, George. *Art, Modernity and Faith: Towards a Theology of Art.* New York: St. Martin's Press, 1991.

Peterson, Linda. "The Feminist Origins of 'Of Queens' Gardens.'" In *Ruskin and Gender,* ed. Dinah Birch and Francis O'Gorman. New York: Palgrave, 2002.

Pickthall, Mohammed Marmaduke, trans. *The Meaning of the Glorious Koran: An Explanatory Translation.* New York: New American Library, 1954.

Plato. *Five Dialogues.* Trans. G. M. A. Grube. Indianapolis, IN: Hackett, 1981.

Pugin, A. W. N. *Contrasts.* New York: Humanities Press, 1969.

Quinton, Anthony. *The Politics of Imperfection: The Religious and Secular Traditions of Conservative Thought in England from Hooker to Oakeshott.* London: Faber & Faber, 1978.

Raven, Charles E. *Christian Socialism, 1848–1854.* London: Macmillan, 1920.

Rawls, John. *A Theory of Justice.* Cambridge, MA: Belknap Press, 1971.

Richards, Thomas. *The Commodity Culture of Victorian England: Advertising and Spectacle, 1851–1914.* Stanford, CA: Stanford University Press, 1990.

Rorty, Richard. "The Historiography of Philosophy: Four Genres." In *Philosophy in History: Essays on the Historiography of Philosophy,* ed. Richard Rorty, J. B. Schneewind, and Quentin Skinner, 49–75. Cambridge: Cambridge University Press, 1984.

———. *Philosophy and the Mirror of Nature.* Princeton, NJ: Princeton University Press, 1979.

———. "The World Well Lost." In *Consequences of Pragmatism (Essays: 1972–1980).* Minneapolis: University of Minnesota Press, 1982.

Rose, Margaret A. *Marx's Lost Aesthetic: Karl Marx and the Visual Arts.* Cambridge: Cambridge University Press, 1984.

Rose, Phyllis. *Parallel Lives: Five Victorian Marriages.* New York: Vintage Books, 1984.

Rosenberg, John D. *The Darkening Glass: A Portrait of Ruskin's Genius.* New York: Columbia University Press, 1980. Originally published, London: Routledge & Kegan Paul, 1963.

Ross, Malcolm Mackenzie. "Ruskin, Hooker and 'the Christian Theoria.'" In *Essays in English Literature from the Renaissance to the Victorian Age: Presented to*

A. S. P. Woodhouse, ed. Millar MacLure and F. W. Watt. Toronto: University of Toronto Press, 1964.

Ruskin, John. *The Works of John Ruskin.* 39 vols. Ed. E. T. Cook and Alexander Wedderburn. London: George Allen, 1903–12.

Ryan, Alan. *The Philosophy of John Stuart Mill.* New York: Pantheon Books, 1970.

———. Introduction to *Utilitarianism and Other Essays: J. S. Mill and Jeremy Bentham.* New York: Penguin Books, 1987.

Sawyer, Paul. *Ruskin's Poetic Argument: The Design of the Major Works.* Ithaca, NY: Cornell University Press, 1985.

Schneewind, J. B. *Backgrounds of English Victorian Literature.* New York: Random House, 1970.

———. "The Divine Corporation and the History of Ethics." In *Philosophy in History: Essays on the Historiography of Philosophy,* ed. Richard Rorty, J. B. Schneewind, and Quentin Skinner. Cambridge: Cambridge University Press, 1984.

———. "Philosophical Ideas of Charity: Some Historical Reflections." In *Giving: Western Ideas of Philanthropy,* ed. J. B. Schneewind. Bloomington: Indiana University Press, 1996.

———. *Sidgwick's Ethics and Victorian Moral Philosophy.* Oxford: Clarendon Press, 1977.

Schudson, Michael. "Delectable Materialism: Second Thoughts on Consumer Culture." In *Ethics of Consumption: The Good Life, Justice and Global Stewardship,* ed. David A. Crocker and Toby Linden. Lanham, MD: Rowman & Littlefield, 1998.

Sedgwick, Peter. *The Market Economy and Christian Ethics.* Cambridge: Cambridge University Press, 1999.

Sen, Amartya. "Capability and Well-Being." In *The Quality of Life,* ed. Martha C. Nussbaum and Amartya Sen. Oxford: Clarendon Press, 1993.

———. "The Living Standard." In *Ethics of Consumption: The Good Life, Justice and Global Stewardship,* ed. David A. Crocker and Toby Linden. Lanham, MD: Rowman & Littlefield, 1998.

———. *The Standard of Living.* Ed. Geoffrey Hawthorn. Cambridge: Cambridge University Press, 1987.

Sen, Amartya, and Martha C. Nussbaum, eds. *The Quality of Life.* Oxford: Clarendon Press, 1993.

Sharpe, Eric J. *Comparative Religion: A History.* 2d ed. Lasalle, IL: Open Court, 1986.

Shaw, George Bernard. *Ruskin's Politics.* London: Ruskin Centenary Council, 1921.

Sherburne, James Clark. *John Ruskin, or the Ambiguities of Abundance.* Cambridge, MA: Harvard University Press, 1972.

Shi, David E. *The Simple Life: Plain Living and High Thinking in American Culture.* New York: Oxford University Press, 1985.

Shrimpton, Nicholas. "Ruskin and the Aesthetes." In *Ruskin and the Dawn of the Modern,* ed. Dinah Birch. Oxford: Oxford University Press, 1999.

———. "Rust and Dust: Ruskin's Pivotal Work." In *New Approaches to Ruskin: Thirteen Essays,* ed. Robert Hewison, 51–67. London: Routledge & Kegan Paul, 1981.

Smart, J. J. C., and Bernard Williams. *Utilitarianism: For and Against.* Cambridge: Cambridge University Press, 1973.

Soenstrom, David. "Millett versus Ruskin: A Defense of Ruskin's 'Of Queens' Gardens.'" *Victorian Studies* 20, no. 3 (1977): 283–97.

Spear, Jeffrey L. *Dreams of an English Eden: Ruskin and His Tradition in Social Criticism.* New York: Columbia University Press, 1984.

Stansky, Peter. *Morris.* In *Victorian Thinkers.* Oxford: Oxford University Press, 1993.

Stoddart, Judith. *Ruskin's Culture Wars:* Fors Clavigera *and the Crisis of Victorian Liberalism.* Charlottesville: University Press of Virginia, 1998.

Stout, Jeffrey. *Democracy and Tradition.* Princeton, NJ: Princeton University Press, 2003.

———. *Ethics after Babel: The Languages of Morals and Their Discontents.* Boston: Beacon Press, 1988.

———. "Homeward Bound: MacIntyre on Liberal Society and the History of Ethics." *Journal of Religion* 69, no. 2 (April 1989): 220–32.

Sussman, Herbert L. *Fact into Figure: Typology in Carlyle, Ruskin and the Pre-Raphaelite Brotherhood.* Columbus: Ohio State University Press, 1979.

Taylor, Charles. *Hegel.* Cambridge: Cambridge University Press, 1975.

———. *Sources of the Self: The Making of Modern Identity.* Cambridge, MA: Harvard University Press, 1989.

Thomas, David Wayne. *Cultivating Victorians: Liberal Culture and the Aesthetic.* Philadelphia: University of Pennsylvania Press, 2004.

Thompson, E. P. *The Making of the English Working Class.* New York: Vintage Books, 1966.

———. *William Morris: Romantic to Revolutionary.* New York: Pantheon Books, 1977.

Thoreau, Henry David. *Journal, vol. 10.* In *The Writings of Henry David Thoreau,* ed. Bradford Torrey. Boston: Houghton Mifflin, 1906.

Tucker, Robert C., ed. *The Marx-Engels Reader.* 2d ed. New York: W. W. Norton, 1978.

Unrau, John. "Ruskin, the Workman and the Savageness of Gothic." In *New Approaches to Ruskin,* ed. Robert Hewison, 33–50. London: Routledge & Kegan Paul, 1981.

Valcanover, Francesco, and Terisia Pignatti. *Tintoretto.* Trans. Robert Erich Wolf. New York: H. N. Abrams, 1985.

Walzer, Michael. *Interpretation and Social Criticism.* Cambridge, MA: Harvard University Press, 1987.

———. *Spheres of Justice: A Defense of Pluralism and Equality.* New York: Basic Books, 1983.

Waterman, A. M. C. *Economics, Revolution and Religion.* Cambridge: Cambridge University Press, 1992.

Waters, Chris. "Marxism, Medievalism and Popular Culture." In *History and Community: Essays in Victorian Medievalism,* ed. Florence S. Boos. New York: Garland, 1992.

Weltman, Sharon Aronofsky. "Myth and Gender in Ruskin's Science." In *Ruskin and the Dawn of the Modern,* ed. Dinah Birch. Oxford: Oxford University Press, 1999.

———. *Ruskin's Mythic Queen: Gender Subversion in Victorian Culture.* Athens: Ohio University Press, 1998.

West, Cornel. "Alasdair MacIntyre, Liberalism, and Socialism: A Christian Perspective." In *Christianity and Capitalism: Perspectives on Religion, Liberalism, and the Economy,* ed. Bruce Grelle and David A. Krueger. Chicago: Center for the Scientific Study of Religion, 1985.

———. *The Ethical Dimensions of Marxist Thought.* New York: Monthly Review Press, 1991.

———. "Religion and the Left." In *Prophetic Fragments.* Grand Rapids, MI: William B. Eerdmans, 1988.

Wheeler, Michael, ed. *Ruskin and the Environment: The Storm-Cloud of the Nineteenth Century.* New York: St. Martin's Press, 1995.

———. *Ruskin's God.* Cambridge: Cambridge University Press, 1999.

Wheeler, Michael, and Nigel Whiteley, eds. *The Lamp of Memory: Ruskin, Tradition and Architecture.* New York: St. Martin's Press, 1992.

Wihl, Gary. *Ruskin and the Rhetoric of Infallibility.* New Haven, CT: Yale University Press, 1985.

Williams, Raymond. *The Country and the City.* New York: Oxford University Press, 1973.

———. *Culture and Society: 1780–1950.* New York: Columbia University Press, 1958, 1983.

———. "John Ruskin." *The Encyclopedia of Philosophy.* Vol. 7, ed. Paul Edwards. New York: Macmillan, 1972.

Wilson, A. N. *God's Funeral: A Biography of Faith and Doubt in Western Civilization.* New York: Ballantine Books, 1999.

Wordsworth, William. Preface to *Lyrical Ballads and Other Poems, 1797–1800.* Ed. James Butler and Karen Green. Ithaca, NY: Cornell University Press, 1992.

Index

Studies in Religion and Culture

Edmund N. Santurri
Perplexity in the Moral Life: Philosophical and Theological Considerations

Robert P. Scharlemann
Inscriptions and Reflections: Essays in Philosophical Theology

James DiCenso
Hermeneutics and the Disclosure of Truth: A Study in the Work of Heidegger, Gadamer, and Ricoeur

David Lawton
Faith, Text, and History: The Bible in English

Robert P. Scharlemann, editor
Theology at the End of the Century: A Dialogue on the Postmodern

Robert P. Scharlemann, editor
Negation and Theology

Lynda Sexson
Ordinarily Sacred

David E. Klemm and William Schweiker, editors
Meanings in Texts and Actions: Questioning Paul Ricoeur

Guyton B. Hammond
Conscience and Its Recovery: From the Frankfurt School to Feminism

Roger Poole
Kierkegaard: The Indirect Communication

John D. Barbour
Versions of Deconversion: Autobiography and the Loss of Faith

Gary L. Ebersole
Captured by Texts: Puritan to Postmodern Images of Indian Captivity

David Chidester
Savage Systems: Colonialism and Comparative Religion in Southern Africa

Laurie L. Patton and Wendy Doniger, editors
Myth and Method

Orrin F. Summerell, editor
The Otherness of God

Langdon Gilkey
Creationism on Trial: Evolution and God at Little Rock

Michael L. Raposa
Boredom and the Religious Imagination

Peter Homans, editor
Symbolic Loss: The Ambiguity of Mourning and Memory at Century's End

Winston Davis, editor
Taking Responsibility: Comparative Perspectives

John P. Burris
Exhibiting Religion: Colonialism and Spectacle at International Expositions, 1851–1893

Jeffrey W. Robbins
Between Faith and Thought: An Essay on the Ontotheological Condition

Michael L. Raposa
Meditation and the Martial Arts

John D. Barbour
The Value of Solitude: The Ethics and Spirituality of Aloneness in Autobiography

Roger Caillois
Pontius Pilate (reprinted edition)

David M. Craig
John Ruskin and the Ethics of Consumption